In *Unspeakable Truths*, Priscilla Hayner delivers a profound, definitive exploration of the world's truth commissions, and the anguish, the injustice, and the legacy of hate they are meant to absolve. She examines the twenty-one major commissions established around the world—paying special attention to South Africa, El Salvador, Argentina, Chile, and Guatemala. Drawing from hundreds of interviews in over a dozen countries, *Unspeakable Truths* takes a critical look at the world's truth commissions, Hayner finds that victims are torn between the need to remember and the need to forget. In the new post-Cold War order, the future of democracy and peace may rest on this debate. For those concerned with the fate of democracy and freedom on the interntional stage, *Unspeakable Truths* is essential reading.

Priscilla Hayner is a program director at the International Center for Transitional Justice in New York City.

UNSPEAKABLE TRUTHS

facing the challenge of truth commissions

WITHDRAWN

PRISCILLA B. HAYNER

LIBRARY ST. MARY'S COLLEGE

Routledge
New York and London

Published in 2002 by
Routledge
29 West 35th Street
New York, NY 10001

Published in Great Britain by
Routledge
11 New Fetter Lane
London EC4P 4EE

Routledge is an imprint of the Taylor & Francis Group.

First Routledge paperback edition, 2002.
Printed in the United States of America on acid-free paper.

10 9 8 7 6 5 4 3

Library of Congress Cataloging-in-Publication Data

Hayner, Priscilla B.
     Unspeakable truths : confronting state terror and atrocity /
     Priscilla B. Hayner
        p. cm.
     Includes bibliographical references and index.
     ISBN 0-415-92477-4 —0-415-92478-2 (pbk.)
     1. Human rights.   2. Political atrocities.   3. Political persecution.
     4. Amnesty   5. Reconciliation.   6. Truth Commissions.   I. Title.

JC571 .H363   2000
323'.044— dc21   00-032315

CONTENTS

acknowledgments

Many individuals and organizations throughout a range of countries contributed to this book.

First, the simple idea of writing a book was launched into an actual book project with a terrific research and writing grant from the John D. and Catherine T. MacArthur Foundation in 1995. A year later, I received additional support from the U.S. Institute of Peace. These two grants made this book possible, and in particular supported the extensive travel that was necessary to fully grapple with the issues at hand. The views expressed in this book do not necessarily reflect those of either of these institutions.

Second, this book was dependent more than most on the willingness of many individuals around the world to sit down with me to describe their experiences and perspectives. I am indebted to the many human rights advocates and survivors of violence, as well as government officials, academics, journalists, church officials, and many others, scattered throughout over a dozen countries, who were so generous with their time and provided such rich and detailed information in response to my queries. This book could not have been written without them.

I was further assisted in my travels by a number of terrific interpreters and guides. In South Africa, Wally Mbhele, S'Kumbuzu Miya, Lucky Njozela, Joseph Dube, and Lebo Molete provided guidance and interpretation in unforgettable visits to the environs of Johannesburg, Durban, and Cape Town, and to Soweto and Daveyton, respectively, during my various visits to the country. Nancy Bernard in Haiti, Hannes Michael Kloth in Berlin, Sören Asmus in Bonn, and Conor Christie and Roberto Luis in Mozambique also provided terrific interpretation and guidance.

As I made my way through foreign lands, I was graciously housed by old friends and new in many cities around the world. I am grateful for the hospitality provided by Roberto Petz in Maputo, Mozambique; Sergio Hevia, Carla Pellegrin Friedman, and Roberto and Valentina Hevia in Santiago; Patricia Bernardi and Luis Fondebrider in Buenos Aires; and Andrew Russell and Judy Kallick in Guatemala City. In South Africa, my warm thanks go to John Daniel and family in Durban, Janet Cherry in Port Elizabeth, and Jeanelle de Gruchy and Madeleine Fullard in Cape Town.

A number of people have read chapters of the book and provided terrifically useful input. I would like to especially thank Bronwen Manby, Mimi Doretti, Peter Rosenblum, Helen Duffy, Alex Vines, Jim Ross, Lisa Inman, Brandon Hamber, Debi Munczek, Michael O'Brien, and my sister Anne and brother John Hayner—all of whom made important contributions. A handful of people—Richard Carver, Douglass Cassel, Margaret Crahan, Ron Kassimir, Naomi Roht-Arriaza, and Paul van Zyl—commented in some detail on the full manuscript, in a near-final draft, which improved the final product considerably. Of course, I am solely responsible for any errors that may remain.

The editors at Routledge have been a great pleasure to work with. I especially would like to thank Eric Nelson, my editor, both for his dedication and for his clear understanding of the intentions of this book. I also thank Krister Swartz, my production editor during the greater part of the book's production, and Amy Shipper and T.J. Mancini, who played critical editorial and production roles at the beginning and end of the process. I am indebted also to my agent, Malaga Baldi, for her guidance and assistance throughout.

Many friends and colleagues provided support, enthusiasm, and input which I have greatly valued, perhaps much more than they realized. First I must thank Mimi Doretti, who provided support and good ideas throughout, and George Lopez, the two people who first encouraged me to write a book on this subject, certainly before the idea had occurred to me. Bronwen Manby instinctively understood the questions I was grappling with, and offered critical input into my endeavor to clarify and fairly present my thoughts. I thank Amie Dorman for her early research assistance, and Jonathan Klaaren, Paul van Zyl, Bill Berkeley, Belinda Cooper, Monroe Gilmour, Gwi-Yeop Son, and many others—I cannot name them all—

who offered assistance, contacts, or welcome enthusiasm for the project at critical points along my journey. My appreciation also goes to the World Policy Institute, at the New School University in New York, where my project was based for over a year.

Particular thanks go to Anthony Romero, Mary McClymont, and Larry Cox at the Ford Foundation, who have been strong supporters of my work on this subject. In the course of my consulting for the Foundation, they have provided the flexibility essential to making my own travels and writing possible. I would also like to thank Robert Crane, the president of the Joyce Mertz-Gilmore Foundation, for providing the leeway for me to undertake a more serious inquiry into this subject while I was still employed with the Foundation through the first part of 1996.

It is unlikely I would have ventured into this subject of inquiry without a fellowship grant in 1992 from the Center for the Study of Human Rights at Columbia University's School of International and Public Affairs, which allowed me to work closely with the truth commission in El Salvador for close to three months. I especially want to recognize the Center's director, Paul Martin, for his constant support and interest. At Columbia University Law School, Alejandro Garro provided early assistance in my first efforts to tackle this subject.

Finally, I want to thank the members of my family for their interest and encouragement throughout. In addition to Anne and John, mentioned above for their editorial input, I want to acknowledge the support of my sisters Marji and Kate Hayner and Irena Hayner Stammer. I warmly dedicate this book to my parents, Norman and Margaret Hayner, whose abundant support, interest, and active concern for the world's affairs have played such an important role in setting me down this path.

FOR MY PARENTS

preface

"How does one make a truth commission?" asked an earnest-looking Burmese girl in the front row. This was spring 2000, and the place was the headquarters of Aung San Suu Kyi's embattled National League for Democracy, surrounded by agents of military intelligence. At Aung San Suu Kyi's invitation, I was speaking about transitions to democracy. What the audience — who risk their freedom and their livelihood by attending such meetings — seemed to like most of all in my remarks was the idea of seeing those who had ruined their golden land sitting and sweating in front of a truth commission.

"How does one make a truth commission?" she asked; and I wish that I could have pressed Priscilla Hayner's book into her hand. For this is the most comprehensive, sober, nuanced and authoritative attempt yet made to answer a question posed not just in Burma, but in many countries that are contemplating or already engaged in the difficult transition from dictatorship. Increasingly, people recognize that such countries can and should learn from the experience of others, not just about how to build a market economy, to write a constitution or to restore the rule of law, but also about how to deal with a difficult past. There are various terms or circumlocutions for this business of past-beating, each of them implying a slightly different priority. Yet all recognize that the problem of "what to do about the past" is a major and intrinsic part of such transitions. Indeed, it can make the difference between success and failure.

Priscilla Hayner locates her study of truth commissions firmly in this wider context. She starts, quite rightly, with the most fundamental question: "to remember or forget?" She sees that the best way forward is almost always some mixture of remembering and forgetting—even, paradoxical though this sounds, of remembering in order to forget. The best way to close old wounds is sometimes to open them again, because, as one of her interlocutors memorably observes, the wounds were badly closed, and you still have to clean out the old infection.

Along the way, she constantly asks how this mode of "past-beating" relates to others, such as vetting (or "lustration") and, particularly, judicial proceedings to punish the perpetrators.

How does the pursuit of truth affect that of justice? While it raises such fundamental, even philosophical issues, the great strength of Hayner's book is its detailed description and analysis of the twenty-one truth commissions that she counts to date. As well as reading the literature, she has been to many of these lands haunted by a bad past and some of her most striking material comes from her extensive interviews. There are human details that will stay with me for a long time.

Hayner is what the French call a *spectateur engagé*. We discover at one point that she had suggested to the U.S. authorities that they should add to their visa-ban lists people clearly found guilty of atrocities by a well-conducted truth commission. (No, it hasn't happened—yet.) Gaining usable knowledge is what this book is all about. Its purpose, she writes at one point, is "to record and learn from the varied models of the past in order to better understand and improve on these exercises in the future . . . " She rightly suggests that one can learn from the small, inconclusive or aborted truth commissions, as well as from those that proceeded to a well-publicized report.

That also means acknowledging the limits of what truth commissions can achieve, in the relatively short period in which they usually sit. She is, for example, skeptical of sweeping claims for a large-scale effect of therapeutic "healing" or national "reconciliation." This is a scrupulous, important and necessary book. It should be widely read. And, as soon as it is printed, I shall send a copy into Burma.

Timothy Garton Ash,
Oxford, June 2000

Introduction

"Do you want to remember, or to forget?" I asked the Rwandan government official in late 1995, just over a year after the genocide in that country had left over 500,000 dead.

He had lost seventeen members of his immediate family during the three and one-half months of slaughter. By chance he was out of the country when it started, and was therefore the only member of his family left alive. When he described the events, he had said with a palpable sense of relief, "With each day, we are able to forget more."

So I asked, "Do you want to remember, or to forget?"

He hesitated. "We must remember what happened in order to keep it from happening again," he said slowly. "But we must forget the feelings, the emotions, that go with it. It is only by forgetting that we are able to go on."

I was sitting with the official as we traveled with a group of international visitors to visit a massacre memorial site, where the bones and decaying clothes of thousands lay strewn in a church. As I observed this site and others over the next days, and tried to fully comprehend the horror of what he and others had experienced, I realized that there was no other answer to my question. One must remember, but one must also sometimes very much want to forget.

I had much the same sensation several months later, while speaking with a weathered farm worker in the far reaches of El Salvador. A United Nations truth commission had, three years earlier, investigated the abuses during the country's twelve-year civil war, and I was visiting his village, in an area known to have been politically active and heavily battered by the war, to ask whether the commission had reached there, and what impact it might have had. When I asked about the war, he described the killings he saw at the hands of the army: how his father's throat was cut, how a neighbor who was pregnant was brutally killed. Had he spoken with the truth commission? I asked. Had he given his testimony? He hadn't. "It's difficult to remember this, it's painful to remember," he said, and you could feel it in how he told his stories. "Oh, how they killed the guerrillas," he said. "I don't like to remember these things. What good would it do to go to the truth commission? I would lose a day of work, and nothing would change." He paused. "It's painful to remember. But it is important to fight for the rule of law."

Remembering is not easy, but forgetting may be impossible. There are a range of emotional and psychological survival tactics for those who have experienced such brutal atrocities. While some victims, such as this Salvadoran man, pleaded to forget, other victims I spoke with were clear that only by remembering could they even begin to recover. Only by remembering, telling their story, and learning every last detail about what happened and who was responsible were they able to begin to put the past behind them. In South Africa, time and again I heard survivors say they could forgive their perpetrators only if the perpetrators admitted the full truth. Almost incomprehensibly, hearing even the most gruesome details of the torture and murder of loved ones seemed to bring some peace. In South Africa, many survivors were able to hear these stories through the public hearings of those seeking amnesty for their crimes. One condition for receiving a grant of amnesty was full disclosure of all details of the crimes, including answering questions directly from victims or surviving family members.

In a township outside of Port Elizabeth, on the south coast of South Africa and in the center of what was fervent antiapartheid activity in the 1980s, I spoke with Elizabeth Hashe, an older black woman whose activist husband disappeared thirteen years earlier with two colleagues. In contrast to much of Latin America and elsewhere, "disappearing" political activists (kidnapping and eventually killing them, and disposing of the body without out a trace) was uncommon in South Africa, and thus the fact that these three men were missing had received a great deal of attention. There was an official investigation when they disappeared, and the police vehemently denied knowing their whereabouts. It was only with the work of the South

African Truth and Reconciliation Commission that their fate was finally uncovered. I spoke to Mrs. Hashe at a tea break in the midst of a grueling two-week public hearing, after listening for four days as former security police testified in great detail about how they kidnapped and killed her husband and the two other men, roasted their bodies over a fire for six hours until they turned to ashes, and dumped the remains into the Fish River. What did she think of the hearing? I asked. What did it mean to her? "At least now I know a bit of the story. It's better to know, to know how they killed him," Mrs. Hashe said.

Monica Godolozi, another of the three widows, was less forgiving. Like most of the audience in the boisterous and crowded hearing room, she was sure that the policemen were not telling the full truth, and were in fact covering up torture that likely took place before the men were killed. As the police officers denied any torture or abuse, the audience hissed loudly; many of the hundreds in attendance had probably once been victims of these same policemen. Mrs. Godolozi told me, "I won't forgive them. There's nothing they could do to make me forgive them — except, *if* they told the truth, then yes. Anybody who tells the truth, I can forgive them. But not someone who tells lies."

Mrs. Hashe disagreed. "Don't we want peace for South Africa? How are we going to find peace if we don't forgive? My husband was fighting for peace for all of South Africa. How can you correct a wrong with a wrong?" One year earlier, Mrs. Hashe had looked tormented as she gave testimony to the commission at one of its first public hearings. Learning what happened to her husband — or at least who killed him, where the ashes of his body were discarded, and many of the details of how he died — changed her; but for Mrs. Godolozi, this was not enough.

Despite the efforts of the Truth and Reconciliation Commission, many South Africans still demanded strict justice and punishment for their perpetrators. Where justice was not possible, the minimal requirement for forgiveness, most insisted, was to be told the full, honest, and unvarnished truth.

These South African widows, the Salvadoran peasant farm worker, and the Rwandan government official reveal the difficulties faced by individual victims and by entire nations after a period of brutal political repression. I had gone to South Africa, El Salvador, and Rwanda, as I was to travel to a number of other countries, to understand how a country and its people might recover from a period of widespread atrocities. Specifically, I was interested in the impact of official truth-seeking, where past horrors are publicly documented and investigated by a special commission, such as was done in El Salvador and South Africa. I heard similar voices everywhere, similar agonizing tales of brutality, pain, struggle, and survival. The details of repression differed widely, as did the range in individual and national response. Yet I soon saw firsthand what anyone might imagine: that such widespread abuses by the state leave behind a powerful legacy. The damage goes far beyond the immediate pain of loss. Where there was torture, there are walking, wounded victims. Where there were killings, or wholesale massacres, there are often witnesses to the carnage, and family members too terrified to fully grieve. Where there were persons disappeared, kidnapped by government forces without a trace, there are loved ones desperate for information. Where there were years of unspoken pain and enforced silence, there are often a pervasive, debilitating fear and, when the repression ends, a need to slowly learn to trust the government, the police, and armed forces, and to gain confidence in the freedom to speak freely and mourn openly.

The world has been overturned with political change in recent years, as many ruthless or repressive regimes have been replaced with democratic or semidemocratic governments. From the civil wars and repression in Central America to the dictatorships in South America; from the end of apartheid in South Africa to the still-turbulent conflicts of Central Africa; from the overthrow of communism in Eastern Europe to the varied political transitions and upheavals in Asia, new governments have swept out the old and have celebrated the chance to start afresh. Many of these changes have taken place since the fall of the Berlin Wall in 1989 and the rapid end of the Cold War, which has removed an incentive for international support for many corrupt and abusive regimes.

When a period of authoritarian rule or civil war ends, a state and its people stand at a crossroads. What should be done with a recent history full of victims, perpetrators, secretly buried bodies, pervasive fear, and official denial? Should this past be exhumed, preserved, acknowledged, apologized for? How can a nation of enemies be reunited, former opponents reconciled, in the context of such a violent history and often bitter, festering wounds? What should be done with hundreds or thousands of perpetrators still walking free? And how can a new government prevent such atrocities from being repeated in the future? While individual survivors struggle to rebuild shattered lives, to ease the burning memory of torture suffered or massacres witnessed, society as a whole must find a way to move on, to recreate a livable space of national peace, build some form of reconciliation between former enemies, and secure these events in the past.

Some argue that the best way to move forward is to bury the past, that digging up such horrific details and pointing out the guilty will only bring more pain and further divide a country. Yet can a society build a democratic future on a foundation of blind, denied, or forgotten history? In recent years, virtually every country emerging from a dark history has directly confronted this question. In some countries, this has been debated during peace negotiations, where "the past" is often the first and most contentious item on the agenda. Elsewhere, the new government has confronted the issue, with accountability for past crimes often one of the most pressing issues before the new administration, especially where there are thousands of victims demanding action. The countries addressed in this book have come out of a wide range of repressive or dictatorial regimes, and emerged from that period through very different types of transitions. Change may come at the end of a civil war, through the downfall of a military regime, or through popular revolt against a repressive regime combined with shifting winds of international support. But in each of these very different types of political transitions, very similar questions and difficulties arise.

This book explores the difficult underside of these questions. Its aim, ultimately, is to better understand how states and individuals might reckon with horrible abuses of the past, and specifically to understand the role played by truth commissions—the name that has been given to official bodies set up to investigate and report on a pattern of past human rights abuses. The South African Truth and Reconciliation Commission succeeded in bringing this subject to the center of international attention, especially through its public hearings of both victims and perpetrators outlining horrific details of past crimes. Although quite a few of such truth commissions existed prior to the South African body, most did not hold hearings in public, and none of the others included such a compelling (if also ethically problematic) offer of individualized amnesty, which succeeded in enticing many South African wrongdoers to confess their crimes in front of television cameras.

Even while a number of new countries are now considering establishing their own truth commissions—in places as diverse as Indonesia, Colombia, and Bosnia—and as new truth commissions are now being established, in Nigeria and Sierra Leone, many aspects of these bodies are still not well understood. There are general misconceptions, for example, in how these bodies typically operate—under what powers and, often, under what significant restraints—as well as in the impact they might have, or might reasonably be expected to have, on victims, policies, and society at large. This book is motivated, perhaps most fundamentally, by a desire to clarify exactly what these bodies are; what they do and have the potential to contribute; and where their limitations lie.

I am often surprised by the way in which notions of truth, and notions of truth commissions, are initially understood and talked about, and the assumptions that are often held about what a process of truth-seeking is and what it might lead to. Unfortunately, many comfortable assumptions have been restated over and again in untested assertions by otherwise astute and careful writers, thinkers, and political leaders. (I am not entirely free of this myself, I should say, in some of my early writing on this topic.) Some of the most oft-repeated statements, and those that we perhaps most wish to be true, are due careful scrutiny. Indeed, they don't always hold up well even under a test of anecdotal evidence.

For example, does truth lead to reconciliation? Or, to state it another way, is it necessary to know the truth in order to advance reconciliation? This is perhaps the most oft-repeated notion in the territory of truth-seeking, and it is possible to point to evidence and to quote survivors to show that it is true; sometimes it is, for some people or in some circumstances. Yet it is easy to imagine that the opposite might sometimes also be true, or, more important, that reconciliation, as hazy a concept as that can be, may be more affected by other factors quite apart from knowing or acknowledging the truth about past wrongs. For example (as I suggest in more detail later), true reconciliation might depend on a clear end to the threat of further violence; a reparations program for those injured; attention to structural inequalities and basic material needs of victimized communities; the existence of natural linkages in society that bring formerly opposing parties together; or, most simply (although often overlooked), the simple passage of time.

As well, it is often asserted that digging into the truth and giving victims a chance to speak offers a healing or "cathartic" experience. Again, this turns out to be a questionable assumption, at least in some cases. Though little scientific evidence is yet available on this question, it is clear that this notion of healing is a bit overstated, at least. Meanwhile, these inquiries are hardly a healing process for those actually responsible for seeking out the truth. Staff and commissioners of these bodies — and sometimes journalists who follow a truth commission's matters — often show many signs of severe stress and trauma themselves after weeks or months on the job, after listening to hundreds upon hundreds of horrific stories. Unexpectedly, perhaps, the administrative staff who are responsible for coding and entering data into the computer — tabulating the dozens of different kinds of torture, abuse, killing, dismemberment, or other heinous atrocity — are sometimes the people within the commission who are the most strongly affected by the information.

But along with any dose of skepticism — or realism, anyway — in what these bodies accomplish, must also come a much better appreciation for the sometimes remarkable but little known contributions that they have occasionally made. In Chile, almost entirely on the basis of the finding of that country's truth commission, the state has paid thousands of families over $5,000 per year in reparation for abuses under the military rule of Augusto Pinochet, in addition to other significant reparations. Likewise, partly on the basis of the truth commission's records in Argentina, the state has committed three billion dollars, in payments of up to $220,000 per family, for the victims of that country's "dirty war." Critical judicial reforms were put in place in El Salvador following the UN truth commission investigations there. In South Africa, very few people will now defend or try to justify the system of apartheid, or question the fact that egregious practices, such as widespread torture in police stations, were used to keep apartheid in place. In some countries, such as Argentina, the commission's report has received a great amount of attention, and continues to sell well even years later.

Perhaps most underappreciated, still, is the sheer difficulty of undertaking these endeavors, of fairly documenting and representing a "truth" — however that is defined in different countries — in the course of a short and intensive period of investigation, when the issues under exploration often remain the most sensitive of the day and when the commission's task is to reach and fairly represent the stories of thousands upon thousands of victims. With a closer look, it becomes clear that truth commissions are of a fundamentally different nature from courtroom trials, and function with different goals in mind. It is also clear that many methodological questions that are central to truth commissions cannot be answered by turning to any established legal norms or general principles, nor can they be well addressed by universal guidelines. Instead, these questions require looking at the specific needs and context of each country. The questions that come up — how a commission should best collect, organize, and evaluate the many accounts from victims and others; whether to hold public hearings or carry out all investigations confidentially; whether it should name the names of specific perpetrators in its report; and many others — will be answered differently in different countries. The task is made even more difficult by the fact that many of these questions are unique to these kinds of broad truth inquires and do not usually come up in relation to trials, for example, where standardized procedures have long been established.

Official truth-seeking, it turns out, is a cumbersome and complicated affair. In the course of my many interviews around the world, where I have had the chance to speak in detail with the commissioners and staff of many past commissions, as well as with victims, advocates, and policymakers who have watched or participated in these processes, a few general points have stood out. First, the expectations for truth commissions are almost always greater than what these bodies can ever reasonably hope to achieve. These hopes may be for rapid reconciliation, significant reparations to all victims, a full resolution of many individual cases, or for a process that results in accountability for perpetrators and significant institutional reforms. Due to a variety of reasons that I will explore throughout the following chapters, few of these expectations can be fulfilled by most truth commissions. Some level of disappointment is not uncommon as a truth commission comes to an end (or as a government accepts but then does not move to implement the recommendations of a truth commission report). While there is certainly room for improvement, some of these expectations are simply not realistic in circumstances where there were thousands upon thousands of victims, where democratic institutions remain very weak, and where the will of perpetrators to express remorse or participate in reconciliatory exercises is tenuous, at best. Ironically, however, these grand expectations and the resulting disappointment often prevent people from appreciating the significant contributions that these bodies do sometimes make.

Second, many of the most difficult problems confronted by truth commissions seem to be almost universal to these kinds of inquiries, as each new commission stumbles on many of the same questions and false assumptions. There is much to be learned from past exercises that might improve the models of the future. Unfortunately, however, many new commissions have begun their work without these lessons at hand.

The third fact, which is becoming apparent only in recent years, is that these truth bodies can have significant long-term consequences that may be entirely unexpected at the start. This is especially true, it seems, in the realm of justice and accountability. Specifically, in recent years, the archives and reports of several truth commissions from long ago have been relied on heavily in efforts to prosecute accused perpetrators in the international arena. Suddenly, the usefulness of having a well-documented record of the crimes of a previous regime has become clear, even where domestic trials are out of the question.

All of these issues are addressed in much more detail throughout this book (the chapter titles should make clear where to find each subject). The book is organized thematically, arranged around the issues that are most often confronted by these commissions themselves, or the questions most often raised by those observing these bodies from the outside. In order to bring out the texture of these processes, I describe five of the more substantial commissions that have existed to date in greater detail — those in Argentina, Chile, El Salvador, South Africa, and Guatemala — and refer to these cases more often throughout the book. A further sixteen commissions are then described more briefly. (A number of supporting charts, including a chronological list of all twenty-one truth commissions to date, can be found in appendix 1.)

This book is intended to help bridge the gap between theory and practice; to fairly represent the experiences of victims, the hopes of human rights advocates, and the dilemmas of policymakers as they embark on or take part in these processes. Ultimately, the decision to dig into the details of a difficult past must always be left to a country and its people to decide, and in some countries there may be reasons to leave the past well alone. But it is a safe assumption, even given the great variation in political circumstance of the transitions on the horizon, that we will be seeing many more examples of truth commissions in the coming years.

two

Confronting Past Crimes

T he 1986 publication of *Transitions from Authoritarian Rule*, a major four-volume work focused on Latin America and Eastern Europe, helped to define the terms of a still-new field, that of studying how (and under what constraints) democratic transitions take shape after a period of repressive rule.[1] While the question of "settling past accounts," as the authors call it, is not the central focus of the study, they note a difficult tension between the desire to bury the past, in order to avoid provoking the ire of powerful wrongdoers, and the ethical and political demand to confront the crimes of the prior regime. The authors highlight this dilemma as one of "immense difficulty" for which they have no satisfactory resolution, and posit in a footnote that an essential difference between this and other transitional problems is that this dilemma is one that "simply cannot be avoided and one that the leaders must attempt to resolve."[2]

The writers move on to suggest that the "worst of bad solutions would be to try to ignore the issue," and that the least worst strategy, based on ethical and political considerations, is to hold trials for the wrongdoers. Leaving aside questions of international law, which the writers are silent on but which today usually frame these questions, what is most interesting in this discussion is the narrow scope of options presented to respond to such crimes. When the book was completed, the National Commission on the Disappeared in Argentina was just under way. There was still virtually no international recognition of nonjudicial truth-seeking as a transitional justice

men's responsibility to action

tool, nor was there much recognition of the range of other nonjudicial strategies now commonly considered during such a postauthoritarian transition. In less than fifteen years, this picture has changed dramatically.

The world now seems to be confronting questions of justice and accountability at every turn, either following the end of a military regime or repressive government, or after a civil war. It has become clear, however, that there are a whole range of needs arising out of these circumstances that cannot be satisfied by action in the courts — even if the courts function well and there are no limits placed on prosecuting the wrongdoers, which is rare. Many alternative and complementary approaches to accountability have thus slowly taken shape. The concrete needs of victims and communities that were damaged by the violence will not be addressed through such prosecutions, except of course in providing some solace if the perpetrators are successfully prosecuted. The institutional or societal conditions that allowed the massive abuses to take place — the structures of the armed forces, the judiciary, or the laws that should constrain the actions of officials, for example — may remain unchanged even as a more democratic and less abusive government comes into place. Many questions may remain open about exactly what took place during the years of repression, and tensions between communities may continue to fester, or deepen, if these are left unaddressed. *things left unaddressed*

It is with these many and multifaceted issues and problems in mind that the field of "transitional justice" has slowly taken shape over the last years, as a subset of the broader field of inquiry into democratic transition. The basic question, that of how to reckon with massive state crimes and abuses (or abuses by groups in opposition to the state), raises a wide range of legal, political, and even psychological questions. This field — to the degree that it has taken shape as a defined field unto itself — has developed in response to the demands and differing circumstances of many transitional states around the world, and the increased public interest and international expectation that accountability is due after atrocity. There is now a widely held belief that these crimes, and the deep legacy of these crimes, must be addressed.[3] *crimes must be addressed | accounted for*

A state may have a number of objectives in responding to past abuses: to punish perpetrators, establish the truth, repair or address damages, pay respect to victims, and prevent further abuses. There may be other aims as well, such as promoting national reconciliation and reducing conflict over the past, or highlighting the new government's concern for human rights and therefore gaining the favor of the international community. Likewise,

ways to respond to past abuses

there are a variety of mechanisms or policies implemented to try to reach these objectives: holding trials in domestic or international courts; purging wrongdoers from public or security posts; creating a commission of inquiry; providing individualized access to security files; awarding reparations to victims; building memorials; or putting in place military, police, judicial, or other reforms.

Justice in the courts is usually the first and most prominent of demands, but also the most difficult. Many attempts to prosecute and punish those responsible for severe abuses under a prior regime have seen little success. Typically, as in El Salvador, South Africa, and Chile, the political transition has involved political compromise, and these compromises have included some form of immunity from prosecution for the repressors of old, perhaps even preserving some of their power or incorporating them into the new government. When dictators or other perpetrators help design the end to their own rule, they usually place limits on any accountability for their own crimes. Despite what are sometimes the best intentions of the new authorities (who may have been active in opposing the former regime, perhaps even imprisoned and tortured for their activities) and despite loud demands for justice from victims and rights advocates, posttransition justice is rare. Where there are trials, they are usually few in number and sometimes fail to convict even those who everyone "knows" are guilty. In virtually every country I visited throughout Latin America, Africa, and elsewhere, I found a difficult struggle for justice and a frustration over the small numbers of victimizers prosecuted and the incapacity of the courts. After a dictatorship or repressive government, the judiciary is often left in shambles: judges politically compromised, corrupt, or timid; expertise lacking; and resources few. The numbers of perpetrators can be overwhelming, so that even in those rare circumstances where the judicial system functions well enough to expect fair trials and there has not been a general grant of amnesty, only a very small number of the total are likely to be prosecuted.

Trials in international courts have also been limited. Compared to the great numbers of accused war criminals, only a relatively small number of persons have been indicted by the International Criminal Tribunal for the Former Yugoslavia and the International Criminal Tribunal for Rwanda, both ad hoc bodies created by the United Nations. It is true that prosecuting the most senior persons responsible for the atrocities, even if few in number, could have a significant effect. But the tribunals, especially the Yugoslavia Tribunal, have had difficulty gaining custody of most of those they have indicted, particularly the most senior of the accused war criminals. The permanent International Criminal Court, agreed to in mid-1998 and expected to start functioning in the next few years, may confront similar problems.

Some Eastern Europe states have employed a strategy of "lustration," which removes persons from public employment based on their affiliation with the prior regime.[4] Yet the practice of lustration has been criticized for lacking due process guarantees and for relying on the sometimes faulty intelligence files of the prior regime. Many lustration policies were implemented without much consideration of how to best protect those wrongly accused, or those whose affiliation with the prior regime was extremely limited or brief.[5] Such lustration policies have not been put in place outside of Eastern Europe. In most circumstances they would not be possible, because it is unusual for a regime to keep such detailed records of collaborators; because the records that do exist are often destroyed during the course of a transition; and because negotiated transitions usually include an agreement that civilian employees of the former regime will not be punished or purged.

Some other states have, however, tried to purge those with a record of human rights abuses from security forces. El Salvador set up a special commission on this matter, the Ad Hoc Commission, as part of the peace accord that brought its twelve-year civil war to an end. This commission recommended that over one hundred senior members of the armed forces be removed; with considerable pressure from the international community (and with the support of the truth commission report that followed), they were all eventually retired from their posts. When Haiti abolished its army and created a new civilian police force, it made an effort to screen applicants and exclude those from the previous force who were known to have been abusive.

Only in Eastern Europe has there been individual access granted to former state security files (most widely in the former East Germany but now also under consideration elsewhere in the region). Because the repression in Eastern Europe was dependent on vast networks of informers, accessing these files has cut to the heart of the former system of repression. Collaborators of the former regime have been discovered at all levels, and individual victims have been able to find and personally confront those who informed on them, all too often their own friends or family members.[6] Yet again, either because such files are not available or because the nature of the repression and the transition have been different in other regions, such a system of providing individualized access to security files has rarely been considered in transitional states outside of Eastern Europe.[7]

In addition to trials, purges, and individualized access to intelligence files, transitional states have struggled with a range of other needs resulting from a period of widespread abuses. These include addressing or repairing the damage done to victims and communities; honoring those persons killed, disappeared, or otherwise victimized; and making institutional or policy changes to prevent further abuses in the future. Such goals may be reached through a range of mechanisms, but are now frequently addressed through a process of investigating and acknowledging the full truth about such abuses of the past.

THE TURN TOWARD TRUTH

It is partly due to the limited reach of the courts, and partly out of a recognition that even successful prosecutions do not resolve the conflict and pain associated with past abuses, that transitional authorities have increasingly turned to official truth-seeking as a central component in their strategy to respond to past atrocities. These broad inquiries into widespread abuses by state forces, sometimes also looking into abuses by the armed opposition, have acquired the generic name of "truth commissions," a term that implies a specific kind of inquiry, even while allowing for considerable variation between the different commissions. I use the term to refer to those bodies that share the following characteristics: (1) truth commissions focus on the *past*; (2) they investigate a pattern of abuses over a period of time, rather than a specific event; (3) a truth commission is a temporary body, typically in operation for six months to two years, and completing its work with the submission of a report; and (4) these commissions are officially sanctioned, authorized, or empowered by the state (and sometimes also by the armed opposition, as in a peace accord). This official status gives a truth commission better access to official sources of information, increased security to undertake sensitive investigations, and a greater likelihood that its report and recommendations will receive serious attention from authorities.

There have been at least twenty-one official truth commissions established around the world since 1974, though they have gone by many different names.[8] There have been "commissions on the disappeared" in Argentina, Uganda, and Sri Lanka, for example; "truth and justice commissions" in Haiti and Ecuador; a "historical clarification commission" in Guatemala; and "truth and reconciliation commissions" in South Africa and Chile. Others have been created in Germany, El Salvador, Bolivia, Chad, and elsewhere. While there is much in common between these various bodies, their specific investigatory mandates and powers have differed considerably to reflect the needs and political realities of each country. Chart 1, in appendix 1, lists these twenty-one truth commissions in chronological order; each is described in greater detail in chapters 4 and 5.

Each of these twenty-one commissions fits within the definition above, though it should be noted that some of these bodies did not at the time of their operation consider themselves to be "truth commissions," nor were they popularly understood to be such by the greater public — especially in comparison with the grander and more successful inquiries that have been seen since. It is awkward, for example, to list two inquiries by the African National Congress (ANC), which took place in the years prior to the transition in South Africa and helped to build the momentum for the larger Truth and Reconciliation Commission that would follow, as consisting of truth commissions themselves. South Africans, for example, do not refer to those earlier inquiries as truth commissions. In other countries, such as Uruguay or Zimbabwe, the commissions were perceived as being too narrow, weak, or politically controlled, or too short-lived to have had an impact, to acquire the title of *truth commission,* and in some of these countries the demand for the establishment of a credible and serious truth commission is still very much alive. If judged only by popular perception, the degree of impact, or the successful unearthing of the truth, then several of the twenty-one commissions on my list would have to be removed. However, for the purposes of this book, which is to record and learn from the varied models of the past in order to better understand and improve on these exercises in the future, these smaller, weaker, or otherwise differently conceived inquiries (such as those of the ANC) must be included. The two ANC inquiries may serve as important examples for some future armed opposition group that has serious intentions of complying with international rights norms and investigating its forces' abuses, for example. The limited or problematic inquiries in Uruguay, Zimbabwe, and Uganda (1974) provide good examples of how not to put together a truth commission. In many ways, these problematic cases make more clear than do the larger and more successful bodies exactly what minimal operating requirements should be met in order to make a contribution.

There are numerous goals that may be attached to these truth bodies — from national reconciliation to advancing healing for individual victims, from ending impunity to putting in place protections to prevent the repetition of abuses in the future—that will be described in chapter 3 and further evaluated throughout the book. Because truth commissions cover many events that could also be subject to trials, many observers mistakenly equate or compare truth commissions to courts, or, alternatively, fear that establishing such a commission somehow reduces the likelihood of a trial on the same matters. But truth commissions should not be equated with judicial bodies, nor should they be considered a replacement for trials. On one level, truth commissions clearly hold fewer powers than do courts. They have no powers to put anyone in jail, they can't enforce their recommendations, and most haven't even had the power to compel anyone to come forward to answer questions. To date, the South African commission was the only one to offer individualized amnesty, and thereby was able to lure some perpetrators into giving full and public accounts of their abuses. Most truth commissions do not interfere with or duplicate any of the tasks of the judiciary. Yet despite the more limited legal powers of truth commissions, their broader mandate to focus on a pattern of events, including the causes and consequences of the political violence, allows them to go much further in their investigations and conclusions than is generally possible in any trial of individual perpetrators. Indeed, the breadth and flexibility of a truth commission are its strength. For example, truth commissions are usually able to outline the full responsibility of the state and its various institutions that carried out or condoned the repression— including not only the military and the police, but sometimes also the judiciary itself. Truth commissions' victim-centered approach of collecting thousands of testimonies and publishing the results of their findings in a public and officially sanctioned report represents for many victims the first sign of acknowledgment by any state body that their claims are credible and that the atrocities were wrong.

Furthermore, most commissions are directed to forward their records to prosecutors or to the courts for possible legal action where they find evidence of criminal wrongdoing. The first well-known truth inquiry, Argentina's National Commission on the Disappeared, was popularly understood to be a preliminary step toward prosecutions that would follow, and indeed the information from this commission was critical to later trials. In other cases, these truth bodies have worked in the context of an amnesty that is already in place, or where a biased and corrupt judiciary makes trials unlikely, and the commission itself has been considered at least a minimal step toward accountability, especially when the commission publicly names those responsible for abuses.

In addition to the four defining characteristics noted above, these twenty-one truth commissions have other essential elements in common: all were created to look into recent events, usually at the point of a political transition; all investigated politically motivated or politically targeted repression that was used as a means to maintain or obtain power and weaken political opponents; and in each of these cases, the abuses were widespread, usually affecting many thousands of persons. Most of these commissions were created to be a central component of a transition from one government to another or from civil war to peace. Whether and how well each played this role is a topic for further consideration, but the intent, timing, and purpose of these commissions were alike in these fundamental ways.

In contrast, there have been other kinds of official inquiry into past human rights abuses that might be called "historical truth commissions." These are present-day government-sponsored inquiries into abuses by the state that took place many years earlier (and that ended years earlier). Such an inquiry is not established as part of a political transition, and indeed may not pertain to today's political leadership or practices, given the time that has passed, but serves instead to clarify historical truths and pay respect to previously unrecognized victims or their descendants. The events investigated by these commissions have generally not been those of widespread political repression, but were targeted practices that may have affected specific ethnic, racial, or other groups. These historical truth commissions are likely to document practices that are largely unknown to the majority of the population, and their reports can thus have a powerful impact despite the years that have passed.

In Australia, for example, the government asked its permanent human rights monitoring body, the Human Rights and Equal Opportunity Commission, to look into the record of state abuse against the country's population. Its year-long investigation documented decades-long state policies of forcibly removing aboriginal children from their families and placing them with white families in order to assimilate them into mainstream Australian society. These practices continued until the early 1970s. With the release of the commission's report, *Bringing Them Home,* in 1997, the story became a national scandal and ultimately a central issue in national elections, as the Australian public was outraged by this previously little-known practice, while the government refused to offer a formal apology in the name of prior governments.[9] Sixty thousand copies of the report were purchased in the first year after its release. An annual "Sorry Day" was created, as recommended by the commission, and "sorry books" were made available for signature by the public. Within a year over 100,000 Australians had signed these books, filling hundreds of volumes.

Canada was also moved to review its policies and relationships with indigenous communities. Heightened tensions between indigenous populations and the Canadian state led to the creation of a special commission tasked to study government policy and make recommendations for improvement. The commission's five-year inquiry included a review of the 500-year history of aboriginal policies, concluding that the policy of assimilation, advanced by the colonial and the Canadian states for over 150 years, was wrong.[10] The government responded with a detailed plan for implementation of the commission's extensive recommendations.[11]

In a similar historical vein, U.S. Energy Secretary Hazel O'Leary appointed an Advisory Committee on Human Radiation Experiments in 1994 to look into the experiments conducted on unknowing medical patients, prisoners, and communities in the United States from the mid-1940s to the mid-1970s. The report of this committee provided an "unprecedented insight into a murky area of American history," according to one observer.[12]

With an eye toward providing reparations to survivors, the U.S. Congress created a Commission on War-Time Relocation and Internment of Citizens in 1982 to study the policies and effect of placing Japanese-Americans in internment camps during World War II. Many of the recommendations of this commission's report have been implemented, including a formal apology from the government and the passage of legislation providing $1.2 billion in compensation to survivors.[13]

There have been other U.S. government practices for which reparations or apologies were offered many years after the fact, though without a formal government inquiry. For example, decades after the press reported on a secret syphilis study done on unknowing poor black men in Tuskegee, Alabama, that began in 1932 and continued into the 1970s, President Bill Clinton offered a formal apology in 1997. The experiments had been well documented by independent writers and the media, and the government had already paid the men and their families over $9 million in an out-of-court settlement, and thus no government inquiry was seen as necessary.[14] (See chart 2 in appendix 1 for a list of these historical truth commissions.)

Finally, there are other examples of official or semiofficial inquiries into past human rights violations which serve some truth-commission-like functions. These were all undertaken during political transitions and served important roles in their respective political circumstances, but were limited in authority or scope, or were undertaken only as a precursor to a possible full-fledged truth commission to follow (see chart 3 in appendix 1). For example, after receiving pressure from the families of victims and from the press, Leo Valladares, the national commissioner for the protection of human rights in Honduras, a government-appointed ombudsman, independently undertook an investigation into 179 disappearances caused by the armed forces in the 1980s and early 1990s. Yet Valladares worked under his own initiative, received no assistance from authorities, and based his investigations primarily on press accounts and other public information. He continued to call for a full truth commission even as he published his report in 1994 documenting the disappearances.[15]

In Northern Ireland, a "victims commissioner" was appointed by the British secretary of state for Northern Ireland in 1997 and given the mandate to "look into possible ways to recognize the pain and suffering felt by victims of violence arising from the troubles of the last 30 years." The commissioner interviewed hundreds of survivors of the violence but did no thorough analysis or investigation. In his report, which was released just weeks after the Good Friday peace agreement in 1998, the commissioner suggested that a truth commission might be considered in the future.[16]

Several years before massive killing in Rwanda took on genocidal proportions, violence in the early 1990s led to an agreement for a commission to investigate past atrocities, part of a negotiated peace accord between the government and the armed opposition. When the government took no action to set up the commission, Rwandan human rights groups invited four international human rights organizations, from the United States, Canada, France, and Burkina Faso, to undertake such an inquiry. Despite the president's public statement welcoming this nongovernmental commission and the assistance provided by some government ministries, it was clear that the president and armed forces resented these investigations, and some witnesses were targeted for attack in what may have been retaliation for their cooperation with the commission. The commission's report, released in 1993, had the greatest impact on European governments, especially France and Belgium, which were then actively supporting the Rwandan government.[17] Yet the report and its recommendations failed to prevent the eruption of genocidal violence that came just one year later.

A full truth-commission-like inquiry and report can also form part of a formal judicial inquiry, although this is rare. In Ethiopia, a Special Prosecutor's Office intended to thoroughly document the broad pattern of abuses under the Mengistu regime, in the course of preparing for trials of over two thousand accused perpetrators, and to publish its broad findings in a report. For several years the office maintained an extensive computerized system and dozens of staff with which to cull names and incriminating details from the extensive documentation that was left behind by the regime. It collected substantial information, but the plan for a truth report was eventually dropped. The Special Prosecutor's Office continues to rely on this documentation in the courtroom, however, arguing that the broad pattern of events points to a policy of genocide under Mengistu. Meanwhile, the prosecutors have used the trials not only to prosecute, but as a public platform to document victims' experiences. Over five hundred witnesses were called to the stand during the first five years of a trial of approximately fifty persons accused; all victims relate similar stories, though little of the testimony directly implicates those on trial, according to observers. There was no end in sight for the trial; after the expected 800 to 1,000 witnesses for the prosecution, it was expected that the defense would call another 800 or more witnesses on its behalf.[18] Meanwhile, over two thousand others accused of similar crimes sat in jail also awaiting trial. Ethiopia's attempt to merge the two goals of broad truth-telling and criminal prosecutions into one process is clearly problematic, and has been criticized by international observers.

Recent years have also produced a number of interesting models of international inquiries that have an official or semiofficial flavor and overlap with the work that is typical of truth commissions. For example, an International Panel of Eminent Personalities to Investigate the 1994 Genocide in Rwanda and the Surrounding Events was created by the Organization of African Unity in late 1998, beginning work in January 1999 and completing its report in June 2000. Its research was focused on the history and circumstances of the conflict in Rwanda that led up to the genocide of 1994 and the resulting impact of the violence, basing its conclusions in part on research papers commissioned from experts. The Rwandan government cooperated with the inquiry. Furthermore, in 1999 the Swedish government created an Independedent International Commission on Kosovo, chaired by South African justice Richard Goldstone, to consider the causes, consequences, and international options for responding to the conflict in Kosovo; it is expected to release a report late in the year 2000.

Finally, there have been a number of war crimes investigations, often referred to as international commissions of inquiry, war crimes commissions, or commissions of experts, which should also be distinguished from truth commissions. These bodies, such as those established to look into events in the former Yugoslavia, Rwanda, and East Timor (and which often have quite long and unwieldy names), have been set up by the United Nations for the purposes of evaluating the evidence available for possible international prosecutions.[19] These commissions collect evidence, and sometimes testimony from victims, and then submit a report, thus overlapping with some of the functions of a truth commission. But these bodies are not authorized by the state under investigation, nor are they aimed at studying the overall patterns, causes, and consequences of the violence, so much as evaluating evidence of criminal wrongdoing and violations of international law. In most cases, these commissions have preceded the appointment of an ad hoc international tribunal, such as in the former Yugoslavia and Rwanda.

There are also important examples of nongovernmental projects that have documented the patterns of abuse of a prior regime, usually undertaken by national human rights organizations, sometimes with church backing. Despite limitations to such private investigations (particularly restricted access to government information), these unofficial projects have sometimes produced remarkable results. In Brazil, for example, a team of investigators was able to secretly photocopy all of the official court papers documenting political prisoners' complaints of torture—some one million pages in total. Working quietly, and with the support of the Archbishop of São Paulo and the World Council of Churches, the team relied on this material to produce *Brasil: Nunca Mais*, a report analyzing the military regime's torture practices over fifteen years' time.[20] In Uruguay, the nongovernmental Servicio Paz y Justicia (SERPAJ) published *Uruguay: Nunca Más*, a far stronger report than that resulting from an earlier parliamentary inquiry, which worked under a very limited mandate and with little political support.[21] The Human Rights Office of the Archbishop of Guatemala undertook an extensive project to document decades of abuses and massacres in advance of the official truth commission there, hoping to both complement and strengthen the commission's work.[22] In Russia, the nongovernmental organization Memorial was set up in 1987 to promote accountability and fact-finding around past events. Its staff has gathered extensive archives on state abuses going back to 1917, and published several books with lists of victims' names and an analysis of state policies of repression.[23]

There are many factors and a range of participants that help shape each country's transitional possibilities and constraints, and thus its posttransition reality. These include the strength of those groups or individuals who were responsible for the abuses and their ability to control transition policy choices; how vocal and organized is a country's civil society, including victims and rights groups; and the interest, role, and involvement of the international community. In addition, the transitional choices will be affected by the type and intensity of the past violence or repression and the political nature of the transition. And finally, there are often aspects of political and social culture — an undefinable set of preferences, inclinations, beliefs, and expectations — that help to shape the parameters of whether and in what manner the past is confronted.

But the actual number of victims does not seem to determine how heavy the past will weigh on the future, nor the intensity of interest in accountability. In some countries, a very small number of victims of government abuse has resulted in serious political repercussions and a strong emotional response from the public. In 1997, Spain was engulfed in political scandal around the deaths of twenty-seven activists in the early 1980s. Surinam, on the northern edge of South America, is still dealing with political repercussions from the assassination of fifteen prominent political activists in 1982, and as late as 1998 the government was entertaining the idea of a commission of inquiry to put those killings to rest. In Uruguay, tens of thousands marched in the street in 1996, 1997, and 1998 to demand a full accounting for the estimated 135 to 190 people who disappeared twenty years earlier. Even with such relatively small numbers of victims, the pressure for full truth and justice can be as great as in those countries where hundreds of thousands were killed.

Some observers, having watched past commissions and the reports they produce, are uncomfortable with the generic name of *truth commission* that these bodies have acquired. "They should be called 'fact and fiction commissions,' or 'some-of-the-truth commissions,'" one person who has long watched these bodies suggested half-seriously. Some people, including former staff of some of these bodies, would prefer the generic *commission of inquiry,* which would lift the pressure to be both perfect and comprehensive. In addition, since the South African commission has attracted widespread international attention, some people have begun to mistakenly equate truth commissions with amnesties. In 1995, for example, a United Nations special envoy to Burundi met strong resistance to his suggestion that a truth commission be established to look into recent violence in that Central African country, as everyone assumed that would mean amnesty for the wrongdoers. When he instead suggested a *commission of inquiry,* his idea quickly gained support, and an International Commission of Inquiry to investigate past violence was created a few months later.[24]

But overall, the *truth commission* name has caught on, and has now become a term with a generally understood meaning: an *official* investigation into a *past pattern of abuses*. Recent commissions have been especially likely to use the name; in Chile, El Salvador, Haiti, and South Africa, some variation of *commission on the truth* has been used. In Guatemala, rights advocates were initially disappointed when their commission on the past was not called a truth commission but instead given the weaker-sounding name "historical clarification commission."[25] On the other hand, the increasing use of *truth and reconciliation commission* as the generic—again, influenced by the well-known South African body—is inaccurate and should be avoided, since many of these commissions on the truth have not held reconciliation as a primary goal of their work, nor assumed that reconciliation would result.

It is certain that more countries will be turning to official truth-seeking in the coming years, and that these inquiries will be shaped in a variety of different ways, with powers, mandates, and expectations changing as local circumstances and priorities dictate. In virtually every state that has recently emerged from authoritarian rule or civil war, and in many still suffering repression or violence but where there is hope for a transition soon, there has been interest in creating a truth commission—either proposed by officials of the state or by human rights activists or others in civil society.[26] The task of these truth bodies will never be easy. Truth commissions are difficult and controversial entities; they are given a mammoth, almost impossible task and usually insufficient time and resources to complete it; they must struggle with rampant lies, denials, and deceit and the painful, almost unspeakable memories of victims to uncover still-dangerous truths that many in power may well continue to resist. At the end of a commission's work, a country may well find the past still unsettled and some key questions still unresolved. Yet despite the inherent limitations, both the process and the product of a truth commission can make a critical contribution in the midst of a difficult transition, fundamentally changing how a country understands and accepts some of the most contentious aspects of its recent history.

Why a Truth Commission?

Far beyond simply finding and stating the truth, official truth bodies have often been given a wide-ranging mission. In a number of cases, they have become the most prominent government initiatives dealing with past crimes and the central point out of which other measures for accountability, reparations, and reform programs are developed. The stated reasons behind setting up a truth commission have differed between countries. For example, some stress national reconciliation and the need to close the book on the past; others have framed it as a step toward prosecutions that will follow; yet others see an inquiry into the past as a means to distance the new government's policies from the former regime and to highlight a new rights-respecting era.

Though presented with varying degrees of emphasis, a truth commission may have any or all of the following five basic aims: to discover, clarify, and formally acknowledge past abuses; to respond to specific needs of victims; to contribute to justice and accountability; to outline institutional responsibility and recommend reforms; and to promote reconciliation and reduce conflict over the past.

TO CLARIFY AND ACKNOWLEDGE THE TRUTH

The most straightforward objective of a truth commission is sanctioned fact-finding: to establish an accurate record of a country's past, clarify uncertain events, and lift the lid of silence and denial from a contentious and painful period of history. The great number of interviews with victims, typical of these commissions, allows a detailed accounting of the patterns of violence over time and across regions, literally recording a hidden history. The detail and breadth of information in a truth commission report is usually of a kind and quality far better than any previous historical account, leaving the country with a written and well-documented record of otherwise oft-disputed events. Beyond outlining overall patterns, some truth commissions have also cracked a number of key cases, even naming the perpetrators or the high-placed intellectual authors of major unsolved crimes. The official and public recognition of past abuses serves to effectively unsilence a topic that might otherwise be spoken of only in hushed tones, long considered too dangerous for general conversation, rarely reported honestly in the press, and certainly out of bounds of the official history taught in schools. In effect, the report of a truth commission reclaims a country's history and opens it for public review.

In some countries, rights activists insist that a truth commission does not find new truth so much as lift the veil of denial about widely known but unspoken truths. Firm denial may especially be present in those countries where the repressive government depended on the active or passive support of the public, or certain sectors of the public, to carry out its policies and maintain power. Antiapartheid activists in South Africa insist that it was impossible for any South African not to have known that torture, killing, and other repressive tactics against opponents were commonplace under the apartheid regime; that unless people consciously chose to put on blinders to block out the truth, they should have known. Some South Africans therefore argue that that commission's most important contribution was simply to remove the possibility of continued denial. While there were initial claims of disbelief from former apartheid supporters when the harsh stories of victims began to emerge, as the commission's hearings continued, and especially as perpetrators took the stand to describe in detail the torture and killings they were involved in, it became impossible for anyone to resist the truth of the testimony. As writer Michael Ignatieff has said, "The past is an argument and the function of truth commissions, like the function of honest historians, is simply to purify the argument, to narrow the range of permissible lies."[1]

Yet compared to many whites, black South Africans were generally not so surprised by the evidence of abuse by state forces: they were victims and witnesses to these abuses themselves. Indeed, in many situations that warrant a post-transition truth commission, the victimized populations may already have a good idea of what took place and who was responsible, and investigations only confirm widely held beliefs about the events or practices in question. In some countries, the atrocities took place with either explicit recognition by the responsible parties (such as political kidnappings, or public announcements about which groups or individuals were targeted), or by uniformed personnel leaving witnesses to their acts (as with the abduction of activists in public, or massacres by armed forces). This sense of victims already knowing the truth, and thus gaining little new truth from a commission, is compounded by the unfortunate fact that few victims who provide testimony to truth commissions are able to learn new information about their own case. Due to the great numbers of testimonies taken and limited time and resources, truth commissions can only undertake serious investigation into a very small number of cases. Most of the thousands of testimonies are recorded exactly as reported by the deponents and used for a statistical analysis of trends, but unfortunately never investigated in depth.

For some victims and survivors, therefore, a truth commission does not so much tell them new truth, as much as formally recognize a truth they may already generally know. In the process of collecting testimony and publishing an official report, a commission offers an official acknowledgment of long-silenced facts. The president may use the occasion of formally accepting a commission report to make a statement of apology on behalf of the state. When President Patricio Aylwin released the Chilean truth report to the public, for example, he made an emotional appeal, broadcast on national television, in which he begged pardon and forgiveness from the families of the victims, often cited by survivors as a powerful moment after having their claims brushed aside for so many years.[2] He then sent a copy of the report to the families of each of the victims listed in the report, with a letter noting the page on which they would find their case listed.

This distinction between *knowledge* and *acknowledgment* has often been noted by observers of truth commissions, first articulated at one of the first major conferences on transitional justice in 1988.[3] "Acknowledgment implies that the state has admitted its misdeeds and recognized that it was wrong," writes Aryeh Neier, president of the Open Society Institute and former executive director of Human Rights Watch.[4] Juan Méndez, a prominent rights lawyer, writes that "Knowledge that is officially sanctioned, and thereby made 'part of the public cognitive scene' . . . acquires a mysterious quality that is not there when it is merely 'truth.' Official acknowledgment at least begins to heal the wounds."[5]

Official acknowledgment can be powerful precisely because official denial has been so pervasive. Some measure the need for official truth, and therefore the appropriateness of a truth commission, in the degree to which a government tried to disguise the true nature of its regime. Aryeh Neier has argued that the need for truth-seeking is determined by how hidden the atrocities were. "The crucial factor is, while abuses were being committed, was the practice one of deception? Certain governments have tried to maintain international legitimacy while engaged in abuses — like a number of Latin American governments, vis-à-vis their relations with the U.S." The crimes in some countries are intentionally committed in a way that can be easily masked: troops wearing civilian clothes and driving unmarked cars, persons disappearing without a trace. "Everything about these crimes was intended to be deniable. Where deception is so central to the abuses, then truth takes on a greatly added significance. The revelation of truth in these circumstances takes on a certain amount of power," explains Neier.[6]

Disappearing a person is the most blatant form of atrocity by deception, with the obvious intent to lie, hide, and conceal. Yet it is not only disappearances that can remain hidden; even large massacres have gone uncounted in some countries, and have been officially and vehemently denied even in the face of significant evidence to the contrary. Hundreds of massacres took place throughout the highlands of Guatemala in the early 1980s during the military's campaign to wipe out armed guerrillas and their supporters. However, access to these areas was blocked to outsiders, preventing news of the massacres from getting out. Even many survivors of the atrocities did not know that similar massacres were taking place elsewhere: prevented by the military from traveling to neighboring villages, often several hours' walk away, many concluded that their village alone was targeted.

Yet even in those circumstances where the events seemed to be well recorded as they took place, basic facts may still be passionately disputed later, sometimes even intentionally misrepresented to serve political ends. Despite close reporting of the Bosnian war, there are three contradictory versions of official truth in Bosnia about what really happened in that war, each version taught in different schools to different communities — Muslim, Croat, or Serb — and reinforcing fundamental points of conflict that could well flare up in future violence. In 1998, Bosnians began to consider the idea of a truth commission in order to establish one agreed-upon and well-documented historical account.

TO RESPOND TO THE NEEDS AND INTERESTS OF VICTIMS

A fundamental difference between trials and truth commissions is the nature and extent of their attention to victims. The function of the judicial system, first and foremost, is to investigate the specific acts of accused perpetrators. During a trial, victims are invited to testify only as needed to back up the specific claims of a case, usually comprising a very narrow set of events which constitutes the crime charged. Usually very few victims are called to testify, and their testimony is likely to be directly and perhaps even aggressively challenged by the defense attorneys in court. (In some cases, victims may also play a critical role in actively moving a case forward for prosecution.)

Most truth commissions, in contrast, are designed to focus primarily on victims. Although commissions may investigate the involvement of individual perpetrators in abuses, and may receive critical information from reaching out to accused perpetrators and others from within the system of repression much of their time and attention is focused on victims. They usually take testimony from a broad array of witnesses, victims, and survivors, and consider all of these accounts in analyzing and describing the greater pattern of events. By listening to victims' stories, perhaps holding public hearings, and publishing a report that describes a broad array of experiences of suffering, commissions effectively give victims a public voice and bring their suffering to the awareness of the broader public. As the South African commission hearings progressed, for example, therapists who worked with torture survivors saw a marked increase in the public's understanding and appreciation of victims' needs. For some victims and survivors, this process may have a cathartic or healing effect.

Commissions may serve victims' needs in other ways: some help to design a reparations program for victims or for families of those killed in political violence, and in a few cases the lists of victims compiled by the truth commission serve as the lists of beneficiaries once a reparations program is established (there will be more on this in chapter 11).

Finally, on a very practical level, many family members of those disappeared want desperately to have the legal status of their loved one officially established. Many civil matters cannot be settled without a death certificate — such as processing a will or accessing money in the disappeared person's bank account. In Sri Lanka, Argentina, and elsewhere, these very practical considerations added significantly to the suffering of survivors. In Argentina, the state designed a new legal status of "forcibly disappeared,"

focus on victims

public certificate

death certificate

functionally equivalent to a death certificate, allowing the processing of civil matters without declaring that the person was dead. This status was applied to all those documented by the truth commission.

TO CONTRIBUTE TO JUSTICE AND ACCOUNTABILITY

Rather than displacing or replacing justice in the courts, a commission may sometimes help contribute to accountability for perpetrators. Many commissions pass their files on to the prosecuting authorities, and where there is a functioning judicial system, sufficient evidence, and sufficient political will, trials may result (there will be more on this in chapter 7). A few commissions have named names of wrongdoers, thus providing a moral sanction, at least. Some have recommended other sanctions that might be instituted without a full trial, such as removing abusers from positions in security forces where they might do further harm. (The difficulty in naming perpetrators in commission reports, and the effect of doing so, is addressed in chapter 8.)

TO OUTLINE INSTITUTIONAL RESPONSIBILITY AND RECOMMEND REFORMS

In addition to addressing the role of individual perpetrators, truth commissions are well positioned to evaluate the institutional responsibilities for extensive abuses, and to outline the weaknesses in the institutional structures or existing laws that should be changed to prevent abuses from reoccurring in the future. It is possible that a commission might help prevent future abuses simply by publishing an accurate record of past abuses, with the hope that a more knowledgeable citizenry will recognize and resist any sign of return to repressive rule. Yet future peace and civility will probably depend much more on changing the institutions in which such abuses have taken place, such as the police and military, as well as those institutions responsible for preventing abuses and punishing wrongdoers, such as the judiciary. Truth commissions are uniquely positioned to undertake this evaluative and prescriptive task, as they can base their conclusions and recommendations on a close study of the record, while standing as an independent institution separate from the systems under review. There is generally no other state body in a position to review the record and deficiencies of the judicial system, for example. In the end, the implementation of reforms recommended by a truth commission depends on the interest and political will of those in power. Most commissions' recommendations have not been mandatory, although they are useful in providing a road map for change and creating pressure points around which the civil society or the international community can push for reforms (for more on this see chapter 10).

TO PROMOTE RECONCILIATION AND REDUCE TENSIONS RESULTING FROM PAST VIOLENCE

Common wisdom holds that the future depends on the past: one must confront the legacy of past horrors or there will be no foundation on which to build a new society. Bury your sins, and they will reemerge later. Stuff skeletons in the closet, and they will fall back out of the closet at the most inauspicious times. Try to quiet the ghosts of the past, and they will haunt you forever—at the risk of opening society to cycles of violence, anger, pain, and revenge. By directly confronting the conflicts of old, it is surmised, these conflicts will be less likely to explode into severe violence or political conflict in the future. Certainly, resolving disagreements and airing latent conflicts can help ease tensions. Yet in some circumstances, in the midst of a delicate transition, truth-telling could also increase tensions, especially when this truth pertains to the culpability of powerful figures or unrepentant armed forces in the commission of large-scale crimes. A government might understandably enter this arena with great care.[7]

In a similar vein, as noted above, many proponents of truth-seeking assert that forgiveness and reconciliation will result from airing the full truth. How can victims forgive without knowing *whom* to forgive and *what* to forgive them for? The goal of reconciliation has been so closely associated with some past truth commissions that many casual observers assume that reconciliation is an integral, or even primary, purpose of creating a truth commission, which is not always true. Whether and how national, political, or even individual reconciliation might result from clarifying the truth, and what other factors are likely to affect this elusive goal, are further explored in chapter 10.

Finally, in addition to these specific purposes for undertaking truth-seeking, some observers argue that finding and making public the truth about abuses is an obligation of the state, as confirmed in international law, and that there is an inherent *right to truth* held by all victims or survivors, or by society as a whole. International human rights law obliges states to investigate and punish gross violators of human rights in most circumstances; implied within that obligation is the inherent right of the citizenry to know the results of such investigations, rights advocates argue. Frank LaRue of the Center for Human Rights Legal Action, in Guatemala, and Richard Carver, formerly of Article 19 in London, were among the first to articulate this right to truth, in 1993. Carver wrote, "Article 19 considers that there is indeed a 'right to know the truth' which is contained within the right to 'seek, receive and impart information' which is guaranteed by Article 19 of the Universal Declaration of Human Rights." He also cites a similar "right to receive information" in the African Charter on Human and Peoples' Rights.[8] Human rights advocates also point to the ruling of the Inter-American Court of Human Rights in the Velásquez Rodríguez case of 1988, which concluded that the state has a duty to investigate the fate of the disappeared and disclose the information to relatives.[9]

These many and varied hopes of a truth commission are compelling reasons for any country to undertake an exercise in official truth-seeking. These ends are certainly important enough to justify considerable energy, expense, time, and effort. Yet unfortunately, the complexity and sensitivity of the task have meant that many commissions have trouble reaching these goals. The following two chapters will begin to suggest why.

four

Five Illustrative
Truth Commissions

The twenty-one commissions described in this and the next chapter represent a broad range of institutions. This list of twenty-one is probably not an exhaustive list, but it certainly includes the great majority and the most important of them to date.[1] The list is growing rapidly: in mid-1999, both Nigeria and Sierra Leone announced the formation of truth commissions, the former through presidential decree shortly after the end of military rule, and the latter agreed to in the peace agreement that ended a nine-year civil war. At the beginning of the year 2000, at least a half dozen additional countries were considering their own truth commissions.

Five of the more substantial truth commissions to date — judged by their size, the impact they had on their respective political transitions, and the national and international attention they received — are described in this chapter at greater length. These five commissions — in Argentina, Chile, El Salvador, South Africa, and Guatemala (in chronological order) — offer significant insights into the workings of these truth bodies, and are referred to more frequently throughout this book. The remaining sixteen commissions are described more briefly in chapter 5.

Four of the five commissions in this chapter were in Latin America, which may suggest, incorrectly, that the majority of truth commissions have existed there. In fact, Africa has had a greater number. For whatever reason, however, the truth commissions in Latin America have tended to be quite substantial affairs, generally presented as central initiatives countering sometimes compromised transitions, and attracting significant public attention. Many of these bodies in Africa have tended to be smaller, less successful, and less prominent. Now, following the great international attention received by the South African Truth and Reconciliation Commission, governments worldwide are approaching these bodies with more seriousness. The truth commissions now being created are much more likely to be larger and more substantial endeavors, and to receive greater international oversight and input. The five commissions here are those most likely to be looked to as examples to follow — or to learn from.

ARGENTINA

The armed forces seized power in Argentina in 1976, and went on to rule the country, in several successive military juntas, for the next seven years. During this time, in a vicious anticommunist campaign to eliminate "subversives," an estimated 10,000 to 30,000 people were disappeared at the hands of the military — arrested, tortured, and killed, the body disposed of so as never to be found, and the fate of the victim never known by agonized family members. It was only after Argentina's war with Great Britain over the Malvinas/Falkland Islands, and the resulting disgrace and public outrage suffered by the armed forces over their loss, that the military acquiesced to popular elections and a return to civilian rule in 1983. Before leaving power, in fear of being held accountable for its crimes, the military junta granted itself immunity from prosecution and issued a decree ordering the destruction of all documents relating to military repression.

The newly elected president, Raúl Alfonsín, tackled the human rights issue immediately upon taking office. An investigative commission on the disappeared was discussed the very first morning of Alfonsin's presidency, according to a key presidential advisor, and within a week the National Commission on the Disappeared (often referred to by its acronym in Spanish, CONADEP) was created through presidential decree.[2] Alfonsin appointed ten commission members "who enjoyed national and international prestige, chosen for their consistent stance in defense of human rights and their representation of different walks of life."[3] Both chambers of congress were also asked to appoint representatives to the commission, although only one complied. The commission was chaired by the widely respected author Ernesto Sábato.

Nongovernmental organizations had lobbied for a parliamentary commission, which could be given much stronger powers than a presidentially appointed body, and were initially resistant to cooperating with Alfonsin's commission because it lacked power to compel the production of information from perpetrators or from military institutions. Most human rights organizations eventually decided to assist the inquiry, turning over great numbers of files on the disappeared, although ultimately their concerns were confirmed: the commission received almost no cooperation from the armed forces, despite repeated requests for information from the commission's investigators.

Although the commission held no public hearings, it maintained a prominent public profile. The commission staff inspected detention centers, clandestine cemeteries, and police facilities; exiles returned from abroad to testify; and statements were taken in embassies and consulates of Argentina around the world. The commission also worked closely with families of the disappeared to locate persons who might still be alive, but it found none. The commission took over 7,000 statements over nine months' time, documenting 8,960 persons who had disappeared. Among those interviewed were over 1,500 people who had survived the military's detention camps, who gave detailed descriptions of conditions in the camps and the kinds of torture used. The commission's primary investigations focused on identifying detention and torture camps, often visiting former camps with survivors to assist in confirming their locations. A list of 365 former torture centers is included in the commission's final report, with accompanying photographs of a number of them.

After nine months, the commission submitted its full report, *Nunca Más* (*Never Again*), to the president.[4] A shorter, book-length version was published by a private publishing house in cooperation with the government. The report was an immediate best-seller: 40,000 copies were sold on the first day of its release, 150,000 copies in the first eight weeks. It has now been reprinted over twenty times, has sold almost 300,000 copies, and is one of the best-selling books ever in Argentina's history. Over fifteen years after it was released, the report can still be found for sale at many sidewalk kiosks throughout Buenos Aires.

Meanwhile, the amnesty that the military regime had granted itself was quickly repealed by the civilian government, and the commission turned its files directly over to the state prosecutor's office. The information collected by the commission, and especially the great number of direct witnesses identified in its case files, was critical in the trial of senior members of the military juntas, succeeding in putting five generals in jail.[5]

CHILE

In September 1973, General Augusto Pinochet overthrew the civilian government of Chile, brutally repressed all opponents, and proceeded to rule Chile for seventeen years. The regime espoused a virulent anticommunism to justify its repressive tactics, which included mass arrests, torture, killings, and disappearances. The worst of the violence was in the first year after the coup, when some twelve hundred people were killed or disappeared, and many thousands more were detained, tortured, and eventually released. The judiciary remained in place, though it did very little to challenge the regime's actions. Meanwhile, nongovernmental organizations, including a church-based human rights project, challenged virtually every case of illegal detention or disappearance in court, which succeeded in establishing a solid record of each case even if rarely gaining the release of the imprisoned. In 1978, Pinochet instituted an amnesty law, which barred prosecution for almost all human rights crimes that had occurred since the coup.

Despite the brutality of his regime, Pinochet maintained the support of a significant number of Chileans, particularly those on the political right, and when he consented to a plebiscite in 1988 on his continued rule, he only narrowly lost. Patricio Aylwin was elected and assumed the presidency in March 1990, though with certain restrictions on democratic rule. Pinochet had amended the constitution in 1980 to ensure his continued power and to preserve the autonomy and political influence of the military; among these changes was the stipulation that he would remain commander in chief of the army until 1998, and would thereafter serve as senator for life.

The amnesty constrained Aylwin's options for responding to the abuses of the Pinochet regime. Deciding that it would not be possible to nullify the amnesty, Aylwin instead turned to a policy of investigating and establishing the truth about the past. Just six weeks after his inauguration, in what became one of the most prominent initiatives of his administration, Aylwin created a National Commission on Truth and Reconciliation through presidential decree. Aylwin appointed eight people to serve on the commission, intentionally selecting four members who had supported Pinochet, including former officials of the Pinochet government, as well as four who had been in opposition, thus avoiding any perception of bias in the commission's work. This strategy proved particularly powerful when the final report received unanimous backing by all eight members. The commission was chaired by a former Senator, Raúl Rettig.

The mandate of the Chilean commission directed it to investigate "disappearances after arrest, executions, and torture leading to death committed by government agents or people in their service, as well as kidnappings and attempts on the life of persons carried out by private citizens for political reasons."[6] Its mandate excluded cases of torture that did not result in death. Thus, although the commission describes practices of torture in some detail in its report, those who were tortured and survived were not listed as victims, their cases were not investigated, and there remains a lack of clarity on the total number of torture survivors (estimates range from 50,000 to 200,000). Torture survivors also did not receive reparations in the program that was established to implement the commission's recommendations.[7]

The commission was given nine months to complete its work. It was greatly assisted by information from nongovernmental organizations, including the detailed records from the thousands of cases that had been taken to court throughout the years of the military regime. In every case, no matter how well documented previously, the commission again took testimony from the families of the missing or killed. Its limited mandate and the relatively small number of cases allowed it to undertake a thorough investigation of each case, relying on its staff of sixty. "As it began to operate," the report explains, "the Commission believed that its primary duty was to determine what really had happened in every case in which human rights had been seriously violated. Only by determining what had happened in each individual instance would the Commission be able to draw up as complete a picture as possible of the overall phenomenon of the violations of these basic rights."[8] The commission also placed advertisements in newspapers around the world asking for information from exiles. It had no power of subpoena, however, and received little cooperation from the armed forces.[9] Of the 3,400 cases brought to it, 2,920 were determined to fit within its mandate.[10]

The commission's eighteen-hundred-page report was completed in February 1991. It is a powerful indictment of the practices of the Pinochet regime, describing both the brutality that took place and the response by domestic and international actors. Of the cases that constituted human rights violations, under the commission's definition, over 95 percent were attributed to State agents.[11] It also addressed the abuses by the relatively small armed left, which the commission found to be responsible for 4 percent of the documented rights violations, although the report debunks one of the central arguments used by the military to justify its violent tactics, that the country had faced an "internal war" that thus demanded significant force against opponents.[12] The impact of the process on the commissioners themselves was powerful. One commission member, who had himself headed an ineffective human rights commission under Pinochet, told the press after the report's release, "What I know now, I would not have imagined."[13]

After taking several weeks to read the report, President Aylwin released it to the public with an emotional statement on national television. Speaking on behalf of the state, he begged forgiveness from the victims and stressed the need for forgiveness and reconciliation, and asked the armed forces to "make gestures of recognition of the pain caused."[14] Pinochet responded with a long statement expressing "fundamental disagreement" with the report and insisted that the army "had saved the freedom and sovereignty of the homeland" by carrying out the coup in 1973. He did not question any specific aspect of the report's conclusions, however.[15]

Relatively few copies of the report were printed, although the full report was reproduced as an insert in a daily newspaper. There were plans to hold national reconciliation and educational events centered around the report. However, in the four weeks following the report's release, three attacks by the armed Left against right-wing members of the political elite, particularly the assassination of the close associate and confidant of Pinochet, Senator Jaime Guzmán, succeeded in shifting the country's attention away from the truth report and toward the threat of leftist terrorists, and all plans for social reconciliation exercises were dropped. The killings "effectively ended public discussion of the Rettig report" according to Human Rights Watch.[16] A year later it was reported that "the Rettig Report, with its deeply disturbing revelations and conclusions, has not re-surfaced since."[17]

Despite the limited public attention to the report, the commission's work had the direct result of prompting a significant reparations program for families of the killed or disappeared. Legislation was passed to establish a follow-up commission, the National Corporation for Reparation and Reconciliation, to search for remains of the disappeared, resolve cases still left open, organize the commission's files so that they could be made available to the public, and institute the reparations program.[18]

Despite the work of the truth commission, the issue of past abuses was not often comfortably discussed by the public or press in Chile for a number of years following. As one torture survivor told me in 1996, to bring up the subject of the abuses under Pinochet in any social context was considered to be "in bad taste." It was not until Pinochet stepped down as commander in chief of the army to take up his post in the senate in early 1998, and was later arrested in London in late 1998 on an extradition request from Spain, that the issue of past human rights violations began to be widely discussed and debated in Chile. The controversy resulting from Spain's request to try Pinochet fundamentally shifted the political landscape in Chile regarding past rights abuses, leading to increased domestic judicial activity on a number of past cases, particularly in reference to the disappeared. Meanwhile, the Spanish judge who asked for Pinochet's extradition relied heavily on Chile's truth commission report in building and presenting his case, even citing the truth report directly in Pinochet's arrest warrant.

EL SALVADOR

With the assistance of $4.5 billion in military and other aid from the United States in the 1980s, the El Salvador government fought a twelve-year war against leftist guerrillas, known as the Farabundo Martí National Liberation Front (or FMLN in Spanish), beginning in 1980 and ending with a United Nations–brokered peace accord in the last days of 1991. The war was marked by tens of thousands of political killings and disappearances, as well as many large-scale massacres of unarmed civilians; it was estimated that 1.4 percent of the Salvadoran population was killed during the conflict.[19] Among the most prominent cases was the killing of six Jesuit priests in 1989, which helped to spur international pressure to end the war.[20] Throughout the war, reports of human rights violations were a point of intense controversy, especially in the U.S. Congress and within the administration of Ronaled Reagan, which vehemently denied the extent of abuses by Salvadoran government forces.

An agreement for a Commission on the Truth for El Salvador was included in the UN-brokered peace accord, initially agreed to in April 1991—just over a year after the Chilean commission concluded its report, which served as the point of reference (and the origin of the idea) for the peace negotiators. The signatories to the accord considered specifying exactly which cases should be investigated by the commission, but they were unable to come to an agreement on key cases, and thus left its mandate open, indicating only that it should investigate "serious acts of violence" that occurred since 1980 whose "impact on society urgently demands that the public should know the truth."[21] The commission was administered by the United Nations and funded through contributions from UN member states (with the largest contributions coming from the United States and several European states), though it had full operational independence in its work.

The mandate granted the commission six months to complete its work, although it obtained a two-month extension to give it a total of eight months to undertake all investigations and submit its report. The commissioners, appointed by the UN secretary-general with the agreement of the two parties to the accords, were highly respected international figures: Belisario Betancur, former president of Colombia; Thomas Buergenthal, former president of the Inter-American Court of Human Rights and professor of law at George Washington University; and Reinaldo Figueredo Planchart, former minister of foreign relations for Venezuela. The commission was supported by approximately twenty staff for its collection of testimony and investigations, with another twenty-five short-term staff added in the last months for data entry and information processing. Due to objectivity concerns, no Salvadorans were included on staff.

The commission took testimony from some two thousand victims and witnesses, reporting on over seven thousand cases of killings, disappearances, torture, rape, and massacres. It also collected information from secondary sources, including national and international human rights groups, relating to over twenty thousand additional victims. It investigated several dozen prominent or representative cases, and brought in the Argentine Forensic Anthropology Team to exhume the remains of a major massacre in the town of El Mozote, which had been at the center of international controversy. Although the armed forces provided little assistance as a whole, a number of senior-level members of the security forces were willing to meet quietly and confidentially with the commission to provide critical inside information—sometimes agreeing only to meet with the commission outside the country, in fear for their safety.[22] Despite intense pressure to soften its report, the commission came to strong conclusions on dozens of controversial cases, naming over forty senior members of the military, judiciary, and armed opposition for their role in the atrocities. The commission concluded that 95 percent of the abuses were committed by those affiliated with the government or armed forces.

The publication of the commission report, *From Madness to Hope,* was "a major political event in El Salvador," according to the Lawyers Committee for Human Rights. In the days leading up to the release of the report, speculation about who would be named in connection with key cases "reached a level of mass hysteria."[23] On the whole, the report itself was well received by human rights activists and organizations in El Salvador and in the United States. However, the commission was criticized for failing to fully report on certain important aspects of the violence, such as the operation of death squads, and on the role of the United States in supporting the government forces. The Salvadoran military responded to the report with a long statement, read on national television by the defense minister, who had himself been named in the report. Flanked by the full military high command, he blasted the report as "unfair, incomplete, illegal, unethical, biased, and insolent" and complained that "the commission does not recognize in its report the nature and origins of the communist attack against El Salvador."[24] The civilian president Alfredo Cristiani, meanwhile, told the press that the report failed to meet the Salvadoran people's "yearning" for national reconciliation, "which is to forgive and forget this painful past."[25]

Five days after the report's release, a sweeping amnesty law was passed that prevented any legal action against the perpetrators, thus considerably deflating the public interest in the truth report.[26] The naming of perpetrators in the commission's report did provide critical support for the removal of human rights violators from the armed forces, however, especially those whom had been previously named by the Ad Hoc Commission, a body established by the peace accords with the task of cleaning human rights violators from the ranks of the armed forces. Those named did not necessarily suffer otherwise, however. Four months after the report's release, for example, Salvadoran Minister of Defense René Emilio Ponce and a number of others named as having participated in major atrocities were retired with full military honors, having completed thirty years of service. In the retirement ceremony, President Cristiani praised the men for performing with "merit, efficiency, and loyalty to the highest duties that the nation can demand."[27]

With strong international pressure, several of the report's key policy recommendations were gradually put in place over the next years, particularly in the area of judicial reform. In retrospect, however, some observers believe that the impact of the truth commission report may have been greater in the United States than in El Salvador. The U.S. government responded to the truth commission report by appointing a panel to examine the implications for foreign policy and the operations of its Department of State, although the panel's report was criticized as too narrow. President Bill Clinton also ordered the review and release of more classified documents pertaining to the U.S. role in the war.

SOUTH AFRICA

After forty-five years of apartheid in South Africa, and thirty-odd years of some level of armed resistance against the apartheid state by the armed wing of the African National Congress (ANC) and others, the country had suffered massacres, killings, torture, lengthy imprisonment of activists, and severe economic and social discrimination against its majority nonwhite population. The greatest number of deaths took place in the conflict between the ANC and the government-backed Inkatha Freedom Party, particularly in the eastern region of the country that is now KwaZulu Natal.

The idea for a truth commission was proposed as early as 1992, but it was not until after Nelson Mandela was elected president in April 1994 that serious discussions began about what form a national truth commission would take.[28] The most contentious issue during the negotiations toward an interim constitution in late 1993 was whether an amnesty would be granted to wrongdoers, as the government and military insisted. In the final hour of negotiations, the parties agreed to a "postamble" to the constitution that stated that "amnesty shall be granted in respect of acts, omissions and offenses associated with political objectives and committed in the course of the conflicts of the past." Only later was this amnesty linked to a truth-seeking process.

After considerable input from civil society, including two international conferences to explore the transitional justice policies instituted in other countries, and after hundreds of hours of hearings, the South African Parliament passed the Promotion of National Unity and Reconciliation Act in mid-1995. Following a public nomination and selection process, seventeen commissioners were appointed, with Archbishop Desmond Tutu as chair. The commission was inaugurated in December 1995, although several months of setup delayed their first hearings and investigations until April 1996.

The commission's empowering act provided the most complex and sophisticated mandate for any truth commission to date, with carefully balanced powers and an extensive investigatory reach. Written in precise legal language and running to over twenty single-spaced pages, the act gave the commission the power to grant individualized amnesty, search premises and seize evidence, subpoena witnesses, and run a sophisticated witness-protection program. With a staff of three hundred, a budget of some $18 million each year for two-and-a-half years, and four large offices around the country, the commission dwarfed previous truth commissions in its size and reach.

The act designed the commission to work in three interconnected committees: the Human Rights Violations Committee was responsible for collecting statements from victims and witnesses and recording the extent of

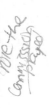

gross human rights violations; the Amnesty Committee processed and decided individual applications for amnesty; and the Reparations and Rehabilitation Committee was tasked with designing and putting forward recommendations for a reparations program.

The commission took testimony from over 21,000 victims and witnesses, 2,000 of which appeared in public hearings. Media coverage of the commission was intense: most newspapers ran a number of stories on the commission every day, and radio and television news often led with a story on the most recent revelations from the commission's hearings. Four hours of hearings were broadcast live over national radio each day, and a *Truth Commission Special Report* television show on Sunday evenings quickly became the most-watched news show in the country.[29]

The commission also held special hearings focused on sectors or key institutions of society and their response to or participation in abusive practices. These institutional hearings focused on the religious community, the legal community, business and labor, the health sector, the media, prisons, and the armed forces. Other special hearings looked at the use of chemical and biological weapons against opponents of the apartheid government, compulsory military service, political party policies, and how youth and women were affected by the violence. The commission also held hearings to address the involvement of specific individuals; the most well known of these was Winnie Mandikizela Mandela, who insisted that her hearing be held in public session rather than in private, as the commission had first planned. The two weeks of intensely covered hearings of Mandikizela Mandela sparked several police investigations into her involvement in criminal acts and effectively ended her pursuit of a prominent political post.

Unfortunately, the commission did not often use the strong powers that it had at its disposal, and was sometimes criticized for holding the mission of reconciliation above that of finding the truth. It employed its subpoena and search and seizures powers only a handful of times; to avoid upsetting various parties, the commission delayed or decided not to issue subpoena or search orders against several key individuals or institutions, among them the headquarters of the South African Defence Force and the ANC, both of which were either slow (in the latter case) or resistant (in the former) to turn over requested information. The commission was also strongly criticized by human rights organizations for not issuing a subpoena against Minister of Home Affairs and Inkatha Freedom Party President Mangosuthu Buthelezi, a decision based largely on the commission's fear of a possible violent reaction.

The greatest innovation of the commission, and the most controversial of its powers, was its ability to grant individual amnesty for politically motivated crimes committed between 1960 and April 1994. The commission received over seven thousand applications for amnesty.[30] Amnesty was granted only to those who fully confessed to their involvement in past crimes and showed them to be politically motivated. For gross violations of human rights (in contrast to politically motivated crimes against property or gun running, for example), the applicant was required to appear in a public hearing to answer questions from the commission, from legal counsel representing victims or their families, and directly from victims themselves.[31] The Amnesty Committee considered a number of factors in determining whether the applicant satisfied the terms for amnesty. Among them, the committee was directed to consider the relationship between the act, omission, or offense and the political objective pursued, and in particular whether there was "proportionality" between the act and the political objective pursued.[32] Any crimes committed for personal gain, or out of personal malice, ill will, or spite were not eligible for amnesty. Neither an apology nor any sign of remorse was necessary to be granted amnesty.

Given the detailed public disclosure that was required to gain amnesty for the most brutal and horrific crimes, it was clear that this truth-for-amnesty offer would only be taken up by those who reasonably feared prosecution. It was hoped that a number of early trials would increase the perceived threat of prosecution. A few high-profile trials for apartheid-era acts did successfully result in convictions and long sentences and spurred an increase in amnesty applications. However, when another important trial — that of the former minister of defense Magnus Malan and nineteen others — ended in acquittal, it was clear that the threat of prosecution would not be strong enough to persuade many senior-level perpetrators to take advantage of the amnesty process. The deadline for applying for amnesty was set for a year before the commission was scheduled to end, with the intention that perpetrators would fear they would be fingered in later amnesty hearings. As well, in order to further increase the pressure on perpetrators to apply for amnesty the commission held some investigative hearings behind closed doors, keeping secret the names mentioned and the crimes detailed. Yet in the end, many former perpetrators took the risk not to apply, particularly political leaders of the apartheid government and senior officers of the army.

A number of key amnesty decisions attracted particular attention. The admitted killers of antiapartheid activist Steve Biko were denied amnesty for the crime on the grounds that the killers claimed his death to be accidental. The panel rejected the argument that an "accidental" killing could be associated with a political objective, and noted that because none of the applicants was admitting to a crime, logic would hold that they could not receive amnesty for it.[33] The panel also questioned whether the applicants had told the full truth.[34] In other cases, the committee ruled that abuses resulting from simple racism could not receive amnesty, in that they lacked both a political motive and the expressed or implied authorization from a political or state body — although there were inconsistencies in the committee's rulings on this and other issues.[35]

This truth commission was the first to have its powers, and its decisions, challenged in a court of law, and it was involved in numerous legal battles throughout the course of its work. Perhaps most important, three prominent victims' families challenged the constitutionality of the commission's amnesty-granting power. The case was decided in favor of the commission by the South African Constitutional Court.[36] Another suit was filed to force the commission to notify in advance those who were to be accused of wrongdoing in a public hearing; the court mandated that the commission must provide reasonable notice to those expected to be named. Charges were brought against former president P. W. Botha after he refused to comply with a subpoena to appear before the commission. His trial turned into an opportunity for the commission to lay out in public its extensive evidence against him, including his knowledge or approval of a long pattern of state crimes. Against this barrage of information, Botha's public support withered. He was convicted, fined $2,000, and given a one-year suspended prison sentence. On appeal, however, the conviction was overturned on a technicality.[37]

The commission's five-volume report was released in October 1998, sparking unexpected controversy in the days before its release. Former president F. W. de Klerk successfully sued to block the commission, at least temporarily, from naming him in the report.[38] In addition, the ANC, unhappy with the commission's conclusions about its past actions, attempted to block publication of the entire report with a clumsy, last-minute court challenge; the court ruled in favor of the commission just hours before the report was due to be released.

The report was formally considered in Parliament several months later, during which Deputy President Thabo Mbeki, speaking in his capacity as president of the ANC, said that the ANC had "serious reservations" about the truth commission's process and report, in particular that they found that "the net effect of [the commission's] findings is to deligitimise or criminalise a significant part of the struggle of our people for liberation."[39] After days of debate and comment, the government made no commitment to implement the commission's many recommendations.

The Amnesty Committee was not able to conclude its review of all amnesty applications by the appointed deadline. It continued to hold amnesty hearings for almost two years after the release of the commission's major report, with a projected completion date late in the year 2000. Meanwhile, the commission's other committees worked to put a reparations program in place, though with minimal funds to match the needs, and to finalize a list of corroborated victims who would be eligible to receive reparations. The full commission was expected to reconvene in the year 2000 to release an addendum to its report that would incorporate the final investigations and amnesty hearings.

GUATEMALA

The civil war in Guatemala, fought between anticommunist government forces and the leftist Unidad Revolucionaria Nacional Guatemalteca (URNG), lasted for over thirty years and resulted in some 200,000 deaths and disappearances. The counterinsurgency strategies of the state were extremely brutal, particularly in the early 1980s when hundreds of villages were razed and tens of thousands of civilians were killed, many in large massacres. The war continued at a lower level into the 1990s, when United Nations–moderated negotiations finally brought the war to an end.

Among the most controversial issues on the table during the negotiations was the question of how past human rights abuses would be addressed during the transition to peace. The Guatemalan negotiations were already under way when the El Salvador truth commission report was released in early 1993, and that example served as Guatemala's main reference point as a truth commission was considered. Most significant was that the Guatemalan armed forces leadership insisted that the Salvadoran model of naming perpetrators would not be repeated in Guatemala. The agreement to establish a Historical Clarification Commission (its full name was actually the Commission to Clarify Past Human Rights Violations and Acts of Violence That Have Caused the Guatemalan People to Suffer) was signed in Oslo, Norway, in June 1994 by the government and the URNG. However, it would be another three years until the final peace accords were signed and the commission would begin work.

The idea of a truth commission attracted intense interest from civil society and victims groups in Guatemala, and they lobbied negotiators heavily in an attempt to influence its terms, but the final terms of reference included several restrictions that these groups strongly opposed. Specifically, they opposed the stipulations that the commission could not "attribute responsibility to any individual in its work, recommendations and report"; that its work "would not have any judicial aim or effect"; and that it was given only six months to conclude its work, with a possible extension of six additional months.[40] The civil society groups directed their anger over the accord at the URNG, for agreeing to sign it; according to some participants in the negotiations, the strong reaction to the truth commission agreement came close to derailing the peace talks altogether.[41]

In time, however, after the commissioners were appointed and the commission hired an impressive team of talented staff, civil society slowly gained confidence in the commission and came to strongly support its work. The inquiry also earned the continued support and trust of the parties to the accord, and it was ultimately allowed to operate for a total of eighteen months, in part by interpreting its twelve-month deadline as pertaining only to its investigative phase.

As designated in the accord, the chair of the commission was a non-Guatemalan, while the remaining two members were Guatemalans. United Nations Secretary-General Kofi Annan appointed Christian Tomuschat, a German law professor who had served as an independent expert on Guatemala for the UN several years earlier, to serve as chair.[42] The remaining two commissioners were appointed by Tomuschat with the agreement of the two parties; the commission mandate directed that one would be "a Guatemalan of irreproachable conduct," and the other would be selected from a list proposed by Guatemalan university presidents.[43] The selected commissioners were Otilia Lux de Cotí, a Mayan scholar, and Edgar Alfredo Balsells Tojo, a lawyer. After a three-and-a-half-month preparation period, the commission was formally installed on July 31, 1997. It operated in several phases, with staff size ranging from two hundred during peak operation (with fourteen field offices) to fewer than one hundred for the months of analysis, investigation, and report writing. Its staff included both Guatemalans and non-Guatemalans, though for security reasons and to project a clear signal of neutrality, none of the field office directors or heads of departments were nationals.

The field offices were open for four to five months to receive testimony. Many Guatemalan villages are very isolated, located far up in the mountains and far from any road. Commission staff sometimes had to trek through back roads and footpaths to reach scattered communities—in some cases walking for six or eight hours through the mountains before arriving at a village to invite testimony from the community. On occasion, staff told me, they arrived to speak with villagers who didn't know there had been a peace agreement and that the civil war was over—especially in villages close to Mexico and on the side of the mountains unable to receive radio signals from Guatemala. In a few cases, during the community meeting where the commission staff introduced themselves, they were accused of being guerrillas—"the guerrillas always come and talk about human rights," it was argued—despite the fact that generally two of the three visiting commission staff were foreigners. Although they seemed to come from persons who probably had something to hide, such accusations were effective in deterring some villagers from giving testimony.

The commission requested the declassification of files from the U.S. government, with the assistance of a nongovernmental organization in Washington, D.C., the National Security Archive. This resulted in the successful declassification of thousands of documents, including detailed information sufficient for the National Security Archive to build a database outlining the structure and personnel of the armed forces in Guatemala over many years' time. Considerably less information was forthcoming from the Guatemalan armed forces itself, which claimed to have no records on the events under investigation.[44]

The commission also incorporated the data from nongovernmental organizations, in particular two projects that were established as alternative truth efforts several years before the start of the official truth commission. The first, the Recovery of Historical Memory Project of the Catholic Church's Human Rights Office (REMHI), collected thousands of statements by training over six hundred local interviewers and working through church networks. Most of this testimony was audiotaped and then transcribed, leaving behind a rich and detailed record in addition to a database of cases and a published report.[45] The second nongovernmental project, the Centro Internacional para Investigaciones en Derechos Humanos (CIIDH), which worked through mass-based, largely indigenous organizations, also collected thousands of testimonies. Its report was completed shortly before the release of the official truth commission's report.[46] The databases from both of these projects were given to the Historical Clarification Commission, which used them to help estimate the total numbers of persons killed or disappeared and to confirm overall patterns.

The commission completed its lengthy and hard-hitting report in February 1999, releasing it to the public in an emotional ceremony attended by thousands of persons in the National Theater in Guatemala City. The report described acts of "extreme cruelty. . . . such as the killing of defenseless children, often by beating them against walls or throwing them alive into pits where the corpses of adults were later thrown; the amputation of limbs; the impaling of victims; the killings of persons by covering them in petrol and burning them alive . . . " and noted that a "climate of terror" permeated the country as a result of these atrocities. "The State resorted to military operations directed towards the physical annihilation or absolute intimidation" of the opposition, such that the "vast majority of the victims of acts committed by the State were not combatants in guerrilla groups, but civilians."[47] In addition to rape, killings, and disappearances, the commission described the military's scorched-earth operations in which civilians, suspected of providing support to the armed guerrillas, were targeted indiscriminately, and whole villages were burned to the ground. For example, in one region, the commission reported that between 70 and 90 percent of villages were razed. The commission also analyzed the economic costs of the armed conflict, concluding that costs of the war, including the loss of production due to death, equaled 121 percent of the 1990 Gross Domestic Product.[48] The commission registered a total of over 42,000 victims, including over 23,000 killed and 6,000 disappeared, and documented 626 massacres. Ninety-three percent of the violations documented were attributed to the military or state-backed paramilitary forces; 3 percent were attributed to the guerrilla forces.

The commission's strongest conclusion, perhaps, was that on the basis of the patterns of violence in the four regions of the country worst affected by the violence, "agents of the State of Guatemala, within the framework of counterinsurgency operations carried out between 1981 and 1983, committed acts of genocide against groups of Mayan people."[49] Finally, although the commission was restricted from naming those responsible, it concluded that the "majority of human rights violations occurred with the knowledge or by order of the highest authorities of the State."[50]

The commission's mandate also directed it to "analyze the factors and circumstances" of the violence, including "internal as well as external" factors.[51] In unflinching language, the report points to racism, structural injustice, and the "anti-democratic nature of institutions" as contributing to the underlying cause of the armed confrontation, as well as the anticommunist National Security Doctrine of the Cold War, and particularly the United States' support for the repressive policies of the Guatemalan state.[52]

In its report, the commission also submitted a long chapter of recommendations. Three weeks after the report's release, the government responded with a long statement that suggested that it considered all relevant matters in the commission's recommendations to be sufficiently addressed in the peace accord.[53] One year later, however, Guatemala's newly elected president Alfonso Portillo made a commitment in his inagural speech to implement the Clarification Commission's recommendations, and brought former commission member Otilia Lux de Cotí into his cabinet.

Shortly thereafter, indigenous leader Rigoberta Menchú Tum filed a case in Spain against the president of Congress in Guatemala, José Efraín Ríos Montt, for his involvement in atrocities in the early 1980s. She submitted the full report of the Historical Clarification Commission to back up her case.

Sixteen Less-Prominent Commissions

W hile the sixteen commissions discussed in this chapter were generally more modest and certainly less internationally prominent than the five in the previous chapter, some of these also played central roles in their respective countries' transitions. Many of these sixteen, which are listed here in chronological order, offer important lessons, particularly in pointing out common problems faced by these exercises, as well as demonstrating the wide range of mandates and operating methodologies that have been employed.

Not all were sucessful. While most of these commissions were carried out in good faith — though not always initially set up with the purest of political motives — some of these inquiries encountered serious trouble in their attempt to document past crimes, or never attracted significant national interest or public trust to become a major force in their respective countries. Due to a lack of political support or changed political circumstances in the course of their investigations, or due to political pressure to undertake a limited inquiry that would not threaten the standing of current leaders or a still-powerful military, some commissions have been unable to complete their task or have encountered serious difficulties in doing so. Two of these commissions (in Bolivia and Ecuador) did not complete their work, ending their investigations and closing the commissions early. Two others completed reports that were kept confidential, at least initially, either considered too risky to release in the quickly changing political environment (Burundi) or, it is presumed, containing information that did not serve the interests of the political leadership (Zimbabwe). Another report, in Haiti, was released by the government only after much delay, and was never made widely available to the public.

Many commissions have stumbled on basic administrative, operational, or fund-raising challenges, lacking the strong leadership necessary to mount a large organizational effort in a very short period of time. At least one commission was set up with the primary purpose of heading off international criticism (the 1974 commission under Idi Amin in Uganda); while that commission made every attempt to carry out a serious investigation, it became clear that the president's interests were not based in advancing human rights. The 1974 Ugandan commission is one of the few commissions included here that did not take place as part of a fundamental political transition, such as the end of dictatorship or a negotiated agreement to end a civil war. In addition, the commission in Zimbabwe, while coming at the end of a repressive period against populations in the south of the country, did not mark a major national political transition.

On the other hand, even with all of these considerable limitations, many of these more modest or comparatively less-prominent commissions had their own small successes and sometimes made surprising contributions, and are well worth studying in an attempt to improve on these bodies in the future.

UGANDA 1974

The Commission of Inquiry into the Disappearance of People in Uganda since 25th January, 1971 was established by President Idi Amin Dada in Uganda in June 1974, with a mandate to investigate the accusations of disappearances at the hands of military forces during the first years of the Amin government.[1] The commission was created in response to increasing pressure to investigate the disappearances, especially from the international community, and was composed of an expatriate Pakistani judge as the chair, two Ugandan police superintendents, and a Ugandan army officer. Established by a presidential legal notice under the Commissions of Inquiry Act of 1914, the commission had the power to compel witnesses to testify and the power to call for evidence from official sources, although access to information was blocked by many sectors of the government, including the military police and military intelligence. The commission heard 545 witnesses and documented 308 cases of disappearances; hearings were generally public unless requested otherwise.

"In view of the considerable practical difficulties it faced and the highly unfavorable political climate in which it operated, the Commission's achievement was remarkable," writes Richard Carver, then research director of the African division of Human Rights Watch. Carver continues, "The Commission concluded that the Public Safety Unit and the State Research Bureau, special security bodies set up by Amin, bore the main responsibility for the 'disappearances.' It also criticized army officers for abuse of powers, as well as the activities of the military police and intelligence."[2] The commission concluded with specific recommendations for reform of the police and security forces and training for law enforcement officials in the legal rights of citizens.

As a commission that worked under and made recommendations to the same government that it was investigating, its first priority was likely to try to prevent future abuses by government forces. Yet the commission was set up without the political will or commitment to real change in human rights policy or practice, and the commission report had little impact on the practices of the Amin government. President Amin did not publish the commission report (nor was he required to under the commission's terms of reference), and none of the recommendations of the commission were implemented. As is now well known, abuses by Amin's forces increased markedly in the following years, earning Amin the nickname "the butcher of Uganda." There is only one known copy of the report in the country.[3]

Carver asks, "So was the whole exercise a waste of time?" He argues that it was not, on three grounds. He cites the importance of the commission report in refuting later revisionist views of the 1970s in Uganda; the fact that disappearances decreased, in the short term, during the period of the commission's investigation; and the fact that this early knowledge of the atrocities places clear responsibility on Amin's international supporters who continued to back him well into the 1970s.[4]

The 1974 Ugandan commission has been all but forgotten in history: in setting up the Ugandan Commission of Inquiry into Violations of Human Rights in 1986, there was no reference made to the similar commission that had operated there just twelve years earlier.[5]

BOLIVIA

The first Latin-American truth commission was in Bolivia, where the government of President Hernán Siles Zuazo created a National Commission of Inquiry into Disappearances just days after the return to democratic rule in October 1982. The eight commissioners, selected to be representative of a cross section of society, were the undersecretary of justice; one member each of the House and of the Senate; one representative each of the armed forces, the labor federation, and the peasants' federation; and one representative from each of the two national human rights organizations. The commission was well known within the country at the time, and collected testimony on 155 disappearances that took place between 1967 and 1982. In some cases the commission was able to locate the remains of disappeared persons, but in the end no cases were conclusively investigated, according to Loyola Guzmán, who was the executive secretary of the commission and was one of the commission's representatives from a human rights organization.[6] Unfortunately, the commission's mandate prevented a full investigation of the truth, as incidents of torture, illegal and prolonged detention, and other abuses were not covered. The commission hired six technical support staff and received limited financial support from the government, but lacked sufficient resources and political support to complete its work, according to Guzman. After two years, the commission disbanded without producing a final report; Guzman has since attempted to gain access to the commission's materials in the hopes of publishing a report.[7]

The commission was quickly overshadowed by trials that began in the mid-1980s of 49 former officials and paramilitary agents of the government of Luis García Meza Tejada (an army commander who seized power in 1980 and ruled the country, with severely repressive tactics, for over a year). In the end, the combination of a truth commission, trials, and private efforts at truth-finding resulted in what Human Rights Watch and others characterized as an overall positive process.[8]

URUGUAY

Following eleven years of military rule, in April 1985 the Uruguayan parliament established the Investigative Commission on the Situation of "Disappeared" People and Its Causes. After seven months, the commission reported on 164 disappearances during the years of military rule, and provided evidence on the involvement of the Uruguayan security force, which they forwarded to the Uruguayan Supreme Court. As in Bolivia, the limited mandate of the commission prevented investigation into many repressive tactics, especially illegal imprisonment or torture, which were actually much more common in Uruguay than disappearances. As Chilean rights advocate José Zalaquett writes, "A systematic practice of 'disappearances' as in Argentina, or, on a lesser scale, as in Chile, was not part of the Uruguayan military's repressive methodology."[9] He continues, "Although it is public knowledge in Uruguay and abroad that torture was systematically practiced during the military rule, there is no officially sanctioned record documenting this practice. The military does not publicly admit to it. In private it attempts to justify torture as a last resort and a lesser evil."[10]

The president of Uruguay generally opposed any attempt to investigate past human rights abuses, as noted by Robert Goldman of American University, who watched the transition closely.[11] Wilder Tayler, then executive secretary of the Institute for Legal and Social Studies of Uruguay, remembers how dissatisfied he was with the commission report. The commission was a political exercise, he says, "not a serious undertaking for human rights."[12] In its report, the commission did conclude that the Uruguayan military had been involved in the disappearances under investigation, and turned its findings over to the courts. However, neither this nor a parallel commission investigating the assassinations of two members of Parliament was "able to find conclusive proof of the institutional decision-making process leading to these crimes," writes Alexandra Barahona de Brito, who closely studied the truth and justice policies of Uruguay and Chile.[13] "Although the coordination of repressive actions between the Argentine and Uruguayan armed forces and the institutional responsibility of the Uruguayan military had been 'proven' by the testimonies of a number of people," Barahona de Brito writes, the commission changed its final report at the last minute, under political pressure, and claimed that it could not conclude that these "irregularities" reflected policy or institutional responsibility.[14]

The commission report, although a public document, was not widely distributed, nor were its findings ever officially announced to the public. The two commissions "failed to produce a national truth" and "their limited coverage elicited no official explanation or response from the previous government and military authorities," writes Barahona de Brito.[15] In response to the limited reach of these parliamentary inquiries, a nongovernmental project soon took up its own truth project, leading to the publication of a much more thorough account of abuses under military rule.[16]

ZIMBABWE

As in Uruguay, the work of the Zimbabwe Commission of Inquiry is also not well known, but for a different reason: its report has never been available to the public, and no one outside of the government has seen it.

The commission of inquiry was established in Zimbabwe in 1985 to investigate governmental repression of "dissidents" in the Matabeleland region of the country. The commission worked under the authority of the president, and was chaired by a Zimbabwean lawyer; after several months of investigation it submitted its report directly to the president in 1984. While the government initially promised to release the commission's findings to the public, over a year after its completion the minister of justice announced without explanation that the commission report would not be made public.[17] Although at the time the commission did not attract much attention inside Zimbabwe, there was increasing pressure from both national and international nongovernmental organizations to publish the report in the years following its completion. While human rights organizations stressed the need for accountability for the crimes committed, the victims' families were interested in formal recognition of the killings, in part so that they could receive compensation. This issue became increasingly controversial as the government refused to recognize the death of several thousand civilians killed in the conflict.[18]

The government resisted publishing the report. Due to tensions between the two main ethnic groups in Zimbabwe, the government claimed that publication of the report could spark violence over past wrongs, and made every effort to quiet the demands for public truth. Twelve years after the end of the Matabeleland violence, a senior government spokesman told me that "if you don't talk about it, it may die a natural death, so that we can build the society we're trying to build."[19] Meanwhile, there were no signs of accountability for the massive abuses. In 1992, the commander of the military brigade responsible for many of the atrocities was promoted to commander of the air force, provoking strong criticism from human rights organizations; many of those involved in the repression continued to hold senior posts in the government.

To counter the government's silence on the matter, two major Zimbabwean human rights organizations produced a report in 1997 that thoroughly documented the repression of the 1980s on the basis of extensive interviews with victims.[20] Before publishing their report, they submitted it to the government for response, but never received a reply.

UGANDA 1986

When the rebel forces led by Yoweri Museveni overthrew the government of Milton Obote in January 1986, the country looked back on over twenty years of terror and brutality at the hands of government forces. Human rights issues were announced as a central concern of the new government, and within months the Museveni government appointed a Commission of Inquiry into Violations of Human Rights to look into past abuses. Set up through the appointing authority of the minister of justice and attorney general and chaired by a High Court judge, the commission was charged with investigating human rights violations by state forces that occurred from Uganda's independence in 1962 up to January 1986, when Museveni came to power (though excluding any abuses by Museveni's rebel force).

The commission's terms of reference were broad, including arbitrary arrest and detention, torture, and killings by government security forces, and called on the commission "to inquire into . . . possible ways of preventing the recurrence" of such abuses.[21] The commission held public hearings around the country, some broadcast live on state-owned radio and television. It was at the center of public attention in its early years, attracting wide popular support and an emotional reaction from the public. Yet the commission was set up without a deadline for finishing its work, and as time wore on, it repeatedly ran out of funds and found its work stalled. As abuses took place under the new government that the commission could not cover, the public lost interest.

In just its second year of operation, the commission completely stopped work for four months due to a lack of funds; it turned to the Ford Foundation for financial support to continue.[22] By early 1991 the commission again reported financial troubles, and received funds from the Danish government to finish its investigation and produce a report.[23] In 1995, after nine years of investigation, the commission of inquiry submitted its report to the government. One thousand copies of the report were printed (and 20,000 copies of a more accessible ninety-page summary), but as of late 1996, when I visited the country, very few people inside or outside of Uganda had seen the report or knew that it might be available. The many boxes of printed reports sat in storage at the commission's old headquarters. The given reason for not distributing the report was that the new human rights commission, which would cover current human rights issues and complaints, first had to be appointed in order to oversee the distribution.[24] But three years later still, after the new commission was appointed and well under way, the thousands of copies of the report and summary still had not been distributed.

NEPAL

The interim government of Prime Minister Krishna Prasad Bhattarai established two commissions of inquiry for Nepal in 1990 to inquire into allegations of torture, disappearances, and extrajudicial executions that had taken place under the Panchayat System from 1961 to 1990. The first commission was dissolved soon after it was appointed; the chair of the commission was seen as a collaborator with the prior regime and was not accepted as credible, so that the other two members, representatives of two human rights groups, soon resigned in protest. A second commission was then appointed, the Commission on Inquiry to Find the Disappeared Persons during the Panchayat Period, which included a founding member of a prominent human rights group in Nepal, the Informal Sector Service Center.

The commission was given the mandate to investigate and identify the final places of detention of those who disappeared, and to identify the victims. It succeeded in investigating about one hundred cases, although it had no powers to name perpetrators or subpoena officials, and the police were generally unresponsive to the commission's requests for information.[25]

The commission completed its two-volume report in 1991. Over the next few years, Amnesty International and local human rights groups repeatedly urged the government to publish the commission's report and ensure that any persons implicated in human rights violations be brought to justice.[26] The report was finally released to the public in 1994, although few of its recommendations have been implemented.

CHAD

On December 29, 1990, one month after coming to power, the new president of Chad, Idriss Déby, created the Commission of Inquiry into the Crimes and Misappropriations By Presidential Decree Committed by Ex-President Habré, His Accomplices and/or Accessories. The decree called on the commission, among other things, "to investigate the illegal imprisonments, detentions, assassinations, disappearances, tortures and practices of acts of barbarity, the mistreatment, other attacks on the physical or mental integrity of persons, and all violations of human rights and illicit trafficking in narcotics" and "to preserve in their present condition the torture chambers and equipment utilized."[27]

The commission was authorized to collect documentation, take testimony, and confiscate material as necessary for "elucidating the truth." The decree appointed twelve individuals to serve as members of the commission, including two magistrates, four officers of the judicial police, two civil administrative officers, and other clerks and secretaries, with the first deputy prosecutor serving as president. In addition to investigating human rights violations, the commission was also directed to look into the embezzlement of state funds by former president Hissein Habré and his associates.

Due to a shortage of office space, the commission was forced to set up its headquarters in the former secret detention center of the security forces, where some of the worst of the torture and killings had taken place, thus deterring many former victims from coming to give testimony.

Like the Ugandan commission, the Chadian commission was severely handicapped by a lack of resources. The commission report describes some of its challenges:

[L]ack of transport . . . paralyzed the Commission for a considerable time. At the start, the Commission was furnished two small urban automobiles, a 504 and a small Suzuki, whereas all-terrain vehicles were actually required for travel to the provinces and the outskirts of N'Djaména.

On 25 August 1991 a Toyota all-terrain vehicle was put at the disposal of the Commission. But during the events of 13 October 1991, unfortunately, the Toyota and the little Suzuki were taken off by combatants. A month later the Toyota was recovered, but the Suzuki was not found until 3 January 1992. . . . This is why the Commission was unable to send investigators to the interior of the country during the entire initial period.[28]

The publication of the report in May 1992 surprised many in its detail, and in its proof of the involvement of foreign governments in the funding and training of the worst violators. Jamal Benomar, then director of the Human Rights Program of the Carter Center, was at the ceremony where the report was released, and described the response:

The findings were shocking: at least 40,000 were killed by the security forces during Habré's regime. Detailed evidence was presented about Habré's personal involvement in the torture and killing of prisoners. The diplomatic corps present at the ceremony was shocked to hear that the investigation uncovered the fact that members of the security service, the DDS [Directorate of Documentation and Security], who carried out all the killings and other abuses, were trained until the collapse of Habré's regime in December 1990 by U.S. personnel both in the USA and N'Djaména. The DDS received a monthly payment of 5 million FCFA from the U.S. government. This amount had doubled since 1989. Iraq also was named as a contributor to the DDS budget, along with France, Zaire and Egypt. A U.S. advisor worked closely with the DDS director at the DDS headquarters where political prisoners were tortured and killed daily.[29]

U.S. involvement in Chad had been discovered by Amnesty International several years earlier, according to Benomar, but the "large scale of the genocide" that was going on made U.S. involvement "hard to believe at the time, even for some in the international human rights community."[30]

The Chadian commission was also the first truth commission to name names of individuals responsible for human rights crimes and the only commission to date to publish the photographs of those named. Some high officials in the new government were included in the list.

The same government of Chad that created this commission has been accused of serious human rights violations itself, which called into question the motivation of the government in setting up the commission. Some human rights observers had the impression that the commission was set up to improve the new president's image. Despite the many years of U.S. support for the Habré regime, one U.S. State Department official, when asked about the commission, said, "Wasn't that just Déby proving that Habré was an SOB?"[31]

Years later, the commission report unexpectedly took on new importance, as international rights advocates turned to it as a primary source of information in their search for evidence to support an international effort to prosecute Habré. While there are significant limitations to the report, these advocates note, it is the only detailed, published record on the rights crimes under Habré, and was thus critical in providing leads to victims and other witnesses who could be used in a trial.[32]

SOUTHERN AFRICA: THE AFRICAN
NATIONAL CONGRESS

In a fascinating case among the array of truth commission models, the African National Congress (ANC) is the only example of an armed resistance group that independently established a commission to investigate and publicly report on its own past abuses.[33]

As is often true of government truth commissions, the ANC did not set up this commission entirely on its own initiative. There had long been reports of abuses in ANC detention camps.[34] Then, in 1991, a group of thirty-two former detainees in ANC camps, all formerly active ANC members held as a result of accusations of being agents of the state, formed a committee to confront the ANC on the detention camp abuses. The Returned Exiles Committee, as they called themselves, brought international attention to the issue, forcing the ANC to investigate. In March 1992, ANC president Nelson Mandela appointed the Commission of Enquiry into Complaints by Former African National Congress Prisoners and Detainees.[35] The commission was directed to focus on events at ANC detention camps located throughout Southern Africa, including Angola, Tanzania, and Zambia.

The terms of reference of the Commission of Enquiry were set out by the ANC at the outset, calling for a "full and thorough investigation" of the complaints by former detainees, and recommendations on action that might be taken by the ANC based on the commission's findings.[36] Two of the three commissioners were ANC members, although the third commissioner and the author of the report was not affiliated with the ANC.

After seven months, the commission submitted to Mandela a strongly worded seventy-four-page report documenting what it called "staggering brutality" in ANC camps over the past years. The report details torture and other abuses regularly inflicted on detainees. Although stopping short of naming names of responsible individuals, it recommended that "urgent and immediate attention be given to identifying and dealing with those responsible for the maltreatment of detainees," and that the ANC take the responsibility to "clean its own ranks."[37] The commission also recommended that the report be made public and that an independent body be appointed to further investigate disappearances and other acts that were outside this commission's terms of reference.

The report was immediately provided to the public and to the press, although the ANC later began questioning the report's accuracy and refused to distribute it further.[38] The report attracted significant international attention and forced the ANC to respond publicly to the accusations: Nelson Mandela accepted collective responsibility on behalf of the leadership of the ANC for the "serious abuses and irregularities" that had occurred, but insisted that individuals should not be named or held personally accountable.[39]

GERMANY

In March 1992, the German Parliament created a commission to investigate and document the practices of the German Democratic Republic (East German) government from 1949 to 1989, the Commission of Inquiry for the Assessment of History and Consequences of the SED Dictatorship in Germany.[40] (The SED, or Socialist Unity Party, was the ruling party of East Germany which tightly controlled the country for over forty years). The commission structure and operation followed the established guidelines for parliamentary commissions of inquiry in Germany, with political parties represented equivalent to their representation in Parliament as a whole. The successor party to the SED, the Democratic Socialist Party, was among those represented on the commission. Twelve of the thirty-six members of the commission were experts from outside of Parliament, primarily historians. Former East German human rights activist Rainer Eppelman served as the commission's chair.

The repression under the East German system was different from the extensive violence seen in other regions under study here. Although there certainly was physical repression against dissidents,[41] many of those who expressed opposition to the system suffered less violent consequences: they were barred from universities, prohibited from working in their chosen profession, or continually harassed by authorities, for example. The commission's mandate thus reached beyond a focus on gross human rights violations to a broader inquiry into government policy and practice. It was directed to "conduct political-historical analysis and make political-ethical assessments" of the structure and practices of the SED party; the human rights violations and environmental degradation that resulted; violations of international human rights conventions and norms, including political, mental, and psychosocial repression; the role of ideology in education, literature, and daily life; the role of the opposition movement; church-state relations; the independence of the judiciary; and relations between West and East Germany.

The commission was largely research based, commissioning over one hundred papers on a wide range of topics, mostly written by academic historians who made use of files opened since the collapse of East Germany. The commission held over forty public hearings where these papers were presented. Although the commission did not reach out to the public for much testimony, over one hundred "contemporary witnesses," including representatives of victims' assistance organizations and a number of victims themselves, gave accounts of suffering and repression in these public hearings. The commission held no subpoena power, and a few former senior government officials who were invited to give testimony declined, in part because they feared their testimony could later be used against them in court.

The full commission report, released at the end of the parliamentary session in 1994, is over 15,000 pages in length, published in eighteen volumes, and includes all the research papers and testimony from the commission's hearings. Even among its members and staff, many saw the commission and its report as more an academic and research-oriented project than a process intended to actively engage the public.[42] Many of the functions that are typical of truth commissions were addressed through other mechanisms in Germany. Files of the East German Stasi, the omnipresent secret police, were made accessible for individual review.[43] These files allowed those who had been victims of Stasi informers to discover who had been reporting on them and to confront those informers in person — either privately or, as was done on a number of occasions, in front of television cameras.[44]

As recommended by the commission, a follow-up body was instituted by the incoming Parliament in 1994, the Commission of Inquiry on Overcoming the Consequences of the SED Dictatorship in the Process of German Unity. In addition to continuing investigations into most of the topics of the first commission, this body was also mandated to look into new areas, such as the economy, education, and daily life in East Germany and the impact of the unification policies since 1990.

AFRICAN NATIONAL CONGRESS II

Shortly after the first ANC commission finished its work in 1992, ANC president Nelson Mandela named a new commission of inquiry to again look into the alleged abuses in ANC detention camps. The first commission had been criticized for its bias (with two of its three commissioners being ANC members) and for not providing sufficient opportunity for accused individuals to defend themselves. The first commission had recommended, in fact, that "consideration be further given to the creation of an independent structure which is perceived to be impartial, and which is capable of documenting cases of abuse and giving effect to the type of recommendations made in this report."[45] The new Commission of Enquiry into Certain Allegations of Cruelty and Human Rights Abuse against ANC Prisoners and Detainees by ANC Members was headed up by three commissioners, one each from the United States, Zimbabwe, and South Africa, who were widely accepted as independent.[46]

The commission was markedly different from the first ANC commission. It structured its proceedings much like those of formal court hearings, hiring counsel to represent the "complainants" and a legal defense team to represent the "defendants," those accused of abuses. The commission held public hearings over a five-week period in the summer of 1993, during which some fifty witnesses were heard, including eleven alleged perpetrators of human rights abuses. The accused were given the opportunity to confront and question their accusers—their alleged victims of torture or abuse—and were allowed representation by attorneys of their choice.

Richard Carver, who observed the hearings for Amnesty International, found the commission's approach awkward and not well thought through, which confirmed his conviction that one "should never mix up [the] two functions" of disciplinary procedures and a truth inquiry.[47] Nevertheless, the commission's report was positively received by most observers, including Carver. Submitted in August 1993, it reached conclusions similar to the first commission, citing severe abuses in ANC detention camps over a number of years. On one detention camp, for example, the commission concluded, "Quadro was intended to be a rehabilitation centre. Instead, it became a dumping-ground for all who fell foul of the Security Department, whether they were loyal supporters accused of being enemy agents, suspected spies or convicts. All were subjected to torture, ill-treatment and humiliation far too frequently to achieve its purpose as a rehabilitation center."[48] The format of the report was also quite different from that of the first ANC truth commission. After briefly describing events, the type and prevalence of abuse, and the structural causes and patterns of abuse, the report concentrates on a description of each case brought before it, concluding with a list of which specific individuals violated the rights of each "complainant" and which rights were violated.

The ANC responded to the report with a long statement congratulating the commission for its work, accepting its general conclusions (while denying that "there was any systematic policy of abuse"), and calling for a truth commission to be set up to cover abuses on both sides of the conflict in South Africa since 1948:

> We regard the Skweyiya and Motsuenyane Commission Reports as a first step in a process of national disclosure of all violations of human rights from all sides. We accordingly call for an establishment of a Commission of Truth, similar to bodies established in a number of countries in recent years to deal with the past. The purpose of such a Commission will be to investigate all the violations of human rights . . . from all quarters. This will not be a Nuremberg Tribunal. Its role will be to identify all abuses of human rights and their perpetrators, to propose a future code of conduct for all public servants, to ensure appropriate compensation to the victims and to work out the best basis for reconciliation. In addition, it will provide the moral basis for justice and for preventing any repetition of abuses in the future.[49]

Just eight months later, the ANC won the country's first democratic presidential elections and proceeded to put their call for a national truth commission into place.

SRI LANKA

In November 1994 the newly elected president of Sri Lanka, Chandrika Bandaranaike Kumaratunga, appointed three Commissions of Inquiry into the Involuntary Removal or Disappearance of Persons with the mandate to investigate "whether any persons have been involuntarily removed or have disappeared from their places of residence" since January 1, 1988. These commissions were also directed to inquire into the present whereabouts of the disappeared persons and to judge the evidence available to bring charges against those accused of involvement. These three commissions were given identical mandates, but each covered a different area of the country, and each operated independently on their assigned area. With little collaboration between them, each interpreted its mandate slightly differently, and established different operational and methodological guidelines for its work.

The period covered by the commissions included both the armed conflict between government forces and the People's Liberation Front in the south from 1987 to 1990, and the conflict between the government forces and the Liberation Tigers of Tamil Eelam in the northeast, which began in June 1990. Human rights organizations objected to the 1988 start date, as it excluded many disappearances that took place earlier.[50] In addition, the conflict with the Tamil Tigers resumed during the course of the commissions' work, with many further disappearances reported, but these too were excluded.[51] Commission access to the northeast to investigate past disappearances was limited as a result of the ongoing conflict.

The three commissions together documented over 27,000 disappearances, with a panel of commissioners listening to each complaint brought forward. After submitting their cases in writing, each deponent was called before a panel for a five-to-fifteen-minute interview to answer basic questions about his or her case.[52] The commissions operated with the equivalent of subpoena power and called a number of officials to testify, primarily from the army, but most of these officials flatly denied accusations of involvement in abuses and insisted that all the records from the period had been destroyed.

The three commissions' final reports were submitted to the president in September 1997. Partly in response to pressure from Amnesty International and other rights groups, the three reports were eventually released in full to the public.[53] Again, the differences between the three commissions were apparent: the most substantial of the three reports, that covering the western and southern provinces, is 178 pages long, with an additional 300 pages of appendices. In contrast, the final report of the commission on the central and northwestern provinces totals just five pages. The third was of a quality and length between these two.[54] A follow-up commission was established to process those cases left unaddressed by these three commissions, headed by the chair of the commission on the western and southern provinces, Manouri Kokila Muttetuwegama.

The ongoing war weakened the impact of the commissions, especially as the president was dependent on the support of the military as the war continued and thus apparently unwilling to criticize or confront the armed forces' human rights record. As a result, she failed to publicly comment on the commissions' reports, did not push for prosecution of perpetrators who were identified, and was slow to address the commissions' recommendations. Financial reparations have been awarded to the families of a number of the victims listed in the commissions' reports, although victims' advocates were frustrated with the small sums paid and the slow implementation of the reparations program.

Over time, however, the work of the commissions did contribute to the prosecution of alleged perpetrators. Amnesty International reported in 1999 that "Investigations into . . . past human rights violations, including cases recommended for further investigation by the three presidential commissions of inquiry . . . continued. According to the Attorney General's department, investigations into 485 of the 3,861 such cases had been completed by mid-October [1998] and 150 alleged perpetrators had been charged in the High Court."[55]

HAITI

Three years after Haitian president Jean-Bertrand Aristide was overthrown in a coup d'état, he returned to power in 1994 with the backing of international troops, a mandate to finish his term, and a public call to deal with the crimes that took place under the three-year de facto military government.

As it had become increasingly clear that Aristide would be reinstated, a group of Haitians in exile and other rights advocates met several times to propose terms for a truth commission to be instituted upon Aristide's return. In part prompted by this work, Aristide announced the creation of the National Commission on Truth and Justice a few months after his return to the country, naming four Haitian and three international members.[56] From the start of its work, however, the commission was plagued by administrative and organizational problems, and especially by a failure to raise sufficient funds to carry out its work. It also failed to reach out to engage the many human rights groups that had initially been very supportive of a truth commission idea, thus sparking yet further criticism from those who should have been its main backers, and failed to gain the broad attention and interest of the general public. Despite its problems, the commission was able to send staff to the field for several months and to collect testimony from close to 5,500 witnesses, pertaining to some 8,600 victims.

After ten months, the commission finished its report in February 1996 and handed it to Aristide just a day before he was to step down. Aristide turned the report over to the incoming president, but it was not until a year later, after considerable pressure from rights advocates, that the report was made public. (Reasons for the delay were never well explained, although the Justice Ministry at one time claimed that the expense of reproducing the report was prohibitive.[57]) Yet the report was never distributed widely in Haiti, and was not easily available to the public. There were no signs that the government was seriously acting to implement its wide-ranging recommendations, many of which pertained to reforming the country's judicial system.

The commission's most surprising recommendation was to the international community, urging that the UN Security Council set up an international tribunal to try those accused of rights violations under the de facto government, since the commission held no faith in the ability of the national justice system to properly handle these cases. The commission attached a list of accused perpetrators to its report submitted to the president, but recommended that it not be made public until appropriate judicial action was taken against those named.

BURUNDI

In late 1993, after an attempted coup and the assassination of President Melchior Ndadaye, widespread interethnic violence broke out in Burundi. With reports of massacres of 50,000 or more, the Burundi government asked the United Nations to establish an international commission of inquiry to investigate, in the hope that this would help to deter a feared cycle of violence.[58] Several UN fact-finding missions also recommended such an inquiry, as did international human rights groups concerned with the situation.

Yet the UN Security Council hesitated to institute an investigation that they feared could spark further violence, especially after Burundi's northern neighbor, Rwanda, tumbled into horrific genocide in April of 1994. Even those who backed the commission proposal recognized the risk of sparking violence. Amnesty International wrote that "the work of the commission will undoubtedly heighten anxiety among the perpetrators of human rights abuses and could create tension in Burundi," but that despite this, it saw the creation of an international commission of inquiry as "a vital step in breaking the cycle of impunity and violence in Burundi."[59]

The UN Security Council finally created the commission through a resolution in July 1995, close to two years after the attempted coup and massacres. The terms of reference adopted for the commission closely followed the recommendation of the secretary-general's special envoy to Burundi, Venezuelan lawyer Pedro Nikken, who had been part of the UN negotiating team in El Salvador several years earlier and had helped to draft the terms for the truth commission there. He recommended a very similar entity for Burundi.[60] The resolution called for the commission to "establish the facts relating to the assassination of the President of Burundi on 21 October 1993, the massacres and other related serious acts of violence which followed," and to "recommend measures of a legal, political, or administrative nature . . . and measures with regard to the bringing to justice of persons responsible for those acts, to prevent any repetition of deeds similar to those investigated by the commission and, in general, to eradicate impunity and promote national reconciliation in Burundi."[61]

After ten months of confidential investigations, the report was due to be released in July 1996; but on the very day that the report was to be released, July 25, a coup overthrew the government of Burundi, and the report was held back. According to the *New York Times*, the report was "withheld from publication by some members of the Security Council who fear that releasing it could lead to more bloodshed in Burundi." A month later, however, the United Nations released the report, which described "acts of genocide" that took place in Burundi in October 1993, recommended that international jurisdiction be asserted over these acts, and suggested that a further inquiry should address events before 1993, as security conditions allow.[62] But violence has continued sporadically in Burundi in the years since, and neither these nor other recommendations of the report have been implemented.

ECUADOR

There have been a number of allegations of grave human rights violations in Ecuador since 1979, when a civilian government took over from military rulers, and there have been repeated calls for a full investigation, the prosecution of those responsible, and reparations awarded for victims. As a result of these demands, the Ministry of Government and Police created a Truth and Justice Commission in September 1996.[63]

The commission was composed of seven members: one was a representative of the Ministry of Government and Police, three were representatives named by international human rights organizations then working in the country, and three were named by national human rights organizations. The commission was authorized to receive testimony pertaining to human rights violations since 1979, carry out investigations, and, as appropriate, submit evidence to the judiciary. It was given one year to conclude its investigations and report, with the possibility of an extension.[64]

After three months, the commission had received information on almost 300 cases, and had investigated unmarked graves of scores of victims of torture or summary execution.[65] Yet despite the government's initial commitment to provide the necessary support and facilities for it to complete its work, commission members expressed frustration in the lack of resources and trained personnel.[66] In February 1997, just five months after it was established, the commission ceased operations. Amnesty International wrote that the failure of the commission to publish any findings "consolidated the impunity surrounding hundreds of cases of torture, disappearances and killings."[67]

NIGERIA

After fifteen years of military rule, Olusegun Obasanjo was elected president of Nigeria in early 1999. Just weeks after taking office, he created a Commission of Inquiry for the Investigation of Human Rights Violations in June 1999. Its members were appointed by President Obasanjo, with a highly respected retired judge, Chukwudifu Oputa, serving as chair.

The commission started off with a very broad mandate and initially was given just ninety days to complete its task. Its mandate called on it to "ascertain or establish the causes, nature and extent of human rights violations or abuses with particular reference to all known or suspected cases of mysterious deaths and assassinations or attempted assassinations committed in Nigeria between the 1st day of January 1984 and the 28th of May, 1999."[68] The Commission first interpreted "human rights violations or abuses" very widely, including cases of dismissal from employment without due compensation. When it first began to accept statements, in just a few weeks' time the commission received close to ten thousand written submissions complaining of violations; it was estimated that nine thousand of these pertained to labor disputes.

After due reflection by the commission, however (and after hosting a retreat with former members of the truth commissions of Guatemala, Chile, and South Africa), the commission reevaluated its plan, refocusing its work on gross violations of human rights.[69] At the commission's request, President Obasanjo also extended its working period to one year, allowed it several months for preparation, and extended the period that it would cover back to 1966, the date of the first military coup in Nigeria. (The commission's initial cutoff date of 1984, the year when the country was last under a civilian government, had been criticized by human rights organizations for excluding the three years that President Obasanjo himself had been the military head of state in the late 1970s.) President Obasanjo expressed strong support for the commission's work, and pledged to appear before the commission to respond to allegations if he was called upon.

The commission was also mandated to "identify the person or persons, authorities, institutions or organizations which may be held accountable" for the abuses under investigation, and to "determine whether such abuses or violations were the product of deliberate State policy or the policy of any of its organs or institutions or . . . whether they were the acts of any political organization, liberation movements or other groups of individuals."[70] The commission was scheduled to begin investigations and hold its first hearings in early 2000, as this book went to press.

SIERRA LEONE

In a peace agreement signed in Lomé, Togo, on July 7, 1999, the government of Sierra Leone and the leadership of the main rebel group, the Revolutionary United Front (RUF), ended a nine-year civil war that had been marked by acts of severe brutality. The war was most well known internationally for the atrocious practice (primarily of rebel forces) of cutting off limbs of civilians, apparently for the sole purpose of spreading terror and somehow discouraging support for the government.[71]

The peace agreement included an unconditional general amnesty for all parties to the war, which was strongly criticized by local and international human rights groups and others.[72] In an attempt to make up for the amnesty, and given domestic and international pressures for some form of accounting for the atrocities of the war, the parties also agreed to the establishment of a Truth and Reconciliation Commission. While providing few details on its operations, powers, or mandate, the peace agreement called on the commission to "address impunity, break the cycle of violence, provide a forum for both the victims and perpetrators of human rights violations to tell their story, [and] get a clear picture of the past in order to facilitate genuine healing and reconciliation."[73]

The United Nations high commissioner for human rights, Mary Robinson, offered to assist the Sierra Leone government in the establishment of the commission, and initiated a broadly consultative process toward drafting terms of reference. This consultative process, which included meetings with a wide range of civil society and government officials in order to work out the preferred investigative mandate, powers, and reach of the commission, resulted in strong terms for the commission and a broad base of support for its work.[74] Robinson's office submitted the final recommendation on the commission's terms of reference to the government of Sierra Leone in December 1999.

The commission's empowering legislation, passed into law by the Parliament of Sierra Leone in February 2000, closely tracked the recommendation from the United Nations, giving the commission broad powers of investigation, including subpoena and search and seizure powers.[75] There was also a broadly consultative process set out for selecting commissioners, intended to ensure credibility and neutrality in a mixed membership of four national and three nonnational members. The commission was due to begin its work in mid-2000 after a three-month preparatory period.

What Is the Truth?

T ruth commissions are obliged to fulfill the direction given them in the written mandate, or terms of reference, upon which they are founded. The mandates of some past commissions have been explicit about what abuses they were to document and investigate, but many provide only general guidance about the kind of abuse to be investigated and exactly what cases should be covered in the investigations. These terms of reference, usually created by presidential decree, national legislation, or as part of a peace accord ending a civil war, can define a commission's powers, limit or strengthen its investigative reach, and set the timeline, subject matter, and geographic scope of a commission's investigation, and thus define the truth that will be documented.

Where the guidelines of truth have been set out very clearly and specifically, some commissions have found themselves restricted to looking at only a portion of the abuses that took place. For example, a number of the truth commissions have been directed to look only into disappearances, such as those in Argentina, Uruguay, and Sri Lanka; but such explicit restrictions risk excluding a significant portion of the truth. The Uruguayan commission missed the majority of the human rights violations that had taken place during the military regime because of such a limited mandate; illegal detention and torture, which constituted the bulk of the abuses, were ignored. In Chile, the commission investigated disappearances, executions, torture leading to death, political kidnappings, and attempts on life by private citizens for political purposes,[1] but its mandate prevented it from investigating incidents of torture that did not result in death, a fact that was criticized by international human rights observers and kept the total count of victims relatively, but unrealistically, low.

For those commissions with a more flexible mandate, a fuller picture of the truth may emerge. The crafters of the terms of reference in El Salvador, deliberating under the pressures of UN-negotiated peace talks, considered specifying which specific cases the commission should look into, but finally left the mandate fairly open, indicating only that the commission should report on "serious acts of violence . . . whose impact on society urgently demands that the public should know the truth."[2] The commission, reading this language, decided to take testimony from thousands of victims, summarize the overall patterns of violence, and report on some thirty cases in depth, all of which went much further than what the crafters originally envisioned. The cases chosen for in-depth investigation were intended to be representative of typical victims, perpetrators, and types of abuse over the twelve years of civil war. The language of the El Salvador commission is a good model: as a general rule, terms of reference should be sufficiently broad and flexible to allow investigation into all forms of rights abuses, leaving to the commission the decision of what specific cases or practices to investigate and report. (See chart 4 in appendix 1 for examples of the acts included and excluded in the investigations of a number of past commissions.)

In addition to explicit limitations in a commission's mandate, commissioners may self-impose restrictions on what the commission will investigate or report. Due to time constraints, limited resources or staff, or insufficient or unreliable information, or in response to political pressure, commissioners may avoid certain topics altogether or decide to omit information from their final report. In South Africa, the commission was directed to investigate gross human rights violations, defined as "killing, abduction, torture, and severe ill-treatment,"[3] but this was not intended to include all abusive practices of apartheid. The commission was particularly criticized for excluding from its inquiry the practice of "forced removals," the apartheid policy that forcibly relocated millions of blacks to barren lands. Excluding this practice from its inquiry may have been justified on grounds of the commission's overwhelming workload and because the forced-removals policy was instituted through law and already well documented, but it prevented many South Africans from seeing their own personal experience reflected in the commission's work. Some observers harshly criticized the commission's failure to include these and other apartheid practices in its net. Ugandan scholar Mahmood Mamdani, based at the University of Cape Town during the years of the commission's work, was one of its strongest critics. He claimed that the commission was creating "the founding myth of the new South Africa" by putting forth a "compromised truth" that "has written the vast majority of victims out of history" in excluding prominent apartheid practices such as forced removals—accusations which, while provocative, often met with strong disagreement from South Africans and seemed to most observers to be overstating the case.[4] The truth commission, for its part, noted that there was a constitutionally established Land Commission that was addressing these very issues, and it did cover the issue of forced removals, in general historical terms, in its report. Nevertheless, because of the great amount of attention that the commission received, and given the quickly fading memory of apartheid in South Africa's youth, it probably would have served history well for the commission to hold at least one televised hearing to highlight legal but abusive apartheid practices, even if these practices were indeed already documented.

A commission's interpretation of "truth" will also be determined by the personality and personal priorities of its leadership. For example, in Sri Lanka, the president created three geographically distinct commissions to investigate disappearances over the previous seven years. The commissions were created on the same date and were given identical mandates, but each worked independently on its assigned third of the country, and each implemented its mandate slightly differently. Rights monitors who observed these commissions in operation and attended commission hearings described how one of the commissions was clearly oriented toward identifying perpetrators and recommending prosecution; another focused more on the financial loss to each family and their reparations needs; and the third took on a more academic tone aimed at reconciliation and the psychology of national healing.[5] One of the three commissions initially chose to hold public hearings, while the other two held all hearings in private (the public hearings eventually had to be closed after some deponents received threats after giving testimony). And although the commissions' mandate was to investigate disappearances (usually meaning kidnapped, and probably killed, but with no body reappearing), one of the three commissions decided to also include victims who were killed outright in their list of the disappeared—interpreting the term as meaning something closer to "disappeared from this world"—though this was clearly not intended in the language of the mandate, according to rights observers.

Some truth commissions have investigated abuses both by state forces and by the armed opposition. After a civil war, investigating both sides can be critical to a commission's popular legitimacy, and important in contributing to national unity and reconciliation. In El Salvador, Guatemala, and South Africa, abuses by the armed opposition were a central piece of the commissions' investigations, though they added up to a relatively small proportion of the total number of abuses reported. On the other hand, in Chile the armed left was very small and its abuses considered fairly insignificant compared to the abuses by state forces. There, many human rights advocates opposed the decision to have the truth commission report on the killings both by the state and by the armed opposition, as they saw this dual focus diminishing the singular outrage of killing, torture, and disappearances by the state.

A particularly interesting issue is the extent to which truth commission reports have included an analysis of or commentary on the role of international actors in the political violence within the country. In virtually every case looked at here, there were international actors — usually foreign governments — that helped to fund, arm, train, or otherwise aid either or both sides of the conflict. Where domestic government forces have committed ongoing, massive human rights violations, the role of foreign governments in supporting such atrocities should be investigated or at least formally recognized in a truth report, especially where the abuses were well known at the time the support took place, as is usually the case.

Most truth commissions have not investigated this international role at any depth; few have addressed the issue at all in their final report. The truth commission in Chad perhaps ventured the furthest in this area. While not entering into in-depth investigation, the commission report names the exact amount of external financial backing provided to the regime, as well as the extent of training for the intelligence service responsible for the worst abuses — facts that were not previously well known by the public or the international human rights community:

> The United States of America heads the list of countries that actively provided the DDS [Directorate of Documentation and Security, the intelligence service] with financial, material, and technical support. America took the DDS under its wing in the very first months of its existence. It trained it, supported it, and contributed effectively to its growth, up to the time of the dictator's fall. . . . The American advisers from the Embassy were regular guests of the DDS director. . . . In addition, France, Egypt, Iraq, and Zaire all contributed . . . financing, training, and equipment, or shared information.

Security cooperation between the intelligence services of the above-
mentioned states and the DDS was intense and continued right up to the
departure of the ex-tyrant.[6]

Despite a long record of international support for parties to the El Salvador civil war, especially the extensive financial assistance from the U.S.
government to the Salvadoran military, the Salvadoran truth commission
report does not comment on the role of international actors, except for describing how the U.S. government "tolerated, and apparently paid little official heed to" a group of Salvadoran exiles in Miami, Florida, who
"directly financed and indirectly helped run certain death squads" in El
Salvador, especially between 1979 and 1983. The report states, "It would be
useful if other investigators with more resources and more time were to
shed light on this tragic story so as to ensure that persons linked to terrorist
acts in other countries are never tolerated again in the United States."[7]
Commissioner Thomas Buergenthal told me that if any foreigner had been
found to be directly involved in actual violations, the commission would
definitely have stated so. The intent of the commission's mandate was not
to study the extent of international involvement, Buergenthal continued; if
the commission had attempted to investigate foreign involvement in the
war—which might include that of Cuba, Nicaragua, and the Soviet
Union, as well as the United States—then it would not have been able to
fulfill its main mission: to clarify the circumstances and extent of the political violence in the country.[8] The release of the truth commission report
did, however, spur the U.S. government to review its past policies on El
Salvador and to release thousands of classified documents to the public.

The Chilean commission report comments at some length on the reaction of the international community to the military regime, including the
suspension of diplomatic relations by a number of governments and the efforts of intergovernmental organizations and international nongovernmental organizations to confront the regime's abuses. It also briefly
outlines the continued U.S. economic and political relations with the
regime, which remained normal during the worst years of repression.[9]

Recent truth commissions seem to be grappling with this issue more
honestly and directly (and, in fairness to the El Salvador commission, more
recent commissions tend to have greater resources and time to undertake a
slightly broader inquiry). The Guatemalan Historical Clarification Commission pointed to the context of the Cold War, including the national security doctrine fervently backed by the United States, as one of the factors

behind that country's brutal civil war. In presenting the report to the public, commission chair Christian Tomuschat noted that "until the mid-1980s, the United States Government and U.S. private companies exercised pressure to maintain the country's archaic and unjust socio-economic structure. In addition, the United States Government, through its constituent structures, including the Central Intelligence Agency, lent direct and indirect support to some illegal state operations."[10] Visiting the country shortly after the report was released, U.S. president Bill Clinton acknowledged the important work of the commission, said that it was "wrong" for the United States to have supported military forces involved in such violent and widespread repression, and noted that "the United States must not repeat that mistake."[11]

Even with a flexible mandate and the intention of fairly gathering information about all patterns of abuse, a commission may well fail to document certain widely experienced abuses. Perhaps the most commonly underreported abuses are those suffered by women, especially sexual abuse and rape. Many commissions have received far less testimony about sexual abuse than in the numbers or proportion that they suspected took place. In South Africa, for example, a very small number of cases of sexual abuse were brought to the commission compared to the widespread practice of rape that was known to have taken place at the hands of the security forces and in the intercommunal violence of the KwaZulu Natal region.[12] The commission was well aware during the course of its operations that the numbers of reports of rape that it was receiving did not accurately represent past realities;[13] other commissions have also been aware of this problem.

This underreporting is due to a number of factors. In many cultures, rape carries great social stigma, embarrassment, and shame for the victim, and women are understandably uncomfortable providing testimony about sexual abuse in public hearings, or even in private hearings if the details would then be published in a public report. There is also sometimes a general tendency by women to downplay their experiences, emphasizing instead the stories of the men in their families.[14] Commissions may unconsciously encourage this tendency: some abuses suffered by women are reported as "secondary experiences," said Beth Goldblatt, a researcher at the Centre for Applied Legal Studies at the University of Witwatersrand in Johannesburg, South Africa, who studied how the commission responded to testimony from women. "Women who spoke to the commission were often portrayed as mothers and sisters and wives," Goldblatt said.[15] The

Guatemalan truth report also describes how, in most testimony that it received, "rape of women is mentioned as a secondary or 'added on' aspect in relation to other violations."[16] Most truth commissions have not been proactive in seeking out, encouraging, or facilitating testimony from women.

Many commissioners come to the position without an understanding of the various factors that serve as impediments to documenting women's experiences, and thus efforts by outsiders to educate the commission can be valuable. In South Africa, nongovernmental victims' advocates and women's rights scholars participated in workshops with truth commissioners, encouraging policies that would be the most inclusive and supportive of women. Partly as a result of this input, the South African commission organized several special hearings focused on women, with a panel of only female commissioners and, in one case, allowing deponents to give testimony from behind a screen, in confidence and out of the view of glaring television cameras. Despite its efforts and its consciousness of the issue, in the end the commission acknowledged in its report that "the definition of gross violation of human rights adopted by the Commission resulted in a blindness to the types of abuse predominantly experienced by women."[17]

A variety of strategies might be put in place that could encourage women to come forward with their stories, but only the most recent commissions have begun to approach this matter in any serious way. The terms of reference of the Haitian truth commission directed it to pay particular attention to "crimes of a sexual nature against female victims that were committed with political ends," resulting in focused attention to the subject throughout its work and a subchapter of its report dedicated to sexual crimes.[18] That approach, of focusing attention to the matter in the mandate, should be seriously considered elsewhere. Truth commissions should also make female statement-takers available to female deponents, in order to put women more at ease in reporting sexual abuse, and should offer confidentiality to victims who don't want their names to appear in print. In some countries, women might also be more willing to report sexual abuse to nonnationals, whom they might feel less risk of running into in their everyday lives, which may be an argument for including foreigners on the statement-taking team. Yet despite these special measures, a commission should not assume that the statements it has collected on certain crimes are representative of the total numbers. While women may choose not to speak out, the practice of rape and other sexual crimes should be fully acknowledged in a commission's report where it is believed such a practice was widespread. If a truth commission does not take special care in addressing this issue, it is likely that it will remain largely shrouded in silence and hidden from the history books—and also likely that few policy, educational, or reparatory measures will be put in place to assist past victims, increase the public understanding of the issue, or reduce the prevalence of sexual abuse in the future.

Recent truth commissions are giving much more attention to this issue. Some commissions have written effectively on this subject even while recognizing, and indeed highlighting, the difficulty of collecting testimony on some aspects of crimes against women. The Guatemala report includes a long and very powerful chapter that describes, with searing quotes from testimony of witnesses, incidents of gang rape and other widespread practices of extreme sexual violence against women. Based on the evidence before it, the commission came to the conviction that "these were not isolated acts or sporadic excesses, but part of a strategic plan" that especially targeted Mayan women.[19]

Truth commissions in the past have occasionally had information about sexual abuse against women but have chosen not to report it, judging that rape did not fall within their mandate of politically motivated crimes. Reporting on a prominent 1980 case, the truth commission in El Salvador chose not to mention in its report that three U.S. nuns and one lay worker had been raped by soldiers before they were killed. Although the commissioners had concluded that rape took place, it reported only that the women were abducted and killed. A commission member told me that since there was no evidence that the rapes resulted from orders from above, and it was assumed that the rapes were at the initiative of the soldiers, they were not considered to be politically motivated acts and were therefore left out of the report.[20] Perhaps that logic would be less likely to be used today. Since 1993, when the Salvadoran commission report was released, rape and sexual abuse have been clearly recognized as war crimes or crimes against humanity under certain conditions,[21] and there has been a heightened appreciation of the importance of more fully describing women's experiences in any historical record of abuses suffered.

This question of when a sexual crime is also a politically motivated crime, and thus an act that falls within the ambit of a truth commission, has apparently been confusing even to more recent commissions. Commissioners serving on the Amnesty Committee of the South African Truth and Reconciliation Commission told me that they threw out an application to receive amnesty for rape, after giving it virtually no consideration, because there was no way, in their logic, that the crime could be political. They cited this case, in fact, to give an example of one of the most far-fetched amnesty applications they had received. "How can someone claim that they raped someone just because she was from another political party? That makes no sense," they reasoned, referring to the violence between the African National Congress and the Inkatha Freedom Party.[22] Yet if the Amnesty Committee members had looked at testimony about gross human rights violations that had been received by the commission from victims, they would have found many reports of rape, some of them perhaps very close to the circumstances referred to in that application for amnesty.

Besides the mandate given to a commission, its report will also reflect the methodology employed in collecting and analyzing information. Many fundamental methodological issues, and the experiences of past commissions in confronting these questions, are addressed in detail later in this book, in chapter 14. The factor that will most fundamentally affect the kind of truth that a commission will document, however, is the information management system that it uses to collect, organize, and evaluate the huge amount of information that may be available to it. In recent years, larger truth commissions have employed sophisticated databases to record and analyze the details collected in thousands or tens of thousands of testimonies from victims and witnesses. Others, including the commissions in the Southern Cone region of South America and the more recent commissions in Sri Lanka, chose to forgo any fancy computerization system, either counting numbers by hand or using a simple computer program to track the most basic information collected in testimonies. The costs and benefits of using a sophisticated computer database, and some of the basic rules, procedures, and necessary resources for taking that route, are also discussed in chapter 14. Many people argue that a powerful database is essential to a truth commission's task. It is true that many kinds of analysis cannot be done without the use of such a program, especially if thousands of cases are being documented. However, less attention has been given to how a database focus to information gathering can have a limiting effect on the final product of the truth that is told.

A few people closely involved with past truth commissions have begun to take a critical look at the standard information-management model of a modern truth commission, which is based on detailed tabulation of specific acts via a database, and have begun to ask whether this approach allows a commission to answer some of the questions that it may want to ask. Janis Grobbelaar, who was an information manager for the South African truth commission, is one of the few sociologists who has staffed a truth commission. When she came to the commission in April 1996, as it was just beginning its work, one of her first questions was about the commission's research or investigation methodology, and she found that the commission had not thought about this issue in much depth. The database-driven approach, she said, reflects a perspective of "acontextual logical positivism, where one focuses on acts, names of perpetrators, and names of victims, but does not ask why and how." She continued, "For practical reasons, this is the right model. Commissioners can buy into value neutrality and positivism. But I'd be more interested in more qualitative variables: looking at the narratives of people's stories, looking at the *why* questions. Do we know why all of this happened? We're only interested in showing *what* happened."[23]

The greater context around specific truths may go unaddressed by a close focus on specific acts. Grobbelaar undertook her own informal survey in order to understand some of these dynamics, interviewing many of the commission's statement-takers who had direct contact with the victims. "Who came to the commission?" she asked. "That's an important question. The answer is: less resourced people, materially and psychologically less resourced. Their experiences and their interest in giving testimony were connected to material deprivation." And, Grobbelaar concluded, most victims were saying to the commission, "'Reconciliation must be materially linked. Give me something that enables me to go on.' How did people experience apartheid in this country? As poverty-stricken people, with very little opportunity to change that. Anything outside of that was white," said Grobbelaar. So the commission's focus on acts, victims, and perpetrators missed a greater reality: how was apartheid experienced, and *from what* is it that people were trying to heal?

Daniel Rothenberg, a U.S. anthropologist who was on the staff of the truth commission in Guatemala in its first months, has begun to ask some of these same questions. He was struck by the fact that no other social scientists were initially on the staff of the commission, and how the commission's information management and field research methodology was crafted by people who, outside of the database consultants, had no experience in field research or large interviewing and data-collection projects. "You realize how much social science has to offer to any inquiry when you see how it's *not* included in truth commission work," he said. The model employed by the commission has its advantages, said Rothenberg, but there is something questionable about deciding on your methodology before deciding on what you want to achieve. Those fundamental questions that should shape the very nature of a truth commission—what kind of truth, and for whom—were perhaps not sufficiently grappled with at the start of the Guatemalan commission. Those shaping the methodological questions approached their task with a legal mind-set, which defined a set of questions on the basis of documenting specific acts of human rights violations. Instead, Rothenberg argued, a truth commission should define its goals first, before bringing in experts to design a database that will shape the final output.[24]

I heard similar questions being asked elsewhere. Over a three-hour conversation in Port-au-Prince, Haiti, Jean Claude Jean, the director general of the Karl Leveque Cultural Institute and former director of a human rights coalition in Haiti, explained how his vision for a truth commission was very different from what ultimately took shape there. He was part of an initial effort of nongovernmental organizations to craft terms for a proposed Haitian truth commission, and supported the idea of creating such a body for Haiti, but after the commission was set up and in operation for a few months, he published a paper that was critical of its work, and particularly of its methodological approach. "You need first to have a methodology, to know what you're going to do with the information," he told me. "Just to produce a technical report on cases is not very useful, nor is it accessible to the population. In order to get to the truth, fight impunity, keep memory alive, and obtain justice, the main condition would be that the population participate in the research and production of the commission's work." More than specific information about cases, the public wanted to know how the repression worked, how different groups operated, and who the masters were behind the repression, he said. "The truth commission should be a public affair. I wanted people to see the process and to locate themselves in the process. I wanted to use the commission to encourage public debate."[25]

Ultimately, these questions come down to what purpose a commission is intended to fill. A truth commission's goals may be multilayered: to reach out to victims, to document and corroborate cases for a reparations program, to come to firm and irrefutable conclusions on controversial cases and patterns of abuse, to engage the country in a process of national healing, to contribute to justice, to write an accessible public report, to outline reforms, or to give victims a voice. Each of these goals may suggest a different approach to its work. Yet because any process that is rooted in detailed testimony-taking and the use of a sophisticated database requires so much focused energy, such an approach tends to define the very nature of a truth commission process and, through its coding and data entry sheets, the truth that the commission will collect. It is not clear exactly what the other possible information-collection models are, but it would be worthwhile for future truth commissions to consider the question seriously before simply following the path taken by commissions in the past. Could a commission document the truth without taking thousands upon thousands of detailed testimonies? Might a commission focus on the sociological, physical, and even psychological effects and tools of repression that fall outside of gross human rights violations, perhaps through a number of case studies on the broader effect of the repression? Some commissions have tried to do this through descriptive chapters on the effect of the violence, as in Guatemala (described below); more of this type of descriptive truth should be considered as future truth commissions sit down to plan their work.

The language of the Guatemalan Historical Clarification Commission's mandate called for an investigation into the "factors and circumstances" of the violence and human rights violations, including "internal as well as external" factors.[26] Staff research teams were established to address causes and origins of the armed conflict, strategies and mechanisms of the violence, and consequences and effects of the violence. This included an analysis of refugee flows, the economic impact of the armed conflict, and other effects of the three-decades-long war. Likewise, some investigators in its field offices undertook extensive interviews with community leaders and others who had no specific case to report, but who could provide detailed contextual information about how their community was impacted by the violence, or the growth and dynamics of the armed opposition in the region over the years. The director of one of the commission's field offices described taking at least one six-to-eight-hour statement from a knowledgeable member of a community who was able to lay out the history and development of the conflict in the region over many years. The researcher took down the whole testimony directly onto his laptop computer. In addition, from its headquarters in Guatemala City, the commission developed a list of "key witnesses" whom they invited to the office to give testimony not about specific cases, but about the larger context of the war and atrocities. These included former presidents, senior members of the armed forces, church leaders, Mayan community leaders, and others. Not all accepted the invitation to come to the commission to give testimony and not all who came were willing to answer all of the commission's questions. But many provided useful contextual information.

Another truth-seeking effort in Guatemala, the Recovery of Historical Memory Project (REMHI), undertaken by the Human Rights Office of the

Archbishop of Guatemala in advance of the official truth commission, suggests an alternative approach to collecting information about past atrocities. The standard interview format used by this project included a self-consciously qualitative — rather than just quantitative or factual — flavor, asking a series of questions that went beyond the act of violence to focus on the context and impact of the event, and was structured to be emotionally and psychologically supportive of the deponent. Beyond gathering the facts pertaining to the specific human rights violation, the interviewer would ask the deponent to describe the victim, including the person's personality (was he a good father? was he cheerful or fun?); to describe how the event affected the deponent and the community as a whole; and to talk about why it happened and what the deponent or the community would like to do now. "Clearly, the complexity and depth of what happened went far beyond violating individual rights," said Marcie Mersky, a senior staff member on the project, noting that it was often the destruction of cultural or religious symbols, or the forced participation by an entire community in the mutilation of the corpse of a community member, for example, which were often the most painful and destructive events, although they wouldn't have fit into a traditional inquiry into human rights violations. To ease the flow of the interview, each session was tape-recorded, and many were transcribed, which allowed extensive quotations from victims and survivors to be included in the REMHI report. "The main idea was to get people to talk," said Mersky.[27] Relying on members of the community to take testimony, after receiving training by the national office, the REMHI project was much more focused on the process and impact of collecting testimony than on the final production of a report.[28]

The question of what kind of information a commission should collect can sometimes carry huge political and emotional baggage. The Argentine commission consciously did not ask survivors about the physical characteristics of the disappeared that could help identify remains, a decision that some people regretted in later years as unidentified skeletons were unearthed. Commission members acknowledge that they were resistant to taking down such information, a reflection of the political and emotional position of many human rights organizations and victims' families at the time, which extended to the commission staff. The position of the families was often unbending: the disappeared were taken alive, and they were expected to be returned alive. "This is explainable and justifiable," one commissioner told me, when asked why the commission didn't take down basic physical data. "This was precisely the argument of the Madres [the activist mothers of the disappeared]: 'They took them alive and we want them alive; we're not going to recognize anything that would presuppose that our children are dead.'"[29] The implied position of the commission was thus that the disappeared should still be presumed to be alive. There was one startling consequence of this position. In the list of the 8,960 disappeared that was printed as an annex to the commission report, the age of each victim is listed not as the age at which the person was disappeared, but the age he or she would have been in 1984, the year the commission report was published — an age, it is now accepted, that none of those on the list ever reached.

It is impossible for any short-term commission to fully detail the extent and effect of widespread abuses that took place over many years' time, nor, in most cases, to investigate every single case brought to it. However, it can reveal a global truth of the broad patterns of events, and demonstrate without question the atrocities that took place and what forces were responsible. If it is careful and creative, it can also go far beyond simply outlining the facts of abuse, and make a major contribution in understanding how people and the country as a whole were affected, and what factors contributed to the violence.

Truth versus Justice

Is It a Trade-Off?

During the negotiations to end the civil war in Guatemala, the Guatemalan armed forces supported the idea of official truth-seeking. In a meeting with international human rights advocates in 1994, Mario Enriquez, then minister of defense, made his position clear. "We are fully in support of a truth commission," he said. "Just like in Chile: truth, but no trials."

This story was related to me by the director of the Americas Division of Human Rights Watch, José Miguel Vivanco, to illustrate the concern among rights advocates that official truth-seeking is sometimes used as a means to avoid trials for rights abusers. In the end, the mandate for the commission in Guatemala explicitly prohibited it from having any "judicial aim or effect," though it was unclear exactly what was intended by this language.[1] (Would it, by the most narrow interpretation, restrict the later use of the commission's information by prosecutors, for example? That was not at first clear.) Other commissions have also raised this concern. In El Salvador, the release of the truth commission report was answered with the immediate passage of a sweeping amnesty law. In South Africa, justice was put up for trade: the truth commission offered freedom from prosecution in exchange for the full truth about politically motivated crimes. These cases and others have led to a suspicion that truth commissions are likely to weaken the prospects for proper justice in the courts, or even that commissions are sometimes intentionally employed as a way to avoid holding perpetrators responsible for their crimes.

Yet a serious review of past experience, and of the actual relationship between truth-finding and prosecutorial endeavors, challenges such a conclusion. Even in those cases where there has been a seemingly clear intention to trade off justice with a weaker inquiry into and statement of the truth, such as suggested regarding Guatemala, El Salvador, and South Africa, the actual relationship between truth and justice endeavors, and the real effect of nonjudicial truth inquiries on prospects for justice, are in fact not so clear. Past experience shows, for example, that truth inquiries have sometimes directly strengthened prosecutions that follow, as will be described below. Furthermore, truth commissions are typically employed in contexts where judicial systems are barely functioning or very weak, or are corrupt and politically biased, and prospects for serious prosecutions are slim— with or without a truth commission—even if no amnesty is in place. And finally, these bodies have often been able to directly contribute to other measures of accountability—and to future prospects for justice—in ways that are out of reach of the courts.[2]

Nonjudicial truth bodies do not and should not be seen to replace judicial action against perpetrators, and neither victims nor societies at large have understood them to do so in those countries where truth commissions have been put in place. While their subject matters may overlap in that they both investigate past crimes, trials and commissions serve different purposes, and neither can fill the role of the other. Scholars and policymakers who have occasionally suggested that a nonjudicial truth-seeking endeavor can successfully take the place of prosecutions—such as in an early suggestion in a *New York Times* op-ed that the International Criminal Tribunal for the Former Yugoslavia should be replaced by a nonjudicial truth inquiry—misunderstand these differing roles, and underestimate the importance of legal prosecutions to victims and society at large.

However, despite these differing roles, it is evident in many peace agreements of recent years, and in the descriptions of those who have been closely involved in many different peace negotiations, that there is a natural and close relationship—or certainly a perception of a close relationship—between nonjudicial truth inquiries and judicial investigations and prosecutions. If an amnesty has been agreed to or is already in place, peace negotiators or new democratic leaders may turn to the idea of a truth commission in search of some form of accounting for past abuses, or may try to modify the amnesty with powers given to a truth commission, for example. They may perhaps use a truth commission as a means to remove perpetrators from positions of authority, even if they cannot be convicted and punished.

They may also decide, at the negotiating table, to reach agreement on a truth commission together with a blanket amnesty, as if one somehow made up for the other, as took place recently in Sierra Leone. But despite the evident fact of a sometimes close relationship between truth commissions and compromised or limited justice, I will argue here that truth commissions should not be seen as a replacement for prosecutions, nor as a second-best, weaker option when "real" justice is not possible, as human rights advocates have sometimes suggested. On the contrary, commissions can, and probably increasingly will, positively contribute to justice and prosecutions, sometimes in the least expected ways.

A basic confusion between truth commissions and courtroom trials, and their differing functions, is understandable, and a distinction between them is necessary in order to understand how they interact. Official truth inquiries and trials of human rights perpetrators are often considered, and may be initiated, at approximately the same time, usually at the point of political transition, and often overlap in the subject matter covered. But trials focus narrowly on identifying individual legal responsibility for specific crimes and punishing those found guilty. In contrast, truth commissions, as noted earlier, have had no power to initiate trials, and only the South African commission has had the power to grant amnesty. Commissions generally investigate and report, and go no further, focusing on describing the broad pattern of events over many years, and the specific policies and practices that caused them, and describing individual cases only as examples of a pattern or to highlight important events.[3] Truth commissions and courts may work with some of the same material, and commissions may make judicial-like decisions in concluding institutional or individual responsibility. But their powers, structures, and goals are quite different.

THE DIFFICULTIES OF REACHING JUSTICE IN THE COURTS

Due to many reasons largely unrelated to the existence of a truth commission, successful prosecution of rights abusers, in countries in transition from authoritarian rule, is rare. Rather than a replacement for judicial action, therefore, in many cases truth commissions have served as a complement to a very weak judicial system, helping to fill the void created by the inaction, incompetence, or inability of the courts to even begin to handle the thousands of crimes that demand prosecution.

A quick glance at recent transitions following a period of widespread rights abuses makes clear that successful trials of perpetrators are uncommon, and where they do take place, they are usually few in number and rarely reach the most senior perpetrators. For example, looking at Guatemala, Haiti, and Uganda together — countries that suffered huge numbers of abuses and where no amnesty laws prevent prosecutions for many of these crimes[4]— there have been only a couple of dozen trials for killings, torture, and other serious rights violations by agents of the previous government. The great majority of these were trials of low-level soldiers, rather than senior officials who planned or directed the atrocities. Rwanda has fared only slightly better: there were close to 150 domestic trials in the three years following the 1994 genocide there, although over 130,000 were in jail awaiting a court date.[5]

There are many reasons why so few trials of rights abusers take place: a barely functioning judicial system, corrupt or compromised officials, and a lack of concrete evidence are common problems. Cash-strapped judicial systems have no witness protection programs and many witnesses fear coming forward with evidence. Police or public prosecutors lack the skills to investigate and present strong cases, judges and prosecutors are underpaid, and courts operate with scant physical and financial resources and without basic administrative support. In some countries, particularly in Latin America, blanket amnesties have been passed to prevent trials for so-called political crimes, often put in place by the abusive regime before leaving power.[6]

Sometimes there is a lack of political will to tackle politically difficult or dangerous cases, perhaps articulated by national leaders who may discourage "divisive" and costly trials, or evident in the resistance of prosecutors or judges to move forward on cases. In Latin America, the powerful armed forces have prevented or limited the prosecution of their members for past abuses, even where an explicit amnesty is not in place. In Colombia and Guatemala, judges have been killed for attempting to investigate abuses by the military, which quickly discourages other judges from doing the same.

Even in South Africa, where there is relative safety and security and a sufficiently well-functioning judiciary to hold serious trials (although still a largely unreconstructed judicial system, with most prosecutors and judges still in place from the apartheid years), the limitations of prosecutions are clear. Two high-profile trials in 1996 for apartheid-era events each took close to two years of intense investigation and cost over eight million dollars for the trials alone, not including the investigation costs. Despite the considerable evidence available, one of these two trials resulted in acquittals for all twenty accused.

This record of impunity exists despite the fact that there is often a legal obligation to prosecute these crimes. Some of these legal obligations are outlined in international treaties, such as the Convention against Torture and Other Cruel, Inhuman or Degrading Treatment or Punishment, or the Convention on the Prevention and Punishment of the Crime of Genocide. Many legal scholars argue that customary international law, which has universal application independent from any treaty, also requires prosecution for crimes against humanity, and therefore makes amnesties for such crimes illegal. The interpretation and reach of international law are under rapid development, and there is disagreement about exactly what is prohibited and what is required. Still, certain obligations, such as those defined in treaties, are very clear.[7] Some rights advocates have also pointed to moral and political reasons to argue strongly that impunity will only encourage more abuses in the future.[8] Yet the point here is that even where international law clearly requires prosecution of those accused of rights crimes, serious prosecutorial action against perpetrators is still uncommon, and many blanket amnesties remain in force.[9]

TRUTH VERSUS JUSTICE: A LOOK AT THE RECORD

The stated intention of most truth commissions has been to strengthen or contribute to justice in the courts. Many have forwarded their case files to the courts or to the prosecutorial authorities and have recommended prosecution, or have suggested measures to strengthen the judiciary for the future. However, whether trials result from the work of the commission has been determined by many factors outside of a commission's control: the strength and independence of the judiciary; the political will of the judiciary and executive branch to challenge powerful perpetrators; the power of the political opposition or nongovernmental organizations that may push for trials and attempt to block or overturn an amnesty; and the prosecution's skill, experience, and resources to move on big cases. Yet there is no inherent reason why a commission cannot contribute to later trials. The following sections explore the relationship between truth commissions and the prospects for justice in six countries: prompting an amnesty in El Salvador; providing evidence to support prosecutions in Argentina, Uganda, and Haiti; working under an amnesty already in place in Chile, and then strengthening later international prosecutions; and offering amnesty in exchange for the truth in South Africa.

Prompting an Amnesty in El Salvador

The blanket amnesty that followed on the heels of the El Salvador truth commission report has colored the memory of the whole commission both for Salvadorans and for others who watched the transition there. El Salvador is the clearest case to date of an amnesty passed into law as a direct response to a truth commission report, but the details of this story make conclusions from the case far from clear.

The El Salvador truth commission's strongly worded report included the names of over forty high-level officials responsible for serious abuses, despite strong pressure from the Salvadoran government not to publish names. In response to the report (and also to rumored threats of a coup by an angry military), the president of El Salvador immediately introduced a bill in Parliament to award "a broad, absolute, and unconditional amnesty" to "all those who in one way or another participated in political crimes, (or) crimes with political ramifications." Just five days after the truth commission report was published, Parliament passed this sweeping amnesty proposal into law, with the support of the former armed opposition.[10]

In fact, the truth commission report had not called for the prosecution of those that it concluded were guilty of horrendous crimes, which was a surprise and disappointment for rights advocates. Nor did it recommend against a blanket amnesty, which could have made it more difficult to pass the amnesty law, since the recommendations of the commission were mandatory, by prior agreement. Many believe that an explicit violation of a commission recommendation so soon after the report's release would have received a sharp rebuke from the international community.[11] According to a senior staff member, the commissioners even considered recommending that an amnesty be passed, given the extremely biased state of the judicial system. Instead, the report takes a full page to underscore the incapacity and bias of the courts, and makes the case that fair trials would be impossible until judicial reforms were put in place—a page that the head of one international rights organization said "undid everything else good in the report" by taking away the expectation and obligation of the judicial system to work.[12] The report states,

> One painfully clear aspect of (the) situation is the glaring inability of the judicial system either to investigate crimes or to enforce the law, especially

when it comes to crimes committed with the direct or indirect support of State institutions. . . . We must ask ourselves, therefore, whether the judiciary is capable, all things being equal, of fulfilling the requirements of justice. If we take a detached view of the situation, this question cannot be answered in the affirmative. . . .

The question is not whether the guilty should be punished, but whether justice can be done. Public morality demands that those responsible for the crimes described here be punished. However, El Salvador has no system for the administration of justice which meets the minimum requirements of objectivity and impartiality so that justice can be rendered reliably. . . .

That being the current situation, it is clear that, for now, the only judicial system which the Commission could trust to administer justice in a full and timely manner would be one which had been restructured in the light of the peace agreements.[13]

The commission was sharply criticized for its silence on the question of amnesty. One expert on El Salvador wrote, "In all likelihood, the Truth Commission could not have prevented the government from passing a sweeping amnesty immediately after issuance of its report. Yet the Commission did not urge prosecutions, gave no opinion about amnesty, did not call for follow-up efforts to determine the fate of victims or identify those responsible, and contributed little to the discussion of possible avenues for compensation. Had the Truth Commission delineated the kinds of crimes that cannot be amnestied under international law or urged that amnesties be contingent upon full revelation of the facts (as in South Africa), it would have upped the cost to the government of such an amnesty."[14]

Despite the strong criticism, commissioner Thomas Buergenthal defended the commission's position, arguing that to recommend prosecutions when serious trials were out of the question would have made things worse. "They would have gone through the motions and acquitted the accused," he says, giving the government an opportunity in effect to retry the commission's findings. "And how would you expect anyone to testify against these people? Who would testify against Defense Minister [René Emilio] Ponce, for example? Trials would have had the opposite effect of what people expect, I am sure. Nobody would have given testimony, and everybody would be acquitted, except those on the left. People were almost too scared to talk to *us*."[15] Yet Buergenthal acknowledged that the commission might have taken a different approach. It may have been a mistake not to say something about an amnesty, he said in retrospect, perhaps, for example, to require an election or some kind of national process or public debate before an amnesty was considered in Parliament.

It is quite possible that the Salvadoran Parliament would have awarded an amnesty for past crimes even if the truth commission had not named perpetrators, and regardless of the commission's recommendations. The 1991 peace accords left the subject unresolved, agreeing only that the issue of amnesty would be considered six months after the completion of the truth commission. Those who opposed the amnesty law, such as the New York–based Lawyers Committee for Human Rights, recognized that a further amnesty may have been inevitable. The Lawyers Committee wrote, "As the government has been quick to point out, the political parties signed an agreement [in 1992] that a general amnesty would be enacted after the Truth Commission report. In dispute were the timing, the scope and how the amnesty relates to the recommendations of the Truth Commission."[16] Whether or not El Salvador would have ended up with a broad amnesty in place, it is clear that the quick passage of the amnesty legislation was in direct response to the commission's naming perpetrators in its report, and was a great disappointment to those who hoped the truth commission would be a step toward accountability.

As described earlier, members of the high command who were named in the report were retired from the armed services several months later, albeit with full honors. Although it was never stated publicly, some observers saw the amnesty as a package deal, by which the military received an amnesty in exchange for its finally agreeing to step down. While this is hardly an impressive example of accountability, at least there did appear to be some direct effect from the commission's firm conclusions.

Evidence to Support Prosecutions: Argentina, Uganda, and Haiti

In sharp contrast to El Salvador, the National Commission on the Disappeared in Argentina played a critical role in the trials against members of the former military junta leadership, serving as a model for the positive relationship that can exist between truth commissions and later prosecutions. The Argentine commission was always perceived by the public to be a predecessor to trials that would follow, and indeed, as the commission concluded its work, it handed its case files directly to the prosecutors, allowing them to quickly build cases against nine of the most senior members of the previous military regime, with access to a large number of primary witnesses.

According to the deputy prosecutor for the most prominent trial, of the senior leadership of the military regime, Luis Moreno Ocampo, the timing and nature of that trial would have been "impossible" without the information from the commission, known as CONADEP. "Perhaps it would have been possible to carry on a trial without CONADEP's files, but we never could have prepared it in such a short time, nor gathered that number of solid cases to present," he told me.[17] In just over five months, the prosecution reviewed the commission's nearly 9,000 case files to choose over 800 witnesses to be presented in the trial, covering some 700 individual cases. The trial began just eighteen months after the military junta left power, when the momentum for accountability and public interest was still strong. The trial was a devastating show of calculated horror, allowing the public to hear firsthand accounts of suffering from those who were caught in the web of the military's torture centers and managed to survive. Because the commission took testimony in private, this and following trials trials were the only opportunity for the public to see witnesses personally recount their stories.

In the end, five of the nine people on trial were convicted of homicide, torture, and other acts of violence, with sentences ranging from four and one-half years to life in prison. While Argentineans were initially angry at the light sentences and acquittals, the world community applauded one of the first successful domestic trials of former rulers in a newly returned democracy. Many other trials were planned, also relying on CONADEP's files, but these trials were soon cut short. Under pressure from the military, restrictive laws were passed that limited prosecutions for abuses during the "dirty war."[18] When President Carlos Menem came into office in 1989, he soon pardoned those few who had been convicted.

Truth commissions in other countries have forwarded their information to the justice system with a recommendation for prosecution, but with less success. In Uganda, for example, the truth commission that operated from 1986 to 1995 forwarded many cases to the police investigation unit when sufficient evidence seemed to warrant prosecution. After investigation, the police were to send each case to the director of public prosecutions. But very few of these cases ever made it to a courtroom.

According to the Ugandan commission chair, Supreme Court Justice Arthur Oder, the commission forwarded about two hundred cases for further investigation; the public prosecutor eventually prosecuted about fifty, and gained convictions in perhaps twelve, mostly for minor offenses such as attempted kidnapping or conspiracy.[19] The commission's report recommended that all those who were implicated in abuses should be prosecuted, but commission members acknowledged that this was unrealistic. Commission chair Oder told me, "There are perhaps fifty thousand people responsible for these crimes. Perhaps ten thousand can be identified. There are some two to three thousand pointed out in the commission documents. But at most, one to two thousand could really be taken on."[20] Yet for a host of reasons, it was clear that one or two thousand was far more than the number that would ever go to court. This failure of the justice system to prosecute these cases, despite solid evidence and thousands of firsthand witnesses, is a reflection of a number of problems, including infrastructural, political, and psychological. Uganda offers a good example of the kinds of challenges that are often confronted by countries struggling to establish a functioning system of justice.

I asked a former director of public prosecutions in Uganda, Alfred Nasaba, why so few of the commission's cases went to court. He claimed only one to three of the commission's cases came to him from the police during the five years that he was public prosecutor, 1991 to 1995. And in each of those cases, his office was unable to find witnesses willing to give testimony. "The witnesses or the complainants reconcile, and then they don't want to come to prove the case," he explained. In other cases, witnesses died or disappeared, or were simply unwilling to cooperate for unexplained reasons.[21]

Uganda's presidential adviser on human rights and former attorney general, George Kanyeihamba, gave the same reason. "It's not a capacity question. It's an evidentiary question. It's difficult to prove these cases in court. Witnesses feel intimidated and are too scared to give testimony."[22] There is a widespread fear of revenge for testifying against someone in court in Uganda. Even the commission found that witnesses would sometimes return after a hearing to withdraw their testimony, sometimes flatly denying what they had said even when it was recorded on video- or audiotape. It was clear they had been pressured to recant their story, particularly if they named perpetrators. Certainly witnesses felt even more hesitation to go to court to help put someone in jail.

In a country known worldwide for the brutality of the Idi Amin and Milton Obote regimes, it is surprising that prosecutions in Uganda could falter for lack of evidence. The minister of justice, Bart Katureebe, told a story to explain how this could be true. When he was a young lawyer in the 1970s, under the government of Idi Amin, he was placed as a low-level employee in the Ministry of Justice. One day, he and his colleagues watched out of their fourth-floor window as soldiers below stuffed a man into the

trunk of their car to take him away — most certainly to suffer serious torture, and probably to be killed. "But if you had taken me into court as a
witness, I wouldn't be able to point out who the soldiers were; I couldn't
recognize them from where we were. And everyone else in the area ran
away. If people see that happening, they're going to run in the other direction. So there's no eyewitnesses to say exactly who was doing it."[23]

Justice Minister Katureebe continued, saying that even the most guilty,
and often those high up in the hierarchy, are sometimes the most difficult
to bring to justice. "If you brought Idi Amin back to Uganda today, you
probably couldn't convict him under our law. *He* wasn't personally involved
in most acts. You need a specific case, and evidence that hasn't been destroyed, to prove the case." Do you dispense with the normal, strict rules of
evidence to convict former despots? he asked. They decided in Uganda that
for the sake of a fair and just rule of law, they would not. "The evidence before the commission is *so* believable you expect people would be convicted.
But when you bring them before a court, with different rules of evidence,
they are acquitted on a specific offense. That discourages others from bringing cases," Katureebe continued. Idi Amin's former vice president and minister of defense lives as a free man in Uganda, since his acquittal in a trial.
"Our policy in Uganda is: If you have a case, charge him. If there is no case,
then he can live as a normal citizen. This policy has paid off."

The argument of Justice Minister Katureebe, that leaders can only be
brought to trial if they were personally involved in specific crimes, is not
exactly correct. In fact, under the theory of "command responsibility," well
accepted in international law, a civilian or military superior may be held
responsible not only for his (or her) own unlawful orders, but for acts of his
subordinates if (1) he knew or had reason to know that the subordinate had
committed, or was about to commit, such acts, and (2) he did not take necessary and reasonable measures to prevent those acts or to punish the subordinate. (The successful prosecution of the junta leadership in Argentina,
for example, relied on this principle.[24])

Prosecutions, however, also require political will. Commission members
in Uganda tell stories of clear-cut cases where written documentation alone
should have been enough to convict, but where the accused would be arrested only briefly, released on bail, and the case never seriously investigated.
There are many known killers wandering freely in Uganda, as the commissioners are all too aware. "I just ran into one of them in the bank," the commission chair Oder said to me. "A high up official in the Muslim community
here. There was clear evidence against him, but he is living freely."[25]

And there are other challenges. The police investigation unit in Uganda is woefully understaffed, underresourced, and short on expertise, partly stemming from massive purges of the police in the 1970s under Idi Amin's reign. Whether or not there is evidence, with few witnesses eager to put a neighbor in jail, overworked and undertrained investigators, and little interest by officials in more trials focused on events of a prior regime, any legal justice relating to events prior to 1986 is not likely in Uganda. Other factors have overshadowed the efforts of the truth commission.

In Haiti it was also intended that the information from the truth commission would be used to prosecute those involved in abuses. The commission's mandate called for information to be sent to the Ministry of Justice. As the commission was finishing its work, Minister of Justice René Magloir (a former member of the commission who stepped down to become the justice minister) told me that his office was preparing to receive the files.[26]

Yet despite efforts to push for high-level prosecutions, few cases have moved forward in the years since democratic rule returned to Haiti in 1994 and the truth commission turned its files over to the Justice Department in early 1996. International lawyers working on some of these cases described intense fear of retaliation on the part of witnesses, lawyers, judges, and even the police, which made prosecutions difficult. Well-armed groups responsible for past abuses were active throughout the country, and many people were not willing to risk their lives by trying to investigate, prosecute, or stand as a witness against these still very dangerous men.

An Amnesty Already in Place in Chile

Chile demonstrates that even with an amnesty in place, information from a truth commission can be used in the courts at least to establish the identity of perpetrators in some individual cases.

The Chilean military granted itself a broad amnesty in 1978, which covered nearly all of its crimes since it took over the government in 1973. When it gave up power in 1990, this amnesty stayed in place. While crimes since 1978 could be prosecuted, the majority of serious abuses had taken place in the first months and years of military rule, and were covered by the law. Trials covering this early period have nevertheless gone forward; the amnesty law has been interpreted to prohibit punishment for crimes, but not to prevent investigation and even court hearings to establish responsibility for crimes.

When President Patricio Aylwin Azocar took power in 1990, he considered overruling the amnesty law, and received considerable pressure from rights groups and victims' families to do so. In the end, he let the amnesty stay in place. Some claim this decision was based on political expediency, as he was under close watch by a still-powerful military. Aylwin and his key policy advisers at the time insisted they simply did not have the votes in Parliament to overturn the amnesty.[27]

Despite the amnesty, the National Commission on Truth and Reconciliation was required to send to the courts any information that it uncovered involving a crime. With the release of the commission's report, President Aylwin announced his position on how the amnesty law should be interpreted, instructing the courts not to apply the law until a case had been thoroughly investigated — what came to be known as the "Aylwin Doctrine." In a nationally televised address, Aylwin said, "Today I submitted a note and a copy of the [commission] report to the Supreme Court asking that it instruct the lower courts to speed up all pending trials involving human rights violations and to begin the new trials that may result from this report. In my opinion, the current amnesty, which this government respects, cannot be an obstacle for court-ordered investigations into responsibilities for human rights violations, particularly in cases of missing people."[28] Under this interpretation of the law, some families have been able to establish in court the identity of perpetrators and even see those individuals face accusations in court.[29]

In 1999, the situation began to change dramatically, when the Chilean Supreme Court ruled that the amnesty no longer applied to cases of disappearances.[30] In the wake of the Pinochet arrest in London in late 1998, a significant number of cases pertaining to severe abuses under the military regime began to move forward in Chilean courts. Suddenly worried about its legal vulnerability, the military hoped that a compromise with human rights lawyers might be reached in which an amnesty for pre-1978 crimes would be applied "in exchange for all information we can acquire for locating where the disappeared are buried," according to one senior military official.[31] These negotiations were still under way as this book went to press.

Amnesty as a Truth-Seeking Tool in South Africa

Only in South Africa has a truth commission been given amnesty-granting powers. Yet this amnesty comes with conditions attached: it is granted on an individual basis only to those who tell all they know about their past crimes and can show that the crimes were politically motivated.

When the new postapartheid government came into power in 1994, it was required by the transitional constitution to institute some form of amnesty, but the interim constitution stated only that "there shall be an amnesty," leaving open how it would be put in place. The new minister of justice, Dullah Omar, spent his first months in office struggling with the problem of how to implement this requirement, or, as he told me, "How to deal with the amnesty requirement in a way that would be morally acceptable to the people." The amnesty was soon linked with the quickly developing proposal for a national truth commission: amnesty would be given only in exchange for the truth. A grant of amnesty would be the carrot to get perpetrators' cooperation in the process, and the threat of prosecution would be the stick.[32]

Over eighteen months after the idea was first proposed, the newly formed Truth and Reconciliation Commission began its first hearings and applications for individual amnesty began to be submitted. The applications for amnesty gained momentum as the deadline for application neared: senior police commanders, hit-squad members, even members of the current ANC-led government applied. In total, there were over 7,000 applications for amnesty for specific crimes. Unfortunately, many of the applications came from persons already in prison, and most senior members of the apartheid government did not apply and continued to deny any crimes. Yet in the hearings that did take place, amnesty applicants provided testimony about exactly how operations were planned, why certain targets were chosen, what forms of brutality and torture victims suffered before they were killed, and who in the line of command — and how far up — gave orders or knew about the acts.

When granted, the amnesty exempted individuals from criminal prosecutions for the acts applied for, and barred civil suits for damages. It also indemnified the state from any liability that might flow from acts committed by those persons granted amnesty.

Prosecutions for past atrocities continued even as the commission was under way. Two special investigation teams were set up soon after the elections in 1994 in order to take up prominent cases of political violence. As those targeted for prosecution felt the heat of the investigations, and as they heard their names come out in the hearings of their former colleagues, a number of violators quickly submitted applications for amnesty. The relationship between the truth commission and the offices of the attorneys general — especially that of the Special Investigation Team of Attorney General Jan d'Oliveira of Transvaal—was sometimes strained. Two-year criminal investigations and near arrests by the attorney general's office were brought to a halt when those accused went to the truth commission to apply for amnesty. In the view of one senior investigator on an attorney general's Special Investigation Team, his team served to "chase all the sheep into the corral of the truth commission. . . . Without us, a lot wouldn't have come out. The 'big breakthroughs' of the [Truth and Reconciliation Commission] were because we started chasing these people."[33] The commission, for its part, was frustrated that the attorney general's office provided the commission's investigators only limited access to its case files. The commission had the power to subpoena the files, but chose not to for lack of time and to avoid straining the relationship further.

TRUTH FROM TRIALS?

Many argue that trials are preferable to truth commissions not only because they impart justice, but because trials in themselves reveal the truth. For example, the trials of the former junta members in Argentina in the mid-1980s received extensive coverage. The media reported on the trials at great length, and a new daily newspaper that was founded to focus solely on the trial was widely read. Although the truth commission report was already a best seller, these trials provided firsthand testimony from hundreds of victims and witnesses, and from real live perpetrators in the dock. The stories were wrenching and the details vivid, and they held the country's attention for months.

The purpose of criminal trials is not to expose the truth, however, but to find whether the criminal standard of proof has been satisfied on specific charges. A measure of the truth may emerge in this process, but trials are limited in the truth that they are able to tell as they must comply with rules of evidence which often exclude important information. In South Africa, several trials running concurrently brought regular press reports of the workings of the government hit squads and the conspiracy of the government to foment political violence in townships during the 1980s. Yet despite the lengthy, high-level, and very public trials in recent years, South Africans have seen the limitations of a prosecutions approach to getting at the truth.

For much of 1996, at least two prominent trials were under way simultaneously in South Africa. One accused the former minister of defense, Magnus

Malan, and nineteen others of planning and carrying out a massacre of thirteen people in 1987. After a difficult trial, with a perfunctory prosecution led by an attorney general who himself was an appointee of the former apartheid government, all defendants were acquitted. They left the courtroom to declare their innocence to the world, to the delight of the previous government and its supporters. The second trial, of Colonel Eugene de Kock, the former head of a secret police assassination unit, resulted in his conviction on eighty-nine charges, including six counts of murder, two counts of conspiracy, and eighty counts of gun running and fraud. Prosecutors were also preparing other high-profile cases.

Paul van Zyl, a lawyer who was a senior staff member of the South African Truth and Reconciliation Commission, argues that "trials have limited explanatory value. They're about individual culpability, not about the system as a whole. Trials set up an 'us versus them' dynamic. A trial is not about *our* complicity. It makes it look like *they're* guilty, not us. So all of white South Africa can look at Eugene de Kock and say, 'evil guy,' and not realize they made him possible. Middle-class suburban housewives and white businessmen voting for the National Party made Eugene de Kock possible. But a trial will never say that."[34] Although there is a secondary explanatory effect of a trial, as van Zyl and others acknowledge, a trial is mostly about establishing guilt in specific instances, not about broader explanations or culpability.

South Africa's judicial system is stronger and more impartial than that of most postauthoritarian transitional countries. Efforts in other countries to try accused perpetrators for politically motivated crimes have sometimes obscured rather than clarified the truth. A trial in El Salvador in 1991 for the 1989 murder of six Jesuit priests, their housekeeper, and her daughter resulted in a welter of conflicting testimony and unusual court procedures. The trial took place before the UN truth commission was set up, and might have provided a degree of accountability for abuses by the state. In a country where trials of military officials are rare, it captured much attention in the press and was followed closely by international rights observers. Yet the trial only succeeded in further discrediting the judiciary. As U.S. law professor Robert Goldman noted in reporting on the trial for the Lawyers Committee for Human Rights, "The conduct of this trial does little to inspire confidence in the existing criminal justice system in El Salvador. Both structurally and operationally, it contains features discarded by many other civil and common law systems, such as a trial judge who performs both investigatory and sentencing functions; a jury virtually free to disregard law and reason in rendering verdicts; antiquated evidentiary guidelines with broad exclusionary rules that are selectively applied; and the admissibility of recanted extrajudicial confessions. . . . If this trial with its unprecedented public scrutiny exemplifies how the system works, then there is cause for concern how defendants in ordinary criminal cases are treated."[35] The defense case was built around an attack on the international community for pressing the government for a trial, and implied threats against the jury in case they took the "wrong decision." The verdict itself (which found two of the nine on trial guilty of murder) was "deeply disturbing and, in one respect, defied rational analysis," according to Goldman. "What occurred in the courtroom in San Salvador brought forth little truth and rendered only partial justice."[36]

HOW TRUTH COMMISSIONS MIGHT CONTRIBUTE TO JUSTICE

As described above in the case of Argentina, a truth commission can most directly strengthen trials through its vast collection of information pertaining to crimes, which can be forwarded directly to prosecuting authorities. It is increasingly clear, in fact, that the record established by a truth commission may serve as a good source of evidence for many years into the future, not only for domestic trials but for prosecutions undertaken on an international level. Baltasar Garzón, the Spanish judge who brought charges against Augusto Pinochet, relied heavily on the Chilean truth commission report to help build his case. Likewise, international human rights groups started with the truth commission report in Chad in their attempts to bring charges against the former ruler of Chad, Hissein Habré. The same could well take place in relation to other countries. In addition, there are other more indirect ways in which truth commissions can contribute to or have an impact on the prospects for justice.

Appraising the Role of the Courts in the System of Repression

Quite apart from referring cases of past abuse for action in the courts, a truth commission can also make a potential contribution in another area that is distinctly out of reach of the courts, and is not easily covered by any other state body: detailing the role of judges and the judicial system as a whole in perpetuating or tolerating abuses by the authorities. In some countries, the judiciary continued to operate relatively independently even during the worst years of repression. In Chile, for example, the military pointed to the courts' independence to try to legitimize its rule and deny rights problems; meanwhile, the courts used none of their powers to stop abuses. South Africa, El Salvador, Guatemala, and other countries have seen similar patterns: judges have either looked the other way or actively supported the authorities' policies and practices, discounting, ignoring, or covering up evidence or simply refusing to move on cases involving abuses by the state. The Guatemalan truth report describes how "[i]mpunity permeated the country to such an extent that it took control of the very structure of the State."[37] Truth commissions can analyze these patterns and fully document the judiciary's role in allowing repression. After all, while it is the military, police, or intelligence officers that may have carried out the physical abuses, it is the judiciary that failed in its duty to provide a check on their authority. If the judiciary had worked well and functioned independently, patterns of violence and abuse by the authorities might have been significantly limited.

The Chilean truth commission report dedicates a whole chapter to the "Behavior of the Courts toward the Grave Human Rights Violations That Occurred between September 11, 1973, and March 11, 1990," spelling out the weaknesses of the judiciary under military rule. The report states that "legal oversight was glaringly insufficient" despite the fact that "the court system continued to operate normally in almost all realms of national activity whose conflicts reached the courts," and that "the judicial power was the only one of the three powers or branches of government that continued to operate."[38] The report goes on to lay blame on the courts for the depth of repression that was reached, saying, "This posture taken by the judicial branch during military rule was largely, if unintentionally, responsible for aggravating the process of systematic human rights violations," thus offering "the agents of repression a growing assurance they would enjoy impunity for their criminal actions, no matter what outrages they might commit."[39]

The Argentina report, *Nunca Más*, also dedicates a long chapter to "The Judiciary during the Repression," highlighting the failure of habeas corpus, the irregular burial of corpses by the judicial mortuary, the judges' authorization of police searches of human rights organizations' offices, and other anomalies. "Instead of acting as a brake on the prevailing absolutism as it should have done, the judiciary became a sham jurisdictional structure, a cover to protect its image."[40] In contrast to Chile, the top levels of the Argentine judiciary were replaced at the time of the coup, including the entire Supreme Court, and the remaining judges had to swear to uphold the objectives of the military junta. The report describes how this newly formed judiciary "condoned the usurpation of power and allowed a host of judicial aberrations to take on the appearance of legality."[41]

The Ugandan commission report includes a chapter on the "Denial of Fair and Public Trial before Independent and Impartial Courts of Law" that outlines the illegal and unfair practices of military and regular courts, providing detailed examples taken directly from court records. It concludes, for example, that the military tribunal "was not independent and impartial. It acted more as a part, and in the interest and service, of the Military Regime than for the purpose of dispensing justice."[42]

The El Salvador report points to problems in the judiciary throughout its analysis. It notes, for example, how judges covered up evidence, rather than acting on it, and the unwillingness of judges to cooperate with the commission's investigations. In one major case, the massacre at El Mozote in December 1981, the report concludes that the president of the Supreme Court, Mauricio Gutiérrez Castro, "interfered unduly and prejudicially, for biased political reasons, in the ongoing judicial proceedings of the case."[43] Finally, the commission concludes that "[t]he situation described in this report would not have occurred if the judicial system had functioned properly."[44] In further detail, it explains, "None of the three branches of government — judicial, legislative or executive — was capable of restraining the military's overwhelming control of society. The judiciary was weakened as it fell victim to intimidation and the foundations were laid for its corruption; since it had never enjoyed genuine institutional independence from the legislative and executive branches, its ineffectiveness steadily increased until it became, through its inaction or its appalling submissiveness, a factor which contributed to the tragedy suffered by the country."[45]

Finally, only the commission in South Africa has gone so far as holding specialized hearings to analyze the role of the judiciary in supporting or allowing state repression. When the judges declined an invitation to participate in the hearing (with the exception of one judge), the commission considered issuing subpoenas to bring them forward to answer questions, but decided against it.

Recommending Judicial Reforms

Understanding the role of the courts in the repression naturally leads to an analysis of what needs to change. Perhaps the most direct contribution toward future justice is to reform the criminal justice system to ensure that the courts, prosecutors, and police are able to prevent further abuses by state forces, and to ensure that accused criminals receive fair treatment. Several past commissions, including those in Chile and El Salvador, have left behind specific and detailed recommendations for judicial reform, and a number of these recommendations have been implemented. In El Salvador, for example, the commission recommended a reduction in the concentration of power over the judicial system that was held by the Supreme Court (and especially by the Court's president) by taking away the Court's centralized power of certification and oversight of lawyers and judges. It also recommended the creation of an independent council with the powers to appoint and remove judges, and another body for the certification of lawyers; an increase in judges' salaries; the creation of new courts; and the strengthening of the judicial training school. In addition, the commission recommended that certain laws be changed to protect the rights of those accused of crimes: that extrajudicial confessions be prohibited as evidence in court (to remove an incentive for torture), and that compliance with maximum time limits for pretrial detention be strictly enforced. Many of these were implemented, and the truth commission should be credited with helping to put these changes in place.

The commission in Chile also recommended a range of changes to strengthen the judiciary and promote respect for human rights. The commission confronted the fact that the judiciary, although not dismantled during the dictatorship, had allowed disappearances and killings to take place with virtually no judicial constraint. Its recommendations were wide ranging, including changes in specific articles of the Chilean Code of Criminal Procedure to require firm evidence before arrest, a reduction in the use of weapons to subdue those being arrested, measures to ensure the compliance by the police with court orders, the creation of an independent body to allow more objective appointment and promotion of judges, and the inclusion of human rights topics in legal training. Other truth commissions have put forward similar recommendations.

Promoting the Rule of Law and Fulfilling International Obligations

Some human rights lawyers suggest that a truth commission can be used as a tool to strengthen the rule of law after a period of lawless authoritarian rule. Most people recognize the practical impossibility of prosecuting everyone implicated in serious rights abuses, when they are in great numbers, and some thus see truth commissions as part of the answer to this problem. If empowered appropriately, commissions can help to fill some of the state's obligations under international law to respond to massive rights abuses.

Rob Weiner, Latin American program director for the Lawyers Committee for Human Rights, in New York, suggests that three steps should be considered minimal requirements of the state after a period of widespread abuses: an inquiry into the facts by relevant authorities, an opportunity for victims to come forward and tell their stories, and a formal finding of the facts.[46] With a description that sounds quite similar to the South African truth commission, Weiner suggests that certain conditions be attached to amnesties: that there be public acknowledgment and publication of the relevant facts by the authorities, including the identity of the perpetrators; that amnesty be provided only to those who individually petition for it; that applicants make full disclosure of their role in the acts or omissions for which amnesty is sought; and that the victim be allowed to seek reparation from the state, even if individual civil liability has been foreclosed (that is, if the amnesty prevents victims from suing perpetrators for damages). (This last suggestion is not in place in South Africa: civil suits against the government are also prohibited under the amnesty.) Weiner also argues that an amnesty application should be decided on by the regular judicial system, rather than an ad hoc body or commission. The South African commission leaves the "regularly constituted judicial system on the side-lines when it should play, and be seen to play, a protagonist's role in rebuilding the legal system's credibility," he writes. Of greatest importance is that "political space be exploited to support the rule of law, even as the state absolves the guilty."[47] Weiner's model assumes a functioning and politically trustworthy judicial system, however, which is often not the case.

Rights advocates have been arguing for a number of years that international human rights treaties require governments to investigate and make known to victims or to their families all that can be established about crimes against humanity. A truth commission is one way that a government may begin to fulfill this obligation.

Is the Full Truth a Form of Justice?

Some victims and family members of those killed say that just having the full truth publicly told can provide some sense of justice. After years of denial and silence, a government's acknowledgment of the harm done can be powerful. And if names of perpetrators are published in the commission report, perhaps that will at least provide moral sanction and public disgrace for the wrongdoers, if there is not to be legal sanction and punishment. Yet the question of naming names goes to the heart of one of the most difficult questions faced by truth commissions: how much truth should a truth commission tell?

Naming the Guilty

F ew issues around truth commissions have attracted as much controversy as the question of whether a commission should publicly name
those individuals it finds to be responsible for human rights crimes. This
question has been hotly debated by many past commissions, and remains a
point of tension for those crafting new bodies.

The disagreement is between two contradictory principles, both of
which can be strongly argued by rights advocates. The first of these is that
due process requires that individuals accused of crimes be allowed to defend themselves before being pronounced guilty. Due process is violated if
a commission, which does not represent a court of law and does not have
the same strict procedures, names individuals responsible for certain
crimes. The second principle is that telling the full truth requires naming
persons responsible for human rights crimes when there is clear evidence
of their culpability. Naming names is part of the truth-telling process, and
is especially important when the judicial system does not function well
enough to expect trials.

The terms of reference for most truth commissions have not addressed
this question, neither prohibiting nor requiring commissions to name
perpetrators, thus leaving the decision to the commissions themselves.
While most commissions have had the power to name perpetrators, however,
only a few have done so: El Salvador, Chad, the second commission of the
African National Congress, and the South African Truth and Reconciliation

Commission. Behind virtually every truth commission there has been turbulence, debate, and disagreement on this issue between the commissioners, between commissioners and their staff, or between the commission and the government to which it is to report.

More recently, as understanding of truth commissions has grown, the mandates of new commissions have been more likely to spell out their powers explicitly. For example, the South African Truth and Reconciliation Commission was mandated to inquire into "the identity of all persons, authorities, institutions and organizations" involved in gross human rights violations, and to "prepare a comprehensive report which sets out its activities and findings,"[1] which was clearly understood to include the names of perpetrators where known. In contrast, the Guatemalan commission's mandate stated that it could not "attribute responsibility to any individual in its work, recommendations, and report," a stipulation that sparked loud protest from disappointed human rights and victims groups who saw this as an unacceptable constraint to its work.

Where this has been left up to a commission, the decision whether to name names has been affected by a number of factors far beyond concerns for due process, as the examples below will show. In some cases, there are explicit or implicit political pressures on a commission to keep names out of the report. Some commissions have been especially concerned about the security risks in naming perpetrators: concerned either for the safety of witnesses who provided the names, for the security of commission members or staff, or about the possibility of revenge (in the form of street justice) taken against those named, especially where there is no chance that justice will be found in the courts. Commissioners must also gauge the quality of their information, the depth of their investigations and the sources on which they have based their conclusions, and whether there is any risk that their conclusions could be wrong. Those truth commissions that have identified perpetrators in their reports have tried to state clearly that the commission report is not a legal judgment and does not determine the persons' criminal liability. Yet regardless of such a caveat, those named in a truth commission report are popularly understood to be guilty, period; the distinction between criminal or legal guilt and a commission's finding of responsibility for a crime will be lost on most readers. Thus, past commissions have struggled with whether and how to state their findings on individual responsibility, under what standards of proof and procedures of due process, and whether the potential fallout of naming names in the midst of a delicate political transition may represent too great of a risk.

DECISIONS BY PAST COMMISSIONS

The first to struggle with this issue was the 1983–1984 National Commission on the Disappeared in Argentina. Over one thousand perpetrators were named in the testimony given to this commission, primarily by witnesses to kidnappings and survivors of detention camps. But its mandate stipulated that "the Commission cannot take judgment on acts and circumstances that constitute material exclusive to the judiciary."[2] As a result, some commission members now argue that they didn't really have an option to publish any perpetrators' names. "According to the presidential decree that established the commission, we had no powers to produce formal statements regarding the responsibility of certain individuals," commissioner Eduardo Rabossi told me. "We were only empowered to inquire into the fate of the disappeared and into the procedures or system of disappearances. We were to leave the rest to the judiciary."[3]

Others tell a more complex and difficult story. The ultimate decision not to make the list of names public was intensely debated within the commission. Senator Graciela Fernandez Meijide, then a senior staff director of the commission and now a prominent political figure in Argentina, sat at the table at each of the commissioners' meetings, though as a staff member she had no voting power. Meijide's own son was disappeared during the "dirty war," and his smiling picture sat on the table next to her in her office when I met with her, a constant reminder of her loss. Meijide played an active part in the debate about naming names, and disagreed with the commissioners' final decision.

The commission had no power to subpoena officials and no capacity to undertake in-depth investigation into individual cases, but Meijide insisted then, as she insists now, that there was considerable objective information based on official sources that could have and should have been published.[4] Through testimony from over six hundred survivors of detention camps, and on-site visits to many of these sites that confirmed their existence, the commission had solid proof of 340 torture centers. It was then simple to gather official records, published in the newspaper at the end of each year, that listed the military command of each area. There is a strict hierarchical and geographical structure to the Argentine military, and thus follows the reasonable assumption that those in command of each area, subarea, zone, or subzone were ultimately responsible for the abuses that took place there. Meijide argued that these names should be published, which would provide at least some moral sanction against abusers.

"The discussion was difficult, it lasted for hours; and it was a discussion that I lost," said Meijide on the commission's debate. "But as I conceded my loss, I said to them that everyone knew that I was losing despite being right." Not all commissioners were against publishing the names, and the decision was ultimately taken by majority vote.

The commission therefore took no position on the responsibility of specific individuals for specific crimes, but its report does include names of some accused of being perpetrators, appearing in the passages of victim and witness testimony that is heavily quoted throughout the text. "We decided that if, in a chosen quotation, names appeared, then we wouldn't erase them. But we wouldn't release the whole list," commissioner Rabossi explained. For example, in a typical passage, one survivor testified,

> The next day I was again beaten up by several people. I recognized the voice of Chief Inspector Roselli . . . and I was able to recognize the voice of the adviser to the Chief of Police, a lieutenant-colonel who also hit me. . . . In the early hours of the 16th I was taken to the toilet by the officer on duty, Francisco Gontero, who, from a distance of four or five meters, loaded his 45-caliber gun and fired three shots, one of which went through my right leg at the height of my knee.[5]

Another testified,

> I was hooded and tortured, and later transferred to the officers' mess of the 9th Infantry Regiment, where they set up simulated executions and also tortured people. One of the visitors I saw myself and was even interrogated by was the then Commander of the 7th Brigade, General Cristino Nicolaides. Another of the visitors was the then Commander of the 2nd Army Corps, General Leopoldo Fortunato Galtieri, who was there in mid-November 1976.[6]

Most prisoners were kept blindfolded for their full period of detention, however, and could neither see nor recognize the voices of their assailants, and thus many passages contain only descriptions of the number of assailants present during torture, or the nicknames that the perpetrators used among themselves.

In an author's note at the beginning of the report, the commission tries to distance itself from any implication that those persons named in testimony should be presumed guilty, stating, "As regards any person named here according to the function they were carrying out, or who are included in the transcription of statements which implicate them in events that may have legal consequences, the National Commission in no way seeks to imply their responsibility for any of the cases mentioned. The Commission has no competence in this respect, since authority for this belongs to the judicial power, in accordance with the statutes of the constitution of Argentina."[7] Meanwhile, the commission attached its own conclusive list of persons responsible for rights abuses to the confidential copy of the report that it submitted to the president. Just after the commission report was made available to the public, someone inside the commission leaked the entire list of perpetrators to the press. "There Are 1,351 Guilty," read the blazing headline, and each of these 1,351 military, civilian, and religious leaders were listed by name, with their position or rank noted.[8]

This list resulted in no concrete effect for the great majority of the 1,351 named (outside the handful who were prosecuted), but a number of former torturers or senior officers in the military regime are often recognized in public, sometimes by those who survived torture at their hands, and they suffer from living in a society that will not forgive them. As international human rights lawyer Juan Méndez described more than twelve years after the end of military rule, "Hundreds of known torturers are free from prosecution and even free from civil actions for damages. But many of them are well-known to the public, and if the state must consider them innocent by operation of the laws and decrees of impunity, society frequently makes clear that their crimes are not forgotten. Whenever they venture into the streets or public places, Videla, Massera, Camps, and several others have experienced spontaneous though nonviolent acts of repudiation: waiters refuse to serve them, other patrons leave the place or sit far away from them, some actually defy their bodyguards and confront them with the opinion that most Argentines have of them."[9] According to the *New York Times* in 1997, retired navy captain Alfredo Astiz, particularly well known for his brutal acts and widely recognized for his baby-faced good looks, "has suffered dozens of assaults in recent years by strangers on the street or people who say he tortured them or their relatives." The same article also notes, however, that many perpetrators "now walk the streets without fear or incident, mainly because few people can identify them."[10]

In Chile, the commission also decided to withhold names of perpetrators from its final report. The Chilean commissioners describe a decision based on prudence and lack of sufficient investigation into each case. As in Argentina, however, this decision was taken with considerable disagreement within the commission, from those who knew these cases well.

The Chilean commission's mandate is a bit more clear on this question than its Argentine predecessor, stating that the commission shall not "assume jurisdictional functions proper to the courts. . . . Hence it will not have the power to take a position on whether particular individuals are legally responsible for the events it is considering."[11] The presidential assistant who drafted the mandate for President Aylwin, Gisela von Muhlenbrok, told me that their intent was to prohibit the naming of perpetrators.[12] The commission itself, however, read this to mean that they were neither prohibited from nor obliged to name perpetrators, as long as any decisions of *legal* culpability were left to the courts, but it did not address the question until six months into its nine-month mandate.

"The question that the commissioners put to me," said then chief of staff Jorge Correa, "was, Do we have enough information to say publicly that such-and-such person is the perpetrator of a specific act? That question was a strong argument: I would have needed another three years of investigations to name with certainty. And it wasn't part of the clear role of the commission.[13]

"Often, we knew who tortured," Correa continued, "but not who pulled the trigger on those who didn't survive. We probably could have said who some were, but it would have required further investigation to track each accusation back to the primary source, the primary witness, and to validate its accuracy. It is *much* more easy to say, 'This person was disappeared,' than to say, 'This person was disappeared, and this is exactly who did it.'"[14]

Some prominent international rights advocates suggest that not naming the perpetrators in Chile was simply a reflection of the power that those perpetrators still held, which left the commission little room, or little desire, for pointing fingers.[15] Indeed, when commissioners in Chile now discuss their decision, you can feel in their descriptions some of the political pressures they were under. "It was an implied must" not to name names, said one commission member, Laura Novoa. "The commission mandate grew out of a political compromise, and we worked under those restrictions."[16] Nonetheless, there was a very long and heated debate when the commissioners met to take their decision on this issue. One commission member remained strongly opposed to omitting the names, but recognizing that he was in the minority, finally accepted the consensus on excluding names.

The commission staff, who knew exactly what information the commission had in its hands, did not take well to this decision. There was a "near revolt" by the staff, said commissioner Novoa, when the commission announced that it would not publish the names of perpetrators. "We met with the staff and had to calm them down. We were older and, maybe, wiser, so we thought we knew better."

Staff members concur with this description of events, but they make it clear why they felt so strongly. "When we started our work, we never dreamed we would obtain the kind of information that we did," says one senior staff member, a practicing lawyer when I met him in 1996. "We investigated every case, and built up thick folders of evidence on each one."[17] As part of their investigations, the staff employed something sounding like a police lineup in a criminal investigation. "There were often witnesses to a kidnapping," he explained. "A neighbor, a spouse, someone else who was detained in the same detention camp and survived. We had obtained photos of those in the armed forces known to be implicated in abuses, and we would show these photos to the witnesses. Witnesses could very often identify the person from the photos."

The commission also received firsthand confessions in some cases. Although there was no official collaboration by the armed forces with the work of the commission, a number of retired officers, about twenty, came forward to testify confidentially. Most who spoke lived outside of Chile (as those in the country feared the consequences of breaking the military's code of silence, I was told). One staff member told me his trip to Europe to take testimony was "life changing."[18] He continued:

> One case we covered was that of a man who was kidnapped off a bus while taking his two small children to school, holding each of their hands in his. The last memory these two children have of their father is that of him being dragged away, literally pulled out of their hands, never to be seen again. When they came to the commission over fifteen years later, it was the first time that they had told their story, and the first time they had talked about how this had affected their lives, carrying this memory for all those years. They had never even talked about it among themselves. It was very emotional. I think we all ended up crying.
>
> Then, when we went to Europe, by chance I was the one to take the testimony of the very person who kidnapped that person off the bus. You can only imagine the kind of impact that had on me.
>
> I'll give you another example: one person, also in Europe, came to give testimony and described how he took people up in helicopters and threw them into the sea. They would be drugged first, but sometimes

they would wake up during the flight, so they would just bludgeon them over the head, kill them probably, and then throw them into the sea.

The very next week, I took the testimony of the daughter of one of those victims, which this guy had just described throwing into the sea. The daughter was just *sure* her father was still alive — on an island somewhere, or kept in some secret prison, in another country, somewhere.

I couldn't say anything. It wasn't for me to effectively kill her father, then, at that moment, after eighteen years of her living with the absolute certainty that he was alive. It came out later in the report, but I couldn't tell her what I knew at that time.

"He knew the identity of each person he killed?" I asked, knowing that in other countries, such as Argentina, this was not the case; but this staff member was uncomfortable telling me more.

"This is still confidential information," he said. "It isn't supposed to come out." Six years had passed since the commission ended, over twenty years since most of these acts took place. I realized that much of this information might never come out.

How many perpetrators' names did you have, how many about which you were sure? I asked. Again, he wouldn't be specific, except to say "many, many more than forty" (which was approximately the number of perpetrators named by the commission in El Salvador).

Armed with this information about individuals responsible for such heinous crimes, the staff was frustrated that the names of the perpetrators would be suppressed. "We very much wanted to publish the names, for a social sanction at least, if there wasn't going to be a judicial sanction. But the decision by the commissioners was not to," said this staff member. "We even suggested that the report say that 'so and so was contacted regarding his involvement in a certain case,' without stating that the commission had clear evidence of guilt. But the commissioners wouldn't go for that.

"In many cases, we had the first and last name of the person who killed someone. It doesn't appear in the report, but if you ask me who threw that man out of the helicopter, I can tell you exactly who."

In contrast to Argentina, this list of names compiled by the Chilean commission has never appeared in public. In fact, most Chileans probably don't know there is such a list, but some insiders say that it is quietly used by the president in his review of senior officers proposed for promotion. No one has been removed from their post for involvement in past abuses, but since 1991, I was told, no one on the truth commission's list of perpetrators has been approved for a high-level promotion.[19]

In the spring of 1993, exactly two years after the Chilean commission was completed, the El Salvador commission was finishing its report, based in its final weeks out of UN headquarters in New York. The commission had gathered significant information on the involvement of senior members of government, the armed forces, and the judiciary in serious abuses of the past, and word leaked out that they planned to publicly name names. As the deadline for completion neared, the commission came under intense pressure from the Salvadoran government to omit those names from the report. Rumors spread about an impending coup if senior military officials were singled out, and the issue captured the attention of the press and the public in San Salvador. Various levels of the UN and international diplomatic community became involved, conferring with or even pressuring the commission on the issue.

The commission was surprised by the Salvadoran government's position on the subject. Commissioner Thomas Buergenthal writes that when they first met with then president Alfredo Cristiani and members of the Salvadoran military high command at the beginning of the commission's work, they had been supportive of the commission's identifying the "rotten apples" within the military that were guilty of abuses, thus protecting the sanctity of "the institution."[20] However, Buergenthal notes, "the attitude of the government began to change dramatically as it became known that the Commission had gathered incriminating evidence against high-ranking government officials, particularly General René Emilio Ponce, the Minister of Defense, and General Juan Orlando Zepeda, his Vice Minister."[21]

The government then began to "mount a fierce diplomatic campaign to force us to omit names from the Report," Buergenthal continues. "President Cristiani led the campaign by urging various Latin American leaders, the United States, and the UN Secretary-General to use their power and influence to prevent the publication of names," as well as sending a government delegation to meet with the commission in New York. "The arguments against publication ranged from the danger to the peace process and national reconciliation, to intimations of imminent coups, and claims of the government's inability to prevent retaliation against those who provided information to the Commission."[22]

Some in the Farabundi Martí National Liberation Front, or FMLN, agreed with the government's position and considered joining the government to amend the commission's mandate, which together they had the power to do. But after a "lengthy and apparently acrimonious debate within the FMLN high command," according to Buergenthal, the FMLN chose to leave the mandate as it was, leaving the decision on names up to the commission.[23]

Despite the intense pressures, the commission proceeded with the evidence before it, naming over forty persons in its report from both sides of the conflict, the majority of them Salvadoran military officers. The report holds individuals responsible for planning and executing assassinations, carrying out massacres of civilians, and obstructing judicial investigations, describing the precise involvement of each person named. On the killing of the Jesuits, for example, the report reads as follows:

> The Commission on the Truth makes the following findings . . :
>
> 1. There is substantial evidence that on the night of 15 November 1989, then Colonel René Emilio Ponce, in the presence of and in collusion with General Juan Rafael Bustillo, then Colonel Juan Orlando Zepeda, Colonel Inocente Orlando Montano and Colonel Francisco Elena Fuentes, gave Colonel Guillermo Alfredo Benavides the order to kill Father Ignacio Ellacuría and to leave no witnesses. . . .
>
> 2. There is evidence that, subsequently, all these officers and others, knowing what had happened, took steps to conceal the truth. . . .
>
> 3. There is full evidence that (a) That same night of 15 November, Colonel Guillermo Alfredo Benavides informed the officers at the Military College of the order he had been given for the murder. When he asked whether anyone had any objection, they all remained silent.[24]

Reporting on the killing of the Archbishop of San Salvador, Monsignor Oscar Romero, while he celebrated mass in 1980, the report reads as follows:

> The Commission finds the following:
>
> 1. Former Major Roberto D'Aubuisson gave the order to assassinate the Archbishop and gave precise instructions to members of his security service, acting as a "death squad," to organize and supervise the assassination.

2. Captains Alvaro Saravia and Eduardo Avila, together with Fernando Sagrera and Mario Molina, were actively involved in planning and carrying out the assassination.

3. Amado Antonio Garay, the driver of former Captain Saravia, was assigned to drive the gunman to the Chapel. Mr. Garay was a direct witness when, from a red, four-door Volkswagen, the gunman fired a single high velocity .22 calibre bullet to kill the Archbishop.

4. Walter Antonio "Musa" Alvarez, together with former Captain Saravia, was involved in paying the "fees" of the actual assassin.

. . .

6. The Supreme Court played an active role in preventing the extradition of former Captain Saravia from the United States and his subsequent imprisonment in El Salvador. In so doing, it ensured, *inter alia,* impunity for those who planned the assassination.[25]

The minister of defense and the president of the Supreme Court were among those named in the report. In expectation of being named, the minister of defense submitted his resignation on the Friday prior to the Monday release of the report (although the president kept him in his post for another four months).

The commissioners described the decision to name names as simple logic. As they explained in the report's introductory chapter,

It could be argued that, since the Commission's investigation methodology does not meet the normal requirements of due process, the report should not name the people whom the Commission considers to be implicated in specific acts of violence. The Commission believes that it had no alternative but to do so.

In the peace agreements, the Parties made it quite clear that it was necessary that the "complete truth be made known," and that was why the Commission was established. Now, the whole truth cannot be told without naming names. After all, the Commission was not asked to write an academic report on El Salvador, it was asked to describe exceptionally important acts of violence and to recommend measures to prevent the repetition of such acts. This task cannot be performed in the abstract, suppressing information . . . where there is reliable testimony available, especially when the persons identified occupy senior positions and perform official functions directly related to violations or the cover-up of violations. Not to name names would be to reinforce the very impunity to which the Parties instructed the Commission to put to an end.[26]

Describing his own assumption that names would be included, right from the beginning of the commission's work, Buergenthal explains, "Until the issue became the subject of a heated debate in and outside of El Salvador towards the end of our investigation, it had certainly never occurred to me that the Report would not name names. On first reading of the Commission's mandate, I concluded that one of our tasks was to identify those who had committed the serious acts of violence we were required to investigate. My colleagues, as I learned later, had reached the same conclusion. . . . How could we make known 'the complete truth' about a murder or massacre, for example, without identifying the killers if we knew their identity?"[27] The commissioners' sentiment was strengthened by the fact that the judiciary was weak and politically biased. According to Buergenthal, "If there had been an effective justice system in El Salvador at the time of the publication of our Report, it could have used the Report as a basis for an independent investigation of those guilty of the violations. In these circumstances, it might have made some sense for the Commission not to publish the names and, instead, to transmit the relevant information to the police or courts for appropriate action. But . . . the Salvadoran justice system was corrupt, ineffective, and incapable of rendering impartial judgments in so-called 'political' cases."[28]

Recognizing that there would not likely be justice or punishment from the courts, and that those named would likely continue to wield power in El Salvador for years to come, the report recommends that those named be removed from their position of employment with the state (either military or civilian), barred from serving in any public position for ten years hence, and permanently barred from the military or security forces. According to the commission's terms of reference, its recommendations were binding, but the government resisted the recommendation to bar persons from running for public office, arguing that such a restriction would be a violation of their constitutional rights. The UN secretary general agreed, allowing that recommendation to be ignored.[29] The report also recommended that the entire Supreme Court resign immediately, to leave room for new members. This was rejected out of hand, with the president of the Supreme Court retorting that "only God" could remove him from his post.[30]

The commission was criticized for naming unevenly and for not explaining their decisions about why they included some names and apparently omitted others. Rights observers were particularly unhappy with the fact that no civilian leaders were named in connection with the death squads, which were widely believed to be financed by the right-wing economic elite, especially after rumors spread that the commission had in fact identified some of those individuals. "Because the Truth Commission for El Salvador was widely seen as having received many more names than it published, the duty should have been incumbent upon it to be more clear and forthright as to the criteria by which some names were published while other names were suppressed," wrote Juan Méndez, calling this one of the commission's major weaknesses.[31]

The fact that the commission named people from only one of the five sectors of the FMLN had a considerable fallout, probably contributing to the breakup of the FMLN shortly thereafter. "The report had the result of unifying the Right and fragmenting the Left," said George Vickers, head of the Washington Office on Latin America, a policy and advocacy group.[32] Yet Vickers and others acknowledge that the split in the FMLN was already in the making, and the commission report probably only accelerated the process.

Buergenthal defends the commission's decisions. Speaking of the FMLN group whose leaders were named, he told me, "We knew it would look like we were after them [People's Revolutionary Army], but we didn't have evidence to name others. It would have been nice to get a nice balance — both between the FMLN and the government, and between the FMLN groups — but we couldn't. We had no choice: we couldn't name people we didn't really have solid evidence on and weren't sure about, and we didn't want to leave out others that we did have the goods on. Unfortunately things don't fall out evenly."[33]

What was the impact of naming names? Some people were removed from their positions, particularly those who had also been named by the earlier Ad Hoc Commission that was set up to purify the armed forces of rights abusers. The president had resisted removing some senior officers named by the Ad Hoc Commission, but did so after they were named again by the truth commission. At least one person was passed over for a prominent appointment because he was named by the commission.[34] When the new Supreme Court was elected a year later (through a new, less-politicized procedure) no members from the old court were reelected, including the court's president, despite his lobbying for reappointment. On the whole, however, those named have seen few repercussions. Some were proposed for senior government posts: the president of the Supreme Court, named in the report for covering up evidence and blocking investigations in cases of serious abuses by government forces, was appointed just a few months later to represent the government on the Inter-American Legal Committee, a subbody of the Organization of American States. In his review of the progress in implementing the truth commission's recommendations, the UN secretary-general called this appointment "inconsistent with the spirit, if not the letter, of the Commission's recommendations."[35] There was certainly a sense among Salvadorans that those purged from the armed forces didn't suffer any serious consequences. As one local activist said bitterly, those purged "were retired with applause and congratulations, with full honors and full benefits. They were all paid off with golden handshakes; they didn't suffer a bit."[36]

This impunity extends to the international level. There are virtually no restrictions on visas to allow travel to the United States by those named, for example. I asked the U.S. State Department's human rights bureau why it was that persons named as responsible for plotting and carrying out massacres were entering the United States for conferences and vacations. The truth commission had been partly funded by the U.S. government, after all, and the conclusions of the report were widely accepted as accurate. My question sparked an enthusiastic response from the senior staff person I spoke with at the bureau in 1996, three years after the El Salvador report was released, who said that such an idea had never occurred to them before, but that perhaps they could set up a system so that those named by a truth commission (and other high-level inquiries) for involvement in past abuses would be flagged in the appropriate U.S. government computers. Minimally, then, an application from such a person for a visa to enter the United States would be reviewed with full knowledge of the fact that the person was implicated in serious abuses. Yet when I called the State Department a year later, I was told that the idea of setting up such a screening procedure had been dropped.

The African National Congress was unsatisfied with the first commission that it set up in 1992 to investigate alleged abuses in ANC detention camps, in part because of a perception that people were accused without being given the opportunity to offer a defense. But only one person is named in the report as abusing prisoners, and the report describes how this person, the head of the ANC Department of Intelligence in the early to mid-1980s, readily admitted abusive practices in testimony to the commission.[37] The commission compiled a confidential list of other persons against whom there were serious allegations of abuse, and sent it to the president of the ANC, Nelson Mandela, but the ANC complained that the commission had interviewed victims only without giving those named a chance to respond. It was in part for this reason that Mandela created a second commission, in 1993, and directed it to inquire into the truth of the allegations and whether those persons accused had breached the ANC Code of Conduct. All questions of methodology and procedure were left to the discretion of the commission.

The proceedings of this second ANC commission looked much like a courtroom, and the commission report reflected this approach. This commission's hearings and report were shaped around the allegations of a number of victims (whom the report calls "complainants") against a number of specific perpetrators (the "defendants"), who were ANC members accused of abuses. One member of the commission, Boston-based lawyer Margaret Burnham, described their methodology as a natural result of the fact that two of the three members were experienced lawyers, and she herself had been a judge. "We worked with what we knew," she said. "We weren't a judicial body, but our job, as we saw it, was to draw factual conclusions about what had occurred and who was responsible."[38]

Eleven accused persons appeared before the commission, each with a team of lawyers (the lead defense lawyer, appointed by the ANC, was the future minister of justice Dullah Omar, who was later to play a central role in crafting the terms for the Truth and Reconciliation Commission). The commission report summarizes the case against each person, and states whether the evidence supports or does not support the allegations against each of them. It further recommends that those persons that it identifies as responsible for human rights abuses "be subject to disciplinary action and/or penalties in accordance with the Code of Conduct of the ANC."[39] The ANC failed to take up this recommendation, instead responding to the report by calling for a national "commission of truth" that would document abuses and perpetrators on all sides of the conflict, propose a code of conduct for all public servants, and ensure appropriate compensation for victims.[40] This proposal eventually led to the formation of the Truth and Reconciliation Commission.

The Haitian commission was perhaps the first to turn to the record of other truth commissions in working out its own decision on what to do with the many names of perpetrators it had collected, although the experiences of earlier commissions gave it few answers to its own difficult dilemma. Given the evidence it had before it and the volatile political and social environment, including the danger that there could be retaliation against anyone named, the commission struggled into its final days with the question of whether and how it might name perpetrators in its report.

Commission staff in Haiti told me that many perpetrators were repeatedly named in testimony by victims or witnesses. Of the five thousand testimonies taken, perhaps half named perpetrators, according to one staff member who helped to compile and tabulate information for the central database. It was common for one person to be named in twenty or twenty-five different testimonies; one individual was named seventy different times by independent witnesses. When the commission staff printed out all of this information, they ended up with a two-hundred-page list of names, each line listing the accused perpetrator, the case reported, and the witness or victim who provided the testimony. Staff hoped that the commissioners would rely on this list to conclude that the names of some accused perpetrators should be published.[41]

In a meeting with the commissioners, the staff suggested that the persons who appeared repeatedly on this list, perhaps those that appeared over twenty times, for example, should be named in the commission report. "Some things were for sure, it was not an issue of proof," said a staff member after the commission's work had ended. "In every region, there were three or four or five names that were absolutely clear, perhaps fifty names in total. When everybody tells the same story, when the whole community is pointing at one man, what else do you need? The proof was overwhelming."[42]

The commission did not have the time or resources to investigate each accusation, so the list produced from the database was based entirely on testimony from victims or witnesses. Staff argued that the report could include the names without implying their definitive guilt, by saying that "these people were named in testimony from victims." They also argued that the commission could rely on the internationally recognized "command responsibility" principle, in which the commander of each district can be held responsible for abuses within his district if he could or should have known about the abuses and did nothing to stop them.[43]

The commissioners felt that due process must be respected, and they attempted to question those persons named who happened to be in jail, to give them a chance to respond to charges, but they did not attempt to find others: some didn't have a fixed address, and many of those named were probably still armed. The commission feared that there could be retaliation against named perpetrators, especially if the public assumed that the possibility of courtroom justice was extremely remote, a reasonable conclusion given the dismal record of trials in Haiti for these kinds of crimes. In the end, the commissioners decided to include names only in a confidential annex to be submitted to the president. Hoping that there would be trials following the commission's report, the commissioners reasoned that justice would best be served by handing the evidence to the judiciary and recommending prosecutions. The report recommends that the names in the confidential annex be made public "after the competent authorities have made the judicial and administrative measures required"—that is, after those on the list had been duly prosecuted.[44] Yet several years later, very few trials had moved forward, and it seemed unlikely that that list would be released anytime soon.

Other commissions have dealt with this issue in still different ways. The truth commission report in Chad, published in 1992, listed names and published the photographs of those it concluded were the worst human rights abusers. When the report was released, many of these individuals were already serving in the new government or its armed forces, mostly in the reconstructed intelligence service or in the army or police. The report makes a strong plea for purging all those who served under the former intelligence service, the Directorate of Documentation and Security (DDS), which was well known for its ruthless practices. "DDS agents were thieves, torturers, and executioners, and as such, they should be excluded from the new special [intelligence] service," says the report,[45] but there were neither purges nor trials after the report's release, and few repercussions for those named.

The terms of reference of two of the most recent truth commissions, in Guatemala and South Africa, addressed the question of naming names directly and unambiguously, but both commissions still had to interpret the exact intent of the language in the mandate, and establish exactly how it would deal with the names of perpetrators that came up in the course of their investigations.

As Guatemalans negotiated a peace accord in 1994 to establish the Historical Clarification Commission, the government and the military did not want to follow the path of their neighbor to the south, El Salvador. "We didn't want what they did in El Salvador," the former chief of the government's negotiating team, Hector Rosada, told me, saying there was nothing

they liked about that commission, but the fact that it named high-level perpetrators was probably the most unattractive aspect.[46] Rosada, who described his own role at the negotiating table as "discussing matters with the
military and finding out what they wanted," said that the negotiations
around a truth commission were very difficult and tense. The final language agreed to prohibited the Guatemalan commission from attributing
"responsibility to any individual in its work, recommendations and report,"[47] a stipulation, as noted earlier, that angered rights advocates and
victims' groups. But even this restriction was open to a bit of interpretation. During the course of the commission's work, the commission chair,
Christian Tomuschat, wrote that "the final report, although it shall not attribute responsibility to any individual, may have to mention the names of
a considerable number of persons who, during the worst years of the conflict, held high positions in the Government or within the structures of the
URNG [the armed opposition]. Clearly, the report itself will not charge
those persons individually with having committed human rights violations, but any attentive observer will be in a position to draw the requisite
conclusions from the facts displayed in the report."[48]

It was also possible that the commission could have described the perpetrators by the positions that they filled, leaving to the press or nongovernmental organizations the task of linking together who filled those positions
at the time described. Rosada suggested that the commission would have
some flexibility in its interpretation of the mandate. As he told me, "It can't
say, 'The responsible person was X,' but it can say that this particular event
happened and persons from such and such unit were there. It just can't put
names in the report. But the commission's archives will surely have names,
and the mandate doesn't say anything about what will happen to that material."[49] Another member of the government negotiating team, Antonio
Arenales Forno, who drafted the commission's terms of reference, acknowledged that the exact meaning of "not individualizing" abuses was
unclear. He thought that this language clearly allowed the commission to
say that "the head of this particular battalion at this time and in this place"
was responsible. "If they don't say at least that, then you wouldn't have
anything," he said.[50]

Yet in the end, the commission chose not to identify individual positions
of responsibility. The closest it came to identifying individual responsibility
for rights crimes was to state that the massive human rights violations had
"occurred with the knowledge or by order of the highest authorities of the
State."[51] Guatemalan rights activists were satisfied that armed with this

statement and the other evidence presented in the report, they had a strong case to bring charges against those persons who headed the government during the worst period of violence.[52]

In contrast to most other truth commissions, names of the accused were publicly broadcast on a regular basis during the work of the South African Truth and Reconciliation Commission, primarily through its public hearings. Victims, witnesses, other perpetrators, and commissioners themselves named individuals that they knew or suspected were responsible for crimes; some of those named later came forward to testify in an amnesty hearing, or were subpoenaed by the commission to answer questions.

Section 30 of the act that created the commission set down that "[i]f during any investigation by or any hearing before the Commission, (a) any person is implicated in a manner which may be to his detriment; or (b) the Commission contemplates making a decision which may be to the detriment of a person who has been so implicated," then the Commission must "afford him or her an opportunity to submit representations to the Commission within a specified time with regard to the matter under consideration or to give evidence at a hearing of the Commission," under procedures to be determined by the commission.[53] Early in its work, the commission was taken to court by two retired policemen who challenged the interpretation of these provisions. Specifically, they challenged how much advance notice and information the accused must receive from the commission before a public hearing. The South African Appeals Court upheld a ruling in favor of the two policemen, holding that the commission had to provide reasonable notice of such allegations, and sufficient documentation by way of witness statements, affidavits, and the like, to enable the alleged perpetrator to identify the incident and respond.[54] Thereafter, the commission established operating procedures that gave twenty-one days' notice in writing to those persons who were expected to be named in a public session.[55] This requirement placed a huge burden on the commission and slowed down its operations considerably.

The commission used the same procedures for those that it planned to name in its report. Commission member Richard Lyster later described the process as follows:

> This took the form of sending a letter to them, advising them of the contemplated finding that the Commission was making against them . . . in effect, sending to them the allegations of their involvement in gross human

rights violations, annexing sufficient supporting documentation to enable them to properly answer the allegations, and to admit, deny, rebut, justify, etc. the allegations, by way of a written response. Thereafter, the response would be examined by the Commissioner who had made the contemplated finding and one other Commissioner, and they would decide whether the written response contained anything to persuade them to change the contemplated finding. If not, the finding would be made final, and was then ratified by the full Commission.

If the written response from the (alleged) perpetrator did contain material or information which tended to change the contemplated finding, this was done, and in a number of instances, the person's name was dropped from the list of perpetrators.[56]

Given the amount of administrative work and the advance time required to notify the accused, these procedures considerably limited how many persons the commission was able to name in its final report.[57] One staff member estimated that she omitted up to 80 percent of the names in her original draft of a section of the report just to ease the administrative burden of sending notices and supplying corroborative evidence. A team covering another region suggested they deleted perhaps 10 percent of the names from their original draft, for the same reasons.[58] Commissioner Richard Lyster estimates that perhaps six hundred names were pulled from the report either because the commission was unable to contact the accused in advance, or, in some cases, because amnesty proceedings were still pending. In such cases, neither the applicant nor anyone implicated in the amnesty application could be named, because applicants had until the date of their personal appearance before the amnesty committee to withdraw or amend their application.[59] "On top of this," said Lyster, "because information was being fed to us literally up to the time of the publishing of the report, we were deprived of the opportunity of sending section 30 notices to about 500 alleged perpetrators, because we wouldn't have had the time to prepare the notices, trace the whereabouts of the perpetrators, send the letters, and formulate our final finding. This was for me one of the most distressing and frustrating aspects of the Commission's work. We knew that we were literally letting thousands of serious perpetrators of human rights violations walk free. This also fed into the ongoing perception about the Commission that it was perpetrator-friendly, and that it bent over backwards to accommodate perpetrators in its dealings with them."[60]

In the end, the commission named hundreds of persons for taking part in or condoning and encouraging gross human rights violations, including former president P. W. Botha, Winnie Mandikizela Mandela, and members of the State Security Council, the inner cabinet of the apartheid government, and recommended that "prosecution should be considered where evidence exists that an individual has committed a gross human rights violation," and where amnesty has not been sought or has been denied.[61] On the day prior to the scheduled release of the commission's report, former president F. W. de Klerk filed a suit in court to prevent the commission from naming him in the report, arguing that the commission had acted in bad faith.[62] Rather than risk a court hearing with no time to read and respond to de Klerk's two-thousand-page complaint, the commission omitted those paragraphs from the report and received a four-month postponement of the court date to review his petition.

THE QUESTION OF WHETHER AND HOW TO NAME NAMES

Most human rights lawyers argue that a commission should name names of perpetrators whenever there is sufficiently convincing information to do so, especially if the courts in the country are hardly functioning, but that they should always respect appropriate due process standards before doing so. For example, Juan Méndez, former professor of law at the University of Notre Dame, then executive director of the Inter-American Institute for Human Rights, and former legal counsel to Human Rights Watch, argues that if there are to be no trials in a country, then it is especially important that a commission name names. He discounts the argument that a commission is overstepping its nonjudicial powers in doing so. "We name people all the time for acts before they are proven. The press often names people. The police give out names all the time. If someone is alleged to have stolen a car, their name is put in print. It's an allegation; it's not a pronouncement of guilt."[63] Many other human rights advocates agree with Méndez, arguing that it can be an important step in counteracting impunity, and that due process guarantees can be established relatively easily.[64]

In contrast, José Zalaquett, a prominent international rights advocate, former member of Amnesty International's executive board, and member of the truth commission in Chile, takes a more restrictive position, warning of the dangers of a nonjudicial body apportioning guilt. In the introduction to the English translation of the Chilean commission's report, Zalaquett writes that in Chile, "To name culprits who had not defended themselves and were not obliged to do so would have been the moral equivalent to convicting someone without due process. This would have been in contradiction with the spirit, if not the letter, of the rule of law and human rights principles."[65] More recently, Zalaquett is quoted as saying that truth commissions "must not trespass that fine line between an ethical commission and a kangaroo court. The moment they start apportioning individual blame, they violate the basic principles of the rule of law."[66]

In an interview, Zalaquett made clear that he accepts that some truth commissions may in fact appropriately name names. He is not in disagreement with the naming of perpetrators by the commission in South Africa, for example, because of that commission's screening and due-process procedures. For most other cases, however — including the commission in El Salvador — Zalaquett argued that naming just a few perpetrators was inherently unfair, leaving perpetrators to "the luck of the draw" since no commission can investigate all accused wrongdoers, and thus only a few perpetrators will be singled out.[67] In correspondence, he stated further that:

> My own position about naming names is based on rights and procedure. . . .
> My position may be characterized as follows: official truth commissions may investigate moral responsibilities of governments, concentrating on victims, which is usually the case. In some cases, as in South Africa, they may come close to touching on legal responsibilities of individuals as well.
>
> When they do concentrate on moral responsibilities, their official character, the solemnity of the whole exercise, etc., means that if they name names, the persons so named would be painted with a brush of guilt, outside due process. This is wrong in legal terms and also in moral terms. The possibilities of failure in judging individual cases outside due process are great. Second, the principle of a bilateral audience, meaning both sides have to be heard, is a sacred one. Third, in reconstructing a society after a major trauma, human rights must be upheld. This means that justice must be sought through just means. It is important that the lesson given by the precedent of truth commission work is that rights were scrupulously respected, despite the fact that others might not have respected them at all in the past.
>
> All that having been said, if procedural safeguards like in South Africa are introduced, I have no qualms about the process. My problem is not with rights or justice. It is with easy righteousness and facile justice.[68]

While due process is important, it is widely agreed that the guarantees required for a commission are less than those of a criminal trial. In a trial, certain minimal requirements are almost universally accepted: the accused must be informed in advance of the charges, and must be given adequate time and opportunity to defend him or herself, including the right to counsel and the right to call and confront witnesses. But due-process requirements are in part determined by the severity of punishment that may result. The consequences of being named by a commission are far less severe than the consequences of being found guilty in court. While perhaps damaging to a person's reputation, a commission generally has no power to punish the named. It may recommend prosecutions or other civil penalties, but these will usually require yet another layer of review before being implemented.

Past commissions have been well aware of these differences in due process standards. Douglass Cassel, a senior advisor to the El Salvador commission, wrote that the commission "made no pretense of affording all the usual elements of due process of law. While the accused were generally advised of the cases in which they were suspected, and given an opportunity to deny or explain their involvement, they were not informed of the identities of witnesses against them, let alone allowed to confront and cross-examine them in a public trial." The commission's chosen procedures, Cassel wrote, were based on "the Salvadoran reality that witnesses are not safe from reprisals and do not perceive themselves to be safe. Given this reality, the *only* way the Commission could arrive at the truth was to deny these usual procedural safeguards."[69]

Each commission that plans to make findings about individual responsibility must establish its own basic due-process requirements and set up a system to ensure that these are respected. The standards and procedures will vary between commissions, though the general outline of these requirements is fairly clear. Most legal experts agree with three basic guidelines. First, individuals who may be named in a report should be informed of the allegations against them and told that the commission intends to name them in a public report. Second, these persons should be given the opportunity to respond to the evidence against them and to offer a defense, either in writing or in an appearance before the commission, in a procedure determined by the commission. However, this right does not necessarily extend to confronting their accusers or even being informed of the source of the allegations, if the commission believes such information could put persons at risk. (Zalaquett also suggests that a report should note that the persons named have denied the allegations against them, when they have, and perhaps provide a brief account of each person's own version.[70] Yet this would surely dilute the commission's conclusions, and most commissions may reasonably choose not to do so, standing by their own judgment. Third, the commission should state clearly that its own conclusions about individual responsibility do not amount to criminal guilt, which must be left to the courts.

The New York–based Human Rights Watch, in a long submission to the South African Truth and Reconciliation Commission, concurred with these due-process standards: it encouraged the commission to "name those whom it believes on good evidence to be responsible for gross abuses, especially those responsible for devising policy at the highest level," and argued that "the full due process protections of the type that are required in criminal trials are not necessary for the purposes of public identification."[71] Human Rights Watch has also suggested other useful guidelines for naming names, saying that "there should be a careful distinction drawn between the different kinds of responsibility involved—for example, if the person directly ordered or carried out specific abuses, or if he or she implemented or devised policies that foreseeably resulted in gross violations," and that, in addition to allowing a response on the substance of the allegations, the commission should "afford each person an opportunity to make representations as to why they should not be named, for example because of concerns as to their own safety, and take those representations into account in its final decision."[72]

While simple in principle, the implementation of these procedural safeguards can be difficult and cumbersome, as described above in South Africa. No other commission has attempted to respect basic due process to the same degree as the South African commission, and that commission's experience makes clear the difficulties of doing this well.

In addition to due-process considerations, a commission must also establish how much evidence is required for it to make a finding, and what standard of proof must be met. For example, the El Salvador commission established a two-source rule, requiring two credible and independent sources as confirmation of a fact. In contrast, the South African commission required only one source, both for corroborating victims' accounts and for deciding the culpability of perpetrators, provided that the source was sufficiently compelling.

The judicial standard for convicting someone of a crime is to establish a level of proof "beyond reasonable doubt." Truth commissions generally do not seek to meet that high level of proof. While there is no uniform practice, the emerging standard for commissions is to rely on a "balance of probabilities" standard (in some countries called "preponderance of evidence"), which means that there is more evidence to show something to be true than not to be true.[73] For example, the South African commission described its methodology, saying, "Given the investigative nature of the Commission's process and the limited legal impact of naming, the Commission made findings on the identity of those involved in gross violations of human rights based on the balance of probabilities. This required a lower burden of proof than that required by the conventional criminal justice system. It meant that, when confronted with different versions of events, the Commission had to decide which version was the more probable, reasonable or likely, after taking all the available evidence into account."[74]

The El Salvador commission established three levels of certainty — where there was *overwhelming, substantial,* or *sufficient* evidence to back up a finding — and stated its degree of certainty for each of its findings throughout the report. According to its report, it applied "strict criteria to determine the degree of reliability of the evidence. . . [and] named names only when it was absolutely convinced by the evidence."[75] According to a senior advisor to the commission, no one was ever named based on the lowest-level test, that of having only *sufficient* evidence. Other commissions that have named perpetrators have not stated what evidentiary standards they used, which is ultimately unfair both to the reader and to the persons named. Future commissions should state clearly in their reports the amount or quality of evidence that backs up their findings (such as one or two primary or secondary sources), as well as what level of certainty their findings represent.

There is an alternative means of including the names of the accused in a commission report that should be considered, short of a commission's stating firm conclusions about the responsibility of specific individuals. Rather than being presented as the commission's equivalent of a court verdict, a commission's report might be equated with a summary of the testimony given in court, the commission playing a role closer to that of reporter rather than of judge or jury. A commission might summarize the evidence before it, including names mentioned by witnesses where they hold credibility, without stating firm conclusions on each individual's culpability. In cases where the commission has investigated further and has drawn its own firm conclusions, it could state these clearly, reverting to the standards and safeguards suggested above. This model is close to the suggestion of the Haitian truth commission staff, who pushed for their commission to state names "as reported to the commission by witnesses," especially those names that appeared repeatedly in testimony. It is similar also to the approach used by the Argentine commission, which printed names of accused perpetrators when they happened to appear in passages of quoted testimony (although that commission's approach was unbalanced, since these excerpts covered only a few of the names which arose in testimony, and thus it was only by chance that some accused perpetrators were named in the report and others were not).

Notwithstanding the important considerations that must be given to the danger of falsely accusing individuals, and the importance of allowing those accused some manner to respond to accusations, a truth commission should seek to tell as much of the full truth as possible, including the names of persons responsible for the abuses. The names of low-level perpetrators might be left out of the report if there is a threat to their safety or to the safety of those who named them, especially when they remain in the community where the crimes took place. A commission should focus attention on those who organized or authorized massive abuses, including those in senior political or military positions who knowingly allowed such acts to take place under their watch. Where justice is unlikely in the courts, a commission plays an important role in at least publicly shaming those who orchestrated atrocities. A commission should also consider recommending nonjudicial sanctions against those named, such as banning them from public positions of authority or from posts in the security or intelligence service, prohibiting them from working in a private security firm, and taking away their right to bear arms. While such recommendations could not be implemented by the commission itself, they could guide lawmakers toward establishing a strategy for accountability and reducing the threat of further abuses by these individuals in the future, outside of the limited possibilities of successfully prosecuting them in court.

Healing from the Past

" **P** eople always ask, 'Why reopen wounds that have closed?'" Horacio Verbitsky, a prominent Argentine journalist, said to me. "Because they were badly closed. First you have to cure the infection, or they will reopen themselves."[1]

With these words, Verbitsky summed up one of the central tenets of those who insist on the need for digging up the truth. Verbitsky lost many friends among the disappeared in the Argentine "dirty war." In 1996, he helped to reopen this subject in Argentina through reporting the confessions of Francisco Scilingo, a retired navy officer who admitted to throwing live political prisoners out of airplanes and into the sea.[2] When Scilingo's stories hit the press, Argentina discovered how much of its difficult past was still unresolved, both emotionally and factually. Despite the work of the National Commission on the Disappeared thirteen years earlier, the issue was once again the center of attention, with articles appearing almost daily in the newspapers for months, and thousands in the streets in demonstrations demanding more truth from the government and armed forces about what happened to the disappeared.

Unhealed wounds of society and of individual victims may continue to fester long after the cessation of fighting or the end of a repressive regime.[3] A country may need to repair torn relationships between ethnic, religious, regional, or political groups, between neighbors, and between political parties. In short, societal healing might be called reconciliation—a society

133

reconciling with its past and groups reconciling with each other, the topic of the next chapter. Individuals, though, suffer most from the intense psychological trauma that may result from extreme events. Many survivors of violent political repression suffer a painful psychological and emotional hell for years. It is true that some survivors of trauma are remarkably resilient: in dire circumstances, or forced by the necessity of daily survival, they effectively suppress their memories and continue to function day to day, or even seem to recover from the experience in sound mind and spirit. But many others are not so lucky, and suffer fiercely from the memory of torture or of witnessing the brutal murder of a loved one.

Many argue that an important function of truth commissions is helping victims heal through providing a forum for them to tell their story. When I asked the chief mental-health specialist of the South African truth commission whether talking led to healing, he quoted his grandmother: "Better out than in," she would say.[4] There is a multitude of studies showing that repressing intense emotional pain leads to psychological trouble. Indeed, one of the cornerstones of modern-day psychology is the belief that expressing one's feelings, and especially talking out traumatic experiences, is necessary for recovery and for psychological health. It is often asserted that following a period of massive political violence and enforced silence, simply giving victims and witnesses a chance to tell their stories to an official commission—especially one that is respectful, nonconfrontational, and interested in their stories—can help them regain their dignity and begin to recover.

Psychologists universally confirm this basic logic. "Past traumas do not simply pass or disappear with the passage of time. . . . Past trauma can always be expected to have emotional consequences for an individual. Repressed pain and trauma generally block emotional life, have psychologically adverse consequences and can even lead to physical symptoms," writes South African psychologist Brandon Hamber, in an early paper about the expected impact of the truth commission there. Summarizing the psychological literature and the opinions of specialists, Hamber continues, "Psychological restoration and healing can only occur through providing the space for survivors to feel heard and for every detail of the traumatic event to be re-experienced in a safe environment."[5] Survivors of intense trauma who try to repress their memories may see the effects play out in physical or psychological symptoms, or in damage to their family or social relationships.

Judith Herman, a professor of psychiatry at Harvard Medical School, points to a tension between victims' desire to speak and their instinct to bury their memories. "The ordinary response to atrocities is to banish them from consciousness. Certain violations of the social compact are too terrible to utter aloud: this is the meaning of the word *unspeakable*. Atrocities, however, refuse to be buried. Equally as powerful as the desire to deny atrocities is the conviction that denial does not work. . . . Remembering and telling the truth about terrible events are prerequisites both for the restoration of the social order and for the healing of individual victims."[6]

Truth commissions or other means of honoring the past may also help to counter what psychologist Yael Danieli calls a "conspiracy of silence" that often develops around political violence and tends to intensify survivors' "already profound sense of isolation, loneliness, and mistrust of society."[7] The official acknowledgment of previously denied events, especially by a state-sponsored body such as a truth commission, can thus be extremely powerful.

Yet those who suggest that "talking leads to healing" are usually making assumptions that do not hold true for truth commissions. Most studies of healing from political violence measure the positive effects of psychological support over a period of time; these studies show that when victims are given a safe and supportive environment to talk about their suffering, most eventually see positive results. Typical symptoms of repressed trauma, such as nightmares, emotional problems, and sleeplessness, often recede.[8] Truth commissions, however, do not offer long-term therapy; they offer survivors a one-time opportunity to tell their story, usually to a stranger whom they will likely never see again. Some anecdotes of the effects on victims of giving testimony to truth commissions are very positive; others are very worrisome. There has been no study to date of the psychological impact of truth commissions on survivors, but the evidence that is available is enough to raise some serious questions.

THE NEED TO TELL ONE'S STORY

Truth commissions seem to satisfy — or least *begin* to satisfy — a clear need of some victims to tell their stories and to be listened to. It may take some months for victim communities to gain trust in a truth commission, but when this trust develops, it is common for long lines to form outside truth commission offices — lines of victims eager to report their stories. In some towns in Haiti, for example, lines of a hundred people or more formed when truth commission staff arrived to take testimony, despite the fact that former perpetrators often lived close by and could see their victims lining up to report their crimes. Many people put themselves at considerable risk in coming forward, in Haiti and elsewhere. They would often wait for hours, returning the next day if necessary. In some countries, survivors have traveled many miles, sometimes on foot, to reach commission offices. It is not always clear what motivates victims and witnesses to come forward. Despite efforts by commission staff to be clear about their purpose and powers, for example, some deponents have expected that a commission would take legal action against known perpetrators, and others have hoped the commission would grant them compensation for their suffering.

Many human rights workers and journalists report what seems to be a very basic need by victims to recount their stories of violence and survival, entirely independent of any commission or official process. Anecdotes abound that make this point: years before the truth commission began work in Guatemala, a Guatemalan forensic anthropology group, which exhumes bones from massacre sites, called a public meeting in a region known for political violence in order to release one of its reports. They expected fewer than one hundred people to attend, but five hundred showed up. The forensic team was amazed to watch the meeting quickly turn into a long series of testimonials. As two of its members explained, "We asked for questions after our presentation, and a long line of people formed — and everyone in line wanted to give testimony about their experiences. All they wanted to do was relate their story — and this was in front of five hundred people, where you didn't know who might be listening — surely someone would report back to the military about who was saying what."[9]

One U.S. citizen living in Guatemala told me that past violence always seemed to unexpectedly crop up in conversation when she visited the highlands. "You could be talking about anything — the price of corn, the weather — and people will suddenly start telling you about the atrocities they suffered."[10]

From South Africa, a similar story: when legislation for the truth commission was being discussed and debated in 1994 and 1995, a small group of victims organized to lobby for a stronger bill. Yet this victims' lobbying group quickly turned into a victims' support group, and suddenly many dozens of people were attending their meetings. "*Everybody* got up and told their story — some forty people at one of the first meetings," said psychologist Brandon Hamber of the Centre for the Study of Violence and Reconciliation, who assisted in the group's formation. "A central part of the group's function quickly became giving people a chance to tell their story."[11]

Truth commissions can offer victims a safe environment in which to relate their experiences. A year into the South African truth commission's work, Hamber was critical of some aspects of the commission, but wrote, "Providing space for victims to tell their stories, particularly in public forums, has been of use to many. It is indisputable that many survivors and relatives of victims have found the public hearing process psychologically beneficial."[12]

This was also true in Chile, at least for some survivors. Elizabeth Lira, a Chilean psychologist who works with victims of political violence, said that the simple act of recognizing a person's traumatic experience could be extremely important to their psychological healing. "In Chile, going to the truth commission was like entering into a family: there was a sense of security, a national flag standing on the table, a mandate from the president, and there was the commission saying, 'We want to hear what you have to say.'" For over fifteen years, the state had cast them aside, telling the world that these claims of persons disappearing were all lies. Suddenly, a state commission was ready to listen to their accounts and publicly acknowledge that disappearances had indeed taken place. Because human rights groups had provided the commission in Chile with details on most cases of disappearances, the testimony taken from the families didn't provide them with much new information, according to Lira: "The symbolic aspect of taking testimony from the families was much more important."[13]

A SENSE OF RELIEF

A South African minister, S.K. Mbande, coordinated the effort to collect statements for the truth commission in the township of Daveyton, an hour outside of Johannesburg. I visited him in his home to ask about his experience taking statements from so many victims.

When some people tell their story, he said, they "stand somewhere between truth and dishonesty, because coming up with the whole truth is still not safe. Some give their statements because they've been told to do so by the government or by their church. But some people are traumatized and fearful, and they feel it's not safe to talk about it. If a woman had been gang raped by the South African Defence Force or the police, it's not easy for her to tell the story, especially in front of her husband or children. So you have to search for what this person is trying to say. Some people have forgotten what happened, or due to trauma, they may tell different stories, or keep changing their story, because they can't remember clearly. From my point of view, telling stories is some sort of healing process, but not for everyone. For some, it makes them feel worse."

"How is it healing?" I asked.

"After telling their story, they relax. They've said what's in their hearts, in their chests, what was closed up. After telling their stories, they want to know where the person's been buried, who killed them — the whys, wheres, and hows. But they are able to open their hearts to a statement-taker, and they often say they feel much better." Another local statement-taker who joined the conversation, Boniwe Mafu, very much agreed.

"Some people don't want to even come to us, to tell their story again. It reminds them, and they feel hurt," said the Reverend Mbande. "Some people come, but they don't talk, they just cry — sometimes for thirty minutes. Or they start talking and in the middle they just start crying."

He paused to think about what he was saying. "In the past, you know, you didn't know you had sick people in this society, traumatized. Only now people are being identified as traumatized, and it's clear that some people need help. It's true that the truth commission is a healing process — if not 100 percent, then 60 percent."

"Sixty percent are healed, or people are healed 60 percent?" I asked.

"Both. Perhaps 60 percent feel better, but those people are only healed 60 percent."[14]

South African Sylvia Dlomo-Jele's teenage son was killed in 1988, and she went to the truth commission to tell her story. I visited her in Soweto, outside of Johannesburg, to ask how she felt about her experience with the commission. "Giving testimony is different for everybody," she told me, "but when I testified at the public hearing, it was very good. It was the first time I'd told what had happened to me. After the death of my son, I stayed many years not talking about it. It was killing me inside. I thought, 'Why me, Lord?' It gave me quite a problem. We depended on our son, as young as he was. Giving testimony, telling the whole world what happened to me — It was painful, but also a relief. The way they listened to me, the interest they showed in my story, that was good for me. But yes, it's true, a lot of people feel worse. One woman I know said, 'I don't want to talk about it; my son won't come back.'"[15]

Sadly, Sylvia Dlomo-Jele died just over a year after I spoke with her, shortly after the amnesty hearing for the killers of her son, Sicelo Dlomo. Unexpectedly, it came out in the hearing that her son had been killed by his

ANC colleagues, though for reasons and in circumstances that were unclear, a fact that seemed too much for her to bear. Although she had been a strong proponent of the right to know the truth, one memorial noted that "Ironically, in the end, it was the stress of [her son's] death and the partial truths about him being killed by his fellow comrades that was too much for her."[16] Her son's killers were granted amnesty in February 2000, with a decision by the Amnesty Committee that was strongly criticized by some observers.[17]

I met up with another South African survivor, Simpson Xakeka, in the Johannesburg truth commission office. He was shot during a march in 1991 in Daveyton. I asked how he felt when he gave his statement to the commission, which he had done some time before. Speaking in his native Zulu, he said, "As I was giving a statement, the actual pains came back. I was made to relive the experience. But as I proceeded into the interview, they eased. It was difficult to talk about it. But it was easier for me to speak out because the statement-taker could empathize; he went along with everything I said.

"Emotionally it helped a great deal. It helped me to come to terms with it. But physically it hasn't helped. I still have bullets in my chest, I'm still in pain. But emotionally it has helped a great deal."

I asked him how it helped. "There's a saying in our culture," he said, "that 'coughing it out relieves everything.' I'm not going to forget what happened to me, but talking about it provides emotional relief. When I get together with others and talk about it, it helps. But I must stress that I won't forget what happened."[18]

Commission staff in many countries talk about how powerful and cathartic the process is for those who give testimony. Telling one's story can be very emotional, especially for those who have never told their story before. But psychologists question the idea of a one-time catharsis resulting in real psychological healing. In clinical counseling settings, in fact, most therapists would avoid pushing someone to address the worst of their pain too quickly, especially if it is rooted in events of extreme trauma.

The central aim of a truth commission is not therapy. It is, instead, to gather as much detailed information from the greatest number of victims as possible to allow an accurate analysis of abuses over a period of time. Guided by these informational needs, victims and witnesses that come to a truth commission are asked to tell their full, horrid story in one relatively short meeting, typically about an hour. The interview is focused on recording specific details of events witnessed or experienced, going to the heart of the deponent's most painful memories. The deponent may show obvious signs of emotional distress by crying, sobbing, wailing, but most interviewers — perhaps lawyers, human rights advocates, or other laypersons hired to take testimony — have little or no training in responding to this level of trauma. In contrast, other deponents may come across as emotionally removed, which may also be misinterpreted or misunderstood by the statement-taker. One staff member in El Salvador, who said she received no training in how to respond to traumatized victims, said, "My recollection is that most people dealt with their loss by becoming almost clinical and detached from what had happened, no matter how horrible it was. I only remember one case of a middle class woman whose son had disappeared in the early eighties and who came with her husband, and was still hysterical as though it had happened yesterday. She still seemed devastated by the loss. I remember someone commenting that she had not been able to deal with what had happened. I think I may have reached out and put my hand on her arm, but it was more from instinct."[19]

Given the great number of victims that come forward and the short period of time that a commission has to complete its work, truth commissions to date have not been able to offer any serious psychological support services, nor generally to respond well to the occasional follow-up phone calls of distress or requests for information on the progress of investigation on a particular case. In South Africa, the truth commission attempted to set up a system to refer distressed victims to independent agencies for further psychological support, but this referral system never functioned well and was not widely used. In addition, many victims live far from any city where such services might be available.

Commissions typically investigate only a few cases in depth, using the vast majority of testimonies only for a statistical analysis of patterns. In those relatively few cases where a commission is able to investigate thoroughly and establish the conclusive facts about what took place and even the location of the remains of someone who was disappeared, survivors seem to find a considerable measure of closure. The amnesty hearings in South Africa, for example, where perpetrators spelled out the brutal details of torture and killings, seemed to bring more peace and closure to survivors. In some cases, the South African commission was able to exhume secret graves and return the remains to family members, even holding memorial services in their honor, which was clearly very powerful and positive for the families.

THE DANGER OF RETRAUMATIZATION

"As long as there is crying going on, there's an assumption that healing's taking place," said Brandon Hamber of the Centre for the Study of Violence and Reconciliation. "For some people, it's the first step; for others, it's the last step, a completion. But there are a lot of people that feel devastated afterwards."[20] Likewise, Harvard psychiatrist Judith Herman told me that "anyone showing interest and providing an opportunity for someone to tell their story can have a therapeutic effect. Some victims may be ready to take advantage of the slightest opportunity in a positive way. For others, it opens them up and leaves them with nowhere to go."[21]

As psychologists readily recognize, and as can clearly be seen by speaking with some of those who have given testimony to truth commissions, victims and witnesses can in effect be retraumatized by giving testimony to a commission, which may be so severe as to result in a multitude of debilitating physical symptoms, such as confusion, nightmares, exhaustion, loss of appetite, and sleeplessness. This set of symptoms may first appear immediately following a traumatic event, but can then come back again years later upon recalling the details of the event. In the field of psychology, this set of physical symptoms is referred to as posttraumatic stress disorder, or PTSD.[22] When victims and witnesses are asked to relate the details of their heart-wrenching story in one sitting, and are then given no follow-up support, the emotional and psychological impact can be great. The difficulty of healing from political violence is even more complicated by the intersection of basic economic and social problems, which may have been exacerbated by the very event in question, such as with the death of the family breadwinner. Sometimes, the trauma may have led to other problems such as substance abuse and the breakdown of personal relationships.

Michael Lapsley, an activist priest in South Africa, has talked with many victims struggling to understand their response to the truth commission. Lapsley lost both hands as a result of a letter bomb sent from the South African authorities in 1990, when he was living in exile in Zimbabwe. He recovered from the bomb, and now lives with metal grips where his hands should be. Since the bombing he has counseled many victims of political violence in South Africa, and while he made clear that he supported the truth commission's work, he stressed the danger of a truth commission approaching healing too simplistically: "If you have a physical wound, you take off the bandage, clean the wound, and rebandage it. But people take their clothes off in front of the truth commission and don't get an adequate opportunity to put their clothes back on. . . . It is naive to think that it takes five minutes to heal. We'll spend the next hundred years trying to heal from our history." When the truth commission arrived for a few days in a town to take testimony, it did give people the chance to come forward to speak, and it brought their suffering to the nation's attention, but Lapsley saw that the hearings often left the townspeople at a loss: "The circus comes to town and the circus leaves — and then what?" they would ask him.

The assumption that knowing the facts about what happened will always contribute to healing is too simplistic, and is sometimes just not true, Lapsley said. In fact, the burden of knowing can be great. "Now that you know who did something — perhaps a loved one was involved in an act, for example — what do you do with that? Now you have to learn to deal with the knowledge that you have."[23]

Marius Schoon, a South African whose wife and daughter were killed by a bomb sent by state security forces, said, "I never really wanted to find out who sent or planted the bomb. I would prefer to hate a system rather than people, and as far as I was concerned the security forces of the National Party government were responsible. That was enough for me," he said. Twelve years after the killings, through the work of the truth commission, he learned exactly who did it. "From March of last year, when I heard [Craig] Williamson [a spy for the apartheid government] was involved, it has been anything but reconciliatory for me in that things I had come to terms with, however ineptly, are suddenly very much in the forefront of my mind again. Now it's personal. There is a good chance that perhaps I might actually shoot him."[24]

South of Johannesburg, in the black township of Sebokeng, I met a mother and son who had survived a massacre of thirty-eight people in their house in the mid-1980s, an atrocity widely known as the 'night vigil massacre.' I visited them in their home in 1996, two weeks after they had gone before the Truth and Reconciliation Commission to tell their story in a public hearing. A Tracy Chapman poster hung on their living room wall, just to the side of the television, just across from the bullet holes that were still in the ceiling from the attack nine years before. My interpreter and I were crowded into their small living room with the mother, Margaret Nangalembe. Her son wasn't home. My interpreter and I only knew that they had recently given testimony, and we were curious about the mother's impressions. She spoke only in general and polite terms about the commission, until I asked her if she thought the truth commission was a good thing.

"I can't say if the truth commission is good or bad, but for me personally, it's made things much worse. My life has deteriorated since the hearing," she said. She described a litany of classic symptoms of PTSD. "It's made me think about these things again. The day that we went to the commission, I started thinking about all of this again, and now all I can think about is the day of the massacre and what happened."[25]

At the public hearing of their case, the mother broke down in such fits of emotion that she had to be taken from the room; her son, Albert "Mandla" Mbalekelwa Nangalembe, finished the presentation of their case. The staff of the truth commission tried to console them afterwards, in the debriefing session that is offered to all who give testimony, but they both went home emotionally distraught. Her physical symptoms started the next morning, and then when she saw clips of the massacre on the following Sunday's Truth Commission Report on television, she became much worse. "I feel dizzy. I have a constant headache. I can't walk far without getting tired: my feet and knees don't work right. I'm not sleeping at night."

After the massacre, she said, "it took me a long time to come to my full senses. I was always confused; it was like everything was dark. My son took me to a specialist doctor in the city and he gave me pills and an injection, and I started getting better. I've gone to the local clinic to ask for treatment again. I was given tablets, but they haven't seemed to work."

I asked if she was sorry she had gone to the truth commission. "I had really wanted to go to the commission to tell the story," she said. "I can't say that I'm sorry. I still would have seen it on TV, since others were going to present the case."

It still wasn't clear, however, what she and her son would get from the truth commission in concrete terms. They wanted assistance in fixing things that were damaged during the attack: the roof still leaked from the bullet holes and the front door wouldn't lock well ever since it was forced open, but the commission hadn't promised anything, not even an investigation.

Her son "Mandla" arrived home and joined the conversation. He was young, bright, articulate, and impressive, perhaps thirty-something in age. He described many of the same symptoms as his mother: he wasn't sleeping, he suffered nightmares, he was having trouble eating. "There's a lot of damage, it's very serious," he said. He called the truth commission a week after the hearing to find out if any progress had been made in the investigation. The commission still hadn't called back. "The truth commission has started something that I'm not sure they're going to be able to finish," he said. "There's a lot of investigation needed. How to heal people, I don't know, but something's got to be done." He also feared retaliation from their perpetrators for speaking to the commission: "We're put in a very dangerous situation. There's a danger we'll be attacked for speaking. They might just say 'let's eliminate them.'"[26]

He had helped form a local support group of victims after the massacre, called the Vaal Victims of Violence. Now the group was focused largely on the truth commission, and most were unhappy with its slow pace. "We're not going to act against the truth commission, but we're in the dark; we don't know what's happening," Mandla said. But the group helped to hold them together. "We meet once a month to see what the truth commission is doing and if there are threats against anyone."

Despite his suffering, he refused to criticize the commission. "We thought it was worth it. We don't say it's worthless; I don't want to be negative. I'm positive. The world should know the truth of the matter."

When he walked us to our car, he thanked us for stopping by. "Maybe I'll be able to sleep tonight, now that I've had a chance to talk about it."

Later, on a visit to Soweto, I heard a far worse story. My guide and interpreter in Soweto worked part time as a statement-taker for the truth commission, and told me about a victim who had been severely tortured while in detention a number of years back. He was left quite disturbed from the torture, barely functioning from day to day, but he chose to give his statement to the truth commission, which required him to describe his torture in detail. As a result of giving his statement, he suffered a severe mental breakdown and had to be immediately admitted to a mental hospital. He remained in the hospital for three months before recovering from his memories sufficiently to be released.[27]

The Trauma Centre for Victims of Violence and Torture in Cape Town has estimated, judging from the hundreds of victims they've worked with, that 50 to 60 percent of those who gave testimony to the commission suffered difficulties after testifying, or expressed regret for having taken part (though recognizing they did not undertake a scientific study or survey on the question).[28] The chief mental-health specialist at the South African truth commission, Thulani Grenville-Grey, acknowledged the dangerous territory on which the commission was treading but defended its work, arguing that it's better to be in pain than to be numb. "It's better to be in touch with your grief. It's not a particularly bad thing to be retraumatized; you have to get worse before you get better, in order to heal. It's horrible, but that makes it a real transformation."[29]

BRIEFERS, REFERRALS, AND OTHER FORMS
OF SUPPORT

The potential for retraumatization is not a surprise to those who counsel victims of political violence. Six months before the South African truth commission began, for example, a South African psychologist warned of the potential for harm: "It is imperative that the Truth and Reconciliation Commission does not unearth painful memories or cause people to re-live difficult times without ensuring that appropriate support services exist for these people. It is far more likely that the truth commission will lead to feelings of revenge, bitterness and anger if people who come into contact with it do not receive appropriate counseling and adequate support and service."[30]

The South African truth commission gave these concerns serious attention, and went further than any other commission in incorporating psychological support into its operational structures. The commission hired four mental-health professionals on its staff, who saw their role as helping to "insure that the commission was psychologically sensitive to trauma," according to Thulani Grenville-Grey, the lead mental-health specialist. He organized his work with the recognition that "a psychologically sensitive or supportive approach to statement-taking is equivalent to a doctor with a good bed-side manner; it makes a huge difference if you do it well, but it's not actually necessary to your primary task."[31]

Training for statement-takers, the commission staff that have the most contact with victims, can be critical since the impact of talking about trauma will be affected by the reaction of the listener. Although commissioners and staff may have the best of intentions, many will come to the commission with no previous training in dealing with such extreme cases of emotional and psychological injury.

Realizing these risks, the South African commission provided at least some basic training for statement-takers on how to respond to signs of trauma. The commission also hired "briefers," as they called them, who had the job of providing constant support to those giving testimony at public hearings. The briefers would introduce the procedure of the hearing and answer questions in a morning meeting, sit next to deponents as they testified, and then debrief them afterwards, offering them words of support and encouragement. Some other truth commissions have incorporated similar support structures into their work, though on a more limited level. In both Chile and Argentina, psychologists and social workers were included on the commissions' staff and attended some of the interviews with victims, for example. Yet truth commissions as a rule are overwhelmed with work, and are thus limited in what they can offer. Apart from those in South Africa, Chile, and Argentina, other commissions have operated with little recognition of the possible retraumatizing effect that their work might have. The commissions in Haiti and El Salvador offered little in the way of basic psychological training for their staff, such as how testimony might be taken in the most sensitive manner, and there was no one on staff dedicated specifically to the needs of victims. No commission outside of South Africa has attempted to set up a system for referral or follow-up for traumatized witnesses.

Of course, formal psychological counseling may not be the appropriate model for helping victims in most countries that are likely to have truth commissions. In many of these countries, there are few formal psychological services available, very few people with the culture or custom to reach out for formal counseling, and few resources available for such relative luxuries. This is true even in relatively developed South Africa. In the entire Northern Province of South Africa, for example, a mostly rural area with a population of over five million people, there are only three private mental-health practitioners, and no clinical psychologists employed by the state health department.[32] In neighboring Mozambique, there are only nineteen psychologists and one psychiatrist in the entire country, and only a few of those are currently in practice.[33] In Sierra Leone, there is only one psychologist in the entire country. Perhaps more important than the lack of personnel or resources, however, is the point that Western psychology may not be the appropriate means of response in some cultures. The impact of culture on how people respond to and recover from extreme trauma is not yet well understood. "In the case of posttraumatic disorders, cultural variability is just starting to be investigated," note two psychiatrists, Cécile Rousseau and Aline Drapeau, based in Montreal. As a starting point, however, they note that "culture provides the tools for grieving. When it comes to trauma, culture, which is obviously involved in the reparative process, may be equally involved in determining how, and how intensely, trauma is relived."[34]

Thus, given resource restrictions and cultural variability, the ideal source of support for victims in many societies may be community organizations, traditional healers, church structures, or extended families and friends. Yet after years of silence and fear, many people who make up these support structures hesitate to talk openly about political violence, and are therefore usually uncomfortable taking on such a supportive role. Furthermore, it is clear that some kinds of violence, particularly rape, are just not going to be easily discussed with community leaders or within a victim's family. For all of these reasons, continued silence about past traumatic events may often be the norm, even within a victim's own home, and even after the victim breaks through this silence by giving a statement to a commission.

Recovery may depend in part on reparations awarded, and many commissions have played an important role in recommending reparation programs. Rather than monetary compensation from the state, according to Harvard psychiatrist Judith Herman, victims may want some kind of restitution from the perpetrators. Victims want to have a "sense that the people who did the damage are made to give something back, or to try to clean up the mess that they made. People are so desperate for those people responsible to be made to face the consequences of their action, and do something about it. It is *that* sense of justice that they are looking for, which is different from punishment."[35]

In the absence of formal structures to help survivors of trauma, a number of self-help support groups have developed. In Argentina and Chile, groups representing families of the disappeared organized even during the dictatorships, first focused on demanding that the disappeared were returned alive. In Argentina, the Mothers of the Plaza de Mayo is famous for its weekly marches in front of the presidential house, which still continue today, though the group has now split into two over political differences. Two decades after the disappearances began in Argentina, Children of the Disappeared groups have now also formed, made up of youths as young as teenagers who are trying to come to terms with missing parents.

In South Africa, groups have organized that go far beyond those seen elsewhere. The largest group, Khulumani, which means "speak out" in Zulu, was initially formed to represent victims' voices in lobbying around the creation of the truth commission, but it quickly took on the additional task of offering support to victims and survivors through support groups. Many of the local Khulumani groups were started around shared concerns about the truth commission — access to information, reparations policy developments, amnesty policies, and so on. Khulumani also dedicated considerable energy in reaching out to educate communities about the truth commission. They produced a powerful play highlighting the tensions, frustrations, and benefits of the truth commission, which toured through black townships. In the process of its work, Khulumani developed strong local roots; by late 1997, the organization had over five thousand members around the country, the vast majority of whom were black and came from the heart of the victimized communities. In addition to following the activities of the commission and the developments of each of their cases, many local Khulumani groups met simply to talk and offer each other support, sometimes holding symbolic memorial services for those killed.

This self-help structure has been very useful to many victims, who stress the importance of these meetings in helping them recover from their pains. Many cite a common "I'm not as bad off as them" phenomenon, when some survivors first start coming to meetings and find others who suffered more. The founders of Khulumani realize that the group never would have formed without the truth commission, though it has now taken on a life of its own. Those who work closely with victims have seen the positive effect of Khulumani and similar organizations and a much lower likelihood of retraumatization symptoms for those who are members of such groups. Many maintain that Khulumani's support provided a much greater sense of healing than the commission itself.[36]

Reverend S. K. Mbande, in Daveyton, told me that these support groups were "one of the fruits of the commission. People coming together and healing themselves—that never would have happened before. Fear was the order of the day. Since the truth commission, things have come out, and it's made people come together."[37]

PSYCHOLOGICAL TRAUMA AFFECTS THE INFORMATION GATHERED

Commissions should be prepared for the discrepancies that may result from collecting information from traumatized witnesses. "People who have survived atrocities often tell their stories in a highly emotional, contradictory, and fragmented manner which undermines their credibility," Judith Herman writes.[38] Exactly when did something take place? What happened first? Who was present? Exactly what did you see? Such details that fade over time become even more confused in the haze of psychological trauma. Faced with a barrage of detailed questions, answers may be unclear or contradictory.

A staff member of the truth commission in Haiti described how testimony from some victims was just one sentence: "My mother was killed." That was all the deponent could say. The interviewers didn't quite know why, but the deponents either didn't know or couldn't say more. Many other statements began strangely, apparently out of order: "they'd start with the last thing first, or they'd begin with the story of their goat being stolen, which seemed irrelevant. It was very common, and very confusing to try to figure out what the story was."[39]

Indeed, the standard American psychiatric reference manual describes one of the common symptoms of PTSD as the "inability to recall an important aspect of the trauma." Furthermore, it continues, "The person commonly makes deliberate efforts to avoid thoughts, feelings, or conversations about the traumatic event. . . . The avoidance of reminders may include amnesia for an important aspect" of the event in question.[40]

Operational choices made by a commission will help determine its psychological impact. Some of these choices are fairly concrete, like the selection of office space. In Chad, the newly installed commission faced a short supply of space, so it set up offices in the empty building that had just been evacuated by the former intelligence service — and which had served as the torture center under the previous government. Victims were understandably wary of coming to the office to give testimony. As the commission wrote in its report, "It must also be conceded that the location of the Commission headquarters itself was not such as to encourage victims to come forward with depositions. . . . [I]t took a great deal of tactful persuasion to reassure and allay the anxieties of hesitant, frightened people."[41]

In El Salvador, the commission set up offices in the heart of the capital's wealthiest neighborhood. The great majority of those who came to give testimony were not comfortable there. In the socioeconomic breakdown of politics and war in the country, that neighborhood was known to house many on the political Right, including supporters of the death squads and the military. Many victims came anyway, but with great hesitation. A priest who offered to drive people to the commission from a nearby city described the dynamics in the car as they approached the commission's office. "The three or four people in the car were terrified that they'd be seen coming to the commission and there'd be retaliation against them. They were really very scared. Even when we left the commission's offices, they all kept saying 'They saw us, they took pictures, they were watching.' The fear of that neighborhood was intense."[42]

"SPONGES OF TRAUMA": SECONDARY TRAUMATIZATION OF COMMISSION STAFF AND JOURNALISTS

The South African commission's mental-health expert, Thulani Grenville-Grey, described commission staff as "sponges" absorbing the grief, pain, and trauma of the stories they heard. "They responded with classic post-traumatic stress symptoms, which is why we have encouraged them to go for weekly debriefing sessions to talk things through."[43] The impact of this trauma was well acknowledged at the commission, manifested in short tempers, aggression, sleeplessness, nightmares, paranoia, headaches, ulcers, substance abuse problems, and other physical and behavioral problems. Commissioners commonly woke at 2:00 or 3:00 a.m., reliving vivid images of the hearings of previous days; staff and commissioners from other truth inquiries have given similar accounts. A few truth commissions have recognized the need to formally address the psychological burden on their own members. The South African and Chilean commissions offered regular debriefing sessions for their staff, for example.

Typically, a truth commission statement-taker might take five to ten statements in one day, but that number can go much higher. In Guatemala, staff told of taking as many as twenty-seven in a day, of working fourteen-hour days, seven days a week, every week—though they resisted telling me that, since they were working under UN contracts and it is against UN regulations to work such hours. After the field offices were closed in Guatemala and the commission realized the toll taken on its staff, it organized a debriefing session with a mental-health expert, but it was perhaps too late to provide much assistance. The most positive accounts that I heard were from directors of field offices in Guatemala who instinctively created outlets to reduce stress, forcing the staff to take breaks from the rhythm of the brutal testimony.

Typically, however, staff are not given many tools to process the pain and agony they hear on a daily basis. A commission staff member in El Salvador, American lawyer Lauren Gilbert, described one experience that stood out in her mind:

> I remember one time (only one time) when I totally fell apart in an interview and had to leave the interview room and go to the rest room. It was the case of a young woman who was the partner of a member of the FMLN [the Salvadoran armed opposition], who was picked up and tortured by the Policía de Hacienda. She was horribly tortured for nearly three weeks (they beat her; they put acid on her blindfold so that when she cried it burned her eyes; they broke her wrist and her teeth; they raped and impregnated her). She couldn't have an abortion because it was "against the law," and she ended up rejecting her baby and becoming grossly obese. Her mother, who gave the testimony, had also lost her

son to the death squads. The mother, like so many others, was almost clinical in the way she gave the testimony; very aloof and detached. I guess that at some point I must have connected with this woman and was grieving for her lost identity, the destruction of her identity by the police. I think it was the first time I really understood the meaning of torture.

I wanted this case to be included in our report. I tried to find the woman, but we were unable to find her home. I went to the prison where she had been held, but they kept only minimal records, so that there was no real way of "corroborating" her testimony to the commissioners' satisfaction. Ultimately her case was not included.[44]

Despite the pain of hearing the stories, however, staff often describe a process that is ultimately positive and rewarding. In El Salvador, for example, Gilbert noted, "In terms of how we dealt with it, or at least how I dealt with receiving all those testimonies, I always felt in each interview that I was writing that person's story, and that by writing the story during our interview at the computer, and reading it back to them for edits and for them to sign, I had done something cathartic for both of us. That feeling of having captured what had taken place was very powerful."[45]

A number of commissions have found that the staff who are the most disturbed by the harrowing tales of torture and abuse are not those taking statements directly from victims, but are instead data entry staff charged with coding and entering the information into the database. Perhaps this is because the statement-takers can see signs of resilience as the victim tells the story, and can put the account in context, thus easing the horror. In addition to having no direct contact with the victims, the coders and data entry staff also process a greater number of statements than do statement-takers, and the data that they are working with is quite harsh. In South Africa, for example, the three-and-one-half-page, single-spaced list of data entry codes spelled out hundreds of different types of violence, torture, and abuse. The list begins with *forcible abduction, amputation,* and *beating of head against a wall,* and continues on to *pulling out of teeth, removal of fingernails, being dragged behind moving vehicle, being buried alive,* and *being burned with chemicals*—and that's all just on the first page. Another 150 terms follow on the next pages: *deprivation of sleep, head submerged in water, intentional spreading of disease, being forced to watch the torture of others, genital mutilation, gang rape, suspension of weights from genitals, decapitation, burning of body parts,* and *disembowelment.* The data coders and processors spend their days reading statement forms, assigning codes, and entering the codes into the computers, often working under considerable time pressure.

Where there have been public hearings and intense media coverage of a commission's work, the journalists that follow a truth commission have also shown signs of secondary traumatization. This was especially true in South Africa, where dozens of print, radio, and television reporters covered the commission full time. A year into the commission's work, journalist Antjie Krog, who led a five-person radio team covering the commission, wrote of the intense and near-debilitating toll the job had taken on her and her colleagues. When the commission began, she writes, a mental-health specialist from the commission addressed the group of journalists working on the truth commission beat, warning them to watch for signs of stress. "You will experience the same symptoms as the victims," they were told. "You will find yourself powerless, without help, without words."

"I was shocked to be a textbook case within a mere ten days," Krog writes; she continues,

> Reporting on the truth commission had indeed left most of us physically exhausted and mentally frayed. . . . Week after week, from one faceless building to the other, from one dusty godforsaken town to the other, the arteries of our past bleed their own peculiar rhythm, tone and image. One cannot get rid of it. Ever.
>
> . . . We develop techniques to lessen the impact. We no longer go into the halls where the hearings take place, because of the accumulated grief. We watch on provided monitors. The moment someone starts crying, we start writing/scribbling/doodling.
>
> . . . My hair is falling out. My teeth are falling out. I have rashes . . . I can talk about nothing else. Yet I don't talk about it at all.[46]

CONCLUSION

From the anecdotal evidence that is available, it is clear that some victims, survivors, and witnesses will feel much better after giving testimony, will be glad for having had the opportunity to speak, and will feel acknowledged and supported by the commission's work. Some will feel an initial rush of adrenaline and relief, especially if they speak in a public hearing, a process often described by participating commissioners and other observers as a powerful and apparently cathartic event. Yet some of these same deponents may feel much worse later, especially if they had high hopes that their cases would be investigated and come to realize they might hear nothing more from the commission. How many will feel better and how many might feel worse is still not known, as no one has closely tracked the short- and long-term impact on victims who participate in the truth commission process.

Besides the direct impact on those who participate in giving testimony, the power of simply having a denied truth recognized must also be appreciated. In Guatemala, the ceremony to release the commission's report to the public, attended by over two thousand people, was an enormously emotional event, with most in the audience in tears from the impact of hearing the truth finally and authoritatively spoken. Even hardened human rights activists referred to the event as "cathartic."

The results of a commission may also have other unintended secondary effects that result in positive benefits for victims. By bringing historical events and their associated trauma into the open, a commission helps to identify the need for basic psychological services for victims. For example, a trauma counselor in Cape Town told me that the work of the truth commission in South Africa had completely changed the public's understanding of the needs of those who had suffered. "Now, if I say 'services for victims,' people understand it." he said. "Before the truth commission, there were just blank stares. The commission is creating a climate where healing can take place. It's a powerful message to say, 'It's OK to start processing this stuff.'"[47]

Meanwhile, however, there are things commissions can do to improve the likelihood that they will have a positive impact for individual victims. For example, a commission should hire a mental health specialist and provide training for statement-takers in how to respond to signs of distress; set up a referral system to outside services and support structures and provide training or basic informational sessions with community, religious, and traditional leaders and others to explain the likelihood of posttraumatic stress disorder and victims' need for support; designate a liaison to respond to individual victim's or organization's questions or concerns; and encourage the development of nongovernmental self-help support groups. Where possible, a commission should facilitate exhumations of persons killed in political violence, working in conjunction with victims' groups and giving due respect to the desires of survivors; in many cultures, an opportunity to provide a proper burial for loved ones is critical for healing to take place. Finally, a commission should aim to stimulate a longer-term healing process, perhaps through targeted recommendations, in recognition that its contribution will represent only the first step of a long process of national and individual recovery.

An Eye to the Future

Reconciliation and Reforms

Perhaps the most important aim of any truth commission should be to prevent further violence and rights abuses in the future. It may hope to do this by breaking the cycle of revenge and hatred between former enemies, somehow encouraging reconciliation between opposing groups who may feel they have much to hate or fear in the other and/or a history to avenge. More concretely, most commissions recommend reforms in the military, police, judiciary, and political systems in the hope of curbing abuses and strengthening the mechanisms that should respond to abuses when they occur.

Both of these aims—advancing reconciliation and promoting institutional reforms—have presented significant challenges to past truth commissions, and while some important contributions have been made, they have often fallen short of obtaining the results initially hoped for. This has been the cause of much disappointment for those who have held high hopes for the transformational powers of individual truth commissions, but in retrospect this should hardly come as a surprise. Both of these goals are dependent on any number of outside actors or elements—political will, legislative or presidential initiatives, and societal and individual readiness to change, among others—such that even heroic efforts by any one truth-speaking commission cannot alone make all of the necessary changes.

Reconciliation is often cited as a goal in national peace processes, but it is rarely clear exactly what is meant by the term. The *Oxford English Dictionary* defines "reconcile" as "to bring (a person) again into friendly relations . . .

after an estrangement. . . . To bring back into concord, to reunite (persons or things) in harmony."[1] In the context of political conflict or violence, *reconciliation* has been described as "developing a mutual conciliatory accommodation between antagonistic or formerly antagonistic persons or groups."[2] It has been widely asserted that knowing the truth about the past is necessary for reconciliation to take place. In places like South Africa, this has been a fundamental tenet in the call for a truth commission, and the international attention to the commission in that country has created the impression that all truth commissions are formed primarily for the purposes of advancing reconciliation. In fact, the degree of emphasis on reconciliation as a goal of truth-seeking has varied greatly among commissions. Not all have framed their work around this goal, but those that have — such as the Truth and Reconciliation Commission in South Africa and the National Commission on Truth and Reconciliation in Chile — have found it to be a difficult mission.

There should be a distinction made between individual reconciliation and national or political reconciliation. The strength of a truth commission process is in advancing reconciliation on a national or political level. By speaking openly and publicly about past silenced or highly conflictive events and by allowing an independent commission to clear up high-profile cases, a commission can ease some of the strains that may otherwise be present in national legislative or other political bodies. An official accounting and conclusion about the facts can allow opposing parties to debate and govern together without latent conflicts and bitterness over past lies. This is not to suggest that the knowledge or memory of past practices should not influence current politics, but if basic points of fact continue to be a source of conflict or bitterness, political relationships may be strained. In a negotiated transition out of civil war, these latent tensions may be of special concern, as opponents can move quickly from the battlefield to the floor of congress.

On an individual level, however, reconciliation is much more complex, and much more difficult to achieve by means of a national commission. There certainly are examples of truth commission processes leading directly to healing and forgiveness for some individuals, but knowing the global truth or even knowing the specific truth about one's own case will not necessarily lead to a victim's reconciliation with his or her perpetrators. Forgiveness, healing, and reconciliation are deeply personal processes, and each person's needs and reactions to peacemaking and truth-telling may be different.

From even before its inception, the Truth and Reconciliation Commission of South Africa was presented as a means to reconcile a fractured nation and heal the wounds of its troubled soul. The message from the commission was clear and unwavering, encouraging an expectation among the public that reconciliation could and would actually be reached in the course of the commission's two and a half years of operation. At its public hearings, a huge sign hung behind the panel of commissioners that read, Truth: The Road to Reconciliation. Posters promoting the commission coaxed, "Let's speak out to each other. By telling the truth. By telling our stories of the past, so that we can walk the road to reconciliation." In some of its first hearings Archbishop Desmond Tutu would sometimes ask victims if they were ready to forgive and reconcile after telling their story (at least one deponent respectfully responded that she could not—and that the commission could not and should not ask her to do so, nor offer forgiveness for her). Even the commission's Amnesty Committee, responsible for deciding the fate of those admitting to wrongs, was influenced by this overarching interest in reconciliation: one Amnesty Committee member told me that they based their decisions in part on their judgment of "what is likely to promote reconciliation" since, they reasoned, that aim was clearly spelled out as the fundamental goal of the commission's work.[3]

As could be expected, the commission's success was thus judged in part on whether and how much "reconciliation" was perceived to have resulted from its work. As it was close to finishing its report in mid-1998, the press and public were overtaken by the realization that widespread reconciliation had not in fact been won. Many, in fact, argued that the country was worse off, that relations between groups in need of reconciling had in fact worsened rather than improved. Market Research Africa released a national poll showing that two-thirds of the public believed that revelations resulting from the truth commission process had made South Africans angrier and led to a deterioration in relations between races. "Among those questioned, 24 percent expected people to feel more angry and bitter, 23 percent said the TRC would cause more hurt and pain. Only 17 percent predicted people would become more forgiving," it was reported.[4] These poll results were referred to in articles worldwide, with the inference that the truth commission in South Africa was not in the end much of a success.[5]

By this time, the commission had long since realized that its initial claims of achieving full reconciliation had been unrealistic. Archbishop Tutu began to argue that a more reasonable goal for the commission was to "promote" reconciliation, rather than to achieve it, as indicated in the name of the Promotion of National Unity and Reconciliation Act that created the commission. Yet despite a general sense of disappointment, there was little serious reflection in the press or public about what reconciliation might really mean, or what might be required to attain it, in a society such as South Africa, where communities had been long separated not only by race and physical space, but also by economic conditions and opportunity.

The commission did not shy away from these frustrations and disappointments in its report. For example, it quoted at length from an outside researcher's report on the community of Duduza, a black township of about 100,000 people, which was perhaps representative of feelings elsewhere:

> The publicity around the establishment and functioning of the Commission, as well as its operation within Duduza, has, at the very least, forced people to examine their own understanding of what reconciliation and forgiveness means to them and their community. For some, this may be primarily an intellectual exercise—looking at existing divisions and formulating some ideas about what should be changed, at what a reconciled community would look like. For others, it is a much more personal reflection, involving feelings of hatred, guilt and fear. Thinking about reconciliation means thinking about a process of overcoming the psychological barriers that they have been living with, often for many years. . . .
>
> While some victims still find the idea of reconciliation, and especially forgiveness, insulting, it appears that for most the Commission has contributed to a greater commitment to the process of reconciliation. It has created the space to pursue reconciliation. . . . It is seen as a forum that provides a platform for storytelling, for revealing the truth, for holding the perpetrator accountable, for reparations, remorse, and forgiveness. These are steps in a process that people now understand and accept as legitimate. . . .
>
> Reconciliation is not an event. People cannot simply one day decide that they want to forgive and forget. Most of the victims in this community are committed to a process of reconciliation. They are not necessarily demanding vengeance. They are, at the same time, not simply willing to move ahead as if nothing happened. They demand to hear the truth and to be given time to consider it. They are often not willing to forgive unless the perpetrators show remorse and some form of reparation is offered. . . .
>
> Victims are not ready to engage in a reconciliation process unless they know more about what happened. They often say they are willing to forgive, but they need to know who to forgive and what they are forgiving them for. A willingness to reconcile is dependent on people's ability to cope with and process this knowledge of what had happened. While the

past remains hidden, a reconciliation process proceeds on very shaky foundations. The Commission has contributed to some of this revealing, but many individuals are still in the dark about the details of their specific cases.[6]

As suggested by this observer in Duduza, where case-specific information was made known, and where perpetrators showed sincere remorse, there were powerful examples of forgiveness and reconciliation that did result directly from the work of the truth commission. There were a number of remarkable community or individual scenes of reconciliation, especially in exchanges between amnesty applicants and victims. One lawyer described hearings that he participated in at Richards Bay, where Inkatha Freedom Party members were seeking amnesty for their murders of African National Congress members. The victims' supporters were initially angry and aggressive toward the amnesty applicants. The dynamics changed radically over the course of the hearing:

Each day there were several hundred people attending the hearings, filling the hall to capacity. As time went on they began to warm to the applicants, as did the committee members, who asked fewer and fewer questions as they realized that the applicants were telling everything that they could remember and were committed to having the whole truth told.

On the penultimate day there was an informal meeting between the community and the applicants at which many questions were asked about specific incidents. Then one by one survivors came forward and forgave the applicants and thanked them for telling everything, allowing them to know what had happened and also telling them who else had been involved and who had given instructions. At the end of the meeting a resolution was taken to forgive the applicants and to tell the committee that the community accepted that the applicants were telling the whole truth within the bounds of the failings of human memory, that the attacks were launched with a political motive and that they would not oppose amnesty.

We then all sang Nkosi Sikelele together, with the applicants tentatively raising their fists, and then Mkhize led everyone in prayer at the request of the community. At the end of the meeting people rushed forward to hug the applicants.[7]

While all, or even most, amnesty hearings certainly did not end on such a tone, there were a number of other similar examples of community or individual reconciliation that were a direct outcome of the official truth-seeking process.

Reconciliation took place on other levels as well, such as in the back room of a large corporation that had never before formally discussed the issue of race. One large sugar-producing concern that participated in the commission's sectoral hearings on the business community used the event to undertake a serious internal review of the company's record. A racially mixed group of about twenty senior company executives met eight times over several months to prepare a company statement to be presented to the truth commission. Yet first, as a senior white executive who took part in the process told me, the group had to come to an agreement on language. "The first meeting was very intense: we spent an hour and a half just on what to call each other: we weren't supposed to say 'black,' which is what the whites thought, but rather 'African.' We wanted to call those of Indian descent 'Asiatic,' but they said 'No, call us Indian.' Thus, we came to understand, 'black' included African, Indian, and coloured. We'd never talked about this before, nor talked about the past. . . . It's really about values, what should and shouldn't have been done. In the end, we were successful in putting together a consensus statement to present to the commission."

During my visit to Chile in 1996, five years after the National Commission on Truth and Reconciliation had concluded its work, I found many Chileans insisting that national reconciliation had been achieved. The director of the follow-up body to the truth commission, Alejandro Gonzalez, defined *reconciliation* as "respecting the rules of the democratic game. There is a civilized dialogue between the government and opposition, and no sector wants to take over anti-democratically."[8] Others suggested much the same. Yet even while insisting that national reconciliation had taken place, many Chileans described personal relationships that remained strained by past events. Former victims and supporters of the regime of Augusto Pinochet worked and lived side by side, but with an unspoken agreement to never bring up the past or their strong differences of opinion. When issues about the past did arise, it was with considerable discomfort.

When Pinochet was arrested in London in late 1998, the depth of these rifts in society became clear. As the country grappled with these tensions, it became ever more clear that there was no consensus about basic facts of right and wrong in the country's past.[9] The breadth and depth of support for the former Pinochet regime, and the level of justification that was used to back up this pro-Pinochet position, were in sharp contrast to South

Africa's postapartheid view of its past (though I am not trying to equate the form and effect of the repression in Chile and South Africa). This form of reconciliation—coming to a generally agreed understanding of a country's history and its wrongs—has been so thoroughly won in South Africa that it is hardly a point of discussion. In contrast to the Chileans supporting Pinochet, very few in South Africa will now even admit to ever having supported apartheid—even though the majority of whites kept the apartheid government in power for forty years. In this widespread, even if clearly dishonest, denial can be found a measure of success in South Africa's reconciliation, for which the South African truth commission should be given considerable credit. Almost no one today would attempt to boast about the benefits of apartheid, as no one would try to deny that torture took place on a wide scale in South African police stations and jails.

In contrast to South Africa and Chile, as noted earlier, some past truth commissions have held no presumption of achieving reconciliation in the course of their work. For example, reconciliation has never been assumed in Argentina, and there is a resistance even to the suggestion of reconciliation taking place under current conditions. As journalist Horacio Verbitsky responded when I mentioned the word, "*Reconciliation* by who? After someone takes away your daughter, tortures her, disappears her, and then denies ever having done it—would you ever want to 'reconcile' with those responsible? That word makes no sense here. The political discourse of reconciliation is profoundly immoral, because it denies the reality of what people have experienced. It isn't reasonable to expect someone to reconcile after what happened here."[10] Patricia Valdez, the former director of the El Salvador truth commission and the head of Poder Ciudadano, an Argentine organization promoting democratic initiatives, told me, "Nobody talks of reconciliation in Argentina, nobody touches it. It's not that anybody is actively opposed to it, it's that the word has no meaning here. Nobody has seriously put that question on the table."[11] Argentine Juan Méndez, former legal counsel to Human Rights Watch and former director of the Inter-American Institute of Human Rights, said that reconciliation in Argentina "was a code word for those who wanted nothing done. *Reconciliation* in Argentina was understood by victims to mean, 'We are being asked to reconcile with our torturers, and they're being asked to do nothing.'" Nongovernmental organizations were painted into a corner, while the military or the government was allowed to define what it meant, said Méndez.[12]

Indeed, few public figures talk of reconciliation in Argentina. One was President Carlos Menem, who cited it as the reason for granting pardons in 1990 to the military leaders then serving time in jail for their crimes under the military regime. The reconciliation justification was a politically convenient claim that had little popular support, as could be seen in the spontaneous reactions of tens of thousands of people who took to the streets to protest the presidential pardons. "Reconciliation is, of course, a worthy goal, but it cannot be imposed by decree on a society," wrote Human Rights Watch in response to Menem's pardons. "It would be easier to understand the reconciliation rationale if there were any sign that the military is genuinely contrite about its role during the 'dirty war,' and is ready to seek reconciliation with their victims. In fact, the opposite is true: the armed forces view the pardons as a step in the direction of full vindication for their victory in 'defeating subversion.' On the date of his release, [the first president of the military regime, General Jorge Rafael] Videla wrote a public letter to the high command stating that the Army had been wrongly accused and that it deserved an apology and vindication from society."[13]

Similarly, the commissions on the forcibly removed and disappeared in Sri Lanka did not suggest that reconciliation or forgiveness would result from their work; they saw their task as documenting who had disappeared and recommending what families should receive reparations.[14] To suggest individual reconciliation would have been unreasonable, rights advocates say, since not one perpetrator in Sri Lanka had stepped forward to express regret or even acknowledge their responsibility. Instead of suggesting forgiveness, the commissions called for justice in the courts and forwarded the names of the accused to prosecutors for further action.

WHAT DOES RECONCILIATION LOOK LIKE?

Reconciliation implies building or rebuilding relationships today that are not haunted by the conflicts and hatreds of yesterday. Yet how might the progress of reconciliation be gauged? If there is a process of reconciling under way, or if a society has achieved a degree of reconciliation, what would be the signs of such a process or end? In short, what does reconciliation look like? To gauge whether reconciliation is taking root, I would propose three questions.[15]

How is the past dealt with in the public sphere? Is there a lack of bitterness over the past in political and other public relationships? Have past conflicts and past abuses been processed or absorbed in such a way that people can talk about these events—if not easily, then at least in a civil manner—even with former opponents?

What are the relationships between former opponents? Specifically, are relationships based on the present, rather than on the past? A constant reference to past wrongs may be a sign of continued antagonism. Examples are plentiful of long and bitter memories that help to foment new violence or are intentionally used by leaders to create tensions between communities. Newly formed relationships between former opponents may depend on new interests or challenges that result in benefits for all. These binding forces or elements might include economic development or reconstruction projects, family or community ties, or even another war against an outside enemy. The Malvinas/Falklands war temporarily rallied Argentines in support of the armed forces, despite years of abusive military rule. In the United States, World War I was critical to psychologically joining the U.S. North and South, fifty years after the bitter end to the Civil War.

Is there one version of the past, or many? To *reconcile* means not only reestablishing friendly relations, but reconciling contradictory facts or stories, "to make (discordant facts, statements, etc.) consistent, accordant, or compatible with each other."[16] As one set of South African writers has noted, reconciliation "is the facing of unwelcome truths in order to harmonize incommensurable world views so that inevitable and continuing conflicts and differences stand at least within a single universe of comprehensibility."[17] These writers continue, "Reconciliation, in this its rich and meaningful sense, is thus a real closing of the ledger book of the past. A crucial element in that closing is an ending of the divisive cycle of accusation, denial and counter-accusation; not a forgetting of these accusations and counter-accusations, but more a settling of them through a process of evaluation—like the accountant's job of reconciling conflicting claims before closing a ledger book."[18]

In countries where simmering conflict and violence have returned in cycles over many years or generations, a root problem has often been fundamental differences in perceptions of the past; the Palestinian-Israeli conflict and the depth of hatred that has arisen between Serbs and their neighbors are examples. In Latin America, fundamental differences in perception of the cause or justifiability of civil wars or military coups have sometimes prevented any real reconciliation from taking root. In El Salvador, senior military officers continued to deny well-documented events, insisting, for example, that the massacre at El Mozote—proven through an extensive exhumation of human remains — was not a massacre at all, but instead a simple battle between the guerrillas and the army.[19] Where there are still fundamentally different versions or continued denial about such important and painful events, reconciliation may be only superficial.

There is never just one truth: we each carry our own distinct memories, and they sometimes contradict each other; but debunking lies and challenging dishonest denial can go far in allowing a country to settle on one generally accurate version of history. There are some facts that are fundamental enough that broad acceptance of their truth is necessary before real reconciliation can take place.

WHAT FACTORS ENCOURAGE RECONCILIATION?

If the above questions help identify where reconciliation exists or is under way, what specific factors or elements might contribute to its development? This question should be considered from the perspective of victims, as perpetrators are more likely to assume that reconciliation has been achieved before victims feel the same. I would propose the following five elements as favorable, and sometimes necessary, for reconciliation to take root. While truth commissions or other mechanisms to address the wrongs of the past clearly can play a role, as suggested in the guidelines above, such mechanisms are not the only, and perhaps are not even the most important, determinants in facilitating reconciliation. Only a few of the following are directly affected by the work of a truth commission.

An end to the violence or threat of violence. This is seemingly an obvious point, but is sometimes overlooked. A transition to peace or democracy implies that war or overt conflict has ended, but this does not mean that all political violence or the threat of violence has ceased; often it has not. Whether in the form of unrestrained paramilitaries that continued to roam Haiti after the democratic government returned there; the threats and skirmishes on the border of Rwanda between the government of Rwanda and armed Hutus based in Congo; or an unrepentant military or paramilitaries that continue to threaten activists in parts of Latin America, threats of political violence and intimidation sometimes continue long after a formal cease-fire or a signed peace. To the degree that such a threat continues, reconciliation may not take root.

Acknowledgment and reparation. Official recognition of the facts of the past, either by perpetrators themselves or by civilian representatives of the bodies under question (such as a statement by the president upon receipt of a commission's report), can be crucial to the process of societal healing. Such acknowledgment serves to recognize one shared understanding of history and to halt widespread denial by some sectors. Victims often say that they cannot forgive their perpetrators, and have no desire or ability to reconcile, until those who caused them pain acknowledge their acts and, ideally, ask for forgiveness and provide some form of symbolic reparation. To be effective, such acknowledgment should go beyond generalities or implied justifications; a statement from authorities that "errors were made" is not sufficient.

Binding forces. In some circumstances, it may be helpful to encourage projects that bring opposing parties together for joint gain, such as development or reconstruction programs. The degree to which there is contact between former opponents will help determine whether reconciliation develops. In some countries, especially in Latin America, there may not be natural linkages between former opponents, if the conflict was played out along sharp political or class lines. Many conflicts in Africa have been fought between ethnic or regional groups which may not have strong links to later bring the groups back together. In order to encourage reconciliation, the question of how to create or re-create such links should be addressed.

Addressing structural inequalities and material needs. Where gross inequalities are a product of past oppression, reconciliation cannot be considered simply a psychological or emotional process. In South Africa, many have stressed the importance of addressing the economic disadvantages suffered by blacks if there is to be any hope for national unity. The Ugandan scholar Mahmood Mamdani, based at the University of Cape Town in 1997, argued that the South African truth commission should not have focused on victims and perpetrators, but rather should have shone the spotlight on victims and *beneficiaries* of apartheid. In Mamdani's view, "Where the focus is on perpetrators, victims are necessarily defined as the minority of political activists; for the victimhood of the majority to be recognized, the focus has to shift from perpetrators to beneficiaries. The difference is this: whereas the focus on perpetrators fuels the demand for justice as criminal justice, that on beneficiaries shifts the focus to a notion of justice as social justice."[20] The truth commission in South Africa recognized the importance of addressing economic issues in order to win reconciliation, even while arguing that that task fell outside its own mandate. The commission report concludes its chapter on reconciliation by stating that "Reconciliation requires a commitment, especially by those who have benefited and continue to benefit from past discrimination, to the transformation of unjust inequalities and dehumanizing poverty."[21]

Time. Reconciliation rarely takes place quickly. Some countries do not begin to seriously grapple with the weight of their past until many decades have passed. In other countries, initial efforts of a truth commission, reparations, or trials begin a process of healing, but the memory of the pain and injury continues to haunt future generations and demand attention for years to come. In the end, societal reconciliation will depend on factors and dynamics that cannot always be predicted or controlled.

RECOMMENDING REFORMS AND OTHER FOLLOW-UP MEASURES

It is difficult for a commission to advance reconciliation because its development so depends on the interest, will, and participation of the greater society, sometimes including perpetrators themselves. Likewise, it is difficult to promote serious policy or institutional reforms because such developments are so dependent on the will of the political leadership and, often, armed forces heads. Despite the serious difficulties in doing so, past truth commissions have made some important contributions in this area.

For example, if you were arrested in El Salvador before the mid-1990s, any confession you offered could be used against you in a trial—including any confession that might have been forced out of you through torture while in detention. Rights advocates have long insisted that the use of such "extrajudicial confession" is problematic, since it can encourage abusive interrogation and because there is often no recourse to retract a forced confession. Yet in El Salvador, the use of such confessions was common.

Furthermore, if you were a Salvadoran judge or lawyer, you depended entirely on the good graces of the Supreme Court, and particularly the president of the Supreme Court, to obtain and retain your position or your authorization to practice law. The Supreme Court was well known for its political bias, actively preventing any investigation into abuses by government forces. The president of the Supreme Court, Mauricio Gutiérrez Castro, was especially notorious for his unabashed progovernment stance and his judicial bullying. The Supreme Court controlled virtually the entire judicial system, and thus few judges or lawyers were able or willing to take a position that challenged the Supreme Court's rightist stance.

In 1997 extrajudicial confessions were invalidated through a constitutional amendment. Torturing suspects to force them to confess and then using that confession against them in court was no longer allowed. In addition, the structure of appointment and review of judges was overhauled: an independent Council of the Judiciary took over the oversight and removal of judges, and functioned under a new broad and democratic system for the election of judges. A number of other reforms of the judicial system were also put in place, such as a reduction in the period of judicial detention and allowing for the indemnification of victims of judicial mistakes. A new Criminal Procedures Code was passed in late 1996 to better protect the procedural rights of defendants and victims.[22]

These reforms were a direct outcome of recommendations made by the El Salvador truth commission, although they did not come easily. According to its terms of reference, the recommendations of the truth commission were mandatory, but the Salvadoran legislature balked on many of the proposed reforms and it took three years of internal debate, deadlock, international pressure, and finally mediation by a senior UN representative sent from New York for a compromise agreement that would put in place many of the suggested judicial reforms.[23] Conservative legislators blocked some of the changes, such as outlawing extrajudicial confessions, because they believed that such confessions were an important tool in fighting rising crime. The final agreement allows for such confessions to be admissible in court only if taken in the presence of a lawyer.

In the years after the truth commission's report was released, the UN paid close attention to the commission's recommendations, applying pressure for their implementation. The UN Mission in El Salvador held monthly meetings with representatives of the two parties to the peace accords (the government and the former guerrillas) to review which truth commission recommendations had been put in place and to push for the implementation of those that were outstanding. The UN secretary-general's office in New York analyzed the recommendations closely, releasing a detailed report on what institution was responsible for which specific recommendation, with further reports that periodically noted which recommendations had been fully implemented.

According to Jeff Thale, a researcher on El Salvador for the Washington Office on Latin America, the new Criminal Procedures Code, which contains many of these basic reforms, "wouldn't have happened without the truth commission's recommendations. It was the truth commission's calling for these judicial reforms which gave the UN the mandate to push for them."[24] Many of these reforms had been suggested before by non-governmental organizations or foreign governments with human rights interests, but the truth commission report focused attention and pressure on them. Unfortunately, however, despite the mandatory nature of these recommendations, many others that were outlined in the report still have not been implemented. U.S. scholar and rights advocate Margaret Popkin, who has watched El Salvador closely, notes that "Unquestionably, more effort has been made to implement the structural and institutional reforms proposed than to implement measures intended to impose administrative sanctions or ban individuals named in the report, or measures intended to contribute to national reconciliation."[25]

While some of the earlier truth commission reports provided only very brief and general recommendations, those in more recent years have been much more extensive, usually including a full and detailed chapter outlining specific reforms across many sectors of government and public life. The El Salvador report's recommendations ran for fifteen pages, South Africa's forty-five pages, and Chile's over fifty-five pages. A commission may gather input from a broad array of advocates and legal scholars in preparing its recommendations, or even hold public sessions seeking discussion and input from interested observers. The Guatemalan commission, for example, invited interested persons to attend a public meeting, and over four hundred people showed up — including legislators and key civil society leaders from across the political spectrum — and together they drafted long lists of proposed policy recommendations.

Commission reports have recommended specific reforms in the judiciary, armed forces, and political sector; the prosecution of perpetrators or their removal from active military or police duty; reparations for victims; further investigation into matters not fully covered by the current commission; measures to instill a human rights culture in society, including through human rights education; and a national commitment to standards of international human rights norms through ratifying international rights treaties. (See chart 5 in appendix 1 for examples of recommendations from past commissions.) Some commissions have recommended reforms so basic that they serve as sharp reminders of how weak the country's political and human rights foundations are. For example, the report of the 1986 Ugandan commission, completed in 1995, recommends that the new constitution provide for a "system of peaceful change of Presidents and governments through regular elections"; that there be a "prohibition of over-staying by Presidents in office after their terms have expired"; and that a system of checks and balances should be set up between different branches of government.[26]

Yet to date only the El Salvador commission's recommendations have been considered mandatory. The legislation creating a Truth and Reconciliation Commission in Sierra Leone, passed into law in February 2000, similarly commits the goverment to implementing the commission's recommendations, stating that "The Government shall faithfully and timeously implement the recommendations of the report that are directed at state bodies and encourage or facilitate the implementation of any recommendations that may be directed to others."[27] Most commissions have only been able to make suggestions of changes needed, with the hope that the momentum of the political transition and the good will of the new democratic leadership would prompt the president or legislature to institute the suggested reforms. Many truth commission recommendations have therefore not been fully implemented, and in some countries, such as in Haiti, they have never been seriously taken up for consideration by policymakers. Yet recommendations of a state-sanctioned commission tend to carry more weight than those from private advocacy organizations, and thus they can help to create pressure points around the most urgent reforms. If done well, a truth commission's recommendations can serve as a road map for advocacy groups and foreign governments or funding agencies to push for change.

A number of commissions have recommended that a follow-up body be created to oversee the implementation of their recommendations. In Chile, a National Corporation for Reparation and Reconciliation was suggested, and legislation was then enacted to create the corporation as "a decentralized public service subject to supervision of the President. . . . The object thereof shall be the coordination, execution and promotion of the actions necessary for complying with the recommendations contained in the Report of the Truth and Reconciliation National Commission."[28] In addition to defining the mandate of the corporation, the law also defines the financial reparations and other benefits to be provided to victims and their families. The two-year mandate of the corporation (later extended to three years) included searching for remains of the disappeared, resolving cases not closed by the commission, organizing the commission's files, and implementing specified reparations.

To date, there has been no thorough review of how many of the hundreds of recommendations by truth commissions have been put in place. Many of these recommendations require legislative action, or even constitutional reform, while others require only presidential initiative or administrative changes. Even years later, some of these items are still under consideration in some countries, or continue to be advocated by nongovernmental activists. It is clear, however, that the record of implementation of truth commission recommendations has been among the weakest aspects of these commissions to date. With no power of enforcement, and often with no official body to watch over and promote the recommendations of a truth commission after it submits its report and closes down, many countries have seen a fine list of recommended reforms receive very little governmental attention. There may be ways to improve this record in the future. The legislation for the Truth and Reconciliation Commission in Sierra Leone, for example, in addition to committing the government to implementation of its final recommendations, calls for the creation of a follow-up committee to track their implementation, and requires the government and the follow-up committee to make public quarterly reports on the progress made.

e l e v e n

Reparations for
State Crimes

F ollowing a period of widespread abuses, victims and survivors often
suffer a range of physical and psychological injuries and sometimes live
under extreme economic conditions as a result of the loss of the breadwinner in the family, the destruction of property, or their physical inability to
work. Many victims are in need of basic medical assistance as a result of the
abuses suffered, such as brutal torture that has left them permanently
scarred or handicapped, but many are unable to pay for even minimal care.

Because most of these abuses were by state forces, in the majority of circumstances, many victims would certainly win substantial awards from the
state if they had the means to bring a case to court and the evidence to back
up their claim; but most victims have neither the solid evidence necessary
nor the legal resources to bring such a case, and in some countries a general
amnesty blocks not only criminal prosecution but also civil claims. Thus,
one the clearest demands to the government following a period of widespread abuses is often for reparations from the state to cover some of the
basic needs of victims. While no amount of money will make up for the
loss of a loved one, even a relatively modest payment can be critical to those
living in poverty and can serve an important psychological role of acknowledging wrongs and providing an official, symbolic apology.

International law clearly establishes an obligation on the part of the state
to provide redress for abuses by state forces. As stipulated in many founda-
tional human rights documents, including regional and international

human rights treaties, and confirmed in decisions put forward by international courts, states must provide reparations to victims of human rights violations.[1] This may take many forms that go beyond the payment of cash to the injured. *Reparations* is a general term that encompasses a variety of types of redress, including *restitution, compensation, rehabilitation, satisfaction,* and *guarantees of nonrepetition*. Restitution aims to reestablish to the extent possible the situation that existed before the violation took place; compensation relates to any economically assessable damage resulting from the violations; rehabilitation includes legal, medical, psychological and other care; while satisfaction and guarantees of nonrepetition relate to measures to acknowledge the violations and prevent their recurrence in the future. Usually, a mix of these types of redress is appropriate.

Many governments will find it impossible to provide direct financial compensation to each and every survivor at anything close to a level that would be proportional to the loss suffered, especially where a family member was killed or disappeared. In very poor states, or where hundreds of thousands of persons were killed or disappeared, substantial individualized monetary compensation may simply not be feasible, even if such compensation is well deserved and such claims in a court of law would be legally sound. Some states have considered instituting some form of reparations tax, or "wealth tax," as South Africans called it when they looked at the idea, but the vast majority of reparations policies to date (and all those considered here) have not relied on any special tax to cover the expense. There is a sad irony, of course, that a newly democratized state must pay for the abusive policies of the prior government, the financial burden ultimately carried by the population as a whole, while the individual perpetrators are not obliged to cover these costs, even if they enriched themselves in the course of their rule (except, of course, in response to suits against individual perpetrators, where not prohibited by an amnesty).

As some victims have strongly argued, establishing the truth about rights violations, offering an apology, and respecting the memory of victims through memorials or other official forms of acknowledgment are one aspect of reparation, and thus the work of a truth commission can be an important piece of a full reparations package. Furthermore, commissions' recommendations to reform state institutions, and their efforts to provide a healing environment for victims who provide testimony, are also important reparatory elements. But many needs of victims may also be partly dependent on monetary payment, especially when medical treatment of injuries is required.

Truth commission staff usually hear many pleas for compensation in the course of taking testimony, and can often see how dire the situation of victims is. Indeed, many victims and survivors approach a commission with the hope that the commission itself will grant them some form of reparation for their suffering. Especially for the very poor, the possibility of receiving financial assistance seems to be a primary reason to come forward to give testimony. Interviews with staff members of many past commissions, and with victims who have given testimony, show that these expectations are often very high, even when a commission tries to be clear that it holds no power to grant awards for damages by the state. After hearing the pleas of so many victims and survivors and seeing the sometimes desperate needs of many deponents, most truth commissions have made strong recommendations that a reparations program be put in place.

Because truth commissions usually produce a list of victims, its records are an obvious source on which to build a reparations program, and in a few cases, such as in Chile and Argentina, significant reparations programs have relied directly on the records of the commission. However, a commission usually documents only a small portion of the total number of victims, and rarely has the resources to corroborate all of the victim statements that it receives. Thus, in most circumstances a truth commission is not in a good position to provide a final list of recommended recipients, nor to outline the specifics of a reparations program. It can better make general recommendations and an overall assessment of need, which can serve as the beginning point for the development of a substantial reparations program to follow. The experiences of a number of countries outlined below show the breadth and variety of reparations programs around the world that depended in part on information from prior truth commissions.

CHILE: SUBSTANTIAL REPARATIONS TO A LIMITED POOL OF VICTIMS

As of 1997, 4,886 Chileans received a check in the mail every month from the government, and most would continue to receive monthly checks for the rest of their lives, as part of the government's "pension plan" for family members of those killed or disappeared under the military dictatorship. The size of the check depends on how many immediate family members are alive: sole survivors receive the equivalent of $345 per month; if there is a surviving spouse, parent, child, and parent of the victim's children, the total monthly allotment split between them will total $482 or more per month. In addition, family members of those killed and disappeared receive generous educational and health benefits and a waiver of mandatory military service. Victims' children receive full coverage of all university or professional education, up to age thirty-five, and an additional monthly stipend to cover the costs of living and school supplies. The total cost to the state for the full reparations program, in the years when the greatest number of survivors were still alive and elegible, was close to $16 million each year.[2] (See chart 6 in appendix 1 for a detailed outline of these reparations.)

This reparations pension program is a direct result of the National Commission on Truth and Reconciliation in Chile, which concluded its report with recommendations for symbolic and financial reparations. A follow-up body, the National Corporation for Reparation and Reconciliation, was put in place to investigate the cases it was not able to close and to implement the commission's recommendations, including reparations.[3] The victims listed in the truth commission final report was established as the official list of beneficiaries, in addition to any further persons determined to be victims through the investigations of the follow-up body.

The reparations payments are slightly higher than the monthly minimum wage in Chile, and some Chileans clearly depend on them for daily survival. For the more wealthy, the checks are not a significant addition to their income but still seen as very important for their symbolic value. "Every time a check arrives, it's a recognition of the crime," the daughter of one victim told me. "After so many years of denial, month by month, it's a recognition that we were right."[4]

Another survivor, Carla Pellegrin Friedman, lost her brother to the violence of the Chilean army. He took up arms against the regime of Augusto Pinochet in 1988, but his group didn't get far before he was captured, tortured, and summarily killed. For her, she told me, the monthly checks from the government represented a "recognition from the state of its own guilt" in killing her brother. Like others, she tried to identify who was responsible for the death through court action, but the amnesty law was applied and the case was closed before determining who was responsible. "Our family has only three things," she told me: "A check that arrives every month, my brother's name in the Rettig truth commission report, and his name on the wall of the memorial at the national cemetery."[5]

The reparations program in Chile is limited, however, by the fact that survivors of torture or illegal imprisonment — the bulk of the victims in Chile — are not covered. The program is constrained by the same definitional boundaries that were given to the truth commission; just as the commission could not investigate individual cases of torture or include survivors of torture in its list of victims, the reparations program provides almost no assistance to such persons. Only the families of those killed and disappeared are eligible to receive pension payments, education benefits, full medical coverage, and a waiver of mandatory military service. The only assistance provided for torture survivors is free access to a state medical program that provides social services, psychological counseling, and medical care, although this program is not well known, is little used by torture survivors, and has received mixed reviews for its quality of care.[6]

Those who staffed the follow-up commission implementing the reparations could see the injustice in excluding torture victims from the reparations program. The chief of staff of the Corporation for Reparation and Reconciliation, Andrés Domínguez Vial, told me that "One woman came into my office and sat down to say, 'The tragedy of my family is that they didn't kill my father. He's destroyed, but they allowed him to live. It would have been better if they had killed him.' Her father is completely destroyed, but her family gets no reparations."[7] Other staff described distraught visitors to the office whose family members had been seriously injured or physically handicapped and in dire need of assistance, such as one person who had been blinded in political violence under the military dictatorship. But there is no recourse for such persons except a referral to the limited state-run medical clinic, or to nongovernmental organizations who try to assist such survivors.

ARGENTINA: A MORE INCLUSIVE PROGRAM

In a small back room on the second floor of the aging building that houses the governmental Human Rights Office in downtown Buenos Aires, there are twelve four-drawer filing cabinets crowded along the walls, a small table in the middle, and a few shelves lined with human rights reports to one side. Eleven of those file cabinets contain the complete collection of the files from the Argentine National Commission on the Disappeared: one file for each of the 8,960 people that the commission reported had disappeared under the military regime. In most of these files, there are just two or three pieces of paper, which constitute the original statement of the victim's family. Whereas the Chilean commission investigated each case in depth, and some of its case files grew to an inch or two thick, the Argentine commission only took testimony from family members or friends of the disappeared, as well as from those who survived "temporary disappearance" and who witnessed others imprisoned. The commission then compiled its victims list based only on this testimony. It generally did not investigate individual cases, except to try to find disappeared persons who might still be alive. Moreover, many of these files, about one-third of the total, only contain information given to the commission from nongovernmental organizations—information based on reports made to these organizations at the time of the disappearances but never repeated directly to the commission.[8]

These 8,960 files serve as the informational heart of the reparations program set up to reach families of the disappeared. The relatives of anyone listed as disappeared by the commission can easily claim reparation, although these cases were never formally corroborated. Since there was no expectation at the time that the commission's work would lead to financial reparations, there is little concern that these files contain false claims. Rather than a monthly pension, as in Chile, family members of the disappeared in Argentina are entitled to receive a lump sum of $220,000, paid in government bonds and distributed among surviving family members.[9]

The twelfth file cabinet in this back room holds records of new cases collected by this governmental Human Rights Office, cases that were never included in the commission's count of the disappeared. The day I visited, I found several elderly men and women sitting in the reception area of the office, waiting to give statements in order to begin the process of claiming reparation. A well-worn copy of the *Nunca Más* appendix, which lists each of the 8,960 cases recorded by the commission, lay on the reception counter; the first question asked to visitors is whether their case was listed by the commission. Newly reported cases must be corroborated either through a mention in the press or a report to a national or international human rights body at the time, or evidence that a habeas corpus petition had been submitted to the courts when the person disappeared in an attempt to establish the person's whereabouts or gain their freedom.

The reparations law for families of the disappeared was not put in place in Argentina until 1994, ten years after the truth commission finished its report, and it was implemented under the administration of the same president, Carlos Menem, who had pardoned the convicted military officers and tried to quiet any further discussion about crimes of the past. There had not been great public demand for reparations, since survivors' priorities were in finding the bodies, establishing the full truth, and prosecuting the guilty, and the idea of being paid for the loss of loved ones was distasteful to some. So it is curious that such a significant reparations program was crafted so many years later.

The reparations program was apparently prompted in part by cases brought to the Inter-American Commission of Human Rights, an organ of the Organization of American States, by a number of former political prisoners demanding compensation for their time in jail. After three years of litigation before the Inter-American Commission, in 1991 the Argentine government reached a friendly settlement with the petitioners.[10] For each day in prison, each petitioner was paid the equivalent of the daily salary of the highest paid Argentine civil servant: $74.00 per day, $2,200 per month, $26,400 per year, up to a maximum of $220,000 (equal to 100 months at this salary). These petitioners were awarded their compensation through executive decree, but the Argentine Congress soon passed a law extending the same reparations to all former political prisoners.[11]

Unique to Argentina, this reparations program was later extended to those forced into exile after arrest — those who, after a period of imprisonment, were literally taken to the airport, put on a plane, and told not to return.[12] For each day in forced exile, these people received the same daily rate as those imprisoned. Juan Méndez, a professor at Notre Dame School of Law and former executive director of the Inter-American Institute of Human Rights, is among those who received compensation for forced exile, in addition to his time in prison. He notes that not everyone who was exiled could claim compensation, saying, "Bear in mind that when we talk about forced exile we refer to a very precise legal category: those of us who were held in administrative detention under the state of siege and allowed at some point to go into exile rather than remain in prison. My guess is that the number is about 1,000 total. Many others were released in Argentina and, if they later went into exile, the government does not pay for that period of exile, since they were nominally free to return. It also does not cover the other, much more frequent form of exile: going abroad a step or two ahead of those bent on arresting, killing or disappearing you."[13]

Three years later, in 1994, in recognition of the unfairness of providing monetary compensation to those jailed but not to the families of the disappeared — and in the face of national court decisions awarding sums of $250,000 to $3 million in "moral damages" to families of the disappeared[14]— the Argentine Congress passed a law which extended reparations to the disappeared and killed.[15] In 1998, the government of Argentina committed to spending up to $3 billion to cover the projected costs of these reparations programs.

For many in Argentina, more important than monetary compensation was the creation of a new legal status of "forcibly disappeared."[16] This new legal category satisfied a number of key demands of surviving families. "Forcibly disappeared" is considered the legal equivalent of death for purposes of civil matters, allowing families to process wills, distribute inheritance, close a disappeared person's estate, and other matters, but it stops short of declaring the person dead. Indeed, the legislation officially holds open the possibility of the person's reappearance—a measure insisted upon by the surviving families. Prior to 1994, in order to process the person's will, sell her (or his) apartment, and close her bank account, a family was forced to declare that the person was "presumed dead," a legal mechanism in Argentine law for those whose whereabouts remained unknown for a long period of time. Such a declaration, which provided no recognition of state responsibility or military involvement, was a psychological and political compromise that many families were unwilling to make (although some were forced to, out of economic necessity).[17] The new law allowing families to obtain a "certificate of forced disappearance" came to be known as the "law on historical sincerity." Argentina was the first state to create this new legal status; other states have since followed suit.

In the process of implementing the reparations laws in Argentina, the government human rights office has been able to document many more cases and a wider array of victims than the truth commission could. The commission was tasked only to document the "disappeared" victims, generally excluding those who were known to be killed outright or those who died in detention and whose bodies were later found and identified. It also did not attempt to count those who survived detention and torture. The 8,960 documented by the commission were those kidnapped by the military or police and never seen again, either dead or alive. In the process of implementing the state reparations programs, the Human Rights Office of the Ministry of Interior began the first full count of the number of non-combatants killed under the military regime (in addition to those disappeared), which they estimated to be in the thousands.[18]

Reparations for families of the disappeared is far more controversial in Argentina than in Chile. In the political maelstrom that continues around the disappeared in Argentina over fifteen years after the end of military rule, one group representing victims' families has denounced state reparations as "blood money," and its members refuse to accept it. "Life doesn't have a price. The reparations only buys your conscience and sells your blood. The president is likely to say to us, 'You can't talk, we paid you,'" Mercedes Meroño of the Mothers of the Plaza de Mayo told me when I visited the organization's office in downtown Buenos Aires. "You can't put a price on life. Some things don't have a price, especially dignity."[19] Yet with time, the majority of families of the disappeared have accepted the reparations, as have former political prisoners.

ELSEWHERE: MORE LIMITED PROGRAMS

Many other truth commissions have recommended financial reparations for victims, and some have resulted in limited programs. The South African truth commission left detailed recommendations for a reparations program, including financial, symbolic, and community or development recommendations. During the course of their work, the commission met with government representatives to get a provisional agreement in support of the commission's proposal, requiring over $600 million in direct financial reparations to over 25,000 victims. With a verbal commitment from the government, the commission thus announced its recommended reparations policy publicly, making clear that only those victims who were on the commission's list would be eligible to take part in the reparations program. The result was a significant increase in numbers of testimonies in some regions (especially in KwaZulu Natal). The commission's proposal was that each victim, or family of those killed, would receive approximately $3,500 each year for six consecutive years; a slightly higher amount would be given to families with many dependents or those in rural areas, where services are more expensive. There was also a hope that monies would be made available during the course of the commission's work for urgent interim reparations, to reach those who came to the commission with pressing medical or other needs. But the first allocation for reparations that was made into the newly created President's Fund at the Ministry of Justice was not until 1998, just months before the commission finished its final report, and the amount allocated was only $16 million (100 million Rand), far short of the commission's recommendation. The government indicated a plan to allocate a further 200 million Rand ($33 million) in the second year and 300 million Rand in the third year of the program. In addition, the governments of Denmark, Switzerland, and the Netherlands each contributed between $150,000 and $250,000 into the President's Fund for reparations.

The new President's Fund was staffed by only three people, and much of the administrative documentation of victims was done by the commission itself. Even after the commission's report was published in 1998, the commission's Reparation and Rehabilitation Committee added staff in order to process reparations claims (as noted earlier, the overall commission continued to operate primarily in order to process outstanding amnesty claims). Each victim who had given a statement to the commission had to be located once again to fill in reparations forms; since many did not have mailing addresses, the commission hired field workers to find each deponent and assist them in filling out the necessary forms. In order to make payments directly into bank accounts, the commission also assisted the many recipients who didn't have them in opening accounts. After a year, some 2,500 payments ranging from 2,000 to 6,000 Rand ($330 to $1,000) had been made in the form of interim reparations, with the hope that further reparation payments to each recipient would follow. It was expected that a total of $100 million Rand ($16 million) would be expended on interim payments alone.[20] However, despite the government's initial commitments, significant additional allocations for reparations did not look likely. This was a point of considerable frustration and disappointment to victims and human rights groups in South Africa, and they continued to try to pressure the government for further attention to this issue into the year 2000.

The reparations question was also of central concern to the Haitian commission, since the majority of victims who came to the commission expected or hoped for some form of assistance, many of them living in abject poverty, some injured and unable to work. The commission's report reflects these concerns, making a strong recommendation for the creation of a follow-up "reparations commission" to determine the "legal, moral, and material obligations" due to victims, and suggesting that funds come from the state, from national and international private donations, and from voluntary contributions of United Nations member states.[21] This recommendation was never seriously taken up by the Haitian government, however, nor have foreign governments or their aid agencies shown much interest. Given the country's extreme poverty, the resource-strapped government, and the basic need for reform and stability in the political sphere, it is very unlikely that this recommendation will be given further attention.

The El Salvador truth commission report also called for the creation of a special fund, administered by "an autonomous body with the necessary legal and administrative powers to award appropriate material compensation to the victims of violence in the shortest time possible," and it recommended that 1 percent of all international assistance to El Salvador be set aside for such a fund.[22] Neither the Salvadoran government nor the international community was enthusiastic about this proposal, however, and the fund was never created. No serious discussions have since taken place around reparations for victims of the abuses that ran rampant during that country's twelve-year war.

Of course, a truth commission is not required for a reparations program to be put in place, nor to establish an authoritative list of victims or beneficiaries. There are important examples of compensation programs instituted after widespread government abuses that have been created through national legislation and independently administered, with no connection to a truth-seeking commission.[23] Germany has instituted the most far-reaching and comprehensive reparations programs to date, a package of domestic legislation and international agreements with foreign states to compensate victims of Nazi crimes. In the past fifty years, over $60 billion has been paid by the German state in cash payments to victims and to families of those killed.[24] Over fifteen years after the end of military rule in Brazil, the Brazilian government set up a reparations commission to provide approximately $100,000 to each of some 135 disappeared persons' families in Brazil.[25] The U.S. government also paid reparations to Japanese-Americans who were interned in camps during World War II, although this program was not put in place until over four decades later, and then paid only directly to survivors who were still alive.[26] Other more limited reparations programs have been put in place in a number of other countries.[27]

THE DIFFICULTIES OF DESIGNING AND IMPLEMENTING A REPARATIONS PROGRAM

Whether designed by a commission or by government or legislative representatives, those who set out to craft a fair program of reparations to victims of political violence usually confront the same set of difficult constraints and dilemmas. The first challenge is in designing a fair and inclusive program. Should cash or a package of services be offered to those who suffered, or a mix of both? How is it possible to quantify the loss of a loved one, or a severe physical injury or handicap, with monetary compensation? Should all victims receive equal compensation, even if some clearly suffered more? If different benefit levels are not established, how can it be fair that a victim who suffered one day of torture receive the same benefit as someone who was jailed and tortured for many years, or a family who lost a loved one? Yet if there are distinctions made between victims, it quickly becomes difficult to categorize degrees of suffering or loss. Furthermore, is it acceptable to exclude some victims — as in the case of Chile's excluding torture victims from any monetary reparations?

Many who have designed past reparations policies have concluded that it was not possible to distinguish between levels of suffering, although some programs do provide different amounts of compensation according to the number of days imprisoned or whether a serious injury was sustained. In South Africa the state followed the recommendation of the commission that it is more cost effective to provide direct cash payments to victims and let them determine what their needs are — be they medical, educational, or other basic services, a tombstone for the person killed, or covering daily living costs — rather than predetermining and parceling out services by the state. The only adjustment made in South Africa, as noted earlier in this chapter, was an increased payment for those with a greater number of dependents or for those who lived in rural areas, where services are more expensive.

The second set of difficulties is in the implementation and administration of a reparations program. An intensely individualized approach requires direct contact with thousands of victims or survivors and some system of corroborating claims. Where truth commissions have been given the responsibility of establishing the list of beneficiaries, as they were in South Africa and Chile, they have had to individually corroborate each victim statement, which is enormously time consuming and, at least in the case of South Africa, distracted the commission's attention from broader investigations into patterns of crimes and responsibility and special investigations into key events. When the South African commission undertook the administrative processing of claims, it required another round of even more intense and individualized case-specific work. These intensive procedures were only possible because the commission's operations were extended for close to two years following the submission of its report. In Argentina, the Human Rights Office of the Ministry of the Interior undertook this administration, while in Chile the follow-up commission to the truth commission took on the task. In the end, some government body must dedicate significant time and resources to administering an individualized reparations program. Given the amount of time and personnel that are necessary to corroborate and administer claims, and because the reparations program should be open to those who do not testify to the truth commission, the implementation of a reparations program should not be done by a truth commission itself.

Furthermore, the truth-seeking function of a commission may be skewed if the commission's mandate includes the job of awarding or recommending reparations to those who come forward to provide testimony, or if there is a direct relationship between the commission's victims list and reparation recipients. The possibility of money following from testimony could provide an incentive for people to give false statements, and thus increases the commission's burden of verifying every statement before the information is used to make general conclusions about past events. The best path to follow is, therefore, for a truth commission to provide general recommendations for a reparations program, and perhaps a general assessment of need, but to leave the details and implementation of a program to a post–truth commission body, allowing the commission to concentrate its time on broader investigations and conclusions.

Ultimately, establishing a broad reparations program will depend on the political interest in formally acknowledging and apologizing for past state crimes, and on a commitment from the state toward repairing its wrongs. Certainly not all reparations need be monetary. Where resources are very limited or where the number of victims is very large, symbolic or community-oriented reparations can be put in place, such as memorials, days of remembrance, or schools or community centers built in the name of victims or in the memory of a major massacre. Such measures may serve an important role in contributing to victims' psychological healing. However, for those left destitute from the loss of a breadwinner in the family, or left emotionally or physically shattered, financial reparation, basic medical benefits, and other support services will be necessary in order to begin to repair the damage.

Leaving the Past Alone

W hy is it that some countries emerge from terrible civil wars or massive state violence and show no interest in digging into the details of their recent past? After watching victims and family members in Argentina, El Salvador, Sri Lanka, South Africa, and so many other countries demand the full truth, one might assume that a full and detailed accounting is a universal good, a universal desire.

Indeed, there is an emerging sentiment in some international advocacy circles that official truth-seeking should always be recommended for countries emerging from authoritarian rule. Policy statements of both Amnesty International and Human Rights Watch, two of the largest international human rights groups, call for investigation into the truth about gross violations of human rights wherever such violations have taken place.[1] Many cite emerging international law to back the "right to the truth" and therefore a government obligation to investigate. Some of these positions are unbending. The senior legal counsel at Human Rights Watch, Wilder Tayler, argues that as a matter of principle, this international obligation to investigate the truth allows no case-by-case exceptions.[2] Amnesty International's position on accountability stresses three principles: the need to uncover the truth, the need to restore the honor and reputation of the victims, and the need to individualize the guilt and bring perpetrators to justice. However, Amnesty International's legal director explained, aspects of this policy will be emphasized or deemphasized in response to the expressed desires and needs of victims in any specific situation.[3]

Likewise, international "principles to combat impunity" proposed in 1997 by United Nations Special Rapporteur Louis Joinet includes a recommendation for a commission of inquiry to establish the truth about the past in a transitional country. "Full and effective exercise of the right to the truth is essential to avoid any recurrence of [gross violations of human rights] in the future," these recommendations state.[4] The document continues, "A people's knowledge of the history of their oppression is part of their heritage and, as such, shall be preserved by appropriate measures in fulfillment of the State's duty to remember. Such measures shall be aimed at preserving the collective memory from extinction and, in particular, at guarding against the development of revisionist and negationist arguments."[5] These various policy recommendations are founded on a desire to combat impunity, build a culture of accountability, and show full respect for victims. In the majority of countries and transitional circumstances, these recommendations are appropriate and indeed helpful in pressuring intransigent authorities who may prefer to hide their crimes. Rapporteur Louis Joinet's focus is in part the preservation of official documentation, which is critically important in any society, with or without a truth-seeking body.

Indeed, there are some examples around the world that seem to confirm the danger of allowing a country or its government the option of simply ignoring the legacy of past state crimes. African rights expert Richard Carver argues persuasively that several countries in Africa have suffered from such a policy, and that there have been clear negative long-term consequences from failing to come to terms with the past. For example, in Malawi, some of the repressive patterns of the past, such as laws allowing censorship, have received support from those who used to oppose them under the old regime. If these laws and the effects that they have "were properly exposed to public view, the repressive tendencies would still be there, but there would be greater public will to resist them," says Carver. He suggests that perhaps there should always be some kind of truth-telling process, but not necessarily always a truth commission; there are, of course, a range of other ways to address and document the past, ranging from historical and academic studies, to theater, to documentation projects of nongovernmental organizations.[6]

Yet there may be cases in which a "truth always" recommendation is not appropriate, or at least in which a recommendation for a formal and official truth-telling project such as a truth commission might be inappropriate. There is little recognition in such blanket recommendations that official truth-seeking is inherently different from other transitional accountability mechanisms. Truth can be painful—to the victims themselves, among others. Digging into the details of past conflicts can be dangerous and destabilizing, even more so than trials, and may disrupt fragile relationships in local communities recently returned to peace. Truth inquiries usually require the active involvement and emotional investment of victims, who are usually asked to testify in the thousands, and demand broad national involvement and significant resources at a point of transition when many urgent priorities may demand attention. None of these are necessarily reasons not to have a truth commission or not to push a government to confront its crimes, but they do point to reasons beyond politics to explain why there may be resistance to a formal process of truth-telling.

I agree that there is a "right to truth" that is articulated in international conventions and has been confirmed by international courts. However, should a society's right to know the truth be turned into an unbending obligation? That is, if those persons most directly affected, the victims themselves, are not interested or not yet prepared to revisit these horrors, should they be obligated to do so? Could there sometimes be aspects of a conflict, a transition, or a people's culture and history that would make such truth-seeking unattractive and unhelpful? I will look at two cases, those of Mozambique and Cambodia, in an attempt to respond to these questions. Both of these countries have seen horrific political violence in recent decades, but in both countries and for different reasons there was a rejection of the idea of broad-scale truth-seeking during their respective political transitions. When I visited Mozambique, I spoke with people across the political spectrum, including victims, academics, government officials and others, and heard eloquent statements that, in sum, said, 'No, we do not want to reenter into this morass of conflict, hatred, and pain. We want to focus on the future. For now, the past is too much part of the present for us to examine its details. For now, we prefer silence over confrontation, over renewed pain. While we cannot forget, we would like to pretend that we can.' Likewise, in Cambodia, while the dynamics around these questions play out differently, there has also been resistance to digging up old horrors.[7]

What would account for this lack of desire to formally establish the truth? Four elements seem to be common in such countries:

- *Fear of negative consequences:* a perception that violence would increase, war could return, or that the current violence or war would not end, if old crimes were revisited.

- *Lack of political interest:* little or no interest by the political leadership in truth-seeking and a lack of significant nongovernmental actors pushing them to do so.
- *Other urgent priorities:* extensive destruction resulting from the war or violence, widespread popular sentiment to focus on survival and rebuilding, and a lack of basic institutional structures that could support a truth-seeking process.
- *Alternative mechanisms or preferences:* indigenous national characteristics may make truth-seeking unnecessary or undesirable, such as unofficial community-based mechanisms that respond to the recent violence or a culture that eschews confronting conflict directly.

The desire for truth-seeking may also be a function of time, as institutions are strengthened and as the tensions that might spark conflict are eased. A country might wait years or even decades before it is able to confront and honestly record some events. This is not to dispute the benefits of undertaking investigations at the moment of transition, as is most common. But in some circumstances this may not be possible or may not fit the needs of a country or its victims.

The establishment and effective operation of a truth commission sometimes requires the encouragement and oversight of the international community, especially to combat resistance from former perpetrators who may still hold power. But ultimately, the decision whether or not to institute broad truth-seeking should be made by the country itself. The question of how the international community can and should judge national interests, and when and how to support local calls for a truth commission, is addressed further below. First, the case of Mozambique, and then Cambodia, suggest that a country may legitimately choose to forgo official truth-seeking at the time of transition.

MOZAMBIQUE: ALTERNATIVE MEANS OF CONFRONTING THE PAST

South Africa's northeastern neighbor, Mozambique, reached a negotiated peace after years of fighting at about the same time that apartheid ended in South Africa. The peace agreement in 1992 ended sixteen years of war and led to national elections in 1994.[8] As in South Africa, "reconciliation" was a central focus of the transition and of the new political order. But reconciliation was understood very differently in these two countries. If in South Africa there was a widely accepted position, at least at the beginning of its truth commission's operations, that "the more truth, the more we talk about the past, then the more reconciliation," in Mozambique the accepted, though largely unstated, belief was "the less we dwell on the past, the more likely reconciliation will be." There has been almost no focus in Mozambique on accountability for past crimes. In a country where some one million civilians were killed, thousands tortured, and some of the most gruesome acts of mutilation and barbarism documented, there have been virtually no calls on the national level for justice, accountability, punishment, or banishment from public office — which is where many of those responsible for orchestrating past crimes now sit, in Parliament or in the armed forces.

A general amnesty for "crimes against the state" was passed by the Mozambique Parliament ten days after the peace accord was signed in 1992, although many senior members of government and the opposition didn't seem to know there was an amnesty even several years after the fact.[9] It is not a point of reference or a point of discussion; the thought of prosecuting individuals for past atrocities was never seriously considered. Fair trials in Mozambique would be very difficult. Alex Vines, the Human Rights Watch expert on Mozambique, explains that the conflict there was "tremendously complicated," that it would be extremely difficult to place clear blame on any one individual, and that there are "few firm facts in Mozambique, and documentation about the big fish has been tampered with." As a result, he says, if there had been trials, people could have easily pointed blame on the innocent for personal revenge or economic gain.[10]

Atrocities Too Numerous to Count

Some people say there is no interest in looking at the past in Mozambique because the past is just too horrible. Those who have watched Mozambique over the past twenty years describe it as experiencing one of the most brutal wars the world has seen. Gruesome tactics were used, particularly by the guerrilla forces, known as Renamo (the Portuguese acronym for the Mozambican National Resistance). "From beginning to end, you couldn't count all the terrible things that happened in Mozambique," Ken Wilson, a Ford Foundation program officer and international expert on Mozambique, noted.[11] A journalist once told me that he had tried to make a list of massacres in the country. "You couldn't keep up. It was pages and pages.

Every week you'd hear of another fifty people killed somewhere," he said. Some say the idea of a truth commission is unrealistic because it would be simply impossible to fairly document the totality of what happened.

The violence was "very confusing at the local level, and difficult to understand what was happening," says Ken Wilson. "How on earth would you get anywhere near to understanding what really happened in Mozambique? It was enormously complicated. The nature of war would change dramatically year to year. And who would you hold to account for what took place? On the government side, how do you establish the accountability of soldiers whose names were never recorded and who were never salaried, when the commander was never there, and where there are no records anyway? And many acts were done by quasi-independent bandit groups. . . . It would be inconceivable to work out who did what."

Renamo was founded by Rhodesia in 1977, and upon Rhodesia's independence (becoming Zimbabwe), support for Renamo was taken over by South Africa, with additional support from private right-wing elements in the West who were intent on overthrowing the Marxist government. While the guerrillas gained internal support after some years, the war was fueled from the outside. The objective of South Africa was to destabilize Mozambique (which they saw as a base of operations for the African National Congress and its armed elements, groups that opposed white rule in South Africa) and they thus used Renamo to terrorize the population and destroy the country's economic infrastructure.[12]

Renamo's tactics included abducting children into the guerrilla army and then forcing them to commit atrocities in their own village to prevent their returning home. Renamo often mutilated its victims in order to spread terror, cutting off ears or lips of the living or the dead. The Mozambique government, known as Frelimo (the Mozambique Liberation Front), was also responsible for serious abuses, although not in the number or severity of those of Renamo. Frelimo's practices included interning thousands in brutal "reeducation" camps, and killing traditional leaders when they were seen as a threat. Many who held senior positions in the government at the time now openly acknowledge the errors of party policy and the seriousness of the abuses.

The numbers were enormous, the details horrid. Every single family in Mozambique is said to have been directly affected by the war — family members were killed, abducted, forced to fight, or uprooted from their home. It was not uncommon for siblings to be fighting on opposite sides of the war.[13]

Perhaps the idea of truth-seeking is of little interest because if people started pointing fingers, they would be pointing too close to home. It may be for this same reason that there has been no evidence of retaliation or revenge after the war ended. Roberto Luis, a Mozambican development specialist who works closely with rural communities, put it succinctly: "Who would retaliate against whom? There wasn't one group against another. Families and communities were put against each other. If it was one ethnic or language group against another, then maybe you could see it. But it's hard to think of how retaliation would be mobilized. It was the Browns vs. the Smiths — but then even families were split up. The conflict is so intricate; no revenge factor is possible." If you were caught up with revenge in Mozambique, the sheer size of the problem might have stopped you. "Would you really be able to kill *all* people who had committed atrocities? If you did, how many people would be left?" asked Luis.

The head of the African-American Institute in Mozambique, Célia Diniz, called the Renamo-Frelimo conflict "a domestic affair. It was the same families, same villages, same tribes, on both sides. At the end of the war, you can't say, 'We won't accept you anymore.' They're part of our lineage."

In the years immediately following the war, Mozambicans were terrified that the conflict would return, even if there was little likelihood of that happening. The same kind of war certainly could not have been repeated, since Mozambique's neighboring governments had changed and were no longer interested in destabilizing the country. Yet there was a palpable sense in Mozambique that if you talked about the war, it might come back; if the war was mentioned, Mozambicans were likely to change the subject, sometimes after acknowledging they lost family and friends. "At the grassroots level, I'm not seeing any signs of trying to remember," said João Paulo Borges Coelho, a professor at the University of Mondlane who studied the war and its aftermath. "Maybe people are too busy trying to recover, and they know that the price to pay for peace is to forget."

The resistance to remembering the past seemed to cut across all levels of society. In preparation for the 1994 presidential elections, some Brazilians came to Mozambique to provide assistance to the ruling party's electoral campaign. "When I met with them, I asked what electoral strategy they were thinking of," a former senior government minister, José Luís Cabaço, told me. "They said they thought the campaign should focus on the abuses of Renamo during the war. 'No, don't do that,' I said immediately. 'That would only create conflict. It would be seen on the ground as 'trying to bring back conflict into our village, when we've solved it already'; of bringing back the spirits of evil to the village."

One man tried such an approach. A candidate from a new political party went to the town of Gaza, organized a big meeting, and denounced Renamo and Frelimo, trying to win support for his new party. He said that Renamo and Frelimo were to blame for the war and for all the atrocities. The response of the crowd was intense anger, and as the speaker continued, passions became heated and the crowd began to attack him, for he was trying to stir up hatred and cause problems in the community after Renamo and Frelimo members had reconciled. "This is the way that the people were saying they'd accepted the reconciliation between Frelimo and Renamo," said Brazão Mazula, rector of the University of Mondlane and former head of the Mozambique electoral commission, who recounted the story. "Today, if we did a truth commission, if we opened up the issue of the past, it would be to restart the hate."

Peace and reconciliation, on the basic level of living together without ongoing conflict, came remarkably quickly to Mozambique. Stories abound of how soldiers of the two warring sides put down weapons and greeted their opponents as brothers. When the peace agreement was signed in Rome, "word came from the top, and the war just stopped. Not another shot was fired," described one observer. The war just "went out," like a fire goes out, said another. From that day on, the former warring enemies have lived in peace virtually without incident.

People often describe this easy peace with a sense of wonder. The Mozambican academic who has studied the postwar transition most closely, João Paulo Borges Coelho, was amazed at what he saw. He described the lack of rancor over past abuses among former enemies now serving together in Parliament and the ease with which soldiers from opposing sides joined together to demand benefits from the government. "There have been *no* reservations toward each other," he noted. "This is all to say, in a few words, that I don't know what is going on. . . . Recently, I had both the son of a Renamo commander and the son of a general in the army who served in the same area, as students in the same class. They discussed this heatedly in class, but after class they went for coffee together, they gave each other rides . . . as if nothing had happened. It's not clear what to think about all this."

As the war ended, national and international organizations were concerned with creating mechanisms to reinforce peace at the local level, but found that their initiatives were not needed. "We were all thinking about how to increase peace and reconciliation, but when we came to the grassroots, they were reconciling already," describes José Luís Cabaço, the former Frelimo government official. "Our ideas were only confusing and stirring up trouble."

A Political Agreement

On the elite political level, a different kind of process was taking place. Since the two parties negotiating the peace accord were both responsible for abuses during the war, neither was much interested in airing their crimes in public or under the painful examining light of the negotiating table. And no one from the outside — neither victims nor the international community — was pushing them to do so. So instead of accountability, truth, or justice, the buzzword that framed the talks was *reconciliation,* and reconciliation was understood to mean "we will talk, and we may govern together, but we will not bring up the past." The issue of past abuses was not even on the agenda during the two years of formal peace talks. The parties quietly agreed in advance to keep it out of the negotiations, but even this prior agreement was never communicated clearly to the public. Everyone watching the negotiations understood that the subject was taboo, however. Two years after the elections, Mozambique expert Ken Wilson described how there was "a tacit agreement not to bring up the past. Certainly, there are skeletons in the cupboard, but they're not rattling, and they're not being brought out of the cupboard very much."

One longtime journalist told me, "It simply would have been impossible to reach an agreement if either side had raised the question," and that "there would be nothing but trouble if you resurrected the old accusations now, four years after the war. The use over and over of the word *reconciliation* to frame the talks made it clearly understood that that wouldn't happen." Recognizing the irony, he added, "I know South Africa's process is called the 'truth and reconciliation commission,' but that has a different meaning. Here, reconciliation meant 'let's not dig up the past.'"

In fact, this issue was one of the first to be aired before negotiations could even begin. "The first condition of the negotiations was 'reconciliation,' that the parties would not use the negatives of the past in the future," described Brazão Mazula, who edited an authoritative book on the Mozambican peace process. "Frelimo first asked Renamo to recognize their crimes as a condition to holding peace talks. Renamo responded by saying Frelimo also had to acknowledge their own past crimes. It took five or six very difficult months before this issue could be worked out, with the Church acting as mediator. It was almost impossible to get beyond this issue to get the negotiations started. Eventually, a policy of 'reconciliation' was agreed to, which was understood to mean that there were crimes, that they were forgiven, and that there would be a general pardon. After this agreement, neither party was obliged to admit their crimes. But it was not easy getting there."

I asked Raul Domingos—who was a senior leader of Renamo for many years, attended the peace negotiations, and then headed the Renamo party in Parliament—if in the negotiations *reconciliation* meant "silence about the past." He agreed: "The word *reconciliation* is a word used to mean forget the past and be tolerant. We killed each other, but we forget this because we are sons, brothers, and we have to live together. Without this, the war would never have ended."[14]

Healing by Other Means

If that agreement served the obvious political interests of politicians, it seems to have coincided well with an apparently natural process of reconciling and healing at the local level. Perhaps the ingredient in Mozambique that most causes it to stand apart from other countries is the strength of traditional healing mechanisms that remain deeply rooted throughout the country. At the end of the war, most soldiers returned home, thus mixing together perpetrators and victims in each community and village, and in many families. They turned to traditional healers to help repair their wounds.

Curandeiros, or traditional healers, are in every town and village, and are widely used and respected. It is difficult to find a Mozambican who does not believe in their powers. In villages, it is unquestioned. "I don't know whether I should believe it or not believe it," said my interpreter and guide, the development specialist Roberto Luis. "It's hard to say 'no, I don't believe any of it,' when you're working with people who believe it *so* much. And then it sometimes seems to be proven—when they call for rain, it rains. So that only strengthens the belief."

"Neotraditional healing mechanisms," as one Mozambican scholar called them, have played a powerful role in reintegrating soldiers into their communities. It works, approximately, like this: if you kill someone, that person's spirit will sit on your shoulders and will give you bad luck. In order to lift that spirit, you must undergo treatment. Your relatives would therefore organize a ceremony to "rehumanize" you, to make you "normal" again. This ceremony is always done by a traditional leader, not someone appointed by the government. It is this ceremony that allows killers back into their communities, and they are then accepted almost without question, even by the relatives of their victims. Luis notes, "It's a very, very big help, especially to the persons involved in the atrocities. It allows them to be accepted in the community again, to not be seen with fear. They have been made a person again, not such a monster."

These ceremonies are particularly important where there have been massacres, especially if the massacre took place in the actual village. "Where many people have died, they do a ceremony to wash away all the blood which has fallen on the land. That ceremony is set up as a spiritual reconciliation between the living and the dead. 'There are so many dead people, we can't live here,' the community would say. 'We need to reconcile ourselves with the dead and reconcile this place with the dead.' It's like, there's a black spirit living in the sky, and you have to chase it away in order to live. I don't know to what extent it works or doesn't work, but there is a very firm belief that it's there. People find the money for these ceremonies, even when they don't have the money — to buy animals to slaughter, prepare the necessary drinks, etc. This is a very powerful force, or structure, within any community," said Luis.

"We know people believe in these things," said a psychologist, Ilídio Silva, who works with a nongovernmental organization in Mozambique trying to merge modern psychotherapy practices with the local healing traditions. "Nothing is better than what you believe. If people believe, then it's positive." With only a very few practicing psychologists in the country, it's clear that Western psychotherapy is not an option for healing those in trauma in Mozambique, just for sheer lack of resources and personnel. However, Western therapy would also probably be inappropriate, as people are likely to respond more effectively to the local belief structures about sickness and healing. Mozambican anthropologist Alcina Honwana notes that "therapies which do not account for the role of ancestral and malevolent spirits in the causation and healing of trauma may actually hamper family and community efforts to provide care," citing studies of war-affected populations in Mozambique that showed that "talking about traumatic experiences does not necessarily help patients 'come to terms' with their distress. In such cases, the performance of complex traditional healing rituals can prove significantly more effective."[15]

When I visited a village ninety minutes north of the Mozambican capital, these descriptions were very much confirmed. One man who lost his father in a battle with Renamo now lives next door to a former Renamo soldier who he thinks took part in the killing, but he has never brought it up with this neighbor, and has no desire to. "Even if I wanted to confront him, the rest of the community would turn against me if I tried. They'd say, 'We've also suffered the same thing,'" he explained. "It's a community issue, not an individual issue."

My two village hosts, one of them the head of the local school, pointed across a grassy field to two men walking by. "There are two of those who committed Renamo atrocities, walking there. They moved here freely; everybody knows them. But they didn't go back to their home village, so they haven't received the 'washing' that can only be done by their home communities. They're not quite normal, not quite right." I tried to get my hosts to explain how the two men were different. "You can see it in their attitude, in the way they talk," they said, unsure of how to answer my question.

In this community of 13,000 people, there are no police. It would take half a day to wait for a bus and travel to the nearest town to find a local police officer. The structure of the community is held together by the power of the traditional leader and his advisors. I asked about the idea of a national commission to investigate the atrocities. One of the men, the headmaster of the school, responded, "If a commission would start, *unless* it was heavily rooted at the community level, and with proper safety and security to make people feel safe, people would be very reluctant to come forward. People would be harassed afterwards. It's important to keep things local. If there was such a commission without security, and you gave testimony, your house would be burned down."

I asked if there had been any revenge attacks since the end of the war four years earlier. There weren't in their village, they said, but that wasn't to say the memory of the war doesn't sometimes erupt in violence. In a nearby town a year before, one man noted, "people got drunk drinking cashew fruit wine. A Renamo guy slipped with his tongue, showing off, bragging about all that he'd done, all the atrocities he'd committed. People were not happy, and they assaulted him. They killed him, I think. Because he was showing off." Clearly, despite local efforts, it would be unrealistic to expect that tensions and difficulties will not continue to arise out of the legacy of such a war.

William Minter, a U.S. scholar who closely followed the Mozambique war and peace process, has concluded that "many of those guilty of atrocities committed them as part of military machines they entered during duress. There will be no Nuremberg trials in Angola or Mozambique, or formal Truth Commission with the impossible task of tracking down responsibility for hundreds of poorly recorded or undocumented incidents stretching over almost two decades of war. The individual truths will emerge, if they do, piecemeal. Historical reflection, however imperative, cannot and will not take priority over the difficult struggle for individual and national reconciliation."[16]

In the end, perhaps Mozambique's process is not about forgetting or denying the past, but about accepting it in its fullness and complexity. The title and founding legislation of the South African truth commission, and the way in which the commission presented itself, presume an ability and desire to reconcile with people and events of the past. One of the top investigative journalists in Mozambique, for example, was one of the most adamant in rejecting the idea of a truth commission. Carlos Cardoso, originally from South Africa and then editor of *MediaFax* in Mozambique, spent years trying to dig up hidden truths. And yet, he said, "I don't believe in truth commissions. To 'reconcile with the past'—people need the right to their own interpretation of the past. I don't want to reconcile myself with the horrendous crimes against the people. Why should I accept it? I want to be able to have contradictions about the past."

Let's look at our past, said Cardoso, but let's not do it by way of a commission telling us there is only one truth. "History is too complex; you can't deep-freeze it. And if you started digging, where would you stop? Who's clean here? It's a quagmire. Everyone was involved in some way, including many, many in the international community."

As I heard over and again that digging into the past made no sense for Mozambique, I began to pose a simple question: in much of the rest of the world, there is an adage that "if you don't study your past, you're bound to repeat it." Is Mozambique somehow the opposite? Most said yes. José Luís Cabaço, former longtime senior member of government, strengthened my supposition: "The past cannot exist in this country," he said. He then thought for a moment and softened his stance. "It must be taught in schools, yes, to not repeat it. But the past is still part of the present, so it's difficult to teach. In five or ten years' time, historians will be able to write a proper history, to unveil the framework and ideologies. But not before five or ten years. It's still about journalism; it's not yet history."[17]

CAMBODIA: TWENTY YEARS LATER

Cambodia is well known internationally for its killing fields of the late 1970s, when the Khmer Rouge government killed between one and two million people, up to one-fifth of the country's population.[18] Whether and how Cambodians want to remember this past, however, is not at all clear.

In the early 1980s, immediately after the Khmer Rouge was driven from power, there was initial interest in recounting stories and letting the world know what had happened, according to David Hawk, who headed the Cambodia Documentation Commission, a nongovernmental organization then pressuring for prosecution of Khmer Rouge leaders under the Genocide Convention.[19] There were spontaneous efforts to record survivors' experiences, and a dozen or so Cambodians wrote autobiographies of their experiences. But civil war continued through the 1980s, suffering continued, and Cambodians expressed a desire to get on with their lives without digging up events from long ago. By the early 1990s, it was often reported that Cambodians wanted to simply forget the past, and that they showed no interest in speaking about that period.[20]

Outside observers concluded that this relative silence about the past was due to both a fear of talking about a still contentious period and the result of the Cambodian and Buddhist tendency not to confront conflict. In 1994, Stephen Marks, head of human rights education and training for the United Nations Mission to Cambodia in 1992 and 1993, outlined a number of reasons why the Cambodian government seemed unlikely to prosecute the Khmer Rouge for its atrocities. These included the fact that many political, military, and financial elites could be implicated, since many in the current government were affiliated with the Khmer Rouge at one time; Cambodians preferred accommodation with the Khmer Rouge rather than continued fighting; the judiciary was too weak to expect serious trials; the Cambodian king, held in high esteem, had proposed a policy of reconciliation with the Khmer Rouge; and Cambodian Buddhism teaches that reconciliation does not require justice or retribution.[21]

Kassie Neou, director of the Cambodian Institute of Human Rights and a former victim of the Khmer Rouge, described to Marks his vision of confronting the past in a way that would be "compatible with the cultural foundations of Cambodian society." The way the past is preserved and displayed is important, he argued. According to Marks, Neou believed "that the current monuments to the genocide in several locations in Cambodia should be replaced by a center with a stupa (a Buddhist shrine) that would be a place of remembrance but not of denunciation, a place where families of victims could come and reflect on the lives of loved ones. The center could also be a place for teaching about human rights, but in the spirit of Buddhist reconciliation. Rather than displaying skulls and bones of victims,

these remains would be incinerated, thus liberating the imprisoned souls."
Neou insisted that "too much blood of the innocent people [has] been spilt
so far. Anything that may jeopardize this peace should not be allowed."[22]

An unsettling outcome of this hushed treatment of the past is a basic
misunderstanding or ignorance of this period of the country's history.
Youths under twenty or twenty-five, not old enough to remember the violence, have very little idea what happened under the Khmer Rouge. On the
rare occasions when survivors tell their stories, the youths tend to think
they're joking or exaggerating. Brad Adams, a U.S. human rights advocate
who lived in Cambodia for several years in the 1990s, argues, "A thorough
and accurate accounting is extremely important to avoid the possibility of a
twisted version of history gaining credence among Cambodians, particularly in the absence of any serious presentation of contemporary Cambodian history in Cambodian schools. It is frightening to hear otherwise
sensible Cambodians whisper that 'the Khmer Rouge were not actually
Khmer but were Vietnamese agents sent here to destroy the Khmer Rouge
people.' More information about what really happened is the best and perhaps only antidote to this potential plague."[23]

While Cambodians saw no hope of justice at home and showed little interest in confronting this period of their history directly, the international
community's interest in accountability for Khmer Rouge crimes of the 1970s
has increased in recent years.[24] As a result of this continued international interest in accountability in Cambodia, an initiative began in the early 1990s in
the U.S. Congress to document Khmer Rouge crimes and push for prosecutions. The office of Senator Chuck Robb, chair of the Senate Sub-Committee
on East Asia, decided that the atrocities of the Khmer Rouge should be thoroughly investigated and documented and the guilty tried.[25] Under the initiative of this senator's office, primarily under the direction of his senior staff
member, Peter Cleveland, a Cambodian Genocide Justice Act was passed in
1994, providing $800,000 to the U.S. Department of State to set up an Office
of Cambodian Genocide Investigations and to award outside research
grants.[26] Funds were provided to Yale University for the bulk of the research
and to independent consultants to consider legal and policy options.[27]

Senator Robb's speech on the floor of Congress made the initiative
sound much like a truth commission, except that it wasn't undertaken by
the authorities of the country under study, nor did it have their backing:

Unfortunately, the factual record on the killing fields in Cambodia is incomplete, and as the years slip by it becomes more difficult to establish in

any comprehensive fashion exactly what happened during those years of terror. History is being whitewashed. . . . However, the legislation I am introducing today will vastly expand our base of knowledge by documenting, collecting, organizing, and evaluating information on the atrocities committed by national Khmer Rouge leaders. . . .

Too many Cambodians died horrible senseless deaths for us to let this slip from our memories, and the future of this country is too important for us to move ahead without properly reflecting on what's happened. . . . Any Cambodian will be able to learn about his or her country's grisly history, and we can hope specific information about how and when and where a relative was executed.[28]

"You can't just say, 'Let genocidal bygones be bygones,'" said the senator's staff member Peter Cleveland in explaining their motivations for the legislation. "The Senator felt you can't ignore that kind of thing, you have to come to terms with it. Morality demands it."[29] Yet in Cambodia, even according to Cleveland, there was virtually no support for the project. He described with amazement the fact that "the Cambodian *government* didn't want this. And Cambodian human rights groups all gathered to meet with me to try to discourage the idea of a genocide investigation." The U.S. Department of State strongly opposed the initiative and only took on the project when forced to when the legislation was passed, according to Cleveland. The State Department warned Senator Robb that his bill could harm bilateral relations if the Cambodian government seriously balked at the investigations, which were sure to touch persons with whom the government was then negotiating. "But you can't ignore the problem just for the sake of getting a deal with the Khmer Rouge," said Cleveland. "At a certain point, you can't allow a country to be its own judge and jury. The international community can't just ignore it."

This U.S.-funded project was limited in one key respect: by narrowing its scope to only the years the Khmer Rouge was in power, it excluded any review of U.S. support for the Khmer Rouge after it left power and, for that matter, the effect of U.S. bombing of Cambodia in the early 1970s, which many blame for fueling the growth of the Khmer Rouge. In an effort to thwart the Vietnam-installed Cambodian government, the U.S. government had provided critical diplomatic support to the Khmer Rouge for many years after it was deposed from power, allowing it to hold on to the Cambodia seat at the United Nations, in coalition with others, despite the atrocities that were then widely known to have taken place under Khmer Rouge rule.

In time, the U.S.-funded initiative made an important contribution to the preservation of documentation. The Yale University project, which received close to half a million dollars over two years from the U.S. government as well as additional grants from private foundations, succeeded in turning up a great number of documents that were previously unknown. The 50,000 to 100,000 pages of documentation, most discovered in a warehouse in Phnom Penh, according to the project director, Ben Kiernan, detail the surveillance practices of the Khmer Rouge secret police and help to outline the structure of the regime. A computerized map of the killing fields, photographs of 16,000 people that were killed in prison, and extensive biographical data of victims and perpetrators have been put up on the World Wide Web.[30] Yale helped set up a documentation center in Cambodia where the documents are stored and processed, and helped the center become an independent Cambodian organization.

As some of the last active Khmer Rouge leaders surrendered in late 1998 (and were warmly welcomed into civilian life by the prime minister) and the Khmer Rouge virtually ceased to exist as a fighting force, there was a clear increase in public interest from Cambodians in trying the top Khmer Rouge command. "The country seems to be embarking, spontaneously, on a long-delayed national conversation about its traumatic past," the *New York Times* reported.[31] One poll showed that 80 percent of respondents wanted the surviving Khmer Rouge leaders to be prosecuted;[32] but reports from Cambodia also showed that Cambodians feared that "instability, crisis and political convulsion have the seeds of returning, immediately, to 1975," as one diplomat put it. "People are so traumatized. They just want to get on with what's left of the rest of their lives."[33]

In early 1999, Cambodian Prime Minister Hun Sen suggested that Cambodia might consider a truth commission in tandem with any trials, and was considering inviting Archbishop Desmond Tutu for a visit (perhaps his intention was to escape the idea of an international tribunal, which was beginning to be discussed by the international community; this was not clear).[34] Meanwhile, several months later, a United Nations–appointed team of legal experts, who were studying accountability options for Cambodia, recommended that a truth commission be considered for Cambodia, but stressed the need for "a process of reflection" by the Cambodian people to determine whether a truth-seeking exercise would be desired, and whether such a commission might be a beneficial complement to prosecutorial endeavors.[35]

It is still largely unknown what the Cambodian public might think of a broad truth inquiry, though there are anecdotal indications that any kind of broad public hearings process might be considered too confrontational or dangerous given that many former Khmer Rouge members are still scattered throughout society. One observer who argued for the importance of clarifying the truth about the past also noted that it is "unlikely that average Cambodians, severely traumatized by unbroken decades of war, mass killings and continuing political repression, would risk playing an active role in a truth commission. There would simply to be too much to lose, and too little to gain."[36] If there were to be a truth commission in Cambodia, it might take a form different from others to date; perhaps, for example, taking testimony from community leaders or others who could describe the effect of the violence in each area, rather than trying to collect individual stories from thousands upon thousands of victims.

WHAT ROLE FOR THE INTERNATIONAL COMMUNITY?

Countries like Cambodia and Mozambique, where for at least a period of time there is a widespread resistance to digging into the past, are rare. Where this reflects a broad consensus, a policy of reconciliation through silence should be acceptable and accepted by the international community. Yet how does one determine a "broad consensus," especially where victims have lived in fearful silence and rights groups have been squashed for years? In the great majority of cases, in fact, there are some groups or sectors of society that do very much want the full truth revealed and others whose interests are better served either by silence or by allowing only a narrow portion of the truth to be revealed. In these circumstances, continued denial may lead to continued conflict and hinder attempts to promote societal healing.

In a number of countries, the international community has played an important role in encouraging a serious truth-seeking effort and provided the funds and sometimes the personnel to make it happen. Where former perpetrators hold too much power in peace negotiations or in the new government, the international community might appropriately push for accountability, including a truth inquiry. Where sectors within the country demand an accounting, it is important for the international community — the United Nations, bilateral partners, international nongovernmental organizations — to back them up and to put pressure on the government where national actors may not have the power or political space to do so.

And where official truth-seeking does take place, the international community should watch that it is done fairly and in good faith. Yet how can outsiders distinguish between politically self-serving motivations to avoid the truth and a legitimate claim that such an exercise is inappropriate for a country at that particular time? What might be looked to that would indicate the usefulness and appropriateness of such an official truth body?

I would rule out certain factors. As noted earlier, neither the quantity nor the type of human rights abuses, nor whether the abuses have already been documented by previous efforts, will determine the suitability or prescribability of official truth-seeking. A relatively small number of cases does not lessen the urgency of the issue.

Instead, the primary measure to determine the importance of a truth commission is found in the desire for a truth-seeking process from within the society under question. It is hard to measure these sentiments in concrete terms. There are few transitional countries that are as sophisticated as South Africa, with the know-how, patience, civil society infrastructure, and resources to dedicate a year and a half to culling ideas and reactions from across the country. Opinion polls are unrealistic in most countries, and fear of speaking publicly about government abuses may continue long after the end of a war or the departure of a repressive regime. Although there may be no means of formal measurement, foreign advocates and governments should look carefully to and be guided by expressed national preferences, especially those of the victims or groups that represent them. In those countries where there is a generalized lack of interest in or resistance to digging up the past, this is likely to be reflected at all political and societal levels: a preference for letting go, an uncomfortableness in talking of the past, an exhaustion with the violence, and a passion for peace and rebuilding. Elsewhere, the demand for truth and accountability is made clear through public demonstrations, lobbying from victims or human rights organizations, or in the negotiating position of the parties to peace talks. There is a striking difference between Mozambique, with its hushed discomfort with talking about the war, and Argentina, where mothers of the disappeared marched (and continue to march) weekly on the public square demanding information; or Guatemala, where nongovernmental organizations organized in advance of the peace negotiations to lobby for a strong truth commission and compiled a great amount of information from their files to present to the commission when it began.

It is true that in some countries there is not a strong civil society to push this issue, with few human rights advocacy organizations or victim support groups. If civil society is so tenuous, or has been so thoroughly squashed, then the passage of time may well strengthen the public voice, making truth-seeking more possible and more reflective of the public's desires at a later point. While there is a risk in postponing an inquiry—primarily in the loss in transitional momentum—it could sometimes be worth waiting until security conditions have improved, or perhaps even until key figures have been prosecuted and removed from the political mix, though that scenario may be unlikely in many circumstances.

Yet even where there is no expressed interest, some international advocates might ask, why not push for official truth-seeking as a standard obligation following widespread abuses? First, if a commission is instituted and fails—if it is disbanded before finishing, fails to complete a report, is given an extremely weak and politically compromised mandate, or fails to gain the attention and interest of victim communities—it is unlikely that another will be created later when the timing is better. Second, if a truth-seeking mechanism is instituted without the support, capacity, resources, or freedom of movement to be done reasonably well, or to articulate its mission clearly to the public, it may not succeed even in its most straightforward areas of inquiry, and will probably unfairly raise expectations that will lead to yet more disappointment for victims and survivors. (Although the public's expectations of a truth commission are often unreasonably high, it is worse if a commission has no hope of even partially succeeding in its aims.) And third, there is a potential to do harm—either in mishandling and retraumatizing victims, or in further inflaming tensions. The fear that accompanies these processes may be an indication of real danger—especially that of sparking further violence—and the view of locals on how serious this danger is should be treated with respect.

A broad official truth-seeking process is different from trials, which should appropriately be pushed as an international obligation wherever there were serious rights crimes (and such prosecutions, for many kinds of human rights crimes, are generally recognized as an obligation in international law). Even while recognizing the limited possibilities for full and fair prosecutions in many transitional societies, for all the reasons outlined in chapter 7, it is appropriate to push for accountability and to push the judiciary to function, or, as is often necessary, to push for judicial reforms so that accountability is possible in the future. Trying those responsible for massive crimes helps to reinforce the rule of law and combat continued impunity.[37]

While avoiding dictating the exact terms or tools of a transition, there are important roles for the international community to contribute to accountability in foreign lands. In many transitional countries, there is a lack of basic knowledge by domestic actors about what their transitional options are, outside of or in addition to prosecuting perpetrators in court, and they often have especially limited understanding of what a truth commission exactly is, how to best set one up, and what might be expected from such a body. The international community can help to make comparative information and expertise available so that domestic actors are better suited to debate options. There are many examples of such efforts. South Africans point to two international conferences in 1994 that helped them to work through ideas leading to the formation of the Truth and Reconciliation Commission.[38] A conference was held in Malawi in 1996 to discuss international examples of accountability and truth-seeking initiatives, to help Malawians explore the idea of a truth commission there.[39] In 1998, a human rights organization in Belgrade, Yugoslavia, hosted an international conference that was partly dedicated to exploring the proposal for a truth commission in Bosnia.

In addition, preserving documentary evidence can be critical to a full investigation or to later prosecutions. Even if a truth inquiry does not take place immediately after a transition, it is very likely that an interest in historical documentation will increase later, either through official or private initiatives. Documents can easily be destroyed as a political transition is under way, or can be lost or damaged over time for lack of attention; there may sometimes be an opportunity for outside actors to help put documents in safekeeping during a tumultuous political transition, or to provide resources for their preservation. The Yale Cambodia project, funded by the U.S. government, has in part done that, preserving and cataloging documentation on the Khmer Rouge period and making much of it available to the public. The Documentation Center of Cambodia, which developed out of this project, became the central collection point for this documentation, and was used in 1998 and 1999 by international legal experts who were evaluating the evidence that could be used to prosecute former Khmer Rouge leaders.[40]

In stark contrast, the U.S. government has done very much the opposite in Haiti. When U.S. forces invaded Haiti in the fall of 1994, they drove trucks straight to the offices of the armed forces and the brutal paramilitary group, the Front for Haitian Advancement and Progress (FRAPH), hauling away documents, photos, videos, and other material that contained extensive evidence of the egregious abuses of these forces, including gruesome "trophy photos" of FRAPH victims. Some foreign rights advocates in Haiti who came into possession of some of this material also handed it over to U.S. troops, relieved that it would be in safer hands. "There wasn't a photocopier working in the entire country, so you couldn't make copies of things, and in the chaos of the moment nowhere else was secure," one person told me. But everyone assumed the material would be returned to Haiti when things settled down. On the contrary, none of these approximately 160,000 pages of documents, photographs, videotapes, or audiotapes have been released by the United States back to the country to which they belong. They remain in U.S. government hands, under the control of the Department of Defense. The assumed reason for this intransigence is not flattering: the United States provided direct support to some of those directly implicated in abuses, paying key FRAPH leaders as intelligence sources, and these documents would almost certainly reveal these connections and the complicity of the U.S. government in supporting known thugs. The United States eventually offered to return the documents only if the Haitian government would agree to restrictions on the use of the material, and after certain portions were blacked out, but the Haitians refused these conditions. Despite formal requests to the U.S. government for access to the documents, the Haitian truth commission completed its work, and a number of important trials have gone forward, without the benefit of any of this damning documentary evidence.[41]

The Haitian case is perhaps the worst example of a foreign power blocking a state's access to its own truth,[42] but the credibility of international efforts to promote accountability for past abuses may always be somewhat dependent on the willingness of these foreign governments to also hold their own policies and actions to account. Even where a transitional state may hesitate, resist, or postpone efforts to document the truth, or where political circumstances make a serious domestic truth effort unlikely, there is no reason why the foreign states that were involved in backing the abusive regime should not review their actions in knowingly supporting, instigating, or providing military training and political cover for abusive forces. Indeed, such a review could, one would hope, have a more direct effect on future policies of such a state, as it considers its relationships with other governments that are known for abusive practices.

The record of the international community is not strong here. In the United States, even where there is direct evidence of complicity in unacceptable and illegal activities — such as training manuals used by the Central Intelligence Agency and U.S. military personnel that provided instructions in the use of torture,[43] or direct backing for a military coup against a democratically elected government[44]— there has been little in the form of serious policy review, and little "truth-telling" outside of what has emerged from nongovernmental organizations' efforts to declassify documents.[45] Perhaps this is unlikely to change: claims of "national security" interests shield many foreign policy decisions from serious review, and few governments are eager to reveal the dark sides of their foreign entanglements or to honestly admit wrongs. Be this as it may, efforts to promote accountability overseas may be viewed with skepticism when advanced by governments that rarely account for their own complicity in these same or similar actions.

Truth Commissions and the International Criminal Court

Conflict or Complement?

Spurred by the increasing calls for justice for heinous crimes, 120 countries agreed in 1998 to the formation of an International Criminal
Court to try individuals accused of crimes against humanity, genocide, and
war crimes.[1] The Court will begin to operate after sixty nations have ratified its statute, expected to take two years or more. The agreement to create this court marks a major advance for the prospects of international
justice, even while recognizing that the reach of the Court, and its capacity
to take on cases, will be limited.

Given the nature of the crimes that fall under the Court's jurisdiction, it
is assumed that states in the midst of or emerging from civil wars or repressive authoritarian rule will produce the most cases for the Court. It is therefore likely that its investigations will focus on those countries where
national truth commissions may also be considered, and that the Court's
and these commissions' subjects of investigation will overlap. This could
raise some delicate legal and political questions, especially around overlapping investigations, access to evidence, and the use of witnesses. Unfortunately, little guidance on these questions is offered from those who worked
out the terms of reference for the Court, since, outside of the question of national amnesties, the issues raised by the Court's relationship with future
truth commissions were never directly discussed during the several years of
intense negotiations around the Court's statute, according to those involved.[2]

Some of the troublesome issues that might arise can be seen in the discussions around a proposed truth commission for Bosnia, and especially in the strong response from the International Criminal Tribunal for the Former Yugoslavia, which opposed the idea of a truth commission that would overlap with its own investigations. The Tribunal, an international court set up by the United Nations on an ad hoc basis to respond to the horrendous crimes in the former Yugoslavia, has an operational mandate similar to any national court: its chief prosecutor investigates and brings charges against individuals, while an international panel of judges hears and decides on each case. After the Yugoslavia Tribunal was under way for a number of years, in 1997 a truth commission was proposed for Bosnia, intended to serve as a complementary body that would work on the national level to document the massive abuses that took place.

The truth commission idea was rooted in the recognition that three contradictory versions of history were being taught by the three ethnic communities of Bosnia—the Serbs, Muslims, and Croats—and that such radically different understandings of the atrocities of the recent war could well lead to future violence. The efforts of the Tribunal did not seem to be having any impact on these local dynamics, and its proceedings and decisions—undertaken in the Hague, the Netherlands—received little attention from the press or public within the country. Those backing the idea of a truth commission argued that only by taking an assertive step toward reconciling such different conceptions of truth and history would Bosnians be able to find common ground and ease tensions between the three groups. The commission's supporters also insisted that such a body, which would be created by the joint presidency of Bosnia and include both national and international commissioners and staff, would be complementary to the work of the Tribunal, and was in no way intended to reduce the Tribunal's powers or effectiveness. On the contrary, they argued, a truth commission might enhance the Tribunal's reach by making more information available to it, especially local language materials. In the process of its investigations, the commission could review, catalog, and summarize thousands of local language documents and press reports and hundreds of videotapes that to date had been out of reach of the Tribunal.[3]

But the leadership of the Tribunal was worried that a Bosnian truth commission could weaken it by creating a parallel structure with overlapping interests, and the Tribunal's president and prosecutor openly opposed the idea of a truth commission while the Tribunal's work was under way. The concerns of the Tribunal's chief prosecutor at the time, Louise Arbour, and its president, Gabrielle Kirk McDonald, were first outlined at a conference in Belgrade, Yugoslavia, in November 1998.[4] They argued that the existence of a truth commission could undermine the Tribunal's work by allowing individuals to cooperate with the commission while continuing to default on their obligations to the Tribunal; that the commission's findings of political responsibility might not be distinguished in the public's eye from those of criminal responsibility, thus leading to unreasonable demands for prosecutions; that there would be a danger that the commission and the Tribunal could arrive at contradictory findings of fact, given the commission's lower standards of evidence; that evidence could be "contaminated" by the commission, especially through repeated interviewing of witnesses; and that the Tribunal already was providing the historical truth, so that a truth commission was not necessary. They also argued that Bosnia was not ready for a truth commission and that the process would likely be manipulated by local political factions. In addition, some observers outside the Tribunal feared that a truth commission, which would depend entirely on international funding, could pull needed funds away from the Tribunal.[5]

While all of these are important concerns, and some would require serious attention before a Bosnian commission were established, many independent legal scholars have concluded that none of these issues should be insurmountable.[6] Whether certain political actors would try to use the truth commission as a means to avoid compliance with the Tribunal is not something the commission could control, except by making public statements to try to deter this ploy. Many countries work under different standards of evidence for different kinds of trials (criminal versus civil), and after mass crimes the public must appreciate that not all of the accused can be tried.[7] The problem of a "contaminated" witness pool is also commonly confronted by prosecutors, and many argue that this should not be a formidable issue for the Tribunal; the commission could further lessen this problem by not taking testimony under oath (to help protect a witness's testimony from being discredited, if a slightly different version were given in court). And finally, it is true that the Tribunal's decisions have included long descriptions of the historical context of each case, thus helping to officially establish the historical record, but unfortunately these decisions are neither easily accessible nor widely read, especially within Bosnia. Whether a truth commission should be established in Bosnia is an open question that ultimately should be decided by Bosnians themselves, not internationals. There may well be important reasons not to have a truth commission at this time— that it would be politically manipulated or not done in good faith could be the strongest arguments against it—but the overlap with the Tribunal is alone not a sufficient reason to drop the commission proposal.

A number of the issues raised by the Yugoslavia Tribunal are likely to be raised in very similar form if the permanent International Criminal Court exists in conjunction with future truth commissions. In addition, there are other questions likely to be pertinent to the International Criminal Court. Perhaps most important, it is not clear how and when information would be shared between a national truth commission and the Court.[8] The Court's statute requires state parties to the treaty to cooperate fully with the Court, and to "comply with requests by the Court to provide . . . assistance in relation to investigations or prosecutions," including "the provision of records and documents, including official records and documents."[9] The timing and nature of how this information would be shared are not spelled out, however, and could be a critical question both to a commission and to the Court. If a commission discovers evidence or receives testimony that links a person to a crime against humanity, genocide, or a war crime, must the commission immediately report this to the Court? Could a truth commission wait until it has completed its work before handing over evidence, even if that evidence implicates persons already under investigation by the Court, or will the Court's prosecutor be able to request and gain access to such evidence at any time? What about truth commissions that operate independently of a government, such as those created by a peace accord—will they be equally obliged to share all information with the Court?

The answer to these questions could have serious implications for a truth commission. If its records must be made available to the Court, a truth commission's ability to grant confidentiality to its witnesses would be at risk, and therefore its investigating powers constrained. Many past truth commissions have offered a screen of strict confidentiality to entice testimony from key witnesses—a particularly important tool for those truth commissions which have no subpoena power and depend on the voluntary willingness of witnesses to come forward. Some victims and other key witnesses may fear speaking to the commission if they do not trust that their information would remain confidential. And certainly, those perpetrators who otherwise might be willing to quietly cooperate with the commission—often a critical source of information—would surely hesitate if they expected that their testimony might be turned over to the Court for prosecution.[10]

There are few past cases to turn to for examples of how a truth commission might interact with ongoing judicial investigations. As described earlier, domestic prosecutions do not often take place while a truth commission is under way—either because an amnesty prevents prosecutions for human rights crimes; because the judiciary is unable or unwilling to move on such cases; or because the prosecutorial authorities wait until a commission has finished and then make use of its information, as took place in Argentina. In South Africa, where there was an overlap in cases investigated by a prosecutor's office and by the truth commission's amnesty committee, the flow of information, such as it was, went from the office of the prosecutor to the truth commission. The official policy of the South African attorneys generals' offices was to allow the commission staff to look at its files and take notes from its documents, although commission staff cite occasions when access was delayed or important documents were held back. Meanwhile, the prosecutorial staff attended some of the commission's amnesty hearings in hopes of learning information useful to its cases, pertaining either to the applicant, in case the amnesty application were to be denied, or to other persons named.

Notwithstanding the potential areas of tension suggested above, the overlap between a truth commission and the International Criminal Court could also result in benefits for both bodies. A commission report's outline of the broad pattern of crimes could help focus the Court's investigations, especially if the commission concludes its work before the Court's prosecutor begins investigations in the country. The commission's report, supporting materials, and interviews with thousands of victims could help identify witnesses and evidence for the prosecutor, as took place in Argentina to greatly strengthen domestic prosecutions there. Even if a commission does not name names in its report, its archives would likely identify persons implicated in crimes. Additionally, as suggested in Bosnia, a national truth commission is more likely to have local experts and facility in the language of the country under study, and could make many local language resources available to the Court, including newspaper reports and videos that may document events under investigation. Finally, most truth commission reports comment in some detail on the strength and independence of the judiciary. This analysis could help the Court determine whether the state is "unwilling or unable" to investigate and prosecute a case, which is a key test for the Court to gain jurisdiction over a matter.[11]

Meanwhile, commissions are likely to appreciate the existence of an international court that could have jurisdiction over the crimes it is investigating.

While some victims may request confidentiality, as suggested above, many who provide testimony to truth commissions are frustrated by the lack of justice and would feel encouraged that their testimony might be used by an international court to prosecute and punish perpetrators. Prospects that its documentation could be used for international prosecutions could add weight to a commission's work, focus its targeted investigations, and help shape or clarify its evidentiary standards.

A "TRUTH COMMISSION" ROLE FOR THE COURT?

It has occasionally been suggested that the Office of the Prosecutor of the International Criminal Tribunal for the Former Yugoslavia could take on the function of a truth commission. For example, in 1997 three international experts on the Tribunal recommended that "[t]he Office of the Prosecutor should be provided with an additional mandate and staff to serve as a high-level truth commission responsible for the purpose of creating an accurate and unbiased historical record of the ethnic cleansing and genocide which occurred in Bosnia."[12] Although that specific recommendation is not likely to be put in place, it raises the question of whether a similar idea might be considered for the permanent International Criminal Court. For a number of reasons, that would be unwise. The Court will not be in a position to fill many of the functions of a truth commission. It would be unfair and unrealistic to ask a prosecutor's office to release a report that makes conclusions on broad events if its own prosecutions around these events are still under way. Given that such prosecutorial action could continue for many years, or could be taken up years after an event if new evidence is discovered, the prosecutor's office would not likely be willing to publish conclusions about the evidence it had in hand. In addition, the prosecutor's office must operate under the evidentiary standards and with the intense individual case focus that is necessary for a trial. It might not be in a position to draw broad conclusions about patterns in the manner of a truth commission. And a prosecutor's office surely would be uncomfortable putting forward policy recommendations pertaining to the country's judiciary, political system or armed forces, or designing a reparations policy to reach all victims. Laying truth commission–like responsibilities onto an international court during the course of its prosecutions would strain the court's abilities and resources, weaken its focus, and unfairly limit the kind of truth that would be reported.

On the other hand, the Court's prosecutor's office is likely to collect much information over the course of its work that will never be revealed in court. Because the materials in its files will pertain to a criminal investigation, it is unlikely that these documents would ever be released for review by any outside party. To take advantage of this wealth of information, and to contribute to a broad public understanding of a conflict or a period of authoritarian rule, it could be useful for the office of the prosecutor to release a summary report of its findings after it has concluded all cases pertaining to a particular country or situation. This follows the model of independent prosecutors in the United States, who submit overview reports at the conclusion of their work. Such report writing is neither prescribed nor prohibited in the Court's statute. However, adding such a responsibility to the prosecutor's duties would require a dedication of resources and time, and, if used at all, should be employed only on a case-by-case basis and at the discretion of the prosecutor. Regardless, given the long wait before the Court is likely to conclude all cases relevant to a particular situation, a prosecutor's final report will generally not be a good replacement for a quickly enacted and independent truth commission.

fourteen

Inside the Commission

Problems and Practicalities

Truth commissions are virtually never smooth, pleasant, well-managed, well-funded, politically uncomplicated bodies. On the contrary, most struggle daily with a barrage of methodological, operational, and political problems, and operate under extreme pressures of time, under the heavy moral and emotional weight of their task and the risk of damaging error in their conclusions. Often they have been the targets of explicit threats of violence from those who feel threatened by their investigations. They are confronted with hundreds of critical operational questions that will determine the kind and quality of truth that will emerge, questions for which there are often no clear right answers. Even in the best of circumstances, with top-notch managers and sufficient resources, the problems are many and the stress intense.

Surprisingly, many of the fundamental methodologies and definitional questions that determine a commission's reach and effectiveness are usually left entirely to the discretion of a commission itself, even though they may be of great political significance. Even the most basic of these questions may well be a point of controversy and disagreement inside and outside a commission as it pursues its work. However, many of these problems and questions are quite similar from commission to commission, and while most must be carefully and differently answered for each different circumstance depending on the needs and possibilities of the situation, much can be learned from the difficulties faced by past bodies.

SPONSORSHIP: WHO CREATES AND
EMPOWERS A COMMISSION?

The majority of truth commissions to date have been established by presidential decree, with the president appointing the commissioners and dictating the commission's mandate without necessarily conferring with others, outside of a set of close advisors. Presidentially appointed commissions can be established quickly and avoid political infighting by a weak or split legislature. In Argentina and Chile, for example, the new civilian presidents decided that passing national legislation in Congress would either take too much time or would require too many compromises, so among their first official acts they each independently created a commission, taking advantage of the initial wave of public support for the civilian governments and, in the case of Argentina, the reduced power of the armed forces. The commissions in Haiti, Sri Lanka, Chad, and Uganda were also put in place through presidential action, with little public debate on their terms.

Less commonly, the national legislature may create a truth commission, usually allowing the possibility of granting stronger powers that may not be possible through a presidential decree, such as the power of subpoena or search and seizure. The South African commission is the best example of the strong powers that can be built into such a parliamentary-empowered body. In an active and functioning democracy with a strong civil society, the process of drafting such legislation can add both to the substance of the commission and the legitimacy it carries in the public and political spheres.

There are now two examples of truth commissions created through a negotiated peace accord. In El Salvador, the peace negotiations worked out terms to the mandate and gained the support and signatures of the parties to the talks before most outsiders even knew that a truth commission was being discussed. In contrast, those involved in the Guatemalan peace talks were under intense pressure from human rights and victims groups, which organized far in advance to push for a strong truth commission. Both the Salvadoran and the Guatemalan commissions were administered by a UN office and had members appointed by the UN, but they operated independently and were not UN bodies per se.[1] The Guatemalan commission, especially, embodied a peculiar legal identity that was "located in a no man's land between domestic and international law," according to the commission's chair, Christian Tomuschat, a German professor in international law.[2] The truth commission in Sierra Leone was also agreed to, in general terms, in a national peace accord, but its terms were then spelled out in national legislation. Crafting this legislation in Sierra Leone was assisted by the input of the Office of the UN High Commissioner for Human Rights, which helped to suggest specific language for the commission's terms.

Finally, the two commissions created by the African National Congress are the only commissions to date established by an armed resistance group to investigate and publicly report on its own past abuses. Even within these four models—commissions created through the authority of a president, parliament, or negotiated peace accord, or independently by an armed opposition group—interesting variations are being developed. For example, the U.S. Institute of Peace, a congressionally funded research and policy institution in Washington, D.C., was asked by the Bosnian government in 1997 to draft a truth commission mandate for Bosnia. If a commission were to be established, the institute might help appoint a selection committee to nominate commissioners. Once inaugurated, the commission would operate independently.[3]

MANAGEMENT AND STAFFING CONSIDERATIONS

Perhaps more than any other single factor, the person or persons selected to manage a truth commission will determine its ultimate success or failure. Several commissions have run into serious problems that were clearly rooted in weak management, leading to staff divisions, misdirected or slow-to-start investigations, and insufficient funding. The strength of an executive director is especially critical when commissioners are not present full-time and do not offer day-to-day management and direction, such as with international commissioners who may be in the country only part-time.

The directorship of a truth commission stands apart from other governmental or nongovernmental posts because of the great public and political pressure under which the person must work, the intense time constraints requiring strong administrative leadership and creative organizational skills, and the range of overlapping activities that the commission must direct, from forensic exhumations to security, to creating a public outreach campaign, to establishing regional field offices. Any commission head must offer strong leadership in overseeing investigations, logistics, recruitment and management of a large and diverse staff, and raising and administering funds.

While commissioners are generally less involved in day-to-day administration, they do usually direct investigations, shape commission policy, and have the final say in what will go into the commission report. As the public face of the commission, the members' personal and political authority can be critical in dealing with recalcitrant authorities. The members of the Salvadoran commission argue that one of the most important qualities of any commissioner is having sufficient personal authority to be able to pick up the phone and get through to almost anyone at any time. The members of that commission, which included the former president of Colombia, Belisario Betancur, and a former president of the Inter-American Court, Thomas Buergenthal, found that their personal connections were critical to accomplishing their task.[4]

Selection of Commissioners

The members of most truth commissions have been appointed through procedures that relied on the good judgment of the appointing authority, usually the state president, but with no consultation with civil society or the public at large. In more recent years, however, several commissions have been appointed through more creative and consultative processes. In Ecuador, a number of the commissioners were selected directly by nongovernmental organizations such that human rights activists served on the commission alongside military representatives. In Guatemala, one of the three commissioners was selected from a list proposed by the presidents of Guatemalan universities.

The legislation creating the South African commission set out a much more consultative process of selection. The legislation indicated only that the commissioners should be "fit and proper persons who are impartial and who do not have a high political profile." A selection committee was formed, including representatives of human rights organizations, which called for nominations from the public. The selection committee received some three hundred nominations, which it then trimmed to fifty people for interviews, which took place in public session and were closely followed by the press. The selection committee narrowed the finalists to twenty-five, which it sent to President Nelson Mandela for the final selection of seventeen commissioners. To provide geographic and political balance, Mandela added two members who did not go through the full selection process.

In Sierra Leone, the act creating the truth commission set out yet another model for selecting commissioners. The special representative of the

UN secretary-general in Freetown was appointed in the act as selection co-ordinator and was directed to call for nominations from the public. Meanwhile, a selection panel was to be formed (with representatives appointed by the two parties of the former armed opposition, the president, the governmental human rights commission, the nongovernmental interreligious council, and a coalition of human rights groups); this panel was to interview the finalists, rank and comment on each, and submit the evaluations to the selection coordinator, who would select the final four candidates. The three international members of the commission were to be selected by the UN high commissioner for human rights, Mary Robinson. The lists of both national and international recommended commission members were to be submitted to the president of Sierra Leone for appointment. (This process was just beginning as this book went to press.)[5]

As with the drafting of the commission's terms, a commission will have greater public support if its members are selected through a consultative process. Those making the final selection should also of course consider specific areas of expertise that may be useful, and should ensure fair representation of political views, ethnic or regional groups, and gender.

Who Should Staff a Truth Commission?

The truth commission in Argentina began its work with staff seconded from the Ministry of the Interior, but these civil servants didn't last long. They had no experience working in human rights and had never before heard the horrific kinds of stories that the commission was to collect. When they began to take testimony, they quickly broke down in tears, emotionally distraught.[6] Seeking persons with the experience, know-how, and emotional wherewithal to handle the subject matter, the commissioners hired staff straight out of national human rights organizations, a decision that they say was critical to the commission's success.

Yet basic human rights experience does not begin to cover the skills needed by such a truth body. Because of the breadth of its work and the nature of its responsibilities, a commission requires a wide range of expertise. In addition to human rights lawyers and investigators, a commission may need social workers or psychologists, computer and information-systems specialists, data coding and data entry staff, logistical coordinators, interpreters, and security personnel. Some specialized expertise that is resource intensive and needed only on a short-term basis can best be obtained through consultancy arrangements with outside experts. Past commissions have turned to nongovernmental forensic teams such as the Argentine Forensic Anthropology Team, which assisted the truth commissions in El Salvador, Haiti, and South Africa, and the Guatemalan Foundation for Forensic Anthropology, which assisted the Guatemalan commission, to undertake exhumations on their behalf. Many commissions also contract out for information management and database expertise.

While a few truth commissions have operated with minimal staff, leaving the great bulk of the work to the commissioners themselves, the trend is clearly in the direction of employing a large and professional staff. The truth commissions in Chile and Argentina had approximately sixty full-time staff members each, considerably larger than other commissions until 1995. But as the complexity and difficulty of these processes have been better appreciated, the size, resources, and sophistication of commissions have grown considerably. South Africa set the high mark for truth commission staff size, with some three hundred staff in four offices between 1996 and 1998; the Guatemalan commission, operating from 1997 to 1999, employed two hundred people at its high point (see chart 7 in appendix 1 for a comparison of resources and responsibilities of past commissions).[7]

It would have been unthinkable to hire members of the national military or police onto truth commission staff in Latin America, since these groups have been so thoroughly implicated in the abuses under investigation, typically having operated with complete impunity at the behest of right-wing governments. This is true in most countries emerging from authoritarian regimes, as independence, impartiality, and confidentiality are essential to the task. Yet in South Africa, the commission did place members of the police force on its investigative staff and was generally supported in doing so (with the exception of one former member of the security police hired by the commission, whose impartiality was questioned). While the majority of torture and killings in South Africa were by the police, the police forces were not so thoroughly corrupt as the security forces in Latin America. Police investigators on the commission staff — and on the staff of South African prosecutorial teams — offered knowledge of the inside workings of the forces under investigation, information considered critical.

Special training may be necessary even for the most experienced staff members, especially for international staff and for all who are to go into the field to take testimony. The detailed and contextual information that past commission staff members have indicated would have been useful include: a basic history of repression in the country; a description of the forms of torture used, and exactly what different kinds of torture are called by locals in different parts of the country; who the elected leaders are in each area where staff are to travel, as well as the key nongovernmental local organizations and their leaders; the political affiliations and divisions between organizations (in order to avoid associating the commission with any one political group); information on the actual threat of danger to commission investigators; distinctions between different regions of the country, including an assessment of continued violence, degree of politicization, and the likely concentration of victims in different areas; how to best deal with the psychological stress of taking testimony; and how to comfort deponents who show signs of psychological trauma.

National or International?

Until 1992, staff and commissioners of all truth commissions were citizens of the country under study. But the Salvadoran commission chose to break this pattern. Set up under the administration and oversight of the UN, the three commissioners and the twenty-five staff members were all non-Salvadorans.[8] The commission generally avoided hiring anyone with previous experience working on Salvadoran human rights issues, as such experience might have suggested a bias that could have colored the neutrality of the commission. Many who knew El Salvador best were thus kept out of the process. Those who backed this approach argued, probably correctly, that in the politically polarized environment of El Salvador, the armed forces' and right-wing challenge to the commission would only have been exacerbated if they could point to any hint of staff bias.[9]

Nonetheless, some observers felt that the commission should have turned more often to the international expertise on El Salvador and worked more closely with Salvadoran human rights organizations, and these critics would later point out weaknesses in the report that they say resulted from a lack of in-depth understanding of the country and its politics. International human rights advocates also argued that a national commission and staff would have left behind Salvadorans who were invested in the report, and thus its impact might have been more long-lasting. While recognizing the difficulties in using national staff and commissioners in El Salvador, the New York–based Lawyers Committee for Human Rights, for example, wrote that "the long-term utility of a truth commission or similar exercise is dubious in the absence of indigenous participants. Salvadorans were not involved in the planning or execution of the work; the team—all foreigners—departed once their research was complete, leaving a vacuum behind them."[10]

But most Salvadorans, including top human rights advocates, insist that a Salvadoran-staffed and-run truth commission was impossible. There were no Salvadorans with the authority and political neutrality to head the commission, they argue, and it is unlikely that a domestic commission would have been able or willing to come to the same strong conclusions that were reached by the international commission. Witnesses would probably have been intimidated from giving their testimony to fellow Salvadorans, unsure of the confidentiality of the process and the political orientation of the statement-taker—a problem experienced by a follow-up commission looking into death squads. Furthermore, the experience of the parallel Ad Hoc Commission, which recommended which members of the armed forces should be removed from their position due to human rights abuses, made the risks clear. The three members of that commission were highly respected and politically centrist Salvadorans, but after submitting their confidential report recommending that over one hundred persons be removed from service, they each received repeated death threats. Two Ad Hoc Commission members were forced to leave the country for over a year in fear for their safety; the third hired bodyguards.

El Salvador is the only truth commission to date to be staffed and run entirely by nonnationals, although a number of commissions since have crafted a "mixed" model of both national and international staff and commissioners. This mixed model works well, allowing national familiarity and international expertise to complement each other, and, in some circumstances, effectively provides training of nationals in international standards of human rights research methodology, a useful skill for the future.[11]

Unless there is a strong argument against doing so, a truth commission should always include nationals both at the commission and the staff levels. Some countries may appropriately choose to exclude foreigners altogether—for reasons of national pride, because the situation under investigation is considered too complex for outsiders, or because the domestic pool of qualified persons from which to draw commissioners and staff is sufficient for the needs.

TIMING: WHEN AND FOR HOW LONG?

Although the circumstances of each country differ, as a general rule a truth commission should begin as soon as possible after a political transition, should carry on for at least nine months and no longer than two or two and one-half years, and should always be given a deadline for completion, even if extendible.

How Soon to Start?

Most countries are well served by a quick start to a truth commission. The political momentum and popular support for such an initiative are generally highest at the point of transition, as a new government takes power or a civil war has just ended, and there is a narrow window to transform this momentum into serious reforms, purges of human rights abusers, or reparations for victims. A quick start to a truth commission can also have the secondary effect of holding off pressure for immediate reforms and other measures of accountability, giving the government time to take stock, plan, and strengthen institutions as necessary to further its other transitional justice initiatives. The former chief of staff of the Chilean commission describes one of the main contributions of that commission as "giving President Aylwin one year of grace, allowing democratic institutions to work for a year before having to deal with the issue of past abuses."[12]

In an odd way, a quickly established truth commission can be the centerpiece of a newfound peace; as an early transitional body, a truth commission often tests the boundaries of the new political dispensation (postwar or postdictatorship) and the willingness of the authorities to cooperate. This, of course, suggests possible limitations on how far a commission might be able to push its investigations, as well as a natural concern for the safety and security of staff members and commissioners, but these are unfortunate by-products of an otherwise advantageous strategy of beginning quickly.

There are important exceptions to this "the quicker the better" rule, however. South Africa spent eighteen months designing its Truth and Reconciliation Commission following democratic elections in 1994. This preparatory time was crucial to developing the commission's complex empowering legislation, to gain the backing from almost all political parties, and to seek input from many outside observers through which the proposed commission gained legitimacy. The Committee on Justice of the South African Parliament held over 150 hours of public hearings on the legislation, taking input from human rights organizations, victims, an association of former police officers, churches, and others. International human rights groups made submissions critiquing the draft legislation. And finally, after the legislation was in place, the very public process of selecting commissioners, as described above, added many months, but these steps greatly improved and strengthened the commission.

The appropriate preparatory period for a truth commission depends on the political culture and circumstances of the country under consideration. The South African opposition had long held a tradition of public input and discussion on policy developments; it would have been politically unacceptable to unilaterally create a truth commission simply under the authority of the new president. In addition, there was little transitional momentum lost in the eighteen months that South Africa took to write and broadly debate the legislation. Serious civil society engagement with a truth commission proposal is important and should be encouraged, but where participatory civil society and democratic institutions are weak, a country may be well served by a rapid start-up, especially where there is likely to be a narrow window of heightened popular support for a transitional government's initiatives.

How Long to Carry On?

Most truth commissions to date have been given six months to a year to complete all investigations and submit a report, sometimes with a possibility of extension. More recent commissions have worked longer: close to three years for the South African commission (and another two years for final wrap-up after submitting its report), one and one-half years for Guatemala (see chart 7 in appendix 1).

For a variety of reasons, it is important to keep a truth commission's tenure relatively short; one year to two and one-half years is probably optimal. Outlining a work plan, collecting and organizing documentation, receiving and processing testimony from thousands of victims, selecting representative cases and completing investigations, and finishing a final report within the allotted time will be difficult even in two years' time. The advantages of finishing quickly are worth the possible sacrifices of investigations cut short, however. It is useful for the report to come out while there is still the momentum of transition under way, when a spirit of reconciliation may still be in the air and recommended reforms are more likely to be implemented. A truth commission cannot hope to document or investigate everything that falls within its mandate; it must choose a few sample cases for investigation and only summarize the rest.

Despite the restrictions of a short deadline for completion, the alternative is worse. The Commission of Inquiry set up in Uganda in 1986 was given no time limit: it took over nine years before it was finished, by then losing the interest and support of the public. On the other extreme, the Salvador commission found that finishing its work in six months was impossible; luckily, it was able to obtain a two-month extension.

Many past truth inquiries have suffered from the same problem: they have lost much time in administrative and logistical preparations, which have cut significantly into their stipulated operating time. Essential activities such as renting and furnishing an office, hiring staff, and creating or adapting a database program, as well as larger tasks such as raising funds and designing a public outreach program, can easily consume months of a commission's time before it even begins to take testimony or start investigations. Such delays have caused considerable consternation on the part of observers frustrated by a commission's slow start. Those establishing future commissions should avoid this pitfall by mandating an explicit setup time, a period of perhaps three to six months, before the commission's operational clock begins. During this period, resources, support, and international consultation should be made available to assist in the commission's preparations.

MONEY MATTERS: BUDGET AND FUNDING

It has been common for truth commissions to run short of funds or struggle under a tight budget — including South Africa's, which was ticking along at $18 million a year (remarkably, "insufficiently resourced" was one of the top complaints from observers of that commission). A shortage of funds was also a problem, at least in the initial stages, of the commissions in Guatemala, with an eigthteen-month budget of $9.5 million, and El Salvador, with an eight-month budget of $2.5 million. Only in Chile did the truth commission executive secretary tell me that resources seemed to be sufficient for the task and that the government had seemed willing to provide all funding necessary for its successful completion. The final cost of that commission ran to about $1 million, although the number of cases dealt with was considerably fewer than for most other truth inquiries.[12]

To the extent possible, full funding for a commission should be committed and available at the start of its work. This is particularly important if the commission is fully or largely funded by the state that is under investigation, so that the question of continued funding cannot be used, or be perceived to be used, as a point of leverage to influence the commission's work. Some commissions have been almost crippled by major cash flow problems and unsuccessful fund-raising. The nine-year commission in Uganda began in

1986 in plush offices, and in its first years was in the center of the public's attention. As the years wore on, however, it lost its hold on the public's attention, repeatedly ran out of funds, and moved offices four times until, when I visited, it was in a back-alley third-floor walk-up in a rundown part of town. The commission had to cease operations several times while it sought further funding. In 1987, the Ford Foundation awarded it a grant of $93,300 to finish up, but it later had to raise yet further funding from the Danish and Canadian governments before finally completing its report in 1994.[13]

The Haitian commission ran into serious problems as well. With apparent administrative and management troubles and the lack of a clear work plan when it began, few foreign governments or private foundations were willing to offer support. These funding problems delayed the commission's start-up, prevented it from offering staff contracts of more than one month (resulting in the loss of the majority of its staff halfway through its work, some of whom were rehired when funds became available), and created a central point of stress and ill-ease throughout its work. In the end, the government of Haiti covered the bulk of the commission's cost, falling considerably short of the original projection that over half of its budget would come from foreign donors.

As the size, complexity, and expense of these commissions have increased over time, the source of their funding has also changed. While the earlier commissions were more likely to be fully funded by the national government, such as in Chile and Argentina, more recent exercises have received considerable financial support from the outside, primarily from foreign governments. The Salvadoran commission's $2.5 million budget was fully funded through voluntary contributions of United Nations members, including $1 million from the U.S. government and much of the rest from Scandinavian countries, and received no funds from El Salvador itself. More commonly now, the national government provides a portion of the funds, and the international community follows, as was true in Guatemala and South Africa. The Guatemalan government contributed over $800,000 to support the work of the Guatemalan commission, toward its budget of $9.5 million. The remaining funds came from thirteen countries and two foundations.[14] Similarly, the South African commission received financial support from a wide range of international donors, although the South African government paid for the bulk of the costs. Chart 8 in appendix 1 outlines the preferable budget, size, powers, and mandate of a truth commission (while recognizing that many decisions must be determined by national circumstances and needs).

HOW TO DO IT? BASIC QUESTIONS
OF METHODOLOGY

Confronted with thousands, tens of thousands, or sometimes hundreds of thousands of victims, a commission must design a system to gather, organize, and evaluate a huge amount of information. In the process, each commission must establish its own operating rules and procedures regarding what cases it will cover; how it will collect data; whether it will use a database and, if so, what kind; due process rules and procedures; on what basis it will make its conclusions of fact; what its relationship will be with the public and press during the course of its investigations; and other questions. Three of the most difficult questions of methodology are addressed here.

The Commission Stage: Public or Private?

Whether a truth commission holds hearings in public for victims to recount their stories, or instead receives testimony only privately, will largely determine the level of engagement by the public during the course of its work.

There are persuasive reasons for a truth commission to hold public hearings. By giving victims and survivors a chance to tell their story before a public audience, a commission formally acknowledges and can even symbolically offer an apology for past wrongs. By bringing the victims' voices directly to the public, especially if the hearings are aired on television or the radio, a commission can encourage public understanding and sympathy for the victims, reduce the likelihood of continued denial of the truth by large sectors of society, and increase the public support and appreciation for the commission's work. Public hearings help to shift a truth commission's focus from *product* (its final report) to *process,* engaging the public as audience and encouraging press coverage of its issues over a longer period of time. A transparent process also helps to assure the public that there is no cover-up of evidence, nor a blatant political bias in the commission's work. In much of Africa, for example, much more so than Latin America, the public tends to be skeptical of inquiries that take place behind closed doors.

In South Africa, the Truth and Reconciliation Commission will be remembered primarily for its hundreds of public hearings, which captured the news every evening with the day's revelations. Media coverage was intense throughout its tenure: a pool of several dozen journalists followed the commission's hearings around the country, and every newspaper carried numerous stories about the previous day's events. The hearings were aired live on the radio for several hours each day, and videotape clips were replayed on the evening television news. The *Truth Commission Special Report*, an hour-long Sunday night television show, had the largest audience of all South African news or current affairs shows.[15] Yet because the commission already had detailed statements from each deponent, which had been taken in advance by commission staff, most victims' hearings provided little new information for the commission. Their primary purpose was to provide a platform on which victims could speak publicly, to offer formal and public acknowledgment of the events reported, and to bring the victims' stories to the public. (The amnesty hearings, in contrast, which were required to process individual applications for amnesty, took much longer, looked closely at the details of each case, and revealed a considerable amount of new information.)

A few other commissions have also held public hearings. The 1986 commission in Uganda interviewed all of its deponents in public sessions. In its first years, the hearings were broadcast live on the radio, and occasionally on the state-run television station, attracting much public attention and interest. Each of the hearings was recorded, transcribed, and eventually published in a fifteen-volume set of commission proceedings. One of the Sri Lankan commissions also held some hearings in public and received a good amount of press coverage, and the second African National Congress commission of inquiry also heard all deponents in a public, courtroom-like session. The commission in Germany held a number of public sessions, but these primarily entailed the presentation of research papers that the commission had requested, rather than testimony from victims. All other truth commissions to date have taken testimony from victims only in private, behind closed doors. No Latin American truth commission has ever held public hearings, nor seriously considered doing so.[16]

Lured by the powerful example of South Africa, a number of analysts have recommended that all truth commissions should hold proceedings in public.[17] This blanket recommendation, however fails to recognize the realities on the ground and the conditions under which these inquiries are undertaken in many countries. There are legitimate reasons why a commission may choose to hold all interviews with victims in private, and this decision should be left to those designing the procedures of each commission. Security is the first concern of most commissions that opt out of public sessions. The continued presence and impunity of known perpetrators, the intense fear of witnesses and survivors, and the impossibility of providing protection to deponents can make public hearings very risky. Some victims are nervous about speaking to a truth commission even behind closed doors, fearing word will get out about what was said. In Sri Lanka, some victims who appeared at public truth commission hearings received death threats, forcing the commission to close its doors to the public and the media.

Beyond concerns for security, commissions may be hesitant to air unchecked accusations in public, given the possibility of causing injury to innocent persons through unsubstantiated allegations. Ideally, persons accused of wrongdoing should be invited to a hearing to defend themselves if the commission knows that they will be named. In Uganda, the 1986 commission operated under the same rules of evidence as used by its judicial system, according to two international observers of its hearings. "The procedures followed seem fair. The alleged perpetrator is afforded an opportunity, with counsel, to refute the allegations," wrote American legal scholars Jonathan Klaaren and Stu Woolman in 1990, after observing the commission's proceedings.[18] The South African commission also allowed those publicly accused to defend themselves.[19]

Given these procedural and due process demands and the great number of victims that may wish to be heard, public hearings can be extremely time and resource intensive. Those on the inside of the South African commission, for example, were painfully aware of the huge cost in time and energy of its many public hearings. The two thousand victims and witnesses heard in public hearings of the Human Rights Violations Committee required close to eighty separate hearings, totaling almost two hundred days of public session spread across the country. Each hearing was held before a panel of several commissioners, taking their time from other commission matters. The commission's many victims' hearings seemed to consume its energies for most of its first year, making in-depth case investigations almost impossible, a frustration clearly felt by the commission staff. Instead of investigating, investigators were asked to cull victim statements to select witnesses for the next hearings, organize logistics, and prepare summary material for the commissioners on each panel. In the end, less than 10 percent of the total number of victims who gave testimony privately to the commission also appeared in a public hearing. The great majority of the 21,000 total victim statements were only taken by commission staff (or by outside statement-takers) behind closed doors. Many asked for a public hearing, but because of the time and resource constraints only a small number were invited back.[20]

Despite the risks involved and the great expense in time and personnel, public "truth" proceedings are potentially powerful enough to at least warrant consideration by all commissions. They should especially be seriously considered in those countries where a primary goal of a truth commission is to advance understanding and reconciliation and to reduce animosities that may hold fast between ethnic, regional, or other groups that stood on different sides of a conflict and have little understanding of the suffering of the other. A commission's impact and reach will be greatly increased if the public is able to observe victims relating their own stories. Of course, public hearings are most possible in those countries with a transitional mix of increased public confidence in speaking the truth openly, reduced fear, and an ability by a commission to protect basic due process rights of those accused. In those countries where public hearings of victims are not possible, other kinds of public sessions might be considered, following the South African model of sectoral hearings; instead of victims, perhaps human rights monitors, church representatives, community leaders, and others could be asked to testify in public to describe the nature of the violence and how various communities or regions were affected.

Defining the Parameters: What Truth Is to Be Recorded, and How?

Truth commissions often ground their work in the collection of testimony from thousands of victims, witnesses, and survivors. In order to cull information about patterns, perpetrators, alleged institutional responsibility, types of victims, types of rights violations, variations in abuses over time, geographic distribution, and other details, a computer database may be necessary to record and analyze the thousands of testimonies, as may be a carefully designed information management system to standardize how interviews are conducted and how they are coded and entered into the computer. Such a system allows complex analysis of information, pointing to information and trends that are otherwise impossible to determine or distinguish in the huge rush of data.

However, the investment necessary to create and oversee the operation of a successful database and information management system is much greater than most commissions expect when they begin. Few commissioners to date have had any experience in data management and analysis, and thus, through no fault of their own, often begin their work with little appreciation for the centrality or complexity of information management, the many, many detailed decisions they will have to make for that system to work well, and the degree to which those information management decisions will determine the quality of the commission's product. While they are a great asset, such systems can also consume a huge amount of a commission's time and staff energy, and should not be set up without a full understanding of what is necessary in order to utilize them well. Virtually every truth commission that has used a sophisticated database has run into serious technical and methodological problems, and these problems have sometimes seemed close to strangling a commission and consuming all of its energy. Fine definitions must be discussed and carefully outlined in order to assure accuracy in coding; even the question of exactly what information should be collected and what questions should be asked of deponents will fundamentally shape the results of the commission. A good portion of a commission staff's energies, certainly over half, can easily be taken up with the detailed work of coding and entering information into the database. Yet if done well, an exacting information collection and management system will serve as a strong foundation to a commission's final conclusions.

The commission in El Salvador worked for months with only minimal computer know-how on staff, borrowing personnel from the UN mission in El Salvador to help design a database. After several months, they hired an information specialist, and later still, dozens of information coders and temporary data entry staff, none of which were originally planned for. The El Salvador commission turned out to be the turning point in truth commissions' taking information management seriously. No previous commission had used a sophisticated data management system; the earlier good-sized commissions in Argentina and Chile kept only simple databases, allowing them to do only basic counts of victims by region, age, occupation, and other characteristics. The larger commissions that followed El Salvador, in Haiti, South Africa, and Guatemala, used sophisticated relational databases and hired dozens of staff to code and input information.

Several truth commissions have turned to outside consultants for help in designing these systems. The Science and Human Rights Program of the American Association for the Advancement of Science (AAAS), a nongovernmental organization in Washington, D.C., has helped design systems for the commissions in South Africa, Haiti, and Guatemala. In the process, the deputy director of the program at the AAAS, Patrick Ball, developed a detailed methodology for data management for large human rights projects that was used by each of these commissions, and his short book on the subject should be closely read by future truth commissions or other large- scale human rights projects that approach this task.[21] Ball applies basic social-science research methodology to the context of rights abuses, suggesting a four-step process to an information management system: *information collection*, wherein interviewers collect thousands of statements from victims, witnesses, and survivors; *data processing* (or *data capturing*), wherein staff standardize the interviews into uniform codes, readying each statement for entry into the database; *data entry*, wherein the coded information is keyed into a computer database; and finally, *analysis* of the information gathered in the database. Consistency and standardized methodology are critical, as any error made upstream in the information flow will impact on the final outcome, says Ball.

Despite the great benefits, this sophisticated and costly approach may not be appropriate for all commissions and all countries. Some commissions in the future may choose not to use computers for statistical analysis, or may not have the means to do so, and not all that use computers will employ such an advanced system. It is possible to tabulate numbers by hand, especially if the abuses are relatively few (thousands rather than tens of thousands), although many kinds of manipulation of the data will not be possible.

Reaching Conclusions: What Level of Proof?

While resulting in no fine, imprisonment, or other judicially imposed punishment, a truth commission's conclusions may well have a negative impact for the persons or institutions that are named as responsible for abuses. In chapter 8, I outlined the due process and evidentiary standards for naming names of perpetrators in a commission's report, which I will not address here. However, some of the same issues are relevant to a commission's overall findings. To assign responsibility for killings or torture to one sector of the military or police might (and should) have implications for the future of that force and the culpability of the commanding officer, even if the officer is not named by the commission. Outlining wide-scale abuses by guerrilla forces, which perhaps converted into a political party at the end of the conflict, might dampen the group's credibility with the international community or its popular support at home. Likewise, conclusions about who the victims were — apolitical civilians caught up in the web of repression, or politicized supporters of armed rebels, or perhaps members of a certain ethnic, regional, or political group — might affect reparations policies or other programs designed to address that population's needs. Finally, the commission risks putting its entire report in question if any serious error is discovered in its report. Thus, a commission should establish clear internal guidelines about what its evidentiary standards and levels of proof will be, and articulate them clearly in its report.

Usually, the picture painted by thousands of victim statements speaks for itself, laying out undeniable patterns. A commission should begin by drawing conclusions from this primary information, and often can make many basic findings simply by studying the patterns that emerge there. In reaching conclusions in specific cases, however, a more precise methodology is needed.

The standards of proof of past commissions have varied considerably, as seen, for example, in the El Salvador and Chilean commissions. The El Salvador report described that commission's approach:

> From the outset, the Commission was aware that accusations made and evidence received in secret run a far greater risk of being considered less trustworthy than those which are subjected to the normal judicial tests for determining the truth and to other related requirements of due process of law, including the right of the accused to confront and examine witnesses brought against him. Accordingly, the Commission felt that it had a special obligation to take all possible steps to ensure the reliability of the evidence used to arrive at a finding. . . .
>
> The Commission decided that, in each of the cases described in this report, it would specify the degree of certainty on which its ultimate finding was based. The different degrees of certainty were as follows:
>
> 1. Overwhelming evidence—conclusive or highly convincing evidence to support the Commission's finding;
> 2. Substantial evidence—very solid evidence to support the Commission's finding;
> 3. Sufficient evidence—more evidence to support the Commission's finding than to contradict it.[22]

In addition, the Salvadoran commission required more than one source or witness before making a finding, including at least one primary source.[23] This two-source policy kept some important information out of the report. One of the more controversial questions before the Salvadoran commission was who was behind the country's death squads: they were widely believed to be controlled and financed by members of the Salvadoran right-wing civilian elite. The commission staff members tasked to investigate this issue reported to the commission that this was true, listing names of civilians who were implicated in the death squad operations, but they could cite only one source for the information, and despite its best efforts the commission was unable to confirm the allegations with a second source. The commission thus deleted from the report the information on death squads that depended on this single source shortly before the report went to press—but not before rumors had spread that this subject would be covered in the report, with names attached. To make up for its lack of attention to the matter, the commission recommended the creation of a follow-up commission to look into the death squads issue more closely.[24] The truth commission's silence on the power and funding behind the death squads was strongly criticized as a major weakness of the report. The commission, for its part, insisted that it would have been risking its credibility if it had published allegations that it could not confirm absolutely to be true.

In Chile, the commission's narrower mandate, limiting its cases to fewer than three thousand killings and disappearances, allowed the commissioners to review and make a decision on each case individually. This commission was also able to collect more case-specific documentation than other commissions have, resulting from staff investigation into every case. As its report describes, "The Commission reached a reasonable and honest conviction about each case based on the testimony of the victims' relatives, of eyewitnesses to relevant events, of current and former government agents, uniformed and civilian, including statements by now-retired high and mid-level ranking officers of the armed forces and police and by former agents of state security; press reports; expert testimony and opinion; some visits to the places where events took place; documentation from human rights organizations; official documents and certificates such as birth certificates, death certificates, autopsy reports, voter registration rolls, criminal records, immigration service records about entry into and departure from the country and many other official documents."[25] The commission "made an effort to always have proof of each specific case. In cases of disappeared prisoners it obtained proof of arrest or that the person was in one of the secret detention sites where the disappeared were often kept."[26]

The emerging standard for truth commissions is to rely on what is sometimes referred to as the "balance of probabilities" standard for basic conclusions of fact. This standard, which is also sometimes called "preponderance of the evidence," suggests that there is more evidence to support than to deny a conclusion, or that something is more likely to be true than not based on the evidence before the commission. (The same standard is used in U.S. courts for civil claims.) Balance of probabilities was the lowest level of proof used by the El Salvador commission, which it described as "Sufficient evidence: more evidence to support the Commission's findings than to contradict it," although it relied on a higher standard of evidence to reach conclusions about the identity of perpetrators. The balance of probabilities standard was also used by the Guatemalan and South African commissions to make their findings.[27]

Challenges and Assistance from the Outside

In addition to the difficulties confronted on the inside of a commission, any truth inquiry will also of course be greatly affected by outside factors—the involvement and information provided by nongovernmental organizations, the level of access that the commission gains to written records of the government or armed forces (or of foreign governments), the willingness of former perpetrators to cooperate with the inquiry, and the possible threat of violence or other forms of intimidation that the commission may confront during the course of its work. The success of past truth commissions has been greatly shaped by these factors, even while recognizing that these outside elements cannot be controlled or determined by the commission itself—although there are a number of things a commission can do to improve the chances that these various actors or factors might work in their favor.

THE ESSENTIAL INGREDIENT: CIVIL SOCIETY

The strength of civil society in any given country—how many and how well organized the nongovernmental advocacy, information, community, and research organizations are—will partly determine the success of any truth commission. Because of their ability to generate public pressure to push for a strong commission, and because of their information, contacts, and expertise in human rights monitoring, the contribution of nongovern-mental organizations (NGOs) can be critical. Nevertheless, the relations between commissions and NGOs have not always been smooth.

Lobbying and Advocacy

The truth commission in South Africa would have looked much different without the active involvement of NGOs during the period in which it was shaped and throughout its tenure. The minister of justice asked the Legal Resources Centre in Johannesburg, a nongovernmental rights organiza-tion, to help draft the bill that would establish the commission; the Centre helped to work through some of the difficulties in the draft legislation and to turn suggestions for changes into legal language before submitting it to Parliament for further drafting, debate, and public hearings. The final draft that came out of Parliament included plans for confidential, closed-door amnesty proceedings, with only the final decisions on amnesty to be announced publicly, a provision that rights groups vehemently opposed. Human rights, church, and victims' organizations mounted an intense lob-bying campaign to lift this mask of secrecy, initially without success. Two dozen of these groups — including virtually every human rights organiza-tion in the country — joined forces and submitted a letter to Parliament: if the legislation was not changed to make the amnesty proceedings public, the commission should expect no cooperation from any of the signatory groups, they warned. Finally, the legislation was changed, allowing confi-dential amnesty hearings only when "it would be in the interest of justice" or "there is a likelihood that harm may ensue to any person as a result of the proceedings being open."[1] This escape clause was rarely used; after two years of amnesty hearings, none had yet been held behind closed doors.[2]

NGOs elsewhere have not always been so successful in shaping commis-sions in the form they preferred. In Guatemala, human rights, indigenous, and victims' groups pushed hard on the parties to the peace negotiations, and on the UN mediator, to change the terms of the proposed truth com-mission mandate, but the final accord creating the commission included a number of limitations these civil society groups had opposed, as described.

A study by Alexandra Barahona de Brito on the truth and justice poli-cies in Chile and Uruguay concludes that a key factor explaining the con-siderable differences in the policies of those two states was "the power of the human rights movement and the Church and their relations with the parties. In Uruguay there were no state-autonomous institutions such as the Church, or powerful human rights organizations capable of successfully challenging party inconsistencies. The human rights organizations were too weak to press for a different outcome."[3]

NGO lobbying is likely to continue during the course of a commission's work, when organizations may pressure it to expand its reach or change its operating policies, press the domestic government or foreign governments to release files to the commission and to cooperate fully with its investigations, and encourage governmental or private funders to provide support to the commission's work. Since a truth commission typically shuts down with the submission of its report, pressure for the implementation of its recommendations must also fall to those outside of the commission, including national and international NGOs, foreign governments, and the United Nations, among others. In addition, some governments have printed very few copies of commissions' reports and may not have found it in their interest to distribute the reports widely. The production of more accessible versions of the report, or wider distribution of the full report, is often left to private actors.

Expertise, Case Files, and Grassroots Contacts

Human rights groups have been an important source of staff members for truth commissions. When the Argentine NGOs lost their battle to have a legislated commission rather than a presidentially appointed commission, the NGOs, disappointed at the weaker model, initially refused to cooperate with the commission. But the commissioners lobbied hard to gain their support. "Without the assistance of the NGOs, our work was impossible," said one Argentine commissioner, Eduardo Rabossi. "We spent the first three weeks of our nine-month mandate trying to convince NGOs to collaborate. We went to NGOs to try to talk to them, visiting each at their offices. Finally, some key individuals agreed to collaborate. They came on as senior staff, bringing others with them. So two or three weeks after the commission officially began, we were able to begin our work."[4]

Not all Argentine NGOs decided to work with the commission. Most important was that the Mothers of the Plaza de Mayo, the most prominent organization representing families of the disappeared, continued to actively oppose the commission throughout its tenure, refusing to cooperate or provide information. In addition to their disappointment that the commission was presidentially appointed, rather than created through Congress, they remained firm in their insistence that the disappeared be brought back alive, and opposed almost any initiative to locate the remains of those killed. Even over fifteen years later, one branch of the organization (which has since split into two) continues to oppose the exhumations of the remains of unknown persons. They do not want their movement of thousands of family members to be split into individual families with the discovery of each person's remains, they explained.[5]

In addition to trained staff, the NGOs in Argentina handed over copies of their case files on the disappeared, each of which was counted in the commission's final list of victims even if the testimony was not taken again by the commission. As a result, even the cases of many of those families who chose not to cooperate with the commission were included in the commission's report based on testimony they had previously given to an NGO.[6] In Chile, the Vicaría de la Solidaridad, the human rights office of the Archbishop of Santiago, closely tracked every reported case of disappearance throughout the years of dictatorship. When the Chilean truth commission opened its doors, the Vicaría handed its well-organized files directly to the commission, which ultimately served as the backbone of its information base. While the commission chose to confirm each reported case by retaking the testimony directly from the families of the disappeared, they knew from the start who to reach out to and what the approximate total number would be. Similarly, NGOs in El Salvador, Guatemala, South Africa, and elsewhere have submitted their files to their respective truth commissions. Even if a commission chooses not to use this secondary information in its report, this case information can offer an important map of where the abuses have taken place, helping to target the allocation of staff and field offices and to highlight special patterns and key cases that call for further investigation.

Many commissions must maintain strict secrecy and confidentiality about their work plan and the cases under investigation, given the sensitivity of their task. While this is justifiable in many circumstances, it can also rob the commission of the expertise of those not on its staff. In El Salvador, the commission was concerned that any close working relationship with human rights groups would color its image of impartiality. While all organizations, political parties, and government and military groups were invited to submit cases to the commission, relations between the commission and local experts were generally distant. In Haiti, human rights groups felt they were left out of the process, and many thought that an opportunity was lost in not using the Haitian truth commission to mobilize and educate victims. Rather than working through rights groups' networks in the field, the Haitian commission usually worked with church or local government structures to gain access to victims and witnesses.

South African commissioner Mary Burton said that that commission initially "thought they'd work in partnership with NGOs, but that didn't work." NGOs suffered significant funding cuts from international donors when apartheid ended, and there was "a lot of hostility from NGOs towards this well-funded commission. They felt that they were being asked to do on a voluntary basis what the commission was being paid to do," such as taking statements from victims to be turned over to the commission and providing trauma counseling in follow-up to commission hearings. The commission eventually sought grants from donors to provide financial support for the organizations' work that directly assisted the commission, but these grants took some time to come through. In addition, said Burton, "there was an ideological difference of opinion" within the commission, with some commissioners worried they might be seen as favoring some groups over others if they established close working relationships, which led them to keep a distance from most of organized civil society and turn down some offers of assistance. "That set us back a lot," Burton explained.[7] In addition, it was clear that some commissioners bristled at the criticism that came from the most vocal and organized victims' group, Khulumani. As a result of all this, the psychological referral networks and other collaborative partnerships originally envisioned in South Africa that would have extended the reach and support of the commission were never well established.

Greater involvement of NGOs would also have facilitated a longer-lasting impact of the commission on the local level in South Africa. Tlhoki Mofokeng of the Centre for the Study of Violence and Reconciliation, who worked closely with local community groups interested in the commission, noted that "If the truth commission had invested more in bringing NGOs on board who are connected to victims, it would have been much better. The commission's impact is on the macro level, but at the micro level its impact is very limited."[8]

Frustrated with poor communication and limited access to the commission, Khulumani, the South African victims' organization, suggested that these kinds of commissions should have an advisory office or a victim's liaison on staff to respond to questions. They suggested that such a person could also provide legal referrals to help victims and their families, to assist families in gaining access to a disappeared person's bank account, for example, or in obtaining a death certificate.[9] Legal clinics based at South African universities provide only minimal support in this respect. While such individualized legal assistance would be beyond the capacity of most overworked truth commissions, it would be useful for commissions to make a staff member available at least for deponents to call for information or to follow up on their case.

ACCESS TO OFFICIAL INFORMATION

Although truth commissions are typically created and funded by the state, working under the authority of the president or a legislative act, many have not had full access to government or military documents in their search for the truth. In El Salvador, the commission had the right, spelled out in its mandate, to enter into any office or compound in search of documents, as well as a formal commitment from the parties to the peace accord to cooperate fully with any request for reports, records, or documents.[10] But the commission found that relatively little official documentation was made available to it, as requests to both the government and the opposition for service and personnel records and other documentation "tended more often than not to be answered with explanations that the files had been destroyed, could not be found, or were incomplete," according to commissioner Thomas Buergenthal.[11]

In many countries, the most important or incriminating information is destroyed long before a commission is created. In Argentina and Chile, the armed forces kept a distance from the commissions, and most requests for information about specific cases were either ignored or turned down with a claim that no information was available.[12] In both countries, in fact, the military forces burned or destroyed evidence before the military left power. The response from the military to the Chilean commission's requests for information was often that the material sought had been burned or destroyed as soon as it became legal to do so. The South African commission dedicated a whole chapter of its report to outlining the problem of destroyed files. In its investigations, it found that the destruction of documents was undertaken "on a massive scale" in the 1990s, and that some departments were still destroying records as late as 1996, some two and one-half years after the first democratic elections and a year into the truth commission's tenure. "The mass destruction of records . . . has had a severe impact on South Africa's social memory. Swathes of official documentary memory, particularly around the inner workings of the apartheid state's security apparatus, have been obliterated," the report states.[13]

The resistance to surrendering information may continue long after a truth commission has ended and well into the tenure of a new democratic government. Some well-intentioned government agencies, working under a strong civilian government and with more time to pursue the subject, have had difficulty gaining access to information from other branches of the government or from the armed forces. In Argentina, the Human Rights Office of the Ministry of the Interior has continued to collect testimony about abuses during the military regime, expanding the files of the Commission on the Disappeared. After a retired captain publicly admitted to throwing prisoners live into the sea from airplanes, there was a public cry for official lists to be released from the files of the armed forces. "The information probably exists, but where?" said Mercedes Assorati, a staff member at the Human Rights Office who oversees the commission archives. "Judges won't get into it. And we can only write a nice letter to branches of the armed forces and say, 'Dear Sirs, please tell us if you have something.' We can't enter their archives or go to the ESMA," she said, referring to a military school that was known to operate as a torture center during the dirty war. "We do know that lists existed of everything: who was kidnapped, who was released, and, if someone was killed, where and when. There were orders to burn all the files before the military left power, and that was thoroughly done. But this information probably does exist in private hands; there are always some people who like to keep this kind of information. But it's probably not in the institutions themselves."[14]

With renewed demands in the late 1990s for the Argentine government and the armed forces to release their lists, the government human rights office was caught in a bind. "We didn't know what to do, so we did nothing. The idea is still hanging there. It's very complicated from a legal viewpoint, and even more complicated from a 'reality' viewpoint. We don't have powers to investigate and adjudicate, only to pressure other departments," said Assorati.

Gaining Access to Foreign Government Documentation

Given the limited access to documentation in domestic files, the records kept by foreign governments can be an important source of information. For a number of reasons, the U.S. government is generally the most important source of such documentation. First, it has maintained strong relations with many abusive governments, especially in Latin America, and its embassies report at great length on activities and political developments. In a number of countries that have had truth commissions, including Guatemala, El Salvador, and Chile, the United States backed or directly funded the governments and militaries responsible for the vast majority of abuses that the commissions were charged with investigating. U.S. military, intelligence, and diplomatic personnel maintained regular contact with many of the worst abusers, commenting on their activities in daily cables to Washington. All of these cables are still on file. Second, since President Jimmy Carter mandated the U.S. Department of State to produce an annual country-by-country report on human rights conditions, the U.S. government has collected extensive information on human rights conditions around the world. While this annual report is public, much of the background intelligence on which the reports are based generally remains classified. And third, it is easier (though certainly not easy) to gain the declassification of official information in the United States, as compared to many other countries, because of the U.S. Freedom of Information Act (FOIA), which allows private individuals to request the declassification of information.[15]

The National Security Archive, a nongovernmental organization based in Washington, D.C., has considerable expertise in how to apply for declassification of U.S. government material. Through many thousands of FOIA requests over the past fifteen years, the Archive has gained access to a wealth of historical material and published collections of declassified records that document U.S. relations with many foreign states over the last decades.[16]

The government's response to a FOIA request can take anywhere from eight months to eight years — not very useful for a short-lived truth commission. Nonetheless, some past commissions have found ways to make use of this declassification system. Because of the National Security Archive's experience with declassification procedures, both the Salvadoran and Guatemalan truth commissions turned to the organization for help. The Salvadoran commission relied primarily on the files of already declassified documents, which the Archive had collected over the previous years, to confirm some of its initial findings. It also applied for the declassification of additional documents, but met considerable resistance from some departments of the U.S. government. With the inauguration of President Bill Clinton in January 1993 cooperation from the government improved, although the commission then had just two months left to complete its investigations and report.[17]

The Guatemalan commission made much more extensive use of U.S. documentation, and relied much more heavily on the assistance of the National Security Archive. Beginning years in advance of the commission's start-up, and in consultation with other rights groups focused on Guatemala, the Archive submitted FOIA requests for information on over three dozen key cases that they expected the commission would investigate.[18] In addition, once the commission was established, the commission made a direct request to President Clinton for the declassification of specific information pertaining to its investigations. The United States set up an interagency group to process its request, which pertained to materials from the Department of State, Department of Defense, Central Intelligence Agency, National Security Council, and the Agency for International Development (regarding AID's public safety programs in the 1960s). In accordance with the commission's request, copies of the documents released were first given to the National Security Archive for processing.[19]

The director of the Guatemala Project at the National Security Archive, Kate Doyle, was responsible for gathering and processing this material over a five-year period, beginning with the submission of the Archive's FOIA requests in 1994. At any given time, two to six people were working on the project at the Archive, reading and organizing released documents and helping to interpret them for the commission. When Doyle traveled to Guatemala, she provided detailed instructions to the commission on how the documents should be read. "It is important to remind researchers that declassified documents are fallible. In addition to often richly detailed and valuable information, they can also contain factual errors, misinformation, or lies," said Doyle. She and her staff also sought documents from the presidential libraries of John F. Kennedy, Lyndon Johnson, Richard Nixon, Gerald Ford, Jimmy Carter, and Ronald Reagan, and searched through the already declassified material in the governmental National Archives and military archives (such as the holdings of the Army War College), looking for information about events dating back to the early 1960s. They then handed the material over to commission investigators and a team of twenty-five leading Guatemalan historians that the commission had gathered in Guatemala to assist in writing the historical account of the Guatemalan conflict (this group was later reduced to a few key historians for the purposes of writing the report). The U.S. documents provided much new information and confirmed other events under investigation. "They explain the nature of the violence, U.S.-Guatemalan relations, and military and insurgent operations. Many of the issues that the commission is concerned with are addressed in these documents. The documents from the 1960s and 1970s are very frank and filled with previously undisclosed details about the war. It makes for riveting reading," said Doyle.[20]

Doyle and her staff also used this material to create a database of military information, the first nongovernmental compilation of detailed information about the Guatemalan armed forces. "There is a dearth of information on the military in Guatemala, and we knew the U.S. worked very closely with the militaries of foreign countries, especially friendly countries, and that the U.S. keeps meticulous records. If you know how to ask for it and where it is, you can get information about military officers, units, operations, et cetera." With this strategic approach, the Archive gained the release of thousands of documents from the U.S. Defense Intelligence Agency and elsewhere. Entered into a database, they added up to eight thousand pieces of data, including military budgets, force size, personal biographies of military commanders, and other details, providing a map of the military structure that was previously unknown. The Archive handed this database to the commission in Guatemala, which could then track where officers were based at any given time, what units were in the region when massacres took place, and many other similar details between 1960 and 1996.[21]

Despite the wealth of information that can be obtained through the U.S. declassification process, the FOIA system is not well suited for most truth commissions, due to the considerable time needed for the processing of requests. With an early start, assistance from NGOs, a supportive U.S. administration, and a direct commission request to speed up the process, however, a truth inquiry in any country where the United States was closely involved may find this to be a very important source of information.

THREATS OF VIOLENCE AND INTIMIDATION

A few months into its work, a member of the truth commission in El Salvador approached the staff person responsible for the commission's documentation center, a room full of bookshelves, file cabinets, and computers holding all of the commission's victims' testimony and other primary and secondary information — the heart of the whole operation. "If there was a military coup tomorrow morning," the commissioner asked this staff member, a Uruguayan, "would you go straight to the airport and take the next plane out of the country, or would you first come to the office and put a match to all these files?"

"I would go straight to the airport," she said, not sure what he hoped to hear.

"Wrong answer," he said. "First, you will come here and burn the files."

There was no coup in El Salvador, but there were indeed threats of a coup and intimidating threats against commission personnel. In October 1992, four months into the commission's work, the U.S. Department of State warned the American commissioner, Thomas Buergenthal, and a senior U.S. staff member to take extreme care while in the country, as there were serious concerns about recent threats against the commission. The commissioners received a number of threats that clearly were intended to intimidate the commission from proceeding with its investigations, including at least one death threat sent by fax. In November, near the end of the commission's mandate, Colin Powell, then chairman of the U.S. Joint Chiefs of Staff, visited El Salvador unexpectedly to meet with the military leadership; many believed that his visit was aimed at squelching plans for a rumored military coup.

At the beginning of January, the truth commission moved its entire operation out of the country, to the United Nations headquarters in New York, for the last two months of report writing. This move was largely based on security concerns, as the commission knew there was no way to ensure the safety of the full staff. In the last days before the commission's report was released, there were again threats and rumors that a military coup would result if the commission named perpetrators in its report. The commission refused to alter its report in response.

Many truth commissions have operated under a constant threat of violence and intimidation. Although very few truth commissions have actually encountered violence, and no staff member or commissioner has yet been seriously injured as a result of their investigations, these bodies have much reason for concern. Certainly many unofficial efforts to dig up the truth about abuses have met with violence. Two days after the church-based truth project in Guatemala released its report documenting years of atrocities in that country's civil war, the project director, Bishop Juan Gerardi Conedera, was brutally bludgeoned to death in his garage. The police work investigating the killing was shoddy and unprofessional, and many months later no motive had officially been established, but the public widely assumed the killer was connected to the armed forces and had acted in response to the rights report.[22]

The very nature of these processes is inherently risky; truth commissions generally start work at the very beginning of a democratic opening, sometimes before a political transition is complete and long before the society has gained confidence in the freedom to speak out against their former repressors. One truth commission secured an executive director only after three people turned down the offer, fearing for their safety. They understood that the commission's work would put their life at risk.

In El Salvador, the armed conflict between the government and Farabundi Martí Liberation Front (FMLN) did not officially end until December 1992, six months into the commission's operations (until then the peace process was operating under a cease-fire agreement). Throughout its tenure, the senior military officers that the commission was investigating still maintained their very powerful positions, and the civilian government that backed them had not changed. The judiciary was still unreformed, and the president of the supreme court, long known for his right-wing bias, tried his best to block the commission's work, especially its exhumations of mass graves. The Salvadoran commission employed five to six full-time security guards on its twenty-five-member staff, sent from UN headquarters in New York. Security guards traveled full-time with the executive director and the commissioners, when they were in the country, and with staff when they went into the field to take testimony.

The truth commission in Chad received a number of threats from former members of the security forces who had been rehired by the new intelligence service, which hampered its work. As the commission described in its final report, "Within the Commission, some members judged the task too hazardous and disappeared altogether. Others reappeared only at the end of the month to pick up their pay and vanished again."[23] When the commission received a four-month extension to its original six-month mandate, it had to replace three-fourths of its original members.

Truth commissions also confront the equally hazardous and troublesome problem of terrified witnesses who fear putting themselves in danger by giving testimony — even when that testimony is given in confidential, closed-door sessions. In Uganda, victims sometimes returned to the commission after giving testimony in public hearings, desperate to retract what they had said. It was clear to the commission that they had been threatened by someone who had been implicated in the testimony.

Witness Protection

Of all truth commissions to date, only the commission in South Africa has had the power and resources to develop a witness protection program aimed at protecting those victims, witnesses, and amnesty applicants who believed they were putting themselves in danger when they testified in public.

When former South African Deputy Attorney General Chris MacAdam was hired to head up the commission's witness protection program, he went first to the Italian consulate for their manual on the Italian witness protection program for Mafia trials. "Mafia crime is similar to political violence. Their witness protection system covers lots of witnesses at low cost. It was the right model for us," he told me.[24] To safeguard threatened witnesses, the commission employed the Italian tactic of "witness camouflaging," which placed people in safe houses outside of their communities while still living under their own name. When a witness expressed concern for his or her safety, either before or after a hearing, the regional commission office would immediately place the person in a safe house for temporary protection, and then begin a formal evaluation of the level of risk. For some, the risk level was determined not to be high enough to justify entering the witness protection program, but the commission would instead help arrange increased community and visible policing, asking the police to make regular contact with the witness. Under the lowest risk level within the protection program, the person would be moved between different safe houses in their home area, accompanied by close police monitoring, making use of one of the one hundred safe houses that the commission maintained around the country. Those under medium risk were placed in another community altogether, but were allowed to leave during the day, only staying in a safe house at night. High-risk cases, those considered to be at risk anywhere in the country, were placed in safe houses outside of their own communities and put under guard. No one would know of a high-risk-case person's whereabouts (including the person's family), and all contact with the family or others would be channeled through the commission. The witness protection staff were investigators seconded from the police, ranging from four to seven people. The commission estimated there would be one hundred witnesses to be protected, all told, and budgeted $400,000 for its work. In the first eighteen months of its work it had already processed more than 230.[25]

"It could be easy to try to fool us by spinning a fancy tale," MacAdam told me. "A lot of people are trying to do that. So we do a full security check, taking their fingerprints, et cetera. One chap is in prison for a year for making false statements to commission. It took us five thousand Rand [$1,000] and a week's investigation to realize his whole story was a lie." It was illegal to make a false statement to the truth commission, even if not in a public hearing. After just six months, there had already been "three or four plants; people trying to get into the system to see the safe houses and meet the witnesses under protection — and then sell the information to the highest bidder — which could be to those perpetrators who had been implicated by the witnesses," said MacAdam.

Other commissions, while lacking the capacity to set up formal witness protection programs, have only been able to provide security through providing strict confidentiality. In El Salvador, for example, some witnesses, such as those from within the state security structures, would only agree to meet with the commission outside the country and with full assurances that the interview would be kept secret. A traditional witness protection program such as used in South Africa would not have been useful to such witnesses, because even the knowledge that they had cooperated with the commission would have put their lives at risk.

There are of course many other problems or difficulties that a truth commission may confront; sometimes they are things that the commission itself has little control over and that may significantly impact upon its work. The rainy season in Sierra Leone nearly shuts the country down for three or four months of the year, making travel to collect testimony or undertake investigations virtually impossible. Those countries with many national languages, such as Guatemala and South Africa, have had to work with interpreters or multilingual staff to take testimony, which carries the risk of affecting the information collected, especially as testimony is generally recorded in a standard language that may be different from that of the majority of statements. In South Africa, for example, commission staff estimated that 80 percent of statements were given in a language other than English; some multilingual statement-takers took testimony in as many as five or six languages. All public hearings in South Africa were equipped with simultaneous translation capacities — a labor-intensive and expensive process but one that allowed deponents to speak in any of eleven national languages. These and other external factors can add significantly to the difficulties of a commission, making its short timeline and the many thousands of cases that it aims to record even more daunting.

As is true with many processes, the quality of a truth commission will be determined largely by the quality of the people that carry it out, though its potential reach and impact may be considerably modified by circumstances and context. In the case of a truth commission, however, as compared to many other processes, there is no time for error, misstarts, or lengthy preparation, and the weight of the task and the importance of getting it right is immense. Unfortunately, there is no one map to guide a commission through the many difficulties that it is likely to confront, though a close study of the paths taken by others may at least provide some general guidance. If done well, however—and given the necessary resources and support—a truth commission can change how a country understands and accepts its past, and through that, if it is lucky, help to fundamentally shape its future.

Looking Forward

February 2000

Next week, I join a team that will travel to Indonesia to assist the government in thinking through its transitional justice program, including the details of a likely Indonesian truth commission to cover the many abuses perpetrated by the thirty-two-year Suharto regime. I then travel to Sierra Leone, on behalf of the United Nations high commissioner for human rights, to help plan for the Truth and Reconciliation Commission of Sierra Leone. Yesterday, I received a call from East Timor about the increasing interest in setting up a truth commission there, independent from the truth commission developments in Indonesia.

As I write, an international conference is under way in Sarajevo to discuss the proposal for a Bosnian truth commission, which has been considered and reconsidered over the last few years, but around which interest now seems to be gaining momentum. A few weeks ago, I received an e-mail from Cambodia describing the discussions under way around a truth commission there to look into the massive killing under Pol Pot, twenty years ago. They are especially grappling with how best to gauge the popular interest in a truth commission in Cambodia, what purpose it might serve, and how such a commission might focus its work when such a large proportion of the population were direct victims. A couple of months ago, a high-level international conference took place in Bogotá that showed a clear consensus that a commission investigating the truth should be part of any Colombian peace agreement, even while it was recognized that a peace

agreement may still be years away. Active discussions around truth inquiries are also now under way in the Philippines, Jamaica, and Burundi,
even though each of these countries is so very different, and in Peru there is
advance planning among some organizations and legislators around the
idea of a future commission whenever a political transition might allow.

What is perhaps most striking about these varied developments, spread
throughout the world and encompassing such a wide range of political circumstances and historical contexts, is that in each case the call for a truth
commission seems to reflect a genuine national desire for truth-telling.
Rather than a suggestion from outsiders, it is generally nationals — nongovernmental advocates, victims' groups, and members of the government
or opposition — who have been pushing for these truth bodies. Simultaneously, there seems to be a recognition in each case that any truth exercise
must be crafted to fit the particular national circumstances of that country.
South Africa may have sparked the idea (it seems all countries have heard
of the South African commission, even if knowing it only from afar and understanding few of its details), but there seems to be a healthy insistence in
all of these countries that they will adapt their own model to fit their needs.

The interest in truth commissions has also gained ground in the international sphere of pundits and policymakers. One of the most startling and
impressive of the recent comments on the subject, for example, was put
forward by Timothy Garton Ash, a perceptive writer on Central Europe
who has closely watched the democratic transitions in that region and elsewhere. In a ten-year review of developments in Europe, he argues that
"with the benefit of hindsight . . . all the countries of Central Europe could
and should have tried the expedient of a truth commission." He concludes,
"So if I were asked to note on a postcard the ingredients of the new model
revolution, I would say: peaceful mass civil disobedience, channeled by an
opposition elite; attention and pressure from the outside world; a transition
negotiated through compromises made at a round table; and then a truth
commission."[1]

What is to be made, then, of this surge of activity around and interest in
official truth-seeking, this intense focus on such a still relatively new mechanism — one that was only recognized as a generic institution in the last
ten or so years? Why are truth commissions suddenly so popular, and
where is this all likely to be leading?

It is perhaps only fair to first recognize that truth commissions have
caught the wind of popularity long before they have been fully understood,
and before the effect of commissions in the past has even been properly

studied. Much of this book makes this clear, especially in regard to the untested assumptions and assertions that are sometimes made on the subject of reconciliation and the healing of wounds. But international peace negotiators and newly installed democratic governments hardly have time to wait for scholarly studies of events elsewhere, and thus they cannot be criticized for leaping — even if relatively blindly — into the truth commission fire.

Clearly, the popularity of truth commissions is a reflection of a real grappling for tools to respond to the challenges that arise with the fall of repressive regimes. It is abundantly clear that domestic judicial systems cannot cope with the great demands for accountability for massive crimes, even in the rare case where there is a functioning and trustworthy judicial system, nor can any international court fully respond to these needs — let alone address the other, parallel issues that fall outside the responsibility of courts but within the central demands of a transition. There are simply too few mechanisms to address the urgent need for accountability, reform, reconciliation, acknowledgment of wrongs, historical preservation, and reparation for victims. Truth commissions are thus turned to with great expectation and hope, although often with little appreciation for the complexity of the process and the difficulty of achieving the hoped-for ends. I do not intend to suggest that the contribution of these commissions will necessarily be minimal or unimportant, only that we should be realistic in our expectations, and about the abilities of any short-term process to satisfy such huge and multifaceted demands.

Once we know more about the real impact (and limitations) of these bodies, then, will their popularity fall off? I would predict, in fact, that it will not. Instead, I expect that truth commissions are fast becoming a staple in the transitional justice menu of options. Because they do respond to such an apparently fundamental and widely felt need — first and foremost, to know and acknowledge the truth, to "unsilence" a long-denied past — it is likely we will only see more of them. I would also predict that with the assistance of the international community, and on the basis of the many lessons from past experience, we are likely to see new and unexpected models develop, perhaps including significant improvements on past examples.

The role of the international community is key here. There is a delicate balance between what should be imported and even insisted on, in the form of international guidelines and lessons learned, and what should be left entirely open for each country to imaginatively design for its own ends. As is abundantly clear throughout this book, new truth commissions that are set up and operate without any international assistance are likely to retrace all the errors and struggle with many of the same difficulties that others have in the past, and thus anything that might help transfer the learned wisdom on these matters should be encouraged. On the other hand, there is no one model of how to do this right; creativity and sensitivity to national needs may be the most important ingredients for setting up successful endeavors.

It seems that the many and varied dimensions of these bodies are now fairly widely recognized, as are their potential contributions and possible risks. Just a few years ago, truth commissions were largely understood as investigative mechanisms that had the primary aim of publishing an authoritative and factual report. How a commission came to these facts, and what kind of societal impact it had in the process of gathering its information, were given little attention. Now, the possibility of holding public hearings, advancing societal and individual healing, and taking part in or promoting a process of reconciliation (however defined) has opened wide the question of means, independent of the final end reached.

In fact, if I were to suggest criteria for evaluating the success of a truth commission, I would point to three different categories of questions, falling under the headings of *process, product*, and postcommission *impact*. As a *process*, such a body should be evaluated by the degree to which it engages the public in understanding unknowns (or in admitting what they have denied), perhaps through holding public hearings; whether it gains full participation from all actors in the course of its investigations, including former perpetrators; and whether its work is positive and supportive to victims and survivors. This is different from the *product* of a commission — the quality and nature of its report and the extent of truth that is revealed, as well as its proposals for reparations and reform. And finally, the *impact* of the commission after it has completed its work may be somewhat independent from either its mode of operation or the quality of its report. The degree to which the commission's work contributes to long-term reconciliation, healing, and reform will be determined in large part by whether perpetrators or state officials acknowledge and apologize for wrongs, whether and how the commission's report is distributed and put to use, and whether its core recommendations are implemented.

Those who are now developing truth commissions seem to already understand that a commission can do much more than write a report outlining the facts. In Sierra Leone, there seems to be a universal desire to see the now-developing truth commission play a role in facilitating an exchange between perpetrator and victim, and thus to facilitate the reincorporation of former combatants into their home communities. This is most likely to take place, Sierra Leoneans say, with the active involvement of paramount chiefs and religious leaders in the commission process, as both would have the authority to encourage or facilitate a process of acknowledgment and forgiveness. Many combatants, especially children, were kidnapped and forced to fight with the rebels in Sierra Leone, and were thus both victim and perpetrator. Many victims, meanwhile, say they are willing to forgive their perpetrators if the perpetrators acknowledge what they have done. Sierra Leoneans also want the commission to address the fundamental *why* questions: Why did Sierra Leone's war become so brutal? Why did cutting off limbs and mutilating bodies become such a common trademark of the war? (Was it the influence of outsiders, drugs, or specific individuals who introduced this form of brutality into the conflict?)

While the driving force to establish new commissions has come from within each country, we are also witnessing an increased internationalization of this area of work in a number of different respects. Each of these countries is reaching out for international assistance in thinking through options — from the United Nations, international nongovernmental organizations or foundations, or from individuals who were closely involved in past truth commissions. There would be risks, of course, in a truth commission crafted and run solely by outsiders, who will never understand the national dynamics and culture as nationals do. It will be a rare case that a country is so politically polarized, as was El Salvador, and for that or for some other reason chooses not to include nationals on the commission. On the other hand, a mixed commission of both national and international members, which is now increasingly common, can be a great asset, combining expertise and international experience with the necessary knowledge of local dynamics and history. This internationalization of truth commissions is of particular importance given that the credibility and trustworthiness of a truth commission will be judged first and foremost by who its commissioners are. Even if starting with a vague or relatively weak mandate, strong commissioners can carry the process far. The composition of its membership will be one of the most important factor in determining the strength and success of a truth commission.

There is much evidence to suggest that history, and particularly a difficult and painful period of history, is remembered and *re*-remembered in different ways over time, and the intensity of public interest in this history may reemerge in cycles. Even in those countries where there is some attempt to confront a difficult period immediately after a transition, this past may again demand serious attention many years later. Both Chile and Argentina have seen years of quiet, and then sudden outbursts of intense interest in their still painful pasts. The interest in a previously hushed history may be even stronger in following generations, as has been seen in Germany in relation to the Holocaust. It may be that a country such as Mozambique, after showing no initial interest in any official truth process, might begin a formal reassessment of its past much later, whenever the political and social circumstances allow, or perhaps future generations will take on a more informal documentation of the horrors of the recent war.

In choosing to remember, in recognizing that it is impossible to forget these events, a country will be in a stronger position to build a more stable future, less likely to be threatened with tensions and conflict emerging from the shadows of a mysterious past. A formal effort to address these painful memories can begin a process that may well need to continue long after a short-lived commission, but can make a vital contribution in recognizing what has long been denied. In the end, a truth commission should not attempt to close these issues. Instead, if done well, it should hope to transform this history from a source of silent pain and conflict to a point of public understanding and acknowledgment, so that the future is not continually hampered by an unresolved past.

An Expanding Universe of Official Truth-Seeking

March 11, 2002

The interest in truth commissions has grown considerably in the time since this book was first published. Since the hardback version went to press eighteen months ago, close to half a dozen new truth commissions have been created (including those in Panama, the Federal Republic of Yugoslavia, Peru, and East Timor), several more countries are rapidly moving toward establishing a truth commission (Ghana, Bosnia-Herzegovina, and Burundi), and a number of other countries are seriously discussing the possibility. Each of these will be described in greater detail below. There have been notable advances in the style, mandate, and powers of some of these new commissions, especially as the interplay between nonjudicial truth-seeking and prosecutions in the courts has in some cases become much more explicit.

The most intriguing new truth commission that is now being established is in East Timor, where not only is there a link with prosecutions, but the commission is explicitly crafted as a tool for reintegrating low-level perpetrators back into their communities. Through a commission-moderated community service program, perpetrators can pay directly for the harm caused, a distinct improvement over the South African amnesty-for-truth model where no requirements were made of the perpetrator other than speaking the full truth. Learning from the limitations and the frustrations that resulted from the South African approach, the East Timorese found a way to serve the interests of both the perpetrators (in responding to their desire to return home safely) and the victimized communities (many of which suffered extensive property damage due to the perpetrators' acts). This arrangement is described in greater detail below.

Working out the appropriate link between truth-seeking and prosecutions has also been a vital question in both Peru and Sierra Leone. In Peru, a special prosecutor (as well as special investigations undertaken by Congress) is moving ahead on a number of cases pertaining to corruption and human rights crimes, overlapping with the human rights matters that will come before the newly appointed truth commission. To resolve any potential conflict, the commission is in regular communication with the office of the attorney general, and there is a clear intent to be mutually cooperative. For example, the commission and prosecutors agreed on a joint plan for exhumations that will involve the commission in any exhumations that are initiated by prosecutors

In Sierra Leone, the question of the relationship between the truth commission and the planned Special Court remains unclear. The way in which this relationship is worked out — whether and how information is shared between the two bodies during the course of their operation, for example — could have a considerable impact on how effective either or both of these institutions will be.

There has also been a greater reliance on indigenous mechanisms or practices in new truth commissions that are being set up. As noted above, East Timor's body was crafted to respond to specific needs on the ground, and relied on existing indigenous mechanisms of community-based conflict resolution in its community reconciliation procedures. Likewise, the Sierra Leone commission is expected to incorporate paramount chiefs and religious leaders in its local village-based processes, which may include cleansing ceremonies rooted in locally held beliefs.

The importance of careful thought and consultation in the setup of any truth commission has become more clear over the past year. In Nigeria, both civil society groups and the commission itself stressed the limitations inherent in the terms of reference that created that country's truth commission. Specifically, there were clear constraints resulting from the reliance on the preexisting Tribunals of Inquiry Act to empower the commission, which some referred to as a "straitjacket" within which the commission had to operate. There was no process of reflection on the means or intended ends of the commission before it was established, leading to lack of clarity and competing demands as it began its work.

In contrast, Peru went through a relatively wide-reaching consultative process in determining the terms of reference for its commission, but little consultation in selecting the members of the commission outside of a small group within government who helped to choose the first members under a short deadline. The first seven members did not reflect a sufficient mix of skills, diversity, and political breadth, which led to the addition of five more members several weeks later in order to further diversify the membership. This selection process cut short an otherwise strong process of consultation in the commission's development, and initially weakened what has been until then an unimpeachable process with strong backing from most parties.

The power of holding public hearings has been highlighted by the huge impact of the hearings held by the presidentially appointed truth commission in Nigeria. The Nigerian public was thoroughly absorbed for a full year in watching the commission's televised sessions, which were aired during the day and then repeated again at night on several channels, as well as played live on numerous radio stations. The great public interest in the commission's work, and especially the appearance of many persons accused of involvement in past abuses, seemed to fundamentally shift the public's understanding of events that took place under military rule. The compelling nature of the South African commission's hearings has led a number of countries, including Peru, East Timor, and Sierra Leone, to include a public hearings component in their mandate, although the way these hearings will be run and the role they will play will differ considerably among the different countries. Nevertheless, the point of making a truth commission more than an exercise of fact collection and report writing—turning it into a process of public engagement rather than an exercise primarily focused on final product—seems to have been thoroughly won.

Transitional justice as a whole has received greater attention over the past year as countries emerging from a bad past have recognized the importance of thinking holistically when designing its policies to respond to past human rights violations. Creative, interlinked approaches to justice offer possibilities for satisfying more of the many needs and demands that a state is likely to confront, as well as fulfilling more of the state's legal obligations. It is now generally recognized that the varied approaches to truth-seeking, prosecutions, reparations, reform, and reconciliation initiatives are strongest when designed from the start to complement and reinforce each other. Some of these demands may be considered during a period of constitutional reform, or during a tense period of negotiating a peace accord. It is important to fully understand the ramifications of decisions taken at an early stage, which may unnecessarily impact the possibility of establishing accountability at a later stage.

As the pace of activities around truth commissions and transitional justice increased in 2000 and 2001, the Ford Foundation took the lead in creating a new organization to assist countries emerging from repressive rule or armed conflict that are struggling to implement transitional justice policies. With the backing of the Ford and other foundations, the International Center for Transitional Justice was founded in March 2001, based in New York City.[1] The center responds to requests for legal and technical assistance from both governmental and nongovernmental actors, helping to craft policies that respond to unique national circumstances. It also undertakes research and provides training and capacity building for in-country actors grappling with transitional justice questions. New developments and new challenges in transitional justice are emerging almost daily. It is clear, at the end of 2001, that the field of transitional justice as a whole—that broad arena of issues, challenges, and policies for addressing a brutal past—is in rapid expansion. The clear trend toward stronger and more deeply-rooted truth commissions is but one sign of this change. More important, there is an increased expectation of accountability at a time of transition, and with it, a sense that creative mechanisms can be found to advance the possibilities of justice on the ground. The forms that such a justice policy takes—and the interplay between the various mechanisms used—may differ dramatically, as demonstrated in the diverse examples described below.

Truth commissions are, of course, just one of the mechanisms for accounting for the past, and they clearly complement but do not replace others. The strength as well as the challenge of these truth-seeking efforts remains in their flexibility and great potential, as well as in the need to carefully shape their plan of work to respond to the needs and realities of each country. The descriptions below show how well some of the new commissions have begun to do that.

NEW TRUTH COMMISSIONS

Panama (January 2001)

Ten years after the fall of the government of Manuel Noriega and the U.S. invasion of Panama, the legacy of years of authoritarian rule remained unsettled. In late 1999 unmarked graves were discovered on the site of an old army base near Panama City's main airport. These graves were discovered after three soldiers confessed to their priests about their existence, and were believed to contain the remains of several opposition activists murdered during the period of military rule.

In response to growing public calls for an investigation, in January 2001 President Mireya Moscoso established the Panama Truth Commission through executive decree.[2] The commission is mandated to examine human rights violations in Panama that were "committed during the military regime," from the coup d'état of October 1968 to late 1989. National and international human rights organizations have provided assistance and information about human rights violations, with a particular focus on disappearances. While initially given a six- to nine-month mandate, the commission received a six-month extension, and is expected to submit a final report in early 2002.

Federal Republic of Yugoslavia (March 2001)

After years of wrenching war in the Balkans that resulted in the break-up of the former Yugoslavia into four independent states, the death of over 200,000 persons and the displacement of millions, the president of the Federal Republic of Yugoslavia, Slobodan Milosevic, was voted out of office in late 2000. Several months later he was arrested and charged with abuse of power and corruption, and then, in July 2001, transferred to the Hague to face charges of crimes against humanity, war crimes, and genocide before the International Criminal Tribunal for the former Yugoslavia (ICTY).

Acting on his own initiative, newly elected president Vojislav Kostunica announced the creation of the Commission for Truth and Reconciliation in March 2001. With little consultation on the terms or membership of the commission, President Kostunica asked the commission to outline its own terms of reference. The commission circulated a draft program for its work to the public for comment, and, with its terms of reference finalized, formally began its work in February 2002. It was given three years to complete its investigations and submit a report. Unfortunately, the commission has met with controversy from the start, as two of its members resigned very soon after appointment.

Given the fact that the much of the war and many of its victims were outside the current state of Yugoslavia, the commission has committed to working regionally and to holding hearings or taking statements, as much as possible, outside of the current state borders. It has also committed to cooperating fully with the ICTY.

Peru (June 2001)

The government of President Alberto Fujimori collapsed in November 2000 in the face of massive evidence of corruption at the highest levels of his government. The end of the Fujimori regime opened up the possibility of assigning accountability for two decades of abuses. Since 1980 the armed conflict between the government and armed opposition groups (the Shining Path and the Tupac Amaru Revolutionary Movement) had been marked by extrajudicial killings, thousands of disappearances, torture, and other serious violations of human rights and international humanitarian law. During the past decade, anti-democratic measures such as the executive's control of judicial and electoral systems contributed to the further erosion of important rights.

Pressure from some sectors of civil society for an official inquiry into past abuses led to a fairly extensive process of reviewing possible terms of such an endeavor, and in June 2001 the interim president issued a decree establishing the Truth Commission (later renamed the Truth and Reconciliation Commission). The commission's mandate directs it to investigate human rights abuses and violations of humanitarian law attributable to the State or to armed insurgent groups between May 1980 and November 2000. In July 2001, after a selection process that invited no public participation or debate, the initial members of the commission were sworn in by the interim president.

Amid public criticism of some initial selections and general concern that the membership was not sufficiently representative, newly elected president Alejandro Toledo named five additional members to the commission in August. The full twelve-person commission (with the head of Peru's Episcopal Conference serving as an observer) had greater human rights expertise and an additional commissioner from outside of Lima. Perhaps most controversial was the appointment of a retired air force general who also serves as Toledo's national security advisor. While the selection process got the commission off to a somewhat rocky start, attention then turned to the substance of the commission's work, which is what will ultimately determine its success.

In his inaugural speech President Toledo pledged his support for the work of the commission and committed his government to implementing the commission's recommendations. The commission has nineteen months to undertake its work, including a four-month preparatory period, plus the possibility of a five-month extension. The commission is directed to determine the conditions that gave rise to the violence, contribute to judicial investigations, draft proposals for reparations, and recommend reforms. The Peruvian commission will also be the first of its kind in Latin America to hold public hearings, which will begin in April 2002.

East Timor (July 2001)

After twenty-five years of stern rule by Indonesia during which an estimated 200,000 East Timorese were killed and many more displaced, East Timor was finally granted the opportunity in August 1999 to vote for either independence or autonomy. The pro-independence vote won by a huge majority, despite active intimidation by Indonesian-backed militias and threats of violence. When the results were announced, the militias reacted with extreme violence, looting and burning large sections of many towns and cities, killing an estimated 1,000 people, and forcibly removing over 200,000 East Timorese across the border to West Timor, a part of Indonesia. After fleeing to West Timor themselves, many of the estimated 10,000 East Timorese militia members feared retribution if they returned to their communities, and were thus hesitant to return home.

The United Nations governed East Timor during the transitional period through the United Nations Transitional Administration for East Timor (UNTAET). When a proposal for a truth commission was put on the table by the main coalition of political parties, the Human Rights Office of UNTAET facilitated a process to incorporate lessons learned from the experiences of truth commissions worldwide.[3]

The truth commission crafted for East Timor—put together under the guidance of a steering committee of representatives of civil society, church, and political party groups, looked different from any other previous truth commission. The Commission for Reception, Truth, and Reconciliation (known in Portuguese as the Comissão de Acolhimento, Verdade, e Reconciliação) was given the mandate of inquiring into human rights violations committed within the context of political conflict in East Timor between April 25, 1974, and October 25, 1999. It was given full powers of subpoena and, with the assistance of the police, the power to search and seize information from any location in the country. It had two years to complete its task, after a two-month preparatory period, with the possibility of an extension of six months.

In addition to these recognizable truth-seeking functions, however, the commission was also crafted to facilitate the return home of low-level perpetrators. The commission offered a bargain: those persons involved in less-serious crimes could admit to and apologize for their crimes, and agree to undertake community service or make symbolic reparatory payments or a public apology as a means of facilitating their return. Loosely based on indigenous East Timorese processes, these arrangements will be expedited and monitored directly by the commission, and brokered through community-based panels organized by regional commissioners with the involvement of the injured community and victims themselves. The final agreements are to be approved by a court, and full compliance with the agreement will result in a waiver of criminal and civil liabilities flowing from the crime.

Persons responsible for murder, sexual offences, organizing or instigating the violence, or undertaking other serious crimes may not enter into the community reconciliation process. Before entering into the community reconciliation process, perpetrators' applications will be reviewed by the office of the prosecutor of UNTAET's Serious Crimes Unit, which has the power to remove the person from the truth commission's process if there is evidence that they took part in a serious crime.

The commission was created in law through a UNTAET regulation in July 2001.[4] A preparatory secretariat was established to prepare logistics, raise funds, and undertake other planning for the commission's startup in early 2002. In December, after extensive consultations coordinated by a representative selection panel, seven national commissioners were selected. In addition, a small advisory board of prominent East Timorese and international members was created to assist the commission. The commission was formally launched, and the commissioners sworn in, in late January 2002.

Other Developments

As of this writing, two other commissions are under way that in many respects should rightly be characterized as truth commissions, though they have a more limited focus and reach than do typical truth commissions of today. In South Korea, the Presidential Truth Commission on Suspicious Deaths was formed in October 17, 2000, to investigate the deaths of democratization activists during past periods of authoritarian regimes.[5] The commission received eighty petitions in the three-month period stipulated for victims to submit claims. In addition to clarifying the circumstances of the deaths, the commission was directed to name persons that it concluded should be prosecuted for these crimes. The commission was able to award the equivalent of $40,000 to persons who provided information, evidence, or documentation that significantly advanced its investigations. The commission is largely focused on individual cases, rather than broad patterns, causes, or overall consequences of past events. It will continue its work into 2002.

In Uruguay, the Peace Commission was created by the recently elected president, Jorge Batlle, in August 2000. It was directed to "receive, analyze, classify, and gather together information regarding the forced disappearances that occurred during the *de facto* regime." At first seen to represent a new opening into the issue of the disappeared after years of neglect and official denial, the commission lost some support after it became clear that its work would be relatively confined. With six commission members and only one staff member, an administrative secretary, the commission showed little inclination and had few powers with which to aggressively investigate individual cases. A final report is expected in early 2002, which is likely to include recommendations for possible reparations to the families of the disappeared.

TRUTH COMMISSIONS IN DEVELOPMENT

It is likely that truth commissions will be created in the following countries, some of them perhaps as soon as in the next months.

Ghana

The government of Ghana proposed the creation of a National Reconciliation Commission in early 2001, suggesting a mandate to cover all periods of military government, including the periods in which Jerry Rawlings was the military ruler. Over the next months, intensive national and international consultation took place to consider the best mandate and reach of the commission, with some arguing for a mandate that would extend back to the date of independence in 1957 and that would include all governments through 1993, when Jerry Rawlings submitted himself to the electoral process and was elected to the presidency. The final legislation, signed into law in January 2002, provided for the commission to focus on the years of unconstitutional government (February 1966 to August 1969; January 1972 to September 1979; and December 1981 to January 1993), but allows the commission to look into any event between March 1957 and January 1993 that may fall outside of these specified years. Civil society organizations, in particular the Center for Democratic Development in Ghana, played a strong role in facilitating a consultative process on the bill. The membership of the commission was being considered as of this writing. The commission is expected to be underway by May or June, 2002.

Bosnia-Herzegovina

After more than three years of discussion, the idea of a truth commission for Bosnia-Herzegovina began to receive much greater attention in 2000 and 2001. Local human rights organizations pushing for a commission have understood the commission to be a complement to the work of the International Criminal Tribunal for the former Yugoslavia, not something that would supplant the tribunal's work. The tribunal, which had initially opposed the idea of a national truth commission, reconsidered its view after consultation with local actors, and came to support the proposal. The proposed terms of reference were changed to ensure a sharing of information from the commission at the tribunal's request, and the commission to defer to the tribunal's jurisdiction. One unique aspect of the proposed mandate directs the commission to document positive actions taken across ethnic or religious lines to assist those in danger during the course of the war.

In early 2002, as of this writing, legislation for the establishment of such a commission was under consideration by the federal legislature of Bosnia, as well as the legislative bodies of Republika Srpska and the Muslim/Croat Federation, the constituent parts of Bosnia-Herzegovina.

Burundi

After eight years of civil strife and an estimated 250,000 killed, a transitional government took power in Burundi on November 1, 2001. The peace accord leading to the transitional government calls for the establishment of both a national truth commission to look at events from 1962 to August 2000 and an international commission of inquiry to look into the question of whether genocide took place and whether an international tribunal is needed. The accord provided that the truth commission would be created within six months of the start of the transitional government. This commission, presuming that it is in fact established, will confront the difficult challenge of trying to establish the truth about a conflict while the conflict is still ongoing: a number of rebel groups did not join the peace accord, and continued violence will likely keep parts of the country out of reach of investigators.

Others

A truth commission has been proposed in Mexico, with support from many human rights advocates and some members of the government of President Vicente Fox, but with skepticism from others. The issue remained on the table in Mexico and continued to receive considerable attention through early 2002. The proposal for a truth commission in Indonesia, which was under serious discussion through 2000 and the beginning of 2001, was left unclear with the incoming of the new president, Megawati Sukarnoputri, in July 2001. Finally, some activists in other countries, such as Croatia, Morocco, and Kenya, were also proposing the formation of truth commissions, for which they are finding some support, but the outlook is still unclear.

UPDATES ON COMMISSIONS DESCRIBED IN CHAPTER FIVE

Two of the commissions described in chapter five have seen important advances since the publication of the first edition of this book. In Nigeria, the commission is now completing its work, while in Sierra Leone, a commission is just about to begin, after considerable delays.

Nigeria

The Oputa Panel, as the Human Rights Violations Investigations Commission was commonly known in Nigeria, began with almost no advance planning and little financial support from the government, and also with few expectations from the public. In time, however, the panel gained an extraordinary level of public interest and support, largely through a year-long process of closely watched public hearings. Broadcast live on television daily and watched by a huge percentage of the Nigerian public, the panel's work seemed to reach all levels of society. It held hearings almost full-time for over a year, traveling to a number of locations around the country and calling forward victims and persons accused in a wide range of events. While the commission held subpoena power, it rarely used it, and most of those accused came forward voluntarily to answer to the charges against them. In a big disappointment to the commission's work, it was not able to question three former heads of state, two of whom obtained court injunctions to prevent their being subpoenaed.

The panel's success was especially striking given the limited resources it had at its disposal — only $450,000 in grants from the Ford Foundation, which covered the cost of the hearings. Its staff, which totaled fewer than a dozen persons, were on loan from the government. Given these constraints, the commission was not able to undertake investigations or corroboration into cases outside of the questioning that took place at the hearings. It did ask the inspector general of the police to create a special unit to investigate cases in which evidence from the commission's hearings suggested that prosecution might be warranted, with approximately thirty-five cases forwarded to this unit from the commission for investigation. It was expected that the panel's report would be finished in early- to mid-2002.

Sierra Leone

Plans for the Truth and Reconciliation Commission in Sierra Leone were slowed after fighting between the rebels and the government was reignited in early 2000. By late 2001 the peace process and disarmament were much further along, and a rigorous process was under way to select the four national and three international commissioners. After receiving over sixty nominations from the public for national commissioners, a representative selection panel conducted interviews of the top candidates and trimmed the list to four national commissioners. The UN high commissioner for human rights, meanwhile, was as of this writing choosing three international members. It is expected that the seven members will be appointed in May 2002, and the work of the commission will begin shortly thereafter.

CONCLUSION

It was only shortly after the U.S. military campaign began in Afghanistan, in fall 2001, that there was first talk of the possibility of a truth commission for that country. Undoubtedly, these discussions were prompted by international personnel in the region who had sufficient experience in other countries to understand both the attraction and the difficulty of such a proposal. As an interim government took power in Afghanistan and questions of accountability for the past remained undefined, it was not clear what the Afghan people would want, or whether a digging up and retelling of the violence suffered over many years would help them to settle their conflicts and heal their wounds. The first question that must be asked, as always, is whether and how the people of any land, and especially those who directly suffered from past policies, want to remember and preserve their past—and, if they do, what the strongest and most appropriate mechanism for accomplishing that is. That question has not yet been answered in Afghanistan, as it has not been answered in many other countries that may, with luck, emerge from abusive rule over the next years.

Whether Afghanistan or any other country decides to take a path toward formal truth-seeking is less important, however, than how the country develops and incorporates a broader vision to halt the culture of impunity that is common in countries emerging from authoritarian rule. A broad view toward the possibility of justice over the long term, including both accountability for the past and prevention of further abuses in the future, must inform the difficult decisions that will have to be made.

NOTES

The sources that are cited frequently throughout the book, particularly truth commission reports, are listed in full in the section that follows, *Frequently Cited Sources,* and are listed in the notes in only abbreviated form.

CHAPTER TWO

1. Guillermo O'Donnell, Philippe C. Schmitter, and Laurence Whitehead, eds., *Transitions from Authoritarian Rule: Tentative Conclusions about Uncertain Democracies* (Baltimore: Johns Hopkins University Press, 1986).

2. Ibid., 75.

3. In the past years, a number of good books and articles have been published in this burgeoning field of transitional justice. Books include, to name just a few, Neil J. Kritz, ed., *Transitional Justice: How Emerging Democracies Reckon with Former Regimes,* vols. 1–3 (Washington, D.C.: U.S. Institute of Peace Press, 1995); Steven R. Ratner and Jason S. Abrams, *Accountability for Human Rights Atrocities in International Law: Beyond the Nuremberg Legacy* (New York: Oxford University Press, 1997); Aryeh Neier, *War Crimes: Brutality, Genocide, Terror, and the Struggle for Justice* (New York: Times Books, 1998); Naomi Roht-Arriaza, ed., *Impunity and Human Rights in International Law and Practice* (New York: Oxford University Press, 1995); James A. McAdams, ed., *Transitional Justice and the Rule of Law in New Democracies* (Notre Dame, IN: University of Notre Dame Press, 1997); Justice and Society Program of the Aspen Institute, *State Crimes: Punishment or Pardon* (Queenstown, MD: the Aspen Institute, 1989). Special issue journals include: M. Cherif Bassiouni and Madeline H. Morris, eds., "Accountability for International Crimes and Serious Violations of Fundamental Human Rights," *Law and Contemporary Problems* 59 (1996); and Madeline H. Morris, ed., "Symposium: Justice in Cataclysm: Criminal Trials in the Wake of Mass Violence." *Duke Journal of Comparative and International Law* 7 (1997). Articles include: Timothy Garton Ash, "The Truth about Dictatorship," *New York Review of Books*, February 19, 1998, 35–40; Luc Huyse, "Justice after Transition: On the Choices Successor Elites Make in Dealing with the Past," *Law and Social Inquiry* 20 (1995), 51–78; Juan E. Méndez, "Accountability for Past Abuses," *Human Rights Quarterly* 19 (1997), 255–82; Aryeh Neier, "What Should Be Done about the Guilty?" *New York Review of Books,* February 1, 1990; Michelle Parlevliet, "Considering Truth: Dealing with a Legacy of Gross Human Rights Violations," *Netherlands Quarterly of Human Rights* 16 (1998), 141–74; Margaret Popkin and Naomi Roht-Arriaza, "Truth as Justice: Investigatory Commission in Latin America," *Law and Social Inquiry: The Journal of the American Bar Foundation* 20 (1995), 79–116; Richard Lewis Siegel, "Transitional Justice: A Decade of Debate and Experience," *Human Rights Quarterly* 20 (1998), 431–54; and José Zalaquett, "Balancing Ethical Imperatives and Political Constraints: The Dilemma of New Democracies Confronting Past Human Rights Violations," *Hastings Law Journal* 43 (1992), 1425–38. A number of excellent country-specific studies of truth commissions have also appeared, which are noted in the footnotes to the country descriptions in this book.

4. The implementation of lustration policies has varied widely. In some states, persons shown to have been affiliated with the prior regime can also lose their employment in the private sector.

5. On the experience of lustration in Eastern Europe generally, see Herman Schwartz, "Lustration in Eastern Europe," *Parker School Journal of East European Law* 1 (1994), 141–71, and Vojtech Cepl, "Ritual Sacrifices: Lustration in the CSFR," *East European Constitutional Review* 1 (1992), 24–26. On the role of lustration in revealing truth, see Maria Łoś, "Lustration and Truth Claims: Unfinished Revolutions in Central Europe," *Law and Social Inquiry* (1995), 117–61.

6. For further exploration of this subject, see especially Tina Rosenberg, *Haunted Lands: Facing Europe's Ghosts After Communism* (New York: Random House, 1995), and Timothy Garton Ash, *The File: A Personal History* (New York: Random House, 1997).

7. There are, of course, examples of individualized access to files kept by intelligence agenices in the United States (through the Freedom of Information Act) and a few other Western non-transitional states.

8. The list of twenty-one truth commissions provided here is not necessarily exhaustive. There may be other past inquiries that would fit the definition of *truth commission* used here, but this list includes the most prominent of such bodies to date. Truth commissions should also be distinguished from what are commonly called national "human rights commissions," which are state bodies established to investigate present-day human rights conditions and violations under the current government. Some human rights commissions have been given briefs that include looking at crimes in the past, thus taking on some truth commission–like functions. These include, for example, a Presidential Committee on Human Rights established by President Corazon Aquino in the Philippines after the fall of the Marcos regime. While many complaints came in pertaining to the Marcos period, this committee was not expected to produce an overall report nor to document the pattern of past abuses, but rather focused its work on responding to individual cases, including filing a number of cases in court.

9. National Inquiry into the Separation of Aboriginal and Torres Strait Islander Children from Their Families, *Bringing them Home: Report of the National Inquiry into the Separation of Aboriginal and Torres Strait Islander Children from Their Families* (Sydney, Australia: Human Rights and Equal Opportunity Commission, 1997).

10. A summary of the Royal Commission on Aboriginal Peoples' report can be found at http://www.inac.gc.ca/rcap/report/word.html.

11. *Gathering Strength: Canada's Aboriginal Action Plan,* of January 1998, can be found at http://www.inac.gc.ca/news/jan98/1–9801.html.

12. Danielle Gordon, "The Verdict: No Harm, No Foul," *The Bulletin of the Atomic Scientists* 52:1 (1996), 33. See also Michael D'Antonio, "Atomic Guinea Pigs," *New York Times Magazine,* August 31, 1997, 38–43.

13. The first checks to the surviving internees were not distributed until 1990. Each internee who was still alive on the date that the legislation was passed (or the heirs of those who died in the interim) received $20,000. See Leslie T. Hatamiya, *Righting a Wrong: Japanese Americans and the Passage of the Civil Liberties Act of 1988* (Stanford, CA: Stanford University Press, 1993).

14. Carol Kaesuk Yoon, "Families Emerge as Silent Victims of Tuskegee Syphilis Experiment," *New York Times,* May 12, 1997, A1. The Tuskegee Syphilis Study was first made public in 1972 through investigative reporting by the Associated Press, and only then was the experiment stopped. This media exposure eventually led to the promulgation of the National Research Act of 1974, which created oversight boards to approve all federally funded research involving human subjects.

15. Leo Valladares, in conversation with the author, September 1995, Washington, DC. See Comisionado Nacional de Protección de los Derechos Humanos, *Los Hechos Hablan por sí Mismos: Informe Preliminar sobre los Desaparecidos en Honduras 1980-1993* (Tegucigalpa, Honduras: Editorial Guaymuras, 1994), or in English, *The Facts Speak for Themselves: The Preliminary Report on Disappearances of the National Commissioner for the Protection of Human Rights in Honduras,* trans. Human Rights Watch and the Center for Justice and International Law (New York: Human Rights Watch, 1994).

16. *We Will Remember Them: Report of the Northern Ireland Victims Commissioner, Sir Kenneth Bloomfield KCB,* April 1998, 8 and 37–38.

17. Human Rights Watch, *Report of the International Commission of Investigation on Human Rights Violations in Rwanda since October 1, 1990 (January 7–21, 1993)* (New York: Human Rights Watch, 1993). The four organizations that jointly sponsored this commission were Human Rights Watch (New York), the International Federation of Human Rights (Paris), the International Center of Human Rights and Democratic Development (Montreal), and the Interafrican Union of Human Rights (Ouagadougou, Burkina Faso).

In previous writing, I identified this commission as a truth commission (see Priscilla B. Hayner, "Fifteen Truth Commissions—1974 to 1994: A Comparative Study," *Human Rights*

Quarterly 16:4 (1994), 629–32, where the commission is described in greater detail). However, despite the quasi-official status it was given with an official government welcome and with roots in the peace accord, this commission was ultimately a nongovernmental effort that is considerably different from the twenty-one official truth commissions described here. Thus, I include it here as a "semiofficial" inquiry into the past.

18. Comments of Dawit Yohannes, Speaker of the House of People's Representatives, Ethiopia, at the International Seminar on Justice, Truth and Reconciliation, December 10, 1998, Geneva.

19. For example, the commission on the former Yugoslavia was called the United Nations Commission of Experts Established Pursuant to Security Council Resolution 780 (1992) to Investigate Violations of International Humanitarian Law in the Former Yugoslavia. It was chaired by M. Cherif Bassiouni, a professor of law at DePaul University.

20. *Brasil: Nunca Mais* (Rio de Janeiro: Editora Vozes, 1985); published in English as *Torture in Brazil: A Shocking Report on the Pervasive Use of Torture by Brazilian Military Governments, 1964-1979*, trans. Jaime Wright (Austin: University of Texas Press, 1998). For a fascinating description of the Brazilian project, see Lawrence Weschler, *A Miracle, A Universe: Settling Accounts with Torturers* (New York: Penguin, 1990; reprint with postscript, Chicago: University of Chicago Press, 1998). Because the Brazil project was carried out secretly, church backing not only provided financial support, but also lent legitimacy to the report.

21. Servicio Paz y Justicia (SERPAJ), *Uruguay Nunca Más: Informe Sobre la Violación a los Derechos Humanos (1972–1985)*, 2nd ed. (Montevideo, Uruguay: SERPAJ, 1989). The parliamentary commission was mandated to investigate disappearances only, which missed the great majority of abuses in the country: illegal imprisonment and torture.

22. The Archbishop of Guatemala's Office of Human Rights project (the Recovery of Historical Memory Project, or REMHI), resulted in a four-volume final report, published in 1998. See *Guatemala: Nunca Más*, 4 vols. (Guatemala City: Oficina de Derechos Humanos del Arzobispado de Guatemala, 1998). A summary of the report has been published in English as *Guatemala: Never Again!* (Maryknoll, NY: Orbis Books, and London: Catholic Institute of International Relations, 1999).

23. See, for example, *Links: Historical Almanac,* vol. 1 (Moscow: Progress Phoenix, 1991) and *List of Executed People, vol. 1: Donskoi Cemetery 1934–1943* (Moscow: Memorial, 1993), both in Russian. For a description of Memorial's activities, see "Making Rights Real: Two Human Rights Groups Assist Russian Reforms," *Ford Foundation Report,* Summer 1993, 10–15, or Nanci Adler, *Victims of Soviet Terror: The Story of the Memorial Movement* (Westport, CT: Praeger, 1993).

24. Pedro Nikken, interview by the author, September 18, 1997, Siracusa, Italy.

25. The formal name of the Guatemalan commission was actually the Commission to Clarify Past Human Rights Violations and Acts of Violence That Have Caused the Guatemalan People to Suffer.

26. The states in which a truth commission has been discussed include Bosnia, Serbia, Indonesia, East Timor, Peru, Colombia, Suriname, Jamaica, Liberia, Mali, Namibia, Malawi, Kenya, Burundi, Rwanda, and the Philippines. In some of these states, a truth commission has been talked about but is probably very unlikely; in others, there is serious interest in the creation of a future truth commission and options are being closely considered; in yet others, a transition has not yet unfolded sufficiently to determine whether a truth-seeking body will take shape.

CHAPTER THREE

1. Michael Ignatieff, "Articles of Faith," *Index on Censorship* 25, no. 5 (1996), 113.

2. "Discurso de S.E. el Presidente de la Republica, Don Patricio Aylwin Azocar, al dar a Conocer a la Ciudadania el Informe de la Comisión de Verdad y Reconciliación," March 4, 1991;

published in English as "Statement by President Aylwin on the Report of the National Commission on Truth and Reconciliation," in Kritz, *Transitional Justice,* vol. 3, 169–73.

3. This conference resulted in the book *State Crimes: Punishment or Pardon* (New York: Aspen Institute, 1989). Professor Thomas Nagel of New York University is credited with first articulating this distinction between *knowledge* and *acknowledgment.*

4. Aryeh Neier, "What Should Be Done about the Guilty?" *New York Review of Books,* February 1, 1990, 34.

5. Juan Méndez, review of *A Miracle, A Universe,* by Lawrence Weschler, in *New York Law School Journal of Human Rights* 8 (1991), 8.

6. Aryeh Neier, telephone interview by the author, July 31, 1996.

7. In fact, no truth commission to date has resulted in or caused any serious incident of violence. The question of the relationship between truth-seeking and conflict resolution, including the possibility of a truth commission's sparking further violence, is addressed at some length in Priscilla B. Hayner, "Past Truths, Present Dangers: The Role of Official Truth Seeking in Conflict Resolution and Prevention," in Paul C. Stern and Daniel Druckman, eds., *International Conflict Resolution After the Cold War* (Washington, DC: National Academy Press, forthcoming 2000).

8. Article 19, "Malawi's Past: The Right to Truth," Censorship News 29 (1993), 3.

9. See, for example, Juan Méndez, "Accountability for Past Abuses," *Human Rights Quarterly* 19 (1997), 255–82, which argues strongly for a right to the truth.

CHAPTER FOUR

1. There have been smaller, subnational commissions that could fit within the definition used here, for example. Some regional governments of Argentina undertook official investigations into the abuses in their respective regions.

2. Jaime Malamud-Goti, interview by the author, December 1998, Geneva, Switzerland. Argentines were conscious of following the example of neighboring Bolivia in proposing a commission of inquiry on past rights crimes; the Bolivian commission is described in the next chapter. Author interview with Mercedes Doretti, Argentine Forensic Anthropology Team, March 26, 1993, New York.

3. *Nunca Más: Report of the Argentine National Commission on the Disappeared,* 428.

4. The full report included over fifty thousand pages of documentation, according to Human Rights Watch. See *Truth and Partial Justice in Argentina: An Update* (New York: Human Rights Watch, 1991), 18.

5. For further information on these trials and other issues of transitional justice in Argentina, see Carlos S. Nino (former advisor to president Alfonsín), "The Duty to Punish Past Abuses of Human Rights Put Into Context: The Case of Argentina," *Yale Law Journal* 100 (1991): 2619–40; Jaime Malamud-Goti (senior presidential advisor to Alfonsín, 1983–1987), "Trying Violators of Human Rights: The Dilemma of Transitional Democratic Governments," in Justice and Society Program of the Aspen Institute, *State Crimes: Punishment or Pardon* (Queenstown, MD: Aspen Institute, 1989), 71–88; Human Rights Watch, *Truth and Partial Justice in Argentina: An Update* (New York: Human Rights Watch, 1991); Alejandro M. Garro, "Nine Years of Transition to Democracy in Argentina: Partial Failure or Qualified Success?" *Columbia Journal of Transnational Law* 31 (1993), 1–102; and Marguerite Feitlowitz, *A Lexicon of Terror: Argentina and the Legacies of Torture* (New York: Oxford University Press, 1998).

6. Decree Establishing the National Commission on Truth and Reconciliation, Supreme Decree No. 355, Chile, April 25, 1990, reprinted in Kritz, *Transitional Justice,* vol. 3, 102.

7. The decision to exclude torture victims from the investigatory mandate of the commission was based on two factors. First, it was clear that no commission could investigate all cases of torture, and there was a desire to avoid opening up the commission to many thousands of cases that could not be fully investigated. Second, as explained by the person who drafted the mandate of

the commission, the state wanted to limit the cases to a reasonable number that could receive compensation; as it was assumed that the commission's records would lead to a reparations program, they therefore excluded survivors of torture from being categorized as victims. Conversation by the author with Gisela von Muhlenbrok, March 13, 1997, Washington, D.C.

8. *Report of the Chilean National Commission on Truth and Reconciliation*, 14.

9. Under Chilean law, the power of subpoena is reserved for the courts.

10. Of these 2,920 cases, 2,025 were determined to be human rights violations by the state security forces; 90 were violations attributable to the armed opposition; 164 were attributed to political violence, such as gun battles; and on 641 cases the commission did not come to a conclusion.

11. Just over 4 percent were attributed to "individuals acting with political pretext," or leftist armed groups.

12. Instead, the report makes clear, there was very little armed resistance to the coup, and many of those who were called turned themselves in to detention centers voluntarily.

13. Human Rights Watch, *Human Rights and the "Politics of Agreements": Chile during President Aylwin's First Year* (New York: Human Rights Watch, 1991), 17, citing *La Epoca*, February 9, 1991.

14. "Discurso de S.E. El Presidente de la Republica, Don Patricio Aylwin Azocar, al dar a Conocer a la Ciudadania El Informe de la Comisión de Verdad y Reconciliación, March 4, 1991; published in English as "Statement by President Aylwin on the Report of the National Commission on Truth and Reconciliation," in Kritz, *Transitional Justice*, vol. 3, 169–73.

15. Human Rights Watch, *"Politics of Agreement,"* 32–33.

16. Ibid., 30. The first killing, of an army doctor who had been censured for having participated in torture sessions, took place just as Aylwin was releasing the report. Human Rights Watch describes, "On March 5, photographs of the doctor's funeral, attended by Pinochet and other senior army officials, competed for front-page space with photographs of Aylwin presenting the Rettig report." Ibid., 29–30.

17. Human Rights Watch, *Chile: The Struggle for Truth and Justice for Past Human Rights Violations* (New York: Human Rights Watch, 1992), 2.

18. Law Creating the National Corporation for Reparation and Reconciliation, Law No. 19, 123, Chile, January 31, 1992; reprinted in Kritz, *Transitional Justice*, vol. 3, 685–95.

19. This percentage is based on an estimate of 70,000 deaths and a population of five million. See Martha Doggett, *Death Foretold: The Jesuit Murders in El Salvador* (New York: Lawyers Committee for Human Rights, and Washington, DC: Georgetown University Press, 1993), 22.

20. For further information on the killing of the Jesuits, see Teresa Whitfield, *Paying the Price: Ignacio Ellacuría and the Murdered Jesuits of El Salvador* (Philadelphia: Temple University Press, 1995), and Doggett, *Death Foretold*.

21. *From Madness to Hope: Report of the Commission on the Truth for El Salvador*, 18.

22. Interestingly, there were some early discussions in El Salvador of employing an "amnesty for truth" strategy, as was later crafted in South Africa. Some staff on the commission discussed the idea with commissioners, but it was never developed further. Later, Jesuit priest José María Tojeira responded to the truth commission report by suggesting that in order to receive a pardon, persons should admit their crimes and ask Salvadoran society for forgiveness. He proposed that there be "two routes: confess and ask society for forgiveness, or stand trial" and emphasized the need for "legal forgiveness." See Doggett, *Death Foretold*, 273.

23. Doggett, *Death Foretold*, 258. The Postscript to this book provides an excellent summary of the reaction to the truth commission report both in El Salvador and in the United States.

24. Ibid., 264.

25. Ibid., 266. A more recent analysis of the truth commission in El Salvador, by U.S.-based El Salvador expert Margaret Popkin, notes that "Although the report did not constitute an official Salvadoran acknowledgment of the truth, it still must be considered an authoritative document, the value of which is not determined by the immediate acceptance or rejection of its findings. . . . [T]he truth commission's report stands as a powerful indictment of the kinds of violations com-

mitted during the war and of the active and passive complicity of state institutions." See Margaret L. Popkin, *Peace without Justice: Obstacles to Building the Rule of Law in El Salvador* (University Park: Pennsylvania State University Press, 2000), 159–60.

26. As has been noted by international legal scholars, however, there is no statute of limitations for crimes against humanity; further political and judicial changes in the future could open the door to legal action against perpetrators.

27. Doggett, *Death Foretold,* 277.

28. Kader Asmal, a leading ANC member, was the first to argue for the importance of truth in a key public lecture at the University of the Western Cape in 1992. See Kader Asmal, "Victims, Survivors and Citizens—Human Rights, Reparations and Reconciliation," *South African Journal on Human Rights* 8, no. 4 (1992), 491–511.

29. There have also been many books and articles published on the South African commission. These include Desmond Tutu, *No Future without Forgiveness* (New York: Doubleday, 1999); Alexander Boraine, *A Country Unmasked: The Story of the South African Truth and Reconciliation Commission* (Cape Town: Oxford University Press, forthcoming); Antjie Krog, *Country of My Skull* (Johannesburg: Random House, 1998, and New York: Times Books, 1999); Martin Meredith, *Coming to Terms: South Africa's Search for Truth* (New York: Public Affairs, 1999); and Charles Villa-Vicencio and Wilhelm Verwoerd, eds., *Looking Back Reaching Forward: Reflections on the Truth and Reconciliation Commission of South Africa* (Cape Town: University of Cape Town Press, and London: Zed Books, 2000).

30. Many of these amnesty applicants, well over half, were already in prison, however; some Amnesty Committee members felt that the majority of the applications were clearly not in relation to political offenses, but were long-shot attempts to obtain freedom.

31. Of the seven thousand amnesty applications, some two thousand pertained to gross human rights violations, requiring a public hearing.

32. Among the factors that the Amnesty Committee considered to determine whether the applicant satisfied the terms for amnesty were (1) motive; (2) the context in which the act, omission or offense took place; (3) the objective of the act, omission, or offense, and in particular whether it was primarily directed at a political opponent or State property or personnel, or against private property or individuals; (4) whether it was carried out as an order, on behalf of, or with the approval of the organization, institution, or liberation movement of which the person who committed the act was a member, an agent, or supporter; and (5) the relationship between the act, omission, or offense and the political objective pursued, and in particular whether there was proportionality between the act and the political objective pursued. In addition, for amnesty to be granted, the act, omission, or offense also had to fall within the bounds of the period covered by the commission (March 1, 1960, to May 11, 1994), and an application for amnesty had to be filed before the deadline of September 30, 1997.

The most controversial aspect of these requirements was how the "proportionality" test was interpreted by the Amnesty Committee. The committee did not spell out any guidelines for interpretation, and there were varying interpretations of its meaning even within the committee itself. Some senior staff held a more restrictive understanding of "proportional," while some committee members told me that most any crime could be considered proportional to one's aim of overthrowing a government, or of protecting one's government from being overthrown; interviews by author with committee members and staff, October 1997, Cape Town and Port Elizabeth, South Africa. In the end, lack of proportionality was rarely the reason for rejecting an application. A year and a half into the committee's work, with over two thousand applications decided (including over one hundred pertaining to gross human rights violations), only one application had been rejected because it failed to meet the proportionality test, according to committee chair Hassan Mall. Yet in its written decisions the committee usually only explained the principal reason for denying amnesty, so even that decision did not explain the committee's reasoning on proportionality. A small number of later decisions also pointed to a lack of proportionality as a major reason for denial of amnesty.

33. On a related issue, persons who were wrongfully convicted of a crime that they did not commit had no recourse in the commission's Amnesty Committee; the committee had no power to grant amnesty for something that someone did not do. In one case, a person who had carried out a murder admitted to it and received amnesty; his partner, who had been wrongfully convicted and was innocent of the crime, remained in jail, requiring him to go through the normal, though more time-consuming, procedures of the courts to overturn his conviction.

34. Suzanne Daley, "Officer Is Denied Amnesty in the Killing of Steve Biko," *New York Times,* January 11, 1999, A8, and Suzanne Daley, "Panel Denies Amnesty for Four Officers in Steve Biko's Death," *New York Times,* February 17, 1999, A4.

35. For example, in the case of Amy Biehl, an American who was killed in a black township in a random antiwhite attack, the applicants were granted amnesty, which seemed to suggest that some race-motivated acts would be accepted as political by the committee. Analysts have noted similar discrepancies in other rulings.

36. This case most fundamentally challenged the work of the South African truth commission by challenging the constitutionality of granting amnesty (and waiving both civil and criminal liability) for gross violations of human rights. The decision of the Constitutional Court was criticized by some legal experts, not because they viewed the decision to be wrong, but because it failed to grapple with important questions of international law that were raised in the case. See John Dugard, "Is the Truth and Reconciliation Process Compatible with International Law? An Unanswered Question: Azapo v. President of the Republic of South Africa," *South African Journal on Human Rights* 13 (1997), 258–68.

37. For a full description of these and other legal battles fought by the commission, see *Truth and Reconciliation Commission of South Africa Report,* vol. 1, chap. 7, "Legal Challenges."

38. The commission wanted to name de Klerk for having known about several bombings, after the fact, and failing to report them. The question of whether the commission could name de Klerk, in an addendum report, was to be resolved in court at a later date.

39. "Statement of the President of the African National Congress, Thabo Mbeki, on the Report of the TRC at the Joint Sitting of the Houses of Parliament, Cape Town," February 25, 1999.

40. "Agreement on the Establishment of the Commission to Clarify Past Human Rights Violations and Acts of Violence That Have Caused the Guatemalan Population to Suffer," UN Doc. A/48/954/S/1994/751, Annex II, June 23, 1994.

41. Various conversations by the author with participants who were at the peace negotiations, 1994 and 1995. The harsh response to the truth commission agreement was seen, for example, in an op-ed in the *New York Times* by one respected writer on Guatemala, who wrote that as compared to the truth commissions of Argentina, South Africa, and El Salvador, according to the writer, "Guatemala has opted for ignorance" because the commission could not investigate and identify wrongdoers. He continued, "Guatemala has been betrayed. The agreement is not a peace treaty, it's a surrender. And what has been surrendered, after a fruitless and horrifying war, is the truth." Francisco Goldman, "In Guatemala, All Is Forgotten," *New York Times,* December 23, 1996.

In fact, most of the restrictions built into the commission's mandate were open to interpretation; even those who signed the accord recognized that the names of the military unit, and the position of the commanding officer who was responsible, could be listed in the report, if the commissioners so chose, and that the persons' names could then be matched up by the press or nongovernmental organizations; interviews by author with signatories to the accord, April 1996, Guatemala City. In addition, it was unlikely that the commission's report could be barred as evidence in court; legal scholars noted that a peace accord cannot unilaterally overrule standard judicial rules and procedures.

42. "Agreement on the Establishment of the Commission to Clarify Past Human Rights Violations and Acts of Violence That Have Caused the Guatemalan Population to Suffer," UN Doc. A/48/954/S/1994/751, Annex II, June 23, 1994. This clause states that the moderator of the peace talks, Jean Arnault, would be appointed by the secretary-general to head the commission, but he was appointed to head up the UN Mission to Guatemala and was therefore unavailable.

43. Ibid.

44. The commission also requested documents from the governments of Argentina, Taiwan, and Israel, but received none.

45. *Guatemala: Nunca Más*, 4 vols., Oficina de Derechos Humanos del Arzobispado de Guatemala (Guatemala City, 1998). A summary of the report has been published in English as *Guatemala: Never Again! The Official Report of the Human Rights Office, Archdiocese of Guatemala* (New York: Orbis Books, and London: Catholic Institute for International Relations, 1999).

46. The CIIDH project also undertook an extensive analysis of the press coverage of the violence, which showed a sharp decline in reporting of killings and disappearances in the very months when they were the greatest, in the early 1980s. See Patrick Ball, Paul Kobrak, and Herbert F. Spirer, *State Violence in Guatemala, 1960-1996: A Quantitative Reflection* (Washington, DC: American Association for the Advancement of Science, 1999).

47. *Guatemala: Memory of Silence (Conclusions and Recommendations)*, 22.

48. Ibid., 32.

49. Ibid., 41. The commission's conclusion that genocide had taken place was particularly important in that genocide was excluded from an earlier amnesty law. The commission had been strongly pressured by organized indigenous groups to state that genocide had taken place in the country.

50. Ibid., 38.

51. "Agreement on the Establishment of the Commission to Clarify Past Human Rights Violations and Acts of Violence That Have Caused the Guatemalan Population to Suffer," UN Doc. A/48/954/S/1994/751, Annex II, June 23, 1994.

52. For example, the report states that the "structures and nature of economic, cultural and social relations in Guatemala are marked by profound exclusion, antagonism and conflict . . . violence was fundamentally directed by the State against the excluded, the poor and above all, the Mayan people, as well as against those who fought for justice and greater social equality." See *Guatemala: Memory of Silence (Conclusions and Recommendations)*, 17.

53. Government of Guatemala, "Posición inicial del Gobierno de la República ante el informe y las recomendaciones de la Comisión de Esclarecimiento Histórico," March 16, 1999.

CHAPTER FIVE

1. Details of this commission are spelled out in Richard Carver, "Called to Account: How African Governments Investigate Human Rights Violations," *African Affairs* 89 (1991).

2. Ibid., 399.

3. Amnesty International also has a copy on microfiche in London.

4. Carver, "Called to Account," 400.

5. There are few references to the first commission in any literature, and even within Uganda it seems to have been forgotten. A commissioner on the 1986 Ugandan Commission of Inquiry into Violations of Human Rights wrote that the 1986 commission was "the second such body in the world, after Argentina." John Negenda, "The Human Rights Commission," in *Uganda 1986-1991: An Illustrated Review* (Kampala, Uganda: Fountain, 1991), 30.

6. Loyola Guzmán, head of the Association of Relatives of the Detained, Disappeared and Martyred for National Liberation), telephone interview by the author, August 12, 1994.

7. Ibid.

8. Human Rights Watch, "Bolivia: Almost Nine Years and Still No Verdict in the 'Trial of Responsibilities,'" (New York: Human Rights Watch, December 1992), 1.

9. Jose Zalaquett, "Confronting Human Rights Violations Committed by Former Governments: Principles Applicable and Political Constraints," in Justice and Society Program of the Aspen Institute, *State Crimes: Punishment or Pardon* (Queenstown, MD: Aspen Institute, 1989), 59.

10. Ibid., 61.

11. Robert Goldman, telephone interview by the author, April 14, 1994.

12. Wilder Tayler, interview by the author, August 2, 1994, New York.

13. Alexandra Barahona de Brito, *Human Rights and Democratization in Latin America: Uruguay and Chile* (New York: Oxford University Press, 1997), 146.

14. Ibid.

15. Ibid.

16. Servicio Paz y Justicia (SERPAJ), *Uruguay: Nunca Más: Informe Sobre La Violación a Los Derechos Humanos (1972–1985)*, 2nd ed. (Montevideo, Uruguay: SERPAJ, 1989). For a description of this project, see Barahona de Brito, *Human Rights*, 145–48.

17. *Breaking the Silence, Building True Peace: A Report on the Disturbances in Matabeleland and the Midlands, 1980 to 1988* (Harare, Zimbabwe: Catholic Commission for Peace and Justice in Zimbabwe and the Legal Resources Foundation, 1997), 61.

18. In contrast, those who died in the struggle for independence received compensation through the 1980 War Victims Compensation Act. No similar law covered the victims of the Matabeleland violence. Generally, see Human Rights Watch, *Zimbabwe: A Break with the Past? Human Rights and Political Unity* (New York: Human Rights Watch, 1989).

19. Bornwell Chakaodza, director of information of the Ministry of Information, interview by author, September 30, 1996, Harare, Zimbabwe.

20. See *Breaking the Silence, Building True Peace*.

21. Legal Notice No. 5 of 1986, established under the Commissions of Inquiry Act (Cap. 56), Uganda.

22. The Ford Foundation provided a $93,300 grant to the Ugandan government, earmarked for the commission, in 1988. *Ford Foundation Annual Report, 1987* (New York: Ford Foundation, 1987).

23. In February 1991 the government-owned newspaper *The New Vision* reported that "The Human Rights Commission this week failed to sit due to lack of funds.... [The secretary of the commission] hoped some funds will be made available to enable the Commission to sit next week." It also reported that "the Commission's vehicles are not in good running condition" to make the investigatory trips that it had planned. Eva Lubwama, "Human Rights Fails," *The New Vision*, February 2, 1991.

The Danish governmental aid agency DANIDA awarded a grant for the commission equivalent to approximately $437,000 in 1992. Over half of the grant was directed toward the printing and publication of the report.

24. Interviews by author, Kampala, Uganda, October 1996.

25. Sushil Pyakurel, executive director, Informal Sector Service Sector, Nepal, telephone interview by author, March 3, 1999.

26. *Amnesty International Report 1993* (New York: Amnesty International USA, 1993), 220.

27. "Relative to the creation of a Commission of Inquiry into the crimes and misappropriations committed by the ex-president, his accomplices and/or accessories," Decree no. 014 /P.CE/CJ/90, Republic of Chad, December 29, 1990, reprinted in Kritz, *Transitional Justice*, vol. 3, 48–50.

28. *Report of the Commission of Inquiry* (Chad), as excerpted in Kritz, *Transitional Justice*, vol. 3, 54.

29. Jamal Benomar, "Coming to Terms with the Past: How Emerging Democracies Cope With a History of Human Rights Violations" (Atlanta: Carter Center, July 1, 1992), 13.

30. Ibid.

31. Official of U.S. Department of State, telephone interview by the author, May 7, 1993.

32. Telephone interviews by the author with Genoveva Hernandez, December 3, 1999, and Reed Brody, Human Rights Watch, December 10, 1999.

33. The two ANC commissions described here are of a different nature from the other commissions, as they were created by a nonstate opposition body rather than by the state itself. But in

the same manner as state-created inquiries, these bodies were self-evaluative and represented the ANC's acknowledgment of its own abuses.

34. See, for example, Amnesty International, "South Africa: Torture, Ill-Treatment, and Executions in African National Congress Camp," (London: Amnesty International, December 2, 1992).

35. The commission was also referred to as the Skweyiya Commission, named for its chair, T. L. Skweyiya.

36. *Report of the Commission of Enquiry into Complaints by Former African National Congress Prisoners and Detainees*, 1992, 6.

37. Ibid., 72.

38. Upon request, the ANC New York office would not provide a copy of the report, saying that the report was not published because it was "not considered to be complete" due to lack of a full hearing of those accused (although names of the accused are not listed in the report).

39. "Statement by Nelson Mandela, president of the African National Congress, on the Report of the Commission of Enquiry into Complaints by Former African National Congress Prisoners and Detainees," released by the African National Congress, October 19, 1992.

40. The commission's name in German is the Enquete-Kommission Aufarbeitung von Geschichte und Folgen der SED-Diktatur in Deutschland.

41. For example, in 1953, hundreds were killed in a violent crackdown on a popular uprising. Between 1961, when the Berlin Wall was built, and 1989, when the wall came down, at least 260 people were killed trying to cross the border from East to West Germany, shot by border guards or killed by land mines. Political prisoners were harshly interrogated; some were tortured, and many were forced into exile. In the 1950s, hundreds of West Germans who fought to change the East German government were kidnapped by East German authorities and imprisoned (and some executed) in the East.

42. Interviews by the author with commission staff, June 1997, Berlin.

43. Access to the files is administered by the Federal Authority on the Records of the Former Ministry for State Security of the German Democratic Republic, commonly known as the Gauck Authority, named for its director, Joachim Gauck.

44. For a description of these televised scenes of reckoning between victim and informant, see Tina Rosenberg, *The Haunted Land: Facing Europe's Ghosts after Communism* (New York: Random House, 1995).

45. *Report of the Commission of Enquiry into Complaints by Former African National Congress Prisoners and Detainees*, 1992, 70–71.

46. The commission was also referred to as the Motsuenyane Commission, after the president of the commission, retired business leader Dr. Samuel M. Motsuenyane.

47. Richard Carver, telephone interview by the author, January 7, 1994.

48. *Reports of the Commission of Enquiry into Certain Allegations of Cruelty and Human Rights Abuse against ANC Prisoners and Detainees by ANC Members*, Johannesburg, August 20, 1993, ii.

49. "African National Congress National Executive Committee's Response to the Motsuenyane Commission's Report," released by the African National Congress, August 31, 1993, 7.

50. Amnesty International documented 680 cases of disappearance between 1983 and 1988, for example. Ingrid Massage, Amnesty International, interview by the author, July 9, 1997, London.

51. In one particularly bad month, July 1996, 365 persons were reported to have disappeared, according to Home for Human Rights, a Sri Lankan human rights organization.

52. Human rights organizations also submitted cases to the commission that were documented in their files. Cases were not included in the commissions' reports if the families did not come forward to give testimony.

53. *Final Report of the Commission of Inquiry into the Involuntary Removal or Disappearance of Persons in the Western, Southern and Sabaragamuwa Provinces*; *Final Report of the Commission of In-*

quiry into the Involuntary Removal or Disappearance of Persons in the Central, North Western, North Central and Uva Provinces; and *Final Report of the Commission of Inquiry into the Involuntary Removal or Disappearance of Persons in the Northern and Eastern Provinces* (Colombo: Sri Lankan Government Publications Bureau, 1997; released to public in January 1998).

54. In addition, each commission published interim reports, some of them quite substantial. The shorter length of the final reports may be explained by the more substantial interim reports, one human rights advocate noted, especially as the commissioners became disillusioned in the lack of action by the government on their interim recommendations.

55. *Amnesty International Report 1999* (London: Amnesty International, 1999).

56. Little has been written about the Haitian truth commission, but a brief summary of its work can be found in Fanny Benedetti, "Haiti's Truth and Justice Commission," *Human Rights Brief* (Washington, DC: Center for Human Rights and Humanitarian Law, Washington College of Law, American University) 3:3, 1996.

57. Human Rights Watch, "Thirst for Justice: A Decade of Impunity in Haiti" (New York: Human Rights Watch, September 1996), 18.

58. The formal request for a commission was reiterated by the government of Burundi in the Convention of Government, September 10, 1994, which is reproduced as an annex to UN Doc. A/50/94/S/1995/190, March 8, 1995.

59. Amnesty International, "Rwanda and Burundi: A Call for Action by the International Community" (London: Amnesty International, September 1995), 23 and 26.

60. Pedro Nikken, interview by the author, September 18, 1997, Siracusa, Italy.

61. UN Security Council Resolution 1012 (1995), August 28, 1995.

62. "UN Reports Burundi Army Slew Civilians by Thousands," *New York Times,* August 4, 1996, A4. The Burundi Commission report has been published as an annex to UN Doc. S/1996/682, August 22, 1996.

63. Ministerial Accord No. 012 (Ecuador), September 17, 1996.

64. This commission is described in *Report on the Situation of Human Rights in Ecuador* (Washington, DC: Organization of American States, 1997), 9–10.

65. *Amnesty International Report 1997* (London: Amnesty International, 1997), 140.

66. *Report on the Situation of Human Rights in Ecuador*, 10.

67. *Amnesty International Report 1998* (London: Amnesty International, 1998).

68. Instrument Constituting a Judicial Commission of Inquiry for the Investigation of Human Rights Violations, published in the *Federal Republic of Nigeria Official Gazette* 86:56, 1999, Lagos (Statutory Instrument 8 of 1999), 1.

69. This retreat, which took place in September 1999, was cohosted by the International Institute for Democracy and Electoral Assistance in Stockholm and the Centre for Democracy and Development in Lagos. Participants from the commissions in South Africa, Chile, and Guatemala attended this meeting; I also attended to provide an overview of lessons learned from past truth commissions.

70. Instrument Constituting a Judicial Commission of Inquiry for the Investigation of Human Rights Violations, 2.

71. For further information on the atrocities in the Sierra Leone war, see the Human Rights Watch reports *Sowing Terror: Atrocities against Civilians in Sierra Leone* (New York: Human Rights Watch, July 1998), and *Getting Away with Murder, Mutilation, and Rape: New Testimony from Sierra Leone* (New York: Human Rights Watch, June 1999).

72. It must be recognized that the government was not negotiating from a strong position. When the peace agreement was reached, rebel groups controlled vast portions of the country. The bulk of the Sierra Leone Army had joined the rebels in the bush after having taken over government in a coup in 1997, ruled the country for nine months, and was then chased from power themselves by the Nigerian-led forces, the Economic Community of West African States Cease-fire Monitoring Group (ECOMOG). Since 1998, the former Sierra Leone Army fought with the rebel

RUF forces against the government. With Nigeria eager to bring its forces home, the government of Sierra Leone felt it had little power to negotiate strong terms when it sat down at the peace table.

The United Nations, which facilitated the peace talks, was especially criticized for signing onto an agreement that included a general amnesty for severe rights crimes. In signing the accord, the special representative of the secretary-general in Sierra Leone, Francis G. Okelo, inserted a note to his signature stating that the United Nations interpreted the amnesty to "not apply to international crimes of genocide, crimes against humanity, war crimes, and other serious violations of international humanitarian law."

73. "Peace Agreement between the Government of Sierra Leone and the Revolutionary United Front of Sierra Leone," July 7, 1999, Article 26.

74. I served as one of the United Nations consultants involved in this process of meeting with interested parties in Sierra Leone and drafting recommended terms.

75. See the Truth and Reconciliation Act of Sierra Leone, 2000, available on the web at www.sierra-leone.org/trc.html.

CHAPTER SIX

1. Executive Branch Supreme Decree No. 355, reprinted in *Report of the Chilean National Commission on Truth and Reconciliation*, 6.

2. *From Madness to Hope: Report of the Commission on the Truth for El Salvador*, 18.

3. Promotion of National Unity and Reconciliation Act, Act No. 34 of 1995 (South Africa).

4. Mahmood Mamdani, partipation on the panel "Legal, Moral, and Political Implications of the South African TRC" at the conference Evaluating South Africa's Truth and Reconciliation Commission, University of Sussex, September 18–19, 1998, Brighton, England (notes on file with author). See also Mamdani, "Reconciliation without Justice," *Southern African Review of Books* 46 (1996), 3–6.

5. One rights observer even wondered whether the president of Sri Lanka created three commissions as an intentional strategy to allow herself more flexibility in responding to the commissions' reports, knowing that they would each make different recommendations, especially on the subject of reparations to victims.

6. *Report of the Commission of Inquiry* (Chad), as excerpted in Kritz, *Transitional Justice*, 45–46.

7. *From Madness to Hope: Report of the Commission on the Truth for El Salvador*, 137.

8. Thomas Buergenthal, interview by the author, April 22, 1994, Washington, DC.

9. The report states, for example, "Relations with the United States nonetheless remained relatively normal. During the Nixon and Ford administrations, the United States helped Chile renegotiate its foreign debt, and U.S. economic aid during 1974–1976 was several times what it was in 1971–1973. Agreements with the U.S. companies that owned the large copper operations that the previous government had nationalized were improved." *Report of the Chilean National Commission on Truth and Reconciliation*, 632.

10. "The Atrocity Findings: 'The Historic Facts Must Be Recognized'" (excerpts of statement by Christian Tomuschat in presenting the report), *New York Times*, February 26, 1999, A8.

11. "Remarks by the President in Roundtable Discussion on Peace Efforts," National Palace of Culture, Guatemala City, March 10, 1999; statement released by the White House Office of the Press Secretary, Washington, DC.

12. Ashnie Padarath, "Women and Violence in KwaZulu Natal," in Meredeth Turshen and Clotilde Twagiramariya, eds., *What Women Do in Wartime: Gender and Conflict in Africa* (London: Zed Books, 1998). Padarath writes that "while the sexual nature of prison torture is the focus of much attention, the sexual brutalization of women believed to be supporters of opposing political parties has received very little emphasis or even acknowledgment" (64).

13. Interviews by the author with Janis Grobbelaar, information manager, and Vanessa Barolsky, researcher, Truth and Reconciliation Commission of South Africa, November 10, 1997, Jo-

hannesburg, and with Beth Goldblatt, researcher, Gender Research Project, Centre for Applied Legal Studies, University of the Witwatersrand, October 24, 1997, Johannesburg. For an analysis of women and the South African commission, see Beth Goldblatt, "Violence, Gender and Human Rights: An Examination of South Africa's Truth and Reconciliation Commission," paper presented at the Law and Society Association annual meeting, May 29–June 1, 1997, St. Louis, Missouri.

14. The South African Truth and Reconciliation Commission describes this phenomenon in its report; see vol. 4, chap. 10, sec. 36–43, 293–94.

15. Beth Goldblatt, interview.

16. *Guatemala: Memoria del Silencio: Informe de la Comisión para el Esclarecimiento Histórico,* vol. 3, chap. 2, par. 37.

17. *Truth and Reconciliation Commission of South Africa Report,* vol. 4, chap. 10, sec. 144, 316. The South African commission met with women's rights scholars and advocates early in its tenure, and received written submissions that urged the commission to "approach the experience of human rights abuses through a gendered lens," suggesting that a failure to do so "will lead to the neglect of women's experiences of abuse and torture, which are often seen as a male preserve." Beth Goldblatt and Sheila Meintjes, "South African Women Demand the Truth," in Turshen and Twagiramariya, eds., *What Women Do in Wartime,* 29. This chapter by Goldblatt and Meintjes is a summary of their submission to the commission.

18. *Si M Pa Rele . . . (If I Don't Cry Out . . .), Report of the National Commission for Truth and Justice,* Haiti, 1996, 40–46.

19. *Guatemala: Memoria del Silencio,* vol. 3, chap. 2, par. 49.

20. On the other hand, the Salvadoran report lists many incidents of rape in its appendix, which documents all victims who provided testimony and the violations that they suffered. These rape victims clearly were considered to fall within the commission's mandate. The commission never explained this discrepancy in its policy.

21. For example, the statute for the creation of the International Criminal Court, agreed to by 120 nations in 1998, defines rape and other forms of sexual violence of comparable gravity as a crime against humanity when committed as part of a widespread or systematic attack directed against a civilian population. The statute also defines rape and similarly grave sexual violence as a war crime, over which the Court would have jurisdiction "when committed as a part of a plan or policy or as part of a largescale commission of such crimes." *Rome Statute of the International Criminal Court,* UN Doc. A/Conf.183/9, July 17, 1998, Articles 7 and 8 (available at www.un. org/icc/romestat.htm). For a summary of the developments in international law that pertain to sexual violence, see Patricia Viseur Sellers, "Rape under International Law," in Belinda Cooper, ed., *War Crimes: The Legacy of Nuremberg* (New York: TV Books, 1999), 159–66.

22. This comment was made in a meeting with three members of South Africa's Amnesty Committee in November 1997.

23. Janis Grobbelaar, interview. Patrick Ball also identifies his approach as *logical positivism,* which he says "assumes that we can classify the world into categories, and can make sense of these categories." Patrick Ball, "Who Did What to Whom: Planning and Implementing a Large Scale Human Rights Data Project," lecture at Columbia University, April 15, 1998.

24. Daniel Rothenberg, telephone interview by the author, November 30, 1998, and comments on a panel at the conference of the Latin American Studies Association, September 26, 1998, Chicago.

25. Jean Claude Jean, interview by the author, December 5, 1995, Port-au-Prince, Haiti; French interpretation by Nancy Bernard.

26. Agreement on the Establishment of the Commission to Clarify Past Human Rights Violations and Acts of Violence That Have Caused the Guatemalan Population to Suffer (UN Doc. A/48/954/S/1994/751, Annex II, June 23, 1994).

27. Marcie Merksy, interview by the author, April 19, 1996, Guatemala City.

28. For a description of the REMHI project and methodology, see Carlos Martín Beristain, "The Value of Memory," *Forced Migration Review* 2 (1998).

29. Eduardo Rabossi, interview by the author, December 11, 1996, Buenos Aires, Argentina.

CHAPTER SEVEN

1. "Agreement on the Establishment of the Commission to Clarify Past Human Rights Violations and Acts of Violence That Have Caused the Guatemalan Population to Suffer," UN Doc. A/48/954/S/1994/751, Annex II, June 23, 1994.

2. *Justice* can mean different things to different people: it may involve symbolic or cash reparations for victims; eye-for-an-eye acts of revenge; or societal or community development to make up for past deprivations and injury. In South Africa, the truth commission suggested that its process was contributing to *restorative justice,* through paying respect to victims, proposing reparations, and advancing national reconciliation, rather than the *retributive justice* of prosecution and punishment of perpetrators. Here I use *justice* as a shorthand for legal action in the judicial system, leading to trials and punishment of those found guilty. It is this form of justice that most victims demand.

3. During the work of the second commission in Uganda, some commission members asked for prosecutorial powers, frustrated with the lack of judicial action on cases it had investigated, but this proposal was rejected. Perhaps a future truth commission's mandate will include this power, though this would surely complicate its functions and overwhelm it with work.

4. An amnesty was passed in Guatemala at the end of 1996, though it exempts many human rights crimes. Previous Guatemalan amnesties prevented prosecutions for acts prior to 1987. Yet between 1987 and 1996, there were many assassinations, disappearances, and other crimes that were not covered by an amnesty but on which little action was taken. An international team of lawyers was based in Haiti to push prosecutions in key rights cases in the years following the end of the coup government, but with little success. On Haiti, see Michael P. Scharf, "Swapping Amnesty for Peace: Was There a Duty to Prosecute International Crimes in Haiti?" *Texas International Law Journal* 31 (1996), 1–41.

5. Domestic trials for the 1994 genocide in Rwanda only slowly began in late 1996, after the passage of a law intended to facilitate the processing of this overwhelming number of cases, which encouraged confessions in exchange for lessened sentences ("Organic Law of 30 August 1996 on the organization of prosecutions for offences constituting the crime of genocide or crimes against humanity since 1 October 1990"). In 1999, the Rwanda government was planning to make use of traditional community structures and practices in order to assist in processing the lower categories of genocide-related crimes. These "Gacaca" tribunals, as they are known, consist of village meetings that allow the community to help determine the appropriate punishment for each perpetrator, which may include direct reparatory measures to their victims. For a full description of these developments, see Stef Vandeginste, "Justice, Reconciliation, and Reparation after Genocide and Crimes against Humanity: The Proposed Establishment of Popular Gacaca Tribunals in Rwanda," paper presented at the All-Africa Conference on African Principles of Conflict Resolution and Reconciliation, Addis Ababa, November 8–12, 1999.

6. Constraints imposed on the posttransition ability to prosecute are not always in the form of amnesty laws. For example, the last apartheid South African government passed a law in 1992 that gave independence and security of tenure to attorneys general appointed by the apartheid government (the Attorneys General Act). While nominally strengthening the rule of law by removing the decision to prosecute from political influence, the law made it difficult for the new government to replace those who were obstructing the prosecution of past perpetrators.

7. See, for example, Michael P. Scharf, "The Letter of the Law: The Scope of the International Legal Obligation to Prosecute Human Rights Crimes," *Law and Contemporary Problems* 59 (1996), 41–61; Diane Orentlicher, "Settling Accounts: The Duty to Prosecute Human

Rights Violations of a Prior Regime," Yale Law Journal 100(1991), 2537–618; Naomi Roht-Arriaza, ed., *Impunity and Human Rights in International Law and Practice* (Oxford: Oxford University Press, 1995); and Steven R. Ratner and Jason S. Abrams, *Accountability for Human Rights Atrocities in International Law: Beyond the Nuremberg Legacy* (Oxford: Oxford University Press, 1997).

8. See, for example, Juan E. Méndez, "Accountability for Past Abuses," *Human Rights Quarterly* 19 (1995), 255–82.

9. For a review of amnesties in Latin America and the international legal response, see Douglass Cassel, "Lessons from the Americas: Guidelines for International Response to Amnesties for Atrocities," *Law and Contemporary Problems* 59 (1996), 197–230.

10. Legislative Decreee 486 (El Salvador), March 20, 1993.

11. UN Secretary-General Boutros Boutros-Ghali expressed his concern that the amnesty law was passed so quickly, saying that "it would have been preferable if the amnesty had been promulgated after creating a broad degree of national consensus in its favor," but most other governmental or intergovernmental observers remained silent. See "Report of the Secretary-General on All Aspects of ONUSAL's Operations," UN Doc. S/25812, May 21, 1993, 2. For a broader discussion of these developments, see Martha Doggett, *Death Foretold: The Jesuit Murders In El Salvador* (New York: Lawyers Committee for Human Rights, and Washington, DC: Georgetown University Press, 1993), 271–76.

12. Michael Posner, Lawyers Committee for Human Rights, interview by the author, March 13, 1996, New York.

13. *From Madness to Hope: Report of the Commission on the Truth for El Salvador,* 178–79.

14. Margaret Popkin, "Judicial Reform in Post-War El Salvador: Missed Opportunities," paper presented at the Latin American Studies Association conference, September 28–30, 1995, 6–7.

15. Thomas Buergenthal, interview by the author, June 14, 1996, Washington, DC.

16. Lawyers Committee for Human Rights, "El Salvador's Negotiated Revolution: Prospects for Legal Reform" (New York: Lawyers Committee for Human Rights, June 1993), 74–75.

17. Luis Moreno Ocampo, interview by the author, December 11, 1996, Buenos Aires, Argentina.

18. The first, the "Punto Final" (Full Stop) law, set a cutoff date for initiating prosecutions for events during the period of military rule; a later "Due Obedience" law prevented the prosecution of those who claimed to be acting under a superior's orders. See *Truth and Partial Justice in Argentina: An Update* (New York: Human Rights Watch, 1991), 47–52.

19. The exact number of cases forwarded for prosecution is unclear. The commission report includes a list of just over forty cases referred to the police or to the director of public prosecutions.

20. Arthur Oder, interview by the author, October 10, 1996, Kampala, Uganda.

21. Alfred Nasaba, interview by the author, October 14, 1996, Kampala, Uganda.

22. George Kanyeihamba, interview by the author, October 11, 1996, Kampala, Uganda.

23. Bart Katureebe, interview by the author, October 13, 1996, Kampala, Uganda.

24. For further description of the principle of command responsibility, see Steven R. Ratner and Jason S. Abrams, *Accountability for Human Rights Atrocities,* 119–20; Michael P. Scharf, "Swapping Amnesty for Peace," 33–34.

25. Arthur Oder, interview.

26. René Magloir, interview by the author, December 6, 1995, Port-au-Prince, Haiti.

27. Francisco Cumplido, secretary general of the University of Chile and former minister of justice under President Patricio Aylwin Azocar, interview by the author, December 1996, Santiago, Chile.

28. "Discurso de S.E. El Presidente de la Republica, Don Patricio Aylwin Azocar, al dar a Conocer a la Ciudadania El Informe de la Comisión de Verdad y Reconciliación, March 4, 1991; published in English as "Statement by President Aylwin on the Report of the National Commission on Truth and Reconciliation," in Kritz, *Transitional Justice,* vol. 3, 169–73.

29. These cases do not always play out so simply, of course. Some families of the disappeared have tried to work their way up the line of command, with limited success. In 1996, the willingness to keep these cases open was waning, dependent on the individual preferences of the judges at hand, and responding to signals of lessening interest from the current president, Eduardo Frei.

30. The Chilean Supreme Court's decision was based on the reasoning that until the bodies of the victims were accounted for, the crime committed was not murder but kidnapping, meaning that the original crime was part of a continuing event that went beyond the cutoff of the 1978 amnesty. See Clifford Krauss, "Chilean Military Faces Reckoning for Its Dark Past," *New York Times,* October 3, 1999, A10.

31. Ibid.

32. Dullah Omar, interview by the author, August 27, 1996, Cape Town, South Africa.

33. Interview by the author, November 7, 1997, South Africa.

34. Paul van Zyl, interview by the author, November 1997, Johannesburg, South Africa.

35. Robert Kogod Goldman, "Report to the Lawyers Committee for Human Rights on the Jesuit Murder Trial," in Doggett, *Death Foretold,* appendix C, 326.

36. Ibid., 324, 328.

37. *Guatemala: Memory of Silence (Conclusions and Recommendations),* 18–19.

38. *Report of the Chilean National Commission on Truth and Reconciliation, vol. I,* 117–18.

39. Ibid., 119.

40. *Nunca Más: Report of the Argentine National Commission on the Disappeared,* 387.

41. Ibid., 386–87.

42. *Report of the Commission of Inquiry into Violations of Human Rights: Findings, Conclusions and Recommendations* (Kampala, Uganda: Commission of Inquiry into Violations of Human Rights, 1994), 234.

43. *From Madness to Hope,* 121.

44. Ibid., 178.

45. Ibid, 172–73

46. Robert O. Weiner, "Trying to Make Ends Meet: Reconciling the Law and Practice of Human Rights Amnesties," *St. Mary's Law Journal* 26 (1995), 857–75.

47. Ibid., 873, 875.

CHAPTER EIGHT

1. Promotion of National Unity and Reconciliation Act, Act no. 34 of 1995, South Africa.

2. Decreto 187/83, Argentina.

3. Eduardo Rabossi, interview by the author, December 1996, Buenos Aires, Argentina.

4. Graciela Fernandez Meijide, interview by the author, December 1996, Buenos Aires, Argentina.

5. Testimony of Luis Alberto Urquiza, in *Nunca Más: Report of the Argentine National Commission on the Disappeared,* 27–28.

6. Testimony of Martha Alvarez de Repetto, in *Nunca Más* (Argentina), English edition, 53.

7. *Nunca Más: The Report of the Argentine National Commission on the Disappeared,* 7.

8. "Los Culpables son 1351," special supplement of *La Voz,* November 4, 1994. This list was first printed in the weekly *El Periodista,* November 2, 1984. See also "Conadep Decries Publication of 'Oppressors' List," *Foreign Broadcasting Information Service,* November 5, 1994.

9. Juan Méndez, afterword to Horacio Verbitsky, *The Flight: Confessions of an Argentine Dirty Warrior* (New York: The New Press, 1996), 165. General Jorge Rafael Videla, Admiral Eduardo Massera, and General Ramon Camps, senior officials in the military regime, had all been convicted for abuses and served some years in prison before being pardoned.

10. Calvin Sims, "Retired Torturer Now Lives a Tortured Existence," *New York Times,* August 12, 1997, A4. For a fascinating and detailed account of Alfredo Astiz and other perpetrators

who walk free in Argentina, see Marguerite Feitlowitz, *A Lexicon of Terror: Argentina and the Legacies of Torture* (New York: Oxford University Press, 1998), esp. 227–28.

11. Supreme Decree No. 355 of the Executive Branch of Chile, April 25, 1990, Article 2.

12. Gisela von Muhlenbrok, in conversation with the author, March 13, 1997, Washington, DC.

13. Jorge Correa, interview by the author, November 26, 1996, Santiago, Chile.

14. Because the commission's mandate empowered it to investigate killings and disappearances but not cases of torture if the victim survived, testimony from survivors was primarily used to try to determine the fate of those imprisoned with them who did not survive, as well as to understand the general practices in the detention centers. Survivors could sometimes identify their own torturers, but could generally not identify others' killers.

15. The constraints on the new democracy were made explicit when General Augusto Pinochet warned the new government not to "touch a single hair of a single soldier," nor ignore the 1978 amnesty, lest he repeat the events of September 1973, when he took over in a coup. "Chile: Editor's Introduction," in Kritz, *Transitional Justice,* vol. 2, 454.

16. Laura Novoa, interview by the author, December 2, 1996, Santiago, Chile.

17. Interview by the author, December 3, 1996, Santiago, Chile.

18. Ibid.

19. Approval by the minister of defense or president is required only for promotions to the most senior levels of the armed forces in Chile.

20. Thomas Buergenthal, "The United Nations Truth Commission for El Salvador," *Vanderbilt Journal of Transnational Law* 27 (1994), 520.

21. Ibid., 520

22. Ibid., 520–21.

23. Ibid., 521.

24. *From Madness to Hope: Report of the Commission on the Truth for El Salvador,* 53.

25. *From Madness to Hope,* 127.

26. *From Madness to Hope,* 25.

27. Buergenthal, "Truth Commission," 519.

28. Ibid., 522.

29. See "Report of the Secretary-General on the Implementation of the Recommendations of the Commission on the Truth," UN Doc. S/26581, Annex, par. 5, October 14, 1993, stating "The United Nations analysis found that only one of the Commission's recommendations, that concerning disqualification by law from holding public office, could not be implemented as it was at variance with fundamental provisions of the Constitution and conflicted with another recommendation made by the Commission concerning the ratification of international human rights instruments under which citizens cannot be deprived of their political rights in the manner recommended by the Commission."

30. Martha Doggett, *Death Foretold: The Jesuit Murders in El Salvador* (New York: Lawyers Committee for Human Rights, and Washington: Georgetown University Press, 1993), 266.

31. Juan E. Méndez, "Accountability for Past Abuses," *Human Rights Quarterly* 19 (1997), 265.

32. George Vickers, in conversation with the author, June 1995, Washington, DC.

33. Thomas Buergenthal, interview by the author, June 14, 1996, Washington, DC.

34. See William Stanley, *Risking Failure: The Problems and Promise of the New Civilian Police in El Salvador* (Cambridge, MA: Hemispheric Initiatives, and Washington, DC: Washington Office on Latin America, 1993), 15. According to this report, Lt. Colonel Manuel Antonio Rivas Mejía, who was a candidate for subdirector of the new civilian national police, was "dropped from consideration after the Truth Commission released its findings." The commission report found Rivas Mejía, then head of the Commission for the Investigation of Criminal Acts, to be responsible for "concealing the truth" and recommending the destruction of incriminating evidence against senior military officers involved in the Jesuit murders. See *From Madness to Hope,* 46–47.

35. "Report of the Secretary-General on the implementation of the recommendations of the Commission on the Truth," U.N. Doc. S/26581, Annex, Par. 3, October 15, 1993.

36. Author interview with local activists in Suchitoto, El Salvador, March 1996.

37. Mzwai Piliso, head of the ANC's Department of Intelligence and Security in the mid-1980s, chose to testify before the commission, although he had the option not to. "Mr. Piliso candidly admitted his personal participation in the beating of suspects in 1981. A plot to assassinate certain senior ANC members had been uncovered and suspects were interrogated over a period of two weeks. These suspects were beaten on the soles of their feet in Mr. Piliso's presence. The soles of their feet were specially chosen, according to Mr. Piliso, because other parts of the body 'easily rupture.' Mr. Piliso justified this treatment on the basis that he wanted information and he wanted it, in his words, 'at any cost.'" As a result of increasing unease with activities of the security department and allegation of abuse, Mr. Piliso was relieved of his duties in 1987 and other changes were made within the ANC. See *Report of the Commission on Enquiry into Complaints by Former African National Congress Prisoners and Detainees*, 1992, 61–62.

38. Margaret Burnham, interview by the author, April 11, 1997, Boston.

39. *Report of the Commission of Enquiry into Certain Allegations of Cruelty and Human Rights Abuse Against ANC Prisoners and Detainees by ANC Members*, August 20, 1993, v.

40. "African National Congress National Executive Committee's Response to the Motsuenyane Commission's Report," statement released by the ANC, August 31, 1993, 7.

41. Fanny Benedetti, former staff member of the Haitian truth commission, interview by the author, March 25, 1997, New York.

42. Ibid.

43. See chapter 7 for more on the principle of command responsibility.

44. *Si M Pa Rele . . . If I Don't Cry Out . . . , Report of the National Commission for Truth and Justice,* Haiti, 1996.

45. *Report of the Commission of Inquiry* (Chad), as excerpted in Kritz, Transitional Justice, vol. 3, 91.

46. Hector Rosada, interview by the author, April 18, 1996, Guatemala City.

47. "Agreement on the Establishment of the Commission to Clarify Past Human Rights Violations and Acts of Violence that have Cause the Guatemalan People to Suffer," UN Doc. A/48/954/S/1994/751, 23 June 1994.

48. Christian Tomuschat, "Between National and International Law: Guatemala's Historical Clarification Commission" *Festschrift Jaenicke* (Heidelberg: Springer, 1998).

49. Hector Rosada, interview by the author, April 18, 1996, Guatemala City.

50. Antonio Arenales Forno, interview by the author, April 19, 1996, Guatemala City.

51. *Guatemala: Memory of Silence (Conclusions and Recommendations)*, 38.

52. Frank LaRue, telephone interview by the author, February 28, 1999.

53. Promotion of National Unity and Reconciliation Act, Act no. 34 of 1995, South Africa, section 30.

54. *Truth and Reconciliation Commission of South Africa Report*, vol. 1, chap. 7, sec. 21–76, 179–90, regarding the case of Van Rensburg and Du Preez vs. the Truth and Reconciliation Commission.

55. In some cases, persons were named in hearings without the commission's advance knowledge; notices were then sent after the fact.

56. Commissioner Richard Lyster, correspondence with the author, November 23, 1998. One senior staff member estimated that perhaps thirty to forty names were deleted in response to the replies from the alleged perpetrators, out of the several hundred who were notified, in most cases because the commission's evidence was weak or was based in part on untested hearsay, and the commission chose to err on the side of caution.

57. Commissioner Richard Lyster explained exactly why these requirements were so limiting:
This placed a huge burden on the TRC. Anyone who was mentioned in the text of the report, even if in passing, was now entitled to receive a section 30 notice, setting out in

some detail exactly what it was he was alleged to have done (he needn't have been accused of committing a gross human rights violation, he just needed to have been mentioned to his detriment), with supporting affidavits and statements, etc. Let us say that one was drafting a section of the report which dealt with, for example, the abduction of ANC activists from Swaziland. There was an incredibly detailed and rich amount of material about this sort of thing, from askaris [turncoats or spies] who had come clean, and from amnesty applicants in particular, security branch policemen who had actually carried out the abducting and, later, torturing and killing of activists. They mentioned in their statements a wide range of people who they relied on in Swaziland for information and assistance: Swazi citizens, policemen and conservative politicians, ANC activists who were corrupted and shopped their colleagues, people who they (the security police) had intimidated through torture and threats against them and their families into complying with their demands.

Simply put, the story of an abduction of a leading ANC activist, her return to South Africa, her subsequent torture over a lengthy period of time and her final murder and secret burial, involved a host of bit part players, all of whom in their own way cooperated with the police, willingly or under duress, to achieve the primary aim of duping someone, abducting them, transporting them illegally across the border, hiding them on a secret farm destination, torturing them, killing them, and burying them. In some cases, we had 30 names of these bit players. All of them were mentioned to their detriment, and therefore were entitled to a notice, with information attached. In most cases we hadn't any idea where they were, and accordingly their names were taken out of the report. Lyster, correspondence with the author, November 29, 1998.

58. John Daniel, correspondence with the author, November 18, 1998.

59. After the Amnesty Committee has completed its work, the commission will submit a supplemental report to summarize the information from these final proceedings.

60. Lyster, correspondence, November 29, 1998.

61. *Truth and Reconciliation Commission of South Africa, Africa Report,* vol. 5, chap. 8, sec. 14, 309.

62. The commission had concluded that de Klerk was an accessory after the fact to a crime because he failed to report it to authorities when he knew about it. De Klerk didn't deny he was informed of the crime, but held that he was not obliged to report it because the perpetrators were soon to apply for an amnesty.

63. Jaun E. Méndez, interview by the author, March 22, 1996, Notre Dame, IN.

64. In interviews, for example, the executive director of Human Rights Watch, Kenneth Roth, and the president of the Open Society Institute, Aryeh Neier, agreed that names should be named by a commission, given basic precautions.

65. *Report of the Chilean National Commission on Truth and Reconciliation*, xxxii.

66. Human Rights Program of the Harvard Law School and the World Peace Foundation, *Truth Commissions: A Comparative Assessment* (Cambridge, MA: Harvard Law School Human Rights Program, 1997), 30.

67. José Zalaquett, interview by the author, November 20, 1996, Guatemala City.

68. José Zalaquett, correspondence with the author, December 2, 1998.

69. Douglass Cassel, "International Truth Commissions and Justice," *Aspen Institute Quarterly* 5, no. 3 (1993), 83–84.

70. José Zalaquett, correspondence with the author, October 29, 1998.

71. Human Rights Watch, "Recommendations to the Truth and Reconciliation Commission," January 1998, 4. This report was written by Human Rights Watch researcher Bronwen Manby.

72. Ibid., 5.

73. *Black's Law Dictionary* defines *preponderance of evidence* as the "evidence which is of greater weight or more convincing than the evidence which is offered in opposition to it; that is,

evidence which as a whole shows that the fact sought to be proved is more probably than not."
Black's Law Dictionary (St. Paul: West Publishing, 1991).

74. *Truth and Reconciliation Commission of South Africa Report*, vol. 1, chap. 4, sec. 155, 91.

75. *From Madness to Hope*, 25.

CHAPTER NINE

1. Horacio Verbitsky, interview by the author, December 10, 1996, Buenos Aires, Argentina.

2. The accounts of Francisco Scilingo are published in Horacio Verbitsky, *The Flight: Confessions of an Argentine Dirty Warrior* (New York: The New Press, 1996).

3. Some people prefer to use the term *survivor* in the place of *victim*, in order to reflect a more empowering and less passive state to those who survived extreme violence. I tend to use the word *victim*, with no intent to imply a negative, but rather to mirror the language most commonly used by these commissions themselves, as well as to avoid the confusion with the use of *survivor* as meaning a family member of someone who was killed.

4. Thulani Grenville-Grey, interview by the author, October 28, 1997, Johannesburg, South Africa.

5. Brandon Hamber, "Do Sleeping Dogs Lie? The Psychological Implications of the Truth and Reconciliation Commission in South Africa," seminar presented at the Centre for the Study of Violence and Reconciliation, Johannesburg, July 26, 1995, 4–5.

6. Judith Lewis Herman, *Trauma and Recovery* (New York: Basic Books, 1992), 1.

7. Yael Danieli, "Preliminary Reflections from a Psychological Perspective," in Theo van Boven, Cees Flinterman, Fred Grünfeld, and Ingrid Westendorp, eds., *Seminar on the Right to Restitution, Compensation and Rehabilitation for Victims of Gross Violations of Human Rights and Fundamental Freedoms* (Netherlands Institute of Human Rights, Maastricht, March 11–15, 1992), 198. See also Yael Danieli, ed., *International Handbook of Multigenerational Legacies of Trauma* (New York: Plenum Press, 1998), 4–6.

8. For example, see Patricia K. Robin Herbst, "From Helpless Victim to Empowered Survivor: Oral History as a Treatment for Survivors of Torture," *Refugee Women and Their Mental Health* 13 (1992), 141–54; Adrianne Aron, "Testimonio: A Bridge between Psychotherapy and Sociotherapy," *Refugee Women and Their Mental Health* 13 (1992), 173–89; and Ana Julia Cienfuegos and Cristina Monelli, "The Testimony of Political Repression as a Therapeutic Instrument," *American Journal of Orthopsychiatry* 53 (1983), 43–51.

9. Fernando Moscoso and Juan Alberto Chamale Gomez, Guatemalan Forensic Anthropology Team, interview by the author, April 18, 1996, Guatemala City.

10. Marcie Mersky, Human Rights Office of the Archbishop of Guatemala, interview by the author, April 19, 1996, Guatemala City.

11. This lobbying group was formed into Khulumani (Speak Out). Brandon Hamber, interview by the author, August 1997, Cape Town, South Africa.

12. Brandon Hamber, "The Burdens of Truth: An Evaluation of the Psychological Support Services and Initiatives Undertaken by the South African Truth and Reconciliation Commission," paper presented at the Third International Conference of the Ethnic Studies Network, Derry, Northern Ireland, June 26–28, 1997, section 4.2.

13. Elizabeth Lira, interview by the author, November 20, 1996, Santiago, Chile.

14. Reverend S. K. Mbande, Anglican Church of Christ the Redeemer, interview by the author (together with Boniwe Mafu and Lebo Molete), October 25, 1997, Daveyton, South Africa.

15. Sylvia Dlomo-Jele, interview by the author, October 26, 1997, Soweto, South Africa.

16. Sylvia Dlomo-Jele died on March 13, 1999. Memorial by the Centre for the Study of Violence and Reconciliation, Johannesburg.

17. Piers Pigou, "Amnesty for Sicelo Dlomo's Killers," *Daily Mail and Guardian* (South Africa), April 14, 2000.

18. Simpson Xakeka, interview by the author, October 27, 1997, Johannesburg, South Africa (interpretation from Zulu by Lebo Molete).

19. Lauren Gilbert, correspondence with the author, December 22, 1997.

20. Brandon Hamber, interview.

21. Judith Lewis Herman, telephone interview by the author, August 2, 1996.

22. The standard psychologists' reference work, the *Diagnostic and Statistical Manual,* points to PTSD symptoms that include "recurrent and intrusive distressing recollections of the event"; "diminished responsiveness to the external world, or 'psychic numbing'"; difficulty sleeping; difficulty concentrating or completing tasks; aggression; and other symptoms. See American Psychiatric Association, *Diagnostic and Statistical Manual of Mental Disorders,* 4th ed. (Washington, DC: American Psychiatric Association, 1994), 424–29.

23. Michael Lapsley, interview by the author, May 1, 1997, New York.

24. Marius Schoon, quoted in Tony Freemantle, "Confession Reignites a Smoldering Pain: Anger Flares as Man Learns Identity of Assassin Who Killed his Family," *Houston Chronicle,* November 18, 1996, A13. Marius Schoon planned to formally oppose the amnesty application of Craig Williamson, but Schoon died of cancer just before the amnesty hearing began. Some believed that the stress from this case had worsened his condition.

25. Interview by the author with Margaret and Albert "Mandla" Mbalekelwa, August 18, 1996, Sebokeng, South Africa; interpretation from Zulu by Wally Mbhele.

26. The fear of revenge is in the context of the intercommunity political violence between the African National Congress and the Inkatha Freedom Party, a conflict that continued long after the end of apartheid and the onset of democratic elections.

27. This account was relayed by Joseph Dube, October 26, 1997, Soweto, South Africa.

28. Suzanne Daley, "In Apartheid Inquiry, Agony Is Relived but Not Put to Rest," *New York Times,* July 17, 1997, A1.

29. Grenville-Grey, interview by the author, 1997.

30. Brandon Hamber, "Dealing with the Past and the Psychology of Reconciliation: The Truth and Reconciliation Commission, a Psychological Perspective," paper presented at the International Symposium on the Contributions of Psychology to Peace, June 27, 1995, 6.

31. Thulani Grenville-Grey, interview by the author, Johannesburg, August 13, 1996, Cape Town, South Africa.

32. Hamber, "The Burdens of Truth," sec. 4.1. Numbers cited were current as of 1997.

33. Ilídio Silva, interview by the author, September 19, 1996, Maputo, Mozambique.

34. Cécile Rousseau and Aline Drapeau, "The Impact of Culture on the Transmission of Trauma: Refugees' Stories and Silence Embodied in Their Children's Lives," in Yael Danieli, *International Handbook,* 465–86.

35. Herman, interview by the author.

36. Tlhoki Mofokeng, Centre for the Study of Violence and Reconciliation, interview by the author, October 28, 1997, Johannesburg, South Africa. Many others echoed this point.

37. Reverend S. K. Mbande, interview.

38. Herman, *Trauma and Recovery,* 1.

39. Fanny Benadetti, interview by the author, March 25, 1997, New York.

40. American Psychiatric Association, *Diagnostic and Statistical Manual,* 424–25, 428.

41. *Report of the Commission of Inquiry,* Chad, as excerpted in Kritz, *Transitional Justice,* vol. 3, 54. It should be noted that at least one other truth commission had this same problem. When the Chilean commission traveled outside of the capital, the commission met with victims and families of the disappeared in municipal buildings, places that had often served as detention and interrogation centers during the dictatorship. See Human Rights Watch, *Human Rights and the "Politics of Agreements": Chile during President Aylwin's First Year* (New York: Human Rights Watch, 1991), 20.

42. Jon Cortina, in conversation with the author, April 12, 1996, San Salvador. The commission in El Salvador later opened offices outside of the capital for brief periods to provide easier access to those who live farther from the capital.

43. "TRC Leaves Deep Scars on Staff," *Mail and Guardian* (South Africa), December 12, 1997.

44. Lauren Gilbert, correspondence with the author, December 22, 1997.

45. Ibid.

46. Antjie Krog, "Overwhelming Trauma of the Truth," *Mail and Guardian* (South Africa), December 24, 1996, 10. For a fuller exploration by Antjie Krog, see her *Country of My Skull* (New York: Random House, 1999).

47. Tom Winslow, Trauma Centre for Victims of Violence and Torture, interview by the author, August 27, 1996, Cape Town, South Africa.

CHAPTER TEN

1. "Reconcile," *The Oxford English Dictionary,* 2nd ed., vol. 13 (Oxford: Clarendon Press, 1989), 352–53.

2. Louis Kriesberg, "Paths to Varieties of Inter-Communal Reconciliation," paper presented at the Seventeenth General Conference of the International Peace Research Association, Durban, South Africa, June 22–26 1998.

3. In conversation by author with Amnesty Committee member, November 1997, Port Elizabeth, South Africa.

4. "Only Half of People Feel TRC Is Fair and Unbiased: Survey," South Africa Press Association, March 5, 1998.

5. Some analysts, however, noted that the poll showed that public attitudes were deeply divided along racial lines. While close to 90 percent of whites "strongly disagreed or tended to disagree" that the commission would bring the races closer together, 54 percent of blacks "strongly agreed or tended to agree" that the races could now interact more harmoniously, with another 24 percent neutral. As the political editor of *Business Day* concluded, "The inference must be that although blacks and whites agree that the commission has made people angry, they differ profoundly on whether it has advanced the cause of reconciliation. There is no necessary contradiction in this," he explained. Since the majority of disclosures were of white security force crimes against black activists, whites were "projecting fear and moral discomfort at the anticipated rage of black people." The article continues, saying, "They are right, as the black respondents confirm. It would be surprising if blacks were not enraged by revelations that the government tried to develop a chemical programme to limit black fertility, or that white policemen cooked meat on one fire while incinerating the body of a murdered township youth on a fire nearby. What is striking, however, is that close to 80 percent of MRA's black respondents do not regard such disclosures as an insuperable obstacle to better racial understanding, and that half believe 'the people in South Africa will now be able to live together more easily.'" Drew Forrest, "Body Has Served National Reconciliation," *Business Day* (South Africa), August 3, 1998.

6. *Truth and Reconciliation Commission of South Africa Report,* vol. 5, chap. 9, sec, 130, 423–28. This passage was excerpted from a report by Hugo van der Merwe, "The South African Truth and Reconciliation Commission and Community Reconciliation" (Johannesburg: Centre for the Study of Violence and Reconciliation, 1998).

7. Angus Stewart, in correspondence with Howard Varney, April 1998, in reference to the Esikaweni incidents in Richards Bay. On file with author.

8. Alejandro Gonzalez, interview by the author, November 1996, Santiago, Chile.

9. As Pinochet's extradition hearing was under way in London, for example, the conservative business daily *La Estrategia* editorialized, "Pinochet supporters, both in Chile and the UK, have made considerable efforts to let the truth be known over what really happened in our country in the years leading up to and after the military takeover in 1973, challenging the international campaign

carried out by Socialists and Communists opposed to General Pinochet and the military. Things have gradually become more clear about the aims of the Unidad Popular [Salvador Allende's leftist coalition, which was deposed in the coup] to impose a Marxist government on our country, the illegality into which that government fell, the infiltration of foreign extremists into our country. The notable political, social and economic successes of the military government are also becoming better known." "The Pinochet Case Is on a Good Track," editorial, *La Estrategia*, January 26, 1999, n.p.

10. Horacio Verbitsky, interview by the author, December 10, 1996, Buenos Aires, Argentina.

11. Patricia Valdez, interview by the author, December 13, 1996, Buenos Aires, Argentina.

12. Juan Méndez, interview by the author, March 22, 1996, Notre Dame, IN.

13. Human Rights Watch, *Truth and Partial Justice in Argentina: An Update* (New York: Human Rights Watch, 1991), 69.

14. Manouri Kokila Muttetuwegama, chair of the Commission of Inquiry into the Involuntary Removals and Disappearances of Persons in the Western, Southern, and Sabaragamuwa Provinces of Sri Lanka, interview by the author, September 18, 1998, Brighton, England.

15. This description of what reconciliation might look like, as well as the following section on the factors that encourage reconciliation, was first published, in slightly longer form, in Priscilla B. Hayner, "In Pursuit of Justice and Reconciliation: Contributions of Truth Telling," Cynthia J. Arnson, ed., *Comparative Peace Processes in Latin America* (Washington, DC: Woodrow Wilson Center Press, and Stanford, CA: Stanford University Press, 1999), 363–83.

16. *The Oxford English Dictionary,* 2nd ed., vol. 13 (Oxford: Clarendon Press, 1989), 353.

17. Kader Asmal, Louise Asmal, and Ronald Suresh Roberts, *Reconciliation through Truth: A Reckoning of Apartheid's Criminal Governance* (Cape Town: David Philip, 1996), 46.

18. Ibid., 47.

19. Mauricio Vargas, interview by the author, April 1996, San Salvador.

20. Mahmood Mamdani, "Degrees of Reconciliation and Forms of Justice: Making Sense of the African Experience," paper presented at the conference *Justice or Reconciliation?* at the Center for International Studies, University of Chicago, April 25–26, 1997, 6.

21. *Truth and Reconciliation Commission of South Africa Report*, vol. 5, chap. 9, sec. 152, 435.

22. For a fuller description of this process of implementing judicial reforms, see Jack Spence, David R. Dye, Mike Lanchin, Geoff Thale, and George Vickers, *Chapúltepec: Five Years Later*, (Cambridge, MA: Hemisphere Initiatives, 1997), 19–20.

23. The terms of reference for the El Salvadoran commission, signed by the government and armed opposition in the peace accords, stated simply that "The Parties undertake to carry out the Commission's recommendations." See "Annex to the Mexico Agreements: Commission on the Truth," UN Doc. S/25500, April 27, 1991, Article 10.

24. Jeff Thale, Washington Office on Latin America, interview by the author, February 4, 1998, Washington, DC.

25. Margaret L. Popkin, *Peace without Justice: Obstacles to Building the Rule of Law in El Salvador* (University Park: Pennsylvania State University Press, 2000), 161.

26. *Report of the Commission of Inquiry into Violations of Human Rights: Findings, Conclusions and Recommendations* (Uganda), October 1994, 584.

27. The Truth and Reconciliation Act of Sierra Leone, 2000, Article 17.

28. Law Creating the National Corporation for Reparation and Reconciliation, Law No. 19,123, Chile, January 31, 1992, reprinted in Kritz, *Transitional Justice,* vol. 3, 685–95.

CHAPTER ELEVEN

1. See "United Nations Commission on Human Rights: Study concerning the Right to Restitution, Compensation and Rehabilitation for Victims of Gross Violations of Human Rights and Fundamental Freedoms: Final Report," Theo van Boven, rapporteur, UN Doc. E/CN.4/Sub.2/1993, July 8, 1993.

2. Details of the Chilean reparations program, and the total costs, are reported in Corporación Nacional de Reparación y Reconciliación, *Informe Sobre Calificación de Víctimas de Violaciones de Derechos Humanos y de la Violencia Política* (Santiago: Corporación Nacional de Reparación y Reconciliación, 1996), 595–602. All monetary amounts are reported here in U.S. dollars.

3. Law Creating the National Corporation for Reparation and Reconciliation, Law No. 19,123, Chile, January 31, 1992, Article 17, reprinted in Kritz, *Transitional Justice*, vol. 3, 685–95.

4. Patricia Verdugo, interview by the author, November 30, 1996, Santiago, Chile.

5. Carla Pellegrin Friedman, interview by the author, December 3, 1996, Santiago, Chile. Reparations payments are not paid to siblings of the victim; in the case of the Pellegrin family, a monthly check will be paid to the victim's daughter, Carla Pellegrin's niece, until she reaches the age of twenty-five.

6. This Program of Reparation and Integral Health Care (known by its Spanish acronym, PRAIS), run through the Ministry of Health, has received little attention; many victims told me they were not aware of it. As of 1995, after five years in operation, only 693 persons had made use of its services, including family members of the disappeared and survivors of detention and torture. See Corporación Nacional de Reparación y Reconciliación, 601.

7. Andres Dominguez Vial, Executive Secretary of the National Corporation for Reparation and Reconciliation, interview by the author, November 27, 1996, Santiago, Chile.

8. The number of cases that were given to the commission from nongovernmental organizations, rather than through direct testimony, can be seen in the final victims list published as an appendix to the Argentine *Nunca Más* report. Those individuals listed without a case number were given to the commission indirectly; those with case numbers (about two out of three) were taken through direct testimony to the commission.

9. Law No. 24,411, Argentina, December 7, 1994, which instituted these reparations.

10. Decree 70/91, Argentina, January 10, 1991. This and following decrees authorized payment to approximately two hundred former political prisoners who had instituted legal proceedings prior to December 10, 1985 (i.e., within the first two years of democratic government). The cases brought to the Inter-American Commission and the friendly settlement with the government of Argentina are described in the *Annual Report of the Inter-American Commission of Human Rights, 1992–93*, OEA/Ser.L/V/II. 83, doc. 14, corr.1, March 12 1993, 35–40.

Information about the reparations programs also obtained in telephone interviews by the author with Alejandro Kawabata, Human Rights Office of the Argentine Ministry of the Interior, February 20, 1998, and Alejandro Garro (legal counsel to petitioners before the Inter-American Commission), Columbia University School of Law, February 16, 1998. See also Human Rights Watch, *World Report 1992* (New York: Human Rights Watch, 1992), 141; and Human Rights Watch, *Truth and Partial Justice in Argentina: An Update* (New York: Human Rights Watch, 1991), 70–71.

11. Those eligible for reparation were (1) those held in custody under the National Executive Authority (political prisoners held without trial); (2) civilians who were imprisoned on orders of a military court; and (3) those who were temporarily disappeared (imprisonment unrecognized by the authorities) whose case was reported at the time or who later gave testimony to the Argentine truth commission. The period covered extended to two years before the military coup of 1976, from the date that a state of siege began under the previous government. See Law No. 24,043, Argentina, November 27, 1991, reprinted in Kritz, *Transitional Justice*, vol. 3, 667–69.

12. Reparations to those forcibly exiled was not explicit in the law, but resulted from an administrative interpretation made by the government's Human Rights Office and the legal advisor to the Ministry of the Interior. Juan Méndez, correspondence with the author, February 13, 1998.

13. Ibid.

14. In April 1992, for example, a court awarded $250,000 for "moral damages" to the father of a young Swedish student, Dagmar Ingrid Hagelin, who disappeared in Argentina during the "dirty war." See "Fuerte indemnización por una desaparecida," *Clarin,* April 4, 1992. In Novem-

ber 1994, a federal district court awarded $3 million to the only survivor of a family of five who disappeared at the hands of the government ($2 million to be paid by former navy admirals previously convicted of causing the disappearances, and $1 million by the state). See "Condenan al Estado, a Massera y a Lambruschini pagar 3 millones," *Clarin,* November 18, 1994, 15. After five years of appeals, the award was finally set at $1 1/4 million, to be split between Emilio Massera and the state of Argentina; Armando Lambruschini was dropped from the suit. See Noga Tarnopolsky, "The Family That Disappeared," *New Yorker,* November 15, 1999, 48–57.

15. Law No. 24,411, Argentina, December 7, 1994.

16. Law No. 24,321, Argentina, May 11, 1994.

17. Law No. 24,321 also allowed those families who had declared a family member "disappeared with the presumption of death" to change their status to "forcibly disappeared."

18. Interview by the author with staff of the Human Rights Office of the Ministry of the Interior, December 11, 1996, Buenos Aires, Argentina.

19. Mercedes Meroño, Madres de la Plaza de Mayo, interview by the author, December 1996, Buenos Aires, Argentina.

20. Interview by the author with Hlengiwe Mkhize, chair of the Reparation and Rehabilitation Committee of the Truth and Reconciliation Commission, Johannesburg, South Africa; and telephone interviews with Thulani Grenville-Grey, staff member of the committee, and Farouk Hoosen, director of the President's Fund, June 1999.

21. *Si M Pa Rele . . . If I Don't Cry Out . . . , Report of the National Commission of Truth and Justice,* Haiti, 1996, 285.

22. *From Madness to Hope: Report of the Commission on the Truth for El Salvador,* 186.

23. For an overview of national reparations programs, see "United Nations Commission on Human Rights: Study Concerning the Right to Restitution, Compensation and Rehabilitation for Victims of Gross Violations of Human Rights and Fundamental Freedoms: Final Report," Theo van Boven, rapporteur. UN Doc. E/CN.4/Sub.2/1993, July 8, 1993.

24. For an exploration of Germany's reparations programs for World War II victims, see Christian Pross, *Paying for the Past: The Struggle over Reparations for Surviving Victims of the Nazi Terror,* trans. Belinda Cooper (Baltimore: Johns Hopkins University Press, 1998). See also summary in van Boven, "United Nations Commission," par. 107–11 and par. 125, as excerpted in Kritz, *Transitional Justice,* vol. 1, 536–38, 543.

25. See Law No. 9,140, Brazil, December 4, 1995. This commission also had some powers to investigate each of these cases of disappearance, and oversaw a number of exhumations undertaken by the Argentine Forensic Anthropology Team.

26. Reparations were also paid to the descendants of those survivors who were still alive on the date that the bill was passed into law. See brief discussion in chapter 2.

27. See van Boven, "United Nations Commission." In addition, some individual victims have gained compensation through suits in national courts or in international fora, such as through the Inter-American Commission on Human Rights or the Inter-American Court of Human Rights, but these decisions have directly affected only the small numbers who are directly involved in the case, as compared to the large classes of people affected by national reparations programs.

CHAPTER TWELVE

1. The Policy Statement on Impunity of Amnesty International states that "there should be a thorough investigation into allegations of human rights violations" and that "the truth about violations must be revealed." The Policy Statement on Accountability for Past Abuses of Human Rights Watch says that there is a "duty to investigate" and argues that "the most important means of establishing accountability is for the government itself to make known all that can be reliably established about gross abuses of human rights. . . . " See Kritz, *Transitional Justice,* vol. 1, 219, 217.

2. Wilder Tayler, interview by the author, New York. In practice, according to other staff, Human Rights Watch also generally takes into account local preferences and would be unlikely to press for a policy on a particular country that was opposed by local rights groups.

3. Nick Howen, former legal director of Amnesty International, interview by the author, July 9, 1997, London.

4. "Set of Principles for the Protection and Promotion of Human Rights through Action to Combat Impunity," Louis Joinet, rapporteur. UN Doc E/CN.4/Sub.2/1997/20/Rev. 1, Annex II, October 2, 1997, Principle 1.

5. Ibid., Principle 2.

6. Richard Carver, telephone interview by the author, August 17, 1999.

7. Spain is another example of a country that showed little desire to investigate past state crimes, after the death of General Francisco Franco and his many decades of sometimes repressive rule. Commentators note that the many years that had passed since the most severe abuses had taken place was the primary reason for the general lack of interest in delving into the subject.

8. For further information on these peace negotiations and related matters, see Jeremy Armon, Dylan Hendrickson, and Alex Vines, eds., *Conciliation Resources: The Mozambique Peace Process in Perspective* (London: Conciliation Resources, 1998), available at www.c-r.org; and Cameron Hume, *Ending Mozambique's War: The Role of Mediation and Good Offices* (Washington, DC: U.S. Institute of Peace Press, 1994).

9. Among those who told me there was no amnesty was the head of opposition in Parliament, Raul Domingos, and the minister of defense, Aguiar Mazula. Domingos explained that the government had offered an amnesty to Renamo, but as Renamo didn't believe that it had broken any laws, "we refused it." All interviews in Mozambique cited in this chapter were undertaken in September 1996.

10. Alex Vines, interview by the author, August 1996, London.

11. Ken Wilson, Ford Foundation program officer for Mozambique, interview by the author, September 1996, Johannesburg, South Africa.

12. For a description of the history and politics of Renamo, see Alex Vines, *Renamo: From Terrorism to Democracy in Mozambique?* (London: James Currey, 1996, revised and updated edition; first published 1991).

13. For a description of the war's abuses, see Human Rights Watch, *Conspicuous Destruction: War, Famine and the Reform Process in Mozambique* (New York: Human Rights Watch, 1992).

14. Renamo did submit a letter to Mozambique president Joaquim Chissano at some point during the negotiations, asking that a truth commission be set up, but never received a reply. Observers who were aware of this letter considered it only to be posturing and not a serious request.

15. Alcinda Honwana, "Sealing the Past, Facing the Future: Trauma Healing in Rural Mozambique," in Armon, Hendrickson, and Vines, eds., *Conciliation Resources*, 77; available at www.c-r.org/acc_moz/honwana.htm. Honwana writes, "In the Mozambican context, as in many other parts of Africa, health is traditionally defined as harmonious relationships between human beings and their natural surroundings, between them and their ancestors, and amongst themselves. . . . Illness is therefore considered primarily a social rather than a physical phenomenon. . . . 'Appeasing the spirits' is thus a mechanism for redressing the wrongs of the past and restoring well-being both within and between communities. Such models of health and healing contradict traditionally Western approaches in which individuals and their social context, the body and the mind, are often perceived as separate, distinguishable entities" (76).

16. William Minter, *Apartheid's Contras: An Inquiry into the Roots of War in Angola and Mozambique* (London: Zed Books, and Johannesburg: Witwatersrand University Press, 1994) 282.

17. It is worth noting that the human rights situation has dramatically improved in Mozambique since the end of the war, much more so than in many other transitional states. The main concerns of human rights observers today are the conditions of prisons and corruption.

18. The total number killed under Khmer Rouge rule is unknown, but estimates range between one and two million people.

19. David Hawk, telephone interview by the author, August 8, 1997.

20. See, for example, Crocker Snow, Jr., "From the Killing Fields, Compassion," *World Paper*, July 1995, 16, and Seth Mydans, "Side by Side Now in Cambodia: Skulls, Victims and Victimizers, *New York Times*, May 27, 1996, A6.

21. Stephen P. Marks, "Forgetting 'the Policies and Practices of the Past': Impunity in Cambodia," *Fletcher Forum of World Affairs* 18, no. 2 (1994), 37–38.

22. Ibid., 40.

23. Brad Adams, "Snatching Defeat from the Jaws of Victory?" *Phnom Penh Post*, January 23, 1999.

24. For an overview of international response to Khmer Rouge crimes and proposals for international accountability measures, see Balakrishnan Rajagopal, "The Pragmatics of Prosecuting the Khmer Rouge," *Phnom Penh Post*, January 8, 1999, and Adams, "Snatching Defeat."

25. The Committee to Oppose the Return of the Khmer Rouge, a coalition of over one hundred human rights and church groups in Washington, lobbied strongly in support of an initiative that would hold the Khmer Rouge accountable for their crimes.

26. While the mass killings by the Khmer Rouge are often referred to as genocide (as in the U.S. legislation and the offices created out of this legislation), much of this violence does not fit that definition. Genocide, as defined by the Genocide Convention, is the "intent to destroy, in whole or in part, a national, ethnic, racial, or religious group" (Convention on the Prevention and Punishment of the Crime of Genocide, 1948, Article 2). Some of the violence by the Khmer Rouge would probably qualify as genocide, such as the campaigns against the ethnic Vietnamese, but most of its abuses were not directed against such specific groups.

27. This study, by two U.S. scholars, resulted in a book outlining accountability options in transitional situations, particularly focused on Cambodia. See Steven R. Ratner and Jason S. Abrams, *Accountability for Human Rights Atrocities in International Law: Beyond the Nuremberg Legacy* (New York: Oxford University Press, 1997).

28. U.S. Congressional Record—Senate, April 10, 1992. It was also hoped that the project would lead to prosecution of the Khmer Rouge. The Cambodian Genocide Justice Act lists among its objectives, "to bring to justice the national political and military leadership of the Khmer Rouge" and "to develop the United States proposal for the establishment of an international criminal tribunal for the prosecution of those accused of genocide in Cambodia." H.R. 2333, 1994.

29. Peter Cleveland, interview by the author, March 12, 1997, Washington, DC.

30. The purpose of putting the photos up on the web, project director Ben Kiernan explained, is to allow survivors to identify those killed (Ben Kiernan, interview by the author, April 25, 1997, New Haven, CT). The address for the website is www.yale.edu/cgp/.

31. Seth Mydans, "20 Years On, Anger Ignites against Khmer Rouge," *New York Times*, January 20, 1999, A1.

32. "Most Cambodians Want Trial for Khmer Rouge: Poll," January 27, 1999, Reuters News Service.

33. Mark McDonald, "Cambodians Brace for UN Trial Proposal: Most Want Leaders Punished, but Resist Opening Old Wounds," *San Jose Mercury News*, February 8, 1999.

34. "Tutu Will Help Cambodia," *Daily Mail and Guardian* (South Africa), January 18, 1999.

35. *Report of the Group of Experts for Cambodia Established Pursuant to General Assembly Resolution 52/135,* UN Doc. A/53/850/S/1999/231, Annex, March 16, 1999, 54.

36. Brad Adams, "Snatching Defeat."

37. Trials are sometimes precluded for reasons of political circumstance (perpetrators hold sufficient power to demand an amnesty, or judges feel too threatened to move on sensitive cases) or incapacity (dysfunctional judicial system, or a limited ability to move on only a select number

of cases). But where trials are possible, they should be advanced, especially for high-level perpetrators (there may sometimes be a question of timing, however, such as waiting until a peace settlement is firmly in place before threatening prosecutions). In contrast, a truth commission may be possible, but may not be preferred, for a variety of acceptable reasons. I recognize that this runs counter to the assumptions of some who would advocate a "truth always, and trials only when they are not too risky" policy.

38. These conferences resulted in two books. See Alex Boraine, Janet Levy, and Ronel Scheffer, eds., *Dealing with the Past: Truth and Reconciliation in South Africa* (Cape Town: Institute for Democracy in South Africa, 1994), and Alex Boraine and Janet Levy, eds., *The Healing of a Nation?* (Cape Town: Justice in Transition, 1995).

39. This conference was cosponsored by the Washington-based Robert F. Kennedy Memorial Center for Human Rights, working in close collaboration with a Malawian university, and was funded by the U.S. Institute of Peace. See *Understanding the Past to Safeguard the Future: Proceedings of a Conference Convened by the University of Malawi and the Robert F. Kennedy Center for Human Rights at Lilongwe, Malawi, 18–19 October 1996* (Washington, DC: Robert F. Kennedy Center, April 1997).

40. See Seth Mydans, "In a Tiny Office, Khmer Rouge Files Tell Grisly Tales," *New York Times*, January 13, 1999, A3.

41. Allan Nairn, "Haiti Under the Gun," *The Nation*, January 15, 1996, 11–15; and "Haiti Under Cloak," editorial, *The Nation*, February 26, 1996, 4–5; and "Danger Signs in Haiti," editorial, *New York Times*, September 9, 1996, A14. The head of FRAPH, Emmanuel Constant, has admitted to working for the U.S. Central Intelligence Agency; although Haiti has asked for his extradition, he lives freely in Queens, New York.

42. In a similar case, the Central Intelligence Agency acquired many sensitive files of the East German Stasi, or secret police, after the fall of the Berlin Wall. The CIA long resisted returning these files, which was a source of tension between the United States and Germany; an accord was reached in late 1999 to return most of them. See Roger Cohen, "Germany's East is Still Haunted by Big Brother," *New York Times*, November 19, 1999, A12.

43. See Tim Weiner, "Interrogation, C.I.A.-Style: The Spy Agency's Many Mean Ways to Loosen Cold-War Tongues," *New York Times*, February 9, 1997, and Dana Priest, "Army's Project Had Wider Audience: Clandestine Operations Training Manuals Not Restricted to Americas," *Washington Post*, March 6, 1997, A1, A16.

44. See, for example, Peter Kornbluh, "Chile's 'Disappeared' Past: US Should Acknowledge Complicity in Murderous Regime," *Boston Globe*, September 13, 1998, E2, and Tim Weiner, "All the President Had to Do Was Ask: The C.I.A. Took Aim at Allende," *New York Times*, September 13, 1998, 4–7.

45. The exceptions are few: In the mid-1970s, the Senate investigated and released a lengthy report on the activities of the intelligence branch of the U.S. government. See *Report of the Senate Select Committee to Study Governmental Operations with Respect to Intelligence Activities*, vols. 1–7 (Washington, DC: U.S. Government Printing Office, 1976, commonly known as the Church Committee Report). After the release of the El Salvador truth commission report, the Clinton administration appointed a panel to "examine the implications" of the report for the "conduct of U.S. foreign policy and the operations of the Department of State," but with a narrow mandate that did not include a full review of U.S. policy toward El Salvador. Experts on El Salvador criticized the report as not very credible. U.S. Department of State, *Report of the Secretary of State's Panel on El Salvador*, July 1993. See also Martha Doggett, *Death Foretold: The Jesuit Murders in El Salvador* (New York: Lawyers Committee for Human Rights, and Washington, DC: Georgetown University Press, 1993), 270. Given this history, some observers have called for a truth commission in the United States to look into the U.S. support for repressive regimes and its complicity in the gross violation of human rights. This has been raised especially in regard to

U.S. involvement in Central America, such as in Thomas Buergenthal, "The U.S. Should Come Clean on 'Dirty Wars,'" *New York Times,* April 8, 1998.

CHAPTER THIRTEEN

1. An "opt out" provision allows countries to reject the Court's jurisdiction over war crimes for the first seven years after the treaty enters into force for the state in question. Furthermore, the crime of "aggression" shall also fall under the jurisdiction of the Court "once a provision is adopted . . . defining the crime and setting out the conditions under which the Court shall exercise jurisdiction with respect to this crime," and with the agreement of seven-eighths of the state parties to make the amendment to the statute. See *Rome Statute of the International Criminal Court,* UN Doc. A/Conf.183/9, July 17, 1998, Article 5, par. 2 (available at www.un.org/icc/romestat.htm).

The United States was among seven nations that voted against the Court's statute. See Alessandra Stanley, "U.S. Dissents, but Accord Is Reached on War-Crimes Court," *New York Times,* July 18, 1998, A3. For analysis and critique of U.S. objections, see Kenneth Roth, "The Court the US Doesn't Want," *New York Review of Books,* November 19, 1998, 45–47.

The International Criminal Court has no jurisdiction over a case unless either the state where the crime took place or the state of nationality of the accused is a member party, or otherwise expressly consents to the Court's jurisdiction. This limitation does not apply where the Security Council refers a situation to the Court acting under the Chapter VII powers of the UN Charter. The Court will also not have jurisdiction if any state is already investigating or prosecuting the case, unless the Court can establish that the state in question is unable or unwilling to carry out genuine proceedings. The Court will not cover crimes that took place before it was established.

2. Many of those who were involved in the development of the Court's statute assumed that the primary issue related to truth commissions that pertained to the Court was the question of national amnesties, which were not to be recognized by the Court. Other questions pertaining to parallel truth investigations were not addressed in the multilateral discussions, according to nongovernmental advocates who closely watched these discussions. Interviews by the author in late 1998 with Helen Duffy, counsel for the ICC Campaign, Human Rights Watch, New York; Jelena Pejic, senior program coordinator for Europe, Lawyers Committee for Human Rights, New York; and Christopher Hall, legal advisor, Amnesty International, London.

3. On the proposal for a truth commission in Bosnia generally, see Neil J. Kritz and William A. Stuebner, "A Truth and Reconciliation Commission for Bosnia and Herzegovina: Why, How, and When?" paper presented at the Victimology Symposium, Sarajevo, Bosnia, May 9–10, 1998. See also Neil J. Kritz, "Is a Truth Commission Appropriate in the Former Yugoslavia?" paper presented at the Conference on War Crimes Trials, Belgrade, November 7–8, 1998. The U.S. Institute of Peace, based in Washington, headed up the discussion and promotion of the Bosnian truth commission idea in 1997 and 1998, at the request of the Bosnian government and working in conjunction with some local Bosnian nongovernmental organizations.

4. See remarks by Ian Martin on the panel "The Need for and Possibility of Truth and Reconciliation Commissions in the Territory of the Former Yugoslavia," Conference on War Crimes Trials, Belgrade, November 7–8, 1998. (Because representatives of the Tribunal were not able to attend the Belgrade conference, their views were relayed by Ian Martin, then deputy high representative for human rights, Office of the High Representative, Sarajevo. His remarks do not necessarily represent the position of the Office of the High Representative.)

5. While defunding the Tribunal in order to provide support to the commission would represent an inaccurate perception on the part of the international community of a truth commission's role, some well-placed observers feared this could take place. Regardless, the size and resource

demands of the two mechanisms are notably different: the fiscal year 1999 budget of the Tribunal was close to $100 million, with a staff of nine hundred. The proposed truth commission, if established, was projected to cost between $15 and $20 million total over the course of two years.

6. Interviews by the author with a range of legal scholars, observers, and supporters both of the Tribunal and the truth commission proposal, 1998 and 1999. In addition, the former chief prosecutor for the Tribunal, South African judge Richard Goldstone, has expressed strong support for a truth commission in Bosnia. See Richard J. Goldstone, "Ethnic Reconciliation Needs the Help of a Truth Commission," *International Herald Tribune*, October 24–25, 1998, 6. See also Tina Rosenberg, "Trying to Break the Cycle of Revenge in Bosnia," *New York Times*, November 22, 1998, sec. 4, 16.

7. The standard of evidence used by truth commissions, versus that used by courts, is discussed in chapters 8 and 14.

8. The powers of the International Criminal Tribunal for the Former Yugoslavia are stronger than that of the International Criminal Court in the area of accessing evidence. The Tribunal has the equivalent of subpoena power and could obtain truth commission material at any time. The Court's powers are weaker, entailing a nonbinding request to a government.

9. The statute also requires "[a]ny other type of assistance which is not prohibited by the law of the requested State, with a view to facilitating the investigation and prosecution of crimes within the jurisdiction of the Court." *Rome Statute of the International Criminal Court,* Article 93, par. 1. A state party may deny the Court's request for assistance if the request concerns "documents or disclosure of evidence which relates to its national security" (although "national security" is left undefined); Article 93, par. 4.

10. While many truth commissions have turned over their files to domestic courts, in some cases, as described in earlier chapters, national amnesties or dysfunctional judicial systems have removed the threat of prosecution, and thus some perpetrators have willingly provided information to the commissions. While the Court's statute states that the Court will "ensure the confidentiality of documents and information, except as required for the investigation and proceedings described in the request," and that the state can request that information transmitted to the Court be used "solely for the purpose of generating new evidence," the possibility of a commission's link to the Court could deter former perpetrators from cooperating with a commission's investigation, especially if the Court gains strength in the coming years. *Rome Statute of the International Criminal Court*, Article 93, par. 8(a) and (b).

11. See *Rome Statute of the International Criminal Court,* Article 17, par. 1(a) and (b), which read:

   1. . . . the Court shall determine that a case is inadmissible where:

   (a) The case is being investigated or prosecuted by a State which has jurisdiction over it, unless the State is unwilling or unable genuinely to carry out the investigation or prosecution;

   (b) The case has been investigated by a State which has jurisdiction over it and the State has decided not to prosecute the person concerned, unless the decision resulted from the unwillingness or inability of the State genuinely to prosecute.

12. Marshall Freeman Harris, R. Bruce Hitchner, and Paul R. Williams, *Bringing War Criminals to Justice: Obligations, Options, Recommendations* (Dayton: The Center for International Programs, University of Dayton, 1997), 25. These authors cite the example of the Special Prosecutors Office in Ethiopia as fulfilling both a prosecutorial and truth commission role; see the description of the Ethiopian prosecutor's office in chapter 2.

CHAPTER FOURTEEN

1. In Guatemala, only the chair was appointed by the UN; in El Salvador, the commissioners were appointed by the UN secretary-general after consultation with the parties to the peace accord.

2. Christian Tomuschat, "Between National and International Law: Guatemala's Historical Clarification Commission," in *Festschrift Jaenicke* (Heidelberg: Springer, 1998). This article offers a fascinating analysis of the tension between the international and national legal foundations to the Guatemalan commission.

3. See Neil J. Kritz and William A. Stuebner, "A Truth and Reconciliation Commission for Bosnia and Herzegovina: Why, How, and When?" paper presented at the Victimology Symposium, Sarajevo, Bosnia, May 9–10, 1998.

4. For example, Buergenthal writes, "Our backgrounds gave us easy access to government officials throughout the Americas; enabled us to obtain the assistance of numerous individuals, government and nongovernmental groups, and institutions; and made it very difficult for the Parties to the Peace Accords to deprecate our views or to discredit us. We were able to use our status and personal connections to overcome a variety of obstacles that were placed in our way, to anticipate problems, and to diffuse potential crises. . . . The more difficult the job a truth commission faces, the more important it is, in my opinion, for at least one or more members of such a body to be distinguished and internationally respected personalities with political, military, diplomatic, or judicial experience." Thomas Buergenthal, "The United Nations Truth Commission for El Salvador," *Vanderbilt Journal of Transnational Law* 27, no. 3 (1994), 543.

5. For a detailed description of the selection process in Sierra Leone, see the Truth and Reconciliation Act of Sierra Leone, 2000, "Schedule," available on the web at www.sierra-leone.org/trc.html.

6. Interviews by author, Buenos Aires and New York. This is also described in *Nunca Más: Report of the Argentine National Commission on the Disappeared*, 429–30.

7. The Guatemalan commission had the greatest number of people during the five to six months when it had a dozen field offices open around the country. After those offices closed, the staff size shrank to the number needed for data processing, research, and drafting the report.

8. In addition, over a period of two to three months, up to twenty additional temporary staff were hired for data processing and data entry.

9. Patricia Valdez, executive director of the Commission on the Truth for El Salvador, interview by the author, March 29, 1993, New York.

10. Lawyers Committee for Human Rights, *Improvising History: A Critical Evaluation of the United Nations Observer Mission in El Salvador* (New York: Lawyers Committee for Human Rights, 1995), 141–42.

11. In Haiti and Guatemala, staff and commission members were approximately half national and half international. In South Africa, the commission staff was predominantly South African, but included a number of foreigners, including professionals on loan from European governments. Perhaps the most difficult aspect of this mixed model is the staff tension that often results from the dramatically different salary levels for national and international employees who are doing the same work, a problem that arises in many contexts where international and national staff work together in the developing world. While there is no easy answer to this problem, it should be recognized as a potential source of bitterness.

12. Jorge Correa, former executive secretary of the Chilean National Commission on Truth and Reconciliation, interview by the author, November 29, 1996, Santiago, Chile.

13. Interviews by author, October 1996, Kampala, Uganda.

14. Funding for the Guatemalan Historical Clarification Commission came from Norway and Switzerland (approximately $1.2 million each); Sweden and the United States ($1 million each); Japan ($750,000); Germany and Denmark ($500,000 each); and Austria, Belgium, Canada, Italy, the Netherlands, and Switzerland ($250,000 or less each). The Ford Foundation and the Open Society Institute also supported the commission with grants or logistical support. Funding details were made available on the commission's website.

15. Max DuPreez, host of *Truth Commission Special Report* (South African Broadcasting Company), interview by the author, October 24, 1998, Johannesburg, South Africa.

16. The Guatemalan and El Salvador commissions' mandates even explicitly prohibited them from holding any public sessions. The Guatemalan accord reads, "The Commission's proceedings shall be confidential so as to guarantee the secrecy of the sources and the safety of witnesses and informants." See "Agreement on the Establishment of the Commission to Clarify Past Human Rights Violations and Acts of Violence That Have Caused the Guatemalan Population to Suffer," UN Doc. A/48/954/ S/1994/751, Annex II, June 23, 1994. The El Salvador mandate states that "The Commission shall have broad powers to organize its work and its functioning. Its activities shall be conducted on a confidential basis." See Annex to the Mexico Agreements, UN Doc. S/25500, Annex, April 27, 1991.

17. Legal scholar Michael P. Scharf, for example, writes, "While there are complications and risks attendant to open proceedings, these can be addressed in less draconian ways than by completely closing the proceedings to the public and press," and argues that "closed proceedings have undermined the integrity of the process, for it is human nature that people do not trust what they cannot see." See Michael P. Scharf, "The Case for a Permanent International Truth Commission," *Duke Journal of Comparative and International Law* 7 (1997), 387–88.

18. Jonathan Klaaren and Stu Woolman, "Government Efforts to Protect Human Rights in Uganda," *Nairobi Law Monthly* 35 (1991), 26–28.

19. The procedures used in South Africa are discussed in chapter 8.

20. In South Africa, there was among those who testified in public less fear of retribution, a fear that is very prevalent throughout Latin America and elsewhere.

21. Patrick Ball, *Who Did What to Whom? Planning and Implementing a Large Scale Human Rights Data Project* (Washington, DC: American Association for the Advancement of Science, 1996). See also Herbert F. Spirer and Louise Spirer, *Data Analysis for Monitoring Human Rights* (Washington, DC: American Association for the Advancement of Science, 1993), which focuses on statistical analysis and presentation of data.

22. *From Madness to Hope*, Report of the Commission on the Truth for El Salvador, 24.

23. Ibid.

24. This follow-up commission was eventually created, but it had difficulty gaining the cooperation of witnesses and was not able to come to firm conclusions about responsibility. See *Report of the Joint Group for the Investigation of Politically Motivated Illegal Armed Groups in El Salvador,* UN Doc. S/1994/989, Annex, October 22, 1994.

25. *Report of the Chilean National Commission on Truth and Reconciliation,* 41.

26. Ibid., 42.

27. The South African report explains that "the Commission is not a court of law. It was set up as a commission of Enquiry and, as such, was not bound by the same rules of evidence as are the courts. In order to make a finding, it had to operate within the framework of a balance of probabilities, which is the standard criterion used in civil litigation. Its conclusions are therefore findings rather than judicial verdicts." *Truth and Reconciliation Commission of South Africa Report,* vol. 5, chap. 6, sec. 64, 208.

CHAPTER FIFTEEN

1. Promotion of National Unity and Reconciliation Act, Act no. 34 of 1995, South Africa.

2. The amnesty hearings continued into the year 2000, and it was likely that this closed-door option would in fact never be used.

3. Alexandra Barahona de Brito, *Human Rights and Democratization in Latin America: Uruguay and Chile* (New York: Oxford University Press, 1997), 193.

4. Eduardo Rabossi, interview by the author, December 11, 1996, Buenos Aires, Argentina.

5. Mercedes Meroño, Mothers of the Plaza de Mayo, interview by the author, December 13, 1996, Buenos Aires, Argentina.

6. Several of the disappeared family members of the Mothers of the Plaza de Mayo whom I spoke with were listed in the report, for example, including Mercedes Meroño. Ibid.

7. Mary Burton, interview by the author, October 29, 1997, Cape Town, South Africa.

8. Tlhoki Mofokeng, interview by the author, October 28, 1997, Johannesburg, South Africa.

9. Interview by the author with members of Khulumani, October 28, 1997, Johannesburg, South Africa.

10. The mandate for the El Salvador commission ("Annex to the Mexico Agreements: Commission on the Truth," UN Doc. S/25500, April 27, 1991) reads:

> 8. For the purposes of the investigation, the Commission shall have the power to:
>
> (a) Gather, by the means it deems appropriate, any information it considers relevant. The Commission shall be completely free to use whatever sources of information it deems useful and reliable. It shall receive such information within the period of time and in the manner which it determines.
>
> (b) Interview, freely and in private, any individuals, groups, or members of organizations or institutions.
>
> (c) Visit any establishment or place freely without giving prior notice.
>
> (d) Carry out any other measures or inquiries which it considers useful to the performance of its mandate, including requesting reports, records or documents from the Parties or any other information from State authorities and departments.
>
> 9. The Parties undertake to extend to the Commission whatever cooperation it requests of them in order to gain access to sources of information available to them.

11. On the other hand, Buergenthal notes that "On the whole, the Commission encountered few difficulties in interviewing any individual it wished to have appear before it. Most civilians, former FMLN combatants, and military personnel presented themselves at the Commission after being summoned by it." (He notes though, that there is an important difference between appearing for questioning and telling the truth or providing the information requested.) See Thomas Buergenthal, "The United Nations Truth Commission for El Salvador," *Vanderbilt Journal of Transnational Law* 27 (1994), 506–7.

12. The Argentine report lists forty-four senior members of the armed forces whom it sent lengthy questionnaires to. Because of the positions they held in the de facto government or armed forces, these persons "could be expected to have the information necessary" to answer the questions on the fate of the disappeared the report states, but to no avail. "There were a few cases in which no answer was forthcoming, and none of the replies received by this Commission have been of use in clarifying the circumstances surrounding the disappearance of people or in helping to trace them." See *Nunca Más: Report of the Argentine National Commission on the Disappeared*, 252–54.

The Chilean commission contacted 160 members of the armed forces and the police to request that they give testimony, but most refused. The heads of the respective branches or their chiefs of staff were consulted for any evidence their institution might have on the events of concern, but most either responded that files had been legally burned or destroyed, or did not respond at all. In a few cases, valuable information was made available. See the *Report of the Chilean National Commission on Truth and Reconciliation*, 17–20.

13. *Truth and Reconciliation Commission of South Africa Report,* vol. 1, chap. 8, sec. 104, 236.

14. Mercedes Assorati, interview by the author, December 9, 1996, Buenos Aires, Argentina.

15. Canada, Sweden, and Australia also have freedom of information laws, though they are structured somewhat differently.

16. Gaining access to this classified material is not easy. The National Security Archive stresses the importance of a targeted approach to any declassification request: the requester should provide as much information as possible not only about the event in question but about the exact division or office where such documents might be stored. For further information on the Freedom of Information Act and how to request the declassification of documents, see the website of the National Security Archive, www.gwu.edu/~nsarchiv.

17. As described by commission member Thomas Buergenthal, "Truth Commission," 507–10.

18. The commission was agreed to in 1994, but did not begin work until mid-1997, after the final peace accord was signed, which gave NGOs over three years to prepare.

19. Meanwhile, documents were also being released on Guatemalan affairs through other parallel processes. Two lawsuits against the U.S. government were brought by U.S. citizens whose husbands were killed in Guatemala, and a parallel government review of U.S. intelligence policy in the country led to the declassification of an additional seven thousand to eight thousand documents.

20. Kate Doyle, interview by the author, March 31, 1998, Washington, D.C.

21. For further information, see Kate Doyle, "Getting to Know the Generals: Secret Documents on the Guatemalan Military," paper presented at the Latin American Studies Association Conference, Chicago, September 24–26, 1998.

22. See, for example, Jo-Marie Burt, "Impunity and the Murder of Monsignor Gerardi," *NACLA Report on the Americas*, May/June 1998, 5.

23. *Report of the Commission of Inquiry* (Chad), as excerpted in Kritz, *Transitional Justice*, vol. 3, 55.

24. In comparison, the United States spends over $50 million each year on witness protection in the context of its judicial proceedings. "There's no way to apply that to South Africa," MacAdam said. Chris MacAdam, interview by the author, October 22, 1997, Cape Town, and September 4, 1996, Durban, South Africa.

25. Ibid.

EPILOGUE

1. Timothy Garton Ash, "Ten Years After," *New York Review of Books*, November 18, 1999, 18.

AFTERWORD

1. I have served as program director for research and technical assistance with the International Center for Transitional Justice since its inception. Information on the work of the center can be found at www.ictj.org, along with information on current developments in over a dozen countries where the center is active.

2. Executive Decree No. 2, 2001. The official website of the Panama Truth Commission, which includes this decree and other background information, can be found at www.comision-delaverdad.org.pa.

3. I was one of two consultants brought to East Timor by the United Nations, visiting the country several times in 2000 and 2001, together with Paul van Zyl, formerly of the South African Truth and Reconciliation Commission and now with the International Center for Transitional Justice in New York.

4. See UNTAET/Reg/2001/10, July 13, 2001, "On the Establishment of the Commission for Reception, Truth, and Reconciliation in East Timor."

5. For further information on the South Korean commission, see the commission's official website at www.truthfinder.go.kr.

Frequently Cited Sources

Truth Commission Reports

Nunca Más: The Report of the Argentine National Commission on the Disappeared (New York: Farrar Straus Giroux, 1986); originally published as *Nunca Más: Informe de la Comisión Nacional sobre la Desaparición de Personas* (Buenos Aires: Editorial Universitaria, 1984). The Spanish edition is available on the web at www.nuncamas.org/index.htm.

Report of the Chilean National Commission on Truth and Reconciliation, trans. Phillip E. Berryman, 2 vols. (Notre Dame, IN: University of Notre Dame Press, 1993). Available on the web at www.derechoschile.com/english/rettig.htm or, in Spanish, www.derechoschile.com/espanol/rettig.htm.

From Madness to Hope: The 12-Year War in El Salvador: Report of the Commission on the Truth for El Salvador, UN Doc. S/25500, Annex, 1993; reprinted in United Nations, *The United Nations and El Salvador: 1990-1995* (New York: United Nations, 1995), 290-414.

Truth and Reconciliation Commission of South Africa Report, 5 vols. (Cape Town: Truth and Reconciliation Commission, 1998, distributed by Juta & Co., Cape Town; and New York: Grove's Dictionaries, 1999). The full report can be found at www. truth.org.za.

Guatemala: Memoria del Silencio: Informe de la Comisión para el Esclarecimiento Histórico, 9 vols. (Guatemala City: Commission for Historical Clarification, 1999; distributed by F&G Editores, Guatemala City). Only the conclusions and recommendations sections of the report have been published in English, as *Guatemala: Memory of Silence: Report of the Commission for Historical Clarification (Conclusions and Recommendations)* (Guatemala City: Commission for Historical Clarification, 1999). Both the Spanish and English versions are available on the web at http://hrdata. aaas.org/ceh.

Report of the Commission of Inquiry into the Crimes and Misappropriations Committed by Ex-President Habré, his Accomplices and/or Accessories, May 7, 1992. An English translation of excerpts of the report can be found in Kritz, Transitional Justice, vol. 3, 51–93. The full report has been published in France as *Les crimes et détournements de l'ex-président Habré et de ses complices: Rapport de la commission d'enquête nationale du ministère Tchadien de la Justice* (Paris: Harmattan, 1993).

Other

Neil J. Kritz, ed., *Transitional Justice: How Emerging Democracies Reckon with Former Regimes,* 3 vols. (Washington, DC: U.S. Institute of Peace Press, 1995).

CHART 1

Twenty-One Truth Commissions

In Chronological Order

Country	Name of truth commission	Title of report and publication date	Date of commission	Dates covered	Created by
Uganda	Commission of Inquiry into the Disappearance of People in Uganda since the 25th January, 1971	Report of the Commission of Inquiry into the Disappearance of People in Uganda since the 25th January, 1971 (1975)	1974	January 25, 1971–1974	President
Bolivia	Comisión Nacional de Investigación de Desaparecidos (National Commission of Inquiry into Disappearances)	Did not complete report (disbanded before finishing)	1982–1984	1967–1982	President

Country	Name of truth commission	Title of report and publication date	Date of commission	Dates covered	Created by
Argentina	Comisión Nacional para la Desaparición de Personas (National Commission on the Disappearance of Persons, or CONADEP)	Nunca Más (Never Again) (1985)	1983–1984	1976–1983	President
Uruguay	Comisión Investigadora sobre la Situación de Personas Desaparecidas y Hechos que la Motivaron (Investigative Commission on the Situation of Disappeared People and Its Causes)	Informe Final de la Comisión Investigadora sobre la Situación de Personas Desaparecidas y Hechos que la Motivaron (Final Report of the Investigative Commission on the Situation of the Disappeared People and Its Causes) (1985)	1985	1973–1982	Parliament
Zimbabwe	Commission of Inquiry	Report kept confidential	1985	1983	President

Uganda	Commission of Inquiry into Violations of Human Rights	The Report of the Commission of Inquiry into Violation of Human Rights: Findings, Conclusions, and Recommendations (October 1994)	1986–1995	December 1962–January 1986	President
Nepal	Commission of Inquiry to Locate the Persons Disappeared during the Panchayet Period	Report of the Commission of Inquiry to Locate the Persons Disappeared during the Panchayet Period (1991; released to public in 1994)	1990–1991	1961–1990	Prime Minister
Chile	Comisión Nacional para la Verdad y Reconciliación (National Commission on Truth and Reconciliation) ("The Rettig Commission")	Informe de la Comisión Nacional de la Verdad y Reconciliación (Report of the National Commission on Truth and Reconciliation) (1991)	1990–1991	September 11, 1973–March 11, 1990	President
Chad	Commission d'Enquête sur les Crimes et Détournements Commis par l'Ex-Président Habré, ses co-Auteurs et/ou Complices (Commission of Inquiry on the Crimes and Misappropriations Committed by the Ex-President Habré, His Accomplices and/or Accessories)	Rapport de la Commission (Report of the Commission) (May 7, 1992)	1991–1992	1982–1990	President

Country	Name of truth commission	Title of report and publication date	Date of commission	Dates covered	Created by
South Africa (ANC)	Commission of Enquiry into Complaints by Former African National Congress Prisoners and Detainees ("The Skweyiya Commission")	Report of the Commission of Enquiry into Complaints by Former African National Congress Prisoners and Detainees (October 1992)	1992	1979–1991	African National Congress
Germany	Enquete Kommission Aufarbeitung von Geschichte und Folgen der SED-Diktatur in Deutschland (Commission of Inquiry for the Assessment of History and Consequences of the SED Dictatorship in Germany)	Bericht der Enquete-Kommission "Aufarbeitung von Geschichte und Folgen der SED-Diktatur in Deutschland" (June 1994)	1992–1994	1949–1989	Parliament
El Salvador	Comisión de la Verdad para El Salvador (Commission on the Truth for El Salvador)	De la Locura a la Esperanza (From Madness to Hope) (March 1993)	1992–1993	January 1980–July 1991	United Nations–moderated peace accord

	Commission	Report (Title and Date)			Establishing Authority
South Africa (ANC)	Commission of Enquiry into Certain Allegations of Cruelty and Human Rights Abuse against ANC Prisoners and Detainees by ANC Members ("The Motsuenyane Commission")	Report of the Commission of Enquiry into Certain Allegations of Cruelty and Human Rights Abuse against ANC Prisoners and Detainees by ANC Members (August 20, 1993)	1993	1979–1991	African National Congress
Sri Lanka	Commissions of Inquiry into the Involuntary Removal or Disappearance of Persons (three geographically distinct commissions)[1]	Final Reports of the Commissions of Inquiry into the Involuntary Removal or Disappearance of Persons (three distinct final reports, plus eight interim reports from each commission) (September 1997)	November 1994–September 1997	January 1, 1988–November 13, 1994	President
Haiti	National Commission for Truth and Justice	Si M Pa Rele ... (If I Don't Cry Out ...) (February 1996)	April 1995–February 1996	September 29, 1991–October 15, 1994	President
Burundi	International Commission of Inquiry	Report of the International Commission of Inquiry (August 1996)	September 1995–July 1996	October 21, 1993–August 28, 1995	United Nations Security Council

Country	Name of truth commission	Title of report and publication date	Date of commission	Dates covered	Created by
South Africa	Truth and Reconciliation Commission	Truth and Reconciliation Commission of South Africa Report (October 1998)	December 1995–2000[2]	1960–1994	Parliament
Ecuador	Truth and Justice Commission	Did not complete report (disbanded before finishing)	September 1996–February 1997	1979–1996	Ministry of Government and Police
Guatemala	Comisión para el Esclarecimiento Histórico (Commission for Historical Clarification) (Formal name: Commission to Clarify Past Human Rights Violations and Acts of Violence That Have Caused the Guatemalan People to Suffer)	Guatemala: Memoria del Silencio (Guatemala: Memory of Silence) (February 1999)	August 1997–February 1999	1962–1996	United Nations–moderated peace accord
Nigeria	Commission of Inquiry for the Investigation of Human Rights Violations	Still underway	1999–2000	1966–May 28, 1999	President

| Sierra Leone | Truth and Reconciliation Commission | Still underway | 2000–2001 | 1991 – July 7, 1999 | Agreed to in peace accord; created through national legislation |

1. In Sri Lanka, there were three geographically distinct commissions that operated simultaneously and with identical mandates: the Commission of Inquiry into the Involuntary Removal or Disappearance of Persons in the Western, Southern and Sabaragamuwa Provinces; the Commission of Inquiry into the Involuntary Removal or Disappearance of Persons in the Northern and Eastern Provinces; and the Commission of Inquiry into the Involuntary Removal or Disappearance of Persons in the Central, North Western, North Central and Uva Provinces. When these three commissions ended, a follow-up body was formed to close the cases outstanding, called the Presidential Commission of Inquiry into Involuntary Removals and Disappearances.

2. The South African Truth and Reconciliation Commission submitted its report in October 1998, but continued to work for approximately two more years in order to conclude amnesty hearings and to help implement a reparations program.

CHART 2

"Historical" Truth Commissions[3]

Country	Name of investigative body	Title of report and publication date	Date of inquiry	Dates covered	Description of investigative body
United States	Commission on Wartime Relocation and Internment of Civilians	Personal Justice Denied (1982; reprinted 1992)	1981–1982	1942–1945	Created by Congressional Commitee on Interior and Insular Affairs
Canada	Royal Commission on Aboriginal Peoples	Looking Forward, Looking Back (vol. I of five-volume report) (November 1996)	August 1991–November 1996	pre-1500–1996	Created by government to recommend improved polices towards indigenous communities; included historical inquiry

| United States | Advisory Committee on Human Radiation Experiments | Report of the Advisory Committee on Human Radiation Experiments (1995) | January 1994–1995 | 1944–1974 | Established by U.S. energy secretary to inquire into radiation experiments on unknowing patients and prisoners |
| Australia | Human Rights and Equal Opportunity Commission | Bringing Them Home: Report of the National Inquiry into the Separation of Aboriginal and Torres Strait Islander Children from Their Families (May 1997) | 1996–1997 | 1910–1975 | Special inquiry undertaken by permanent governmental human rights monitoring body |

3. See discussion of these commissions in chapter 2.

CHART 3

Alternative Forms of Official or Semiofficial Inquiry into the Past[4]

Country	Name of investigative body	Title of report and publication date	Date of inquiry	Dates covered	Description of investigative body
Ethiopia	Office of the Special Prosecutor	Prosecutions ongoing; plans for overall "truth" report have been dropped	1993–present	1974–1991	Special prosecutor focused on crimes of prior regime
Rwanda	International Commission of Investigation on Human Rights Violations in Rwanda since October 1, 1990	Report of the International Commission of Investigation on Human Rights Violations in Rwanda since October 1, 1990 (March 1993)	1993	October 1990–1993	Composed of four international nongovernmental organizations; granted quasi-official status and some cooperation from authorities

Honduras	National Commissioner for the Protection of Human Rights in Honduras	Los Hechos Hablan por sí Mismos: Informe Preliminar sobre los Desaparecidos en Honduras 1980–1993 (The Facts Speak for Themselves: Preliminary Report on the Disappeared in Honduras 1980–1993) (January 1994)	1993	1980–1993	Government human rights ombudsman; inquiry into disappeared taken at his own initiative
Northern Ireland	Northern Ireland Victims Commissioner	We Will Remember Them (April 1998)	November 1997– April 1998	1967–1997	Special one-person commission established by British secretary of state for Northern Ireland

4. See discussion of these commissions in chapter 2.

CHART 4

What Rights Violations Do Truth Commissions Cover?

A Selected List

	Key language in commission terms of reference that defines what acts it should cover	*Principal acts documented by the commission*	*Significant violations or acts not investigated by commission, or not included in its final report*
Argentina	"clarify the acts related to the disappearance of persons," and, if possible, determine the location of their remains.	• disappearances (kidnapping with no reappearance of body)	• killings by armed forces in real or staged "armed confrontation" • temporary disappearances, when person was released or body was found and identified • forced exile • detention and torture (survivors were interviewed by the commission and their stories included as witness accounts, but they were not included in list of victims) • acts of violence by armed opposition • disappearances by government forces before the installation of military government in 1976

	Definition		
Uganda 1986	"mass murders and all acts or omissions resulting in the arbitrary deprivation of human life . . . arbitrary imprisonment and abuse of powers of detention; denial of a fair and public trial . . . torture, massive displacement of persons . . . and discriminatory treatment by virtue of race, tribe, place of origin, political opinion, creed or sex" on the part of public officials.	•murder and arbitrary detention of life •arbitrary arrest, detention, or imprisonment •denial of fair and public trial before independent and impartial court •torture, cruel and degrading treatment •displacement and expulsion of peoples •discriminatory treatment by public officials •denial of fundamental freedoms such as freedom to worship, freedom of the press, and freedom of association	•abuses by armed opposition groups •abuses by the government after the date the commission was set up (controversial because the commission continued work for nine years and no other government rights body yet existed)
Chile	"disappearance after arrest, execution, and torture leading to death committed by government agents or people in their service, as well as kidnappings and attempts on the life of persons carried out by private citizens for political reasons."	•disappearances •torture resulting in death •executions by government forces •use of undue force leading to death •death of combatants and noncombatants in the firefight immediately after coup •killings "by private citizens for political reasons," particularly the armed Left	•torture not resulting in death (torture practices were described, but survivors were not listed as victims) •illegal detention, if released and survived •forced exile

	Key language in commission terms of reference that defines what acts it should cover	Principal acts documented by the commission	Significant violations or acts not investigated by commission, or not included in its final report
El Salvador	"serious acts of violence . . . whose impact on society urgently demands that the public should know the truth."	• massacres by armed forces • extrajudicial executions by agents of the state • assassinations by death squads • disappearances • torture by government forces • killings by armed opposition • kidnappings by armed opposition	(No significant acts excluded.)
South Africa	"gross violations of human rights," defined as "the killing, abduction, torture, or severe ill-treatment of any person," or the "conspiracy, incitement, instigation, or command" of such acts "which emanated from conflicts of the past . . . within or outside of the Republic, and the commission of which was advised, planned, directed, commanded or ordered by any person acting with a political motive."	• killings by agents of the state inside and outside of the country • disappearances • torture and abuse by police and armed forces • raids into neighboring countries by armed forces to attack opposition • killings, primarily by bombs and land mines, by the armed opposition • abuses in detention camps of the armed opposition outside South Africa's borders • violence by private individuals for political purposes	• the forced removal and displacement of millions of people based on race • everyday policies and practices of apartheid that did not result in killings, abduction, torture, or severe ill-treatment as defined by the commission

Guatemala

"clarify with all objectivity, equity and impartiality the human rights violations and acts of violence that have caused the Guatemalan population to suffer, connected with the armed conflict."

- acts of genocide by government forces (No significant acts excluded.) against the Mayan population
- massacres and arbitrary killings by government forces and by the armed opposition
- disappearances and kidnappings by the state forces and by the guerrillas
- acts of violence by the economically powerful (landowners or business people) with the support of state forces
- massive forced displacement and militarized resettlement by the state
- forced recruitment by the guerrillas

CHART 5

Past Truth Commission Recommendations

A Selected List

The following offers only a sampling of recommendations from previous truth commissions, selected to show the variety, type, and level of detail across a range of subject areas. (This is a select list. Some reports include hundreds of recommendations across many areas. For a full listing, please consult the commissions' reports.) See chapter 10 for a discussion of these recommendations and resulting reforms.

1. THE ADMINISTRATION OF JUSTICE AND REFORM OF THE JUDICIARY

Uganda 1986 Only confessions made to magistrates should be admissible in criminal cases, not confessions to police officers.

     The office of the attorney general and minister of justice should be separated and held by different persons, in order to reduce the concentration of power in the hands of one individual.

Chile   An ongoing system of evaluating judges should be created.
Law schools should devote particular attention to the question of human rights.

     Appointment of Supreme Court judges and prosecutors should be done by an independent body rather than by the president of the country.

     Military tribunals should be used in limited circumstances and under the supervision of the Supreme Court

     Extrajudicial confessions obtained after arrest by police should not be given evidentiary weight if the person retracts the confession in the presence of the judge.

     There should be limitations in the use of solitary confinement, with access to an independent doctor and safeguards for the prisoner's physical and mental health.

El Salvador The current members of the Supreme Court should resign immediately from their posts, to make way for the appointment of a new Supreme Court.

     Judges should be appointed and removed by an independent National Council of the Judiciary, rather than by the Supreme Court of Justice.

Granting authorization to practice as a lawyer should be attributed to a special independent body, rather than to the Supreme Court of Justice.

Extrajudicial confessions should be invalidated.

South Africa   Imbalances in the racial and gender composition of judges in the high court should be urgently addressed, as well as in the gender composition of the magistry.

A code of conduct for prosecutors should be drawn up to ensure that the interests of victims are properly considered.

2. REFORM OF THE ARMED FORCES, POLICE, AND INTELLIGENCE SERVICES

Uganda 1986   Uganda's army should be national in character, reflecting the ethnic composition of geographical areas of the country as a whole.

The army should not be used for the purpose of perpetuation of a single leader or political organization in power.

The army should never be used to suppress internal political dissent or differences or for solving political conflicts.

Antagonism and rivalry between the army and the police should be eradicated.

The police should not be staffed with undisciplined, ill-trained, ill-prepared and profession-phobic officers.

There should be an increase in the payment to police personnel to raise morale and efficiency.

Chile   Redefine the functions of the intelligence services, limiting them to gathering information.

The application of "due obedience," while important, should not serve as an excuse for violating human rights.

The functions of safeguarding public order and security should fall exclusively to the police.

Members of the armed forces and police and their families should be encouraged to be more integrated into society, by incorporating them into common social and cultural activities, and insofar as possible not providing separate housing arrangements for them. Knowing one another is a first step on the way to reconciliation.

Chad   Reexamine the powers and structures of the new special intelligence service so that it does not become a machine of torture and oppression.

Chad, *continued*   Eliminate detention centers under control of intelligence service and police security branch, keeping only those provided for in the code of criminal procedures.

El Salvador   Subordinates should be protected when they refuse to obey illegal orders.

Military curricula should include thorough training in human rights.

Remove all links between the new civilian police and the former security forces and other branches of the armed forces.

South Africa   The South African National Defence Force should not be entitled to engage in any covert activities not specifically authorized by the minister of defense and another minister with an unrelated portfolio.

Guatemala   The government should promote a new military doctrine for the Guatemalan army that should establish the basic principles for the appropriate relationship between the army and society within a democratic and pluralist framework: the army should be apolitical; subordinate to political power; respect the Constitution; and recognize that sovereignty resides in the Guatemalan people.

With the aim of respecting the Mayan cultural identity, the army should no longer use names of particular Mayan significance and symbolism for its military structures and units.

3. POLITICAL REFORMS

Uganda   The new Constitution should provide for a system of peaceful change of presidents and governments through regular elections; prohibition of overstaying by presidents in office after their terms have expired; and separation of powers with checks and balances.

Laws for the investigation and prosecution of corruption should be strengthened.

Abolition of government monopoly of the public media (radio, TV, and newspapers), and recognition by the government of the rights of others with different views or opinions to disseminate them through the media.

4. INSTILL HUMAN RIGHTS INTO THE NATIONAL CULTURE

Argentina   Laws should be passed that make the teaching and diffusion of human rights obligatory in state educational establishments, including civilian, military, and police academies.

Uganda

Qualification in human rights education should be a requirement for admission to all stages of education after primary education, for appointment to public offices, and for standing for elective office at local and national levels.

The people of Uganda should overcome their passive response to government abuses and develop a culture of solidarity to fend for their rights and protect those whose rights are violated.

Chile

The Chilean government should ratify all international agreements in the area of human rights to which Chile is not yet a signatory.

South Africa

The truth commission report, as well as accompanying video and audio tapes, should be made widely available as a resource for human rights education.

5. PROSECUTE PERPETRATORS OR REMOVE THEM FROM POSITIONS OF AUTHORITY

Argentina

The body that replaces us should speed up the procedures involved in bringing before the courts the documents collected during our investigation.

Uganda

All those implicated in crimes before the commission should be prosecuted.

No time limit should be imposed with regard to when prosecution may be instituted.

Any person proven to have violated human rights should be barred from holding any political, public, or civic office.

Chad

The authors of rights crimes, especially assassinations, abductions, and torture, should be prosecuted.

All former intelligence agents who have been rehabilitated and employed by the new intelligence service should be removed from their position.

El Salvador

Since it is not possible to guarantee a proper trial for all those responsible for the crimes described here, it is unfair to keep some of them in prison while others who planned the crimes or also took part in them remain at liberty. This can only be resolved, in some circumstances, through a pardon after justice has been served.

Those named by the commission as personally implicated in the perpetration or cover-up of serious acts of violence should be dismissed

El Salvador,
continued

from their posts and discharged from the armed forces, or dismissed from the civil service or judicial posts they currently occupy.

Perpetrators named in the report should be disqualified from holding any public post or office for a period of not less than 10 years, and should be disqualified permanently from any activity related to public security or national defense.

South Africa

Where amnesty has not been sought or has been denied, and where evidence exists that an individual has committed a gross human rights violation, prosecution should be considered.

Attorneys general must pay rigorous attention to the prosecution of members of the South African police service who are found to have assaulted, tortured and/or killed persons in their care.

In order to avoid a culture of impunity and to entrench the rule of law, the granting of a general amnesty in whatever guise should be resisted.

Guatemala

Where the current amnesty law does not prohibit prosecution, particularly in reference to crimes of genocide, torture, and forced disappearance, appropriate persons should be prosecuted, tried, and punished, paying particular attention to those who instigated and promoted such crimes.

6. MEASURES TO ADVANCE RECONCILIATION

Chile

It is hoped that those who are in a position to help advance reconciliation with some gesture or specific act will do so. They could, for example, make available the information they may have on the whereabouts of those who disappeared after arrest or the location of the bodies of those who were executed or tortured to death and have not yet been found.

It is absolutely necessary that a space for broad public debate on human rights be opened immediately through public forums, cultural activities on human rights day, and the like.

Symbols that are divisive for Chileans should be eliminated.

El Salvador

There is a need for a process of collective reflection on the reality of the past few years. One bitter but unavoidable step is to look at and acknowledge what happened and must never happen again.

South Africa

The government should accelerate the closing of the gap between the advantaged and disadvantaged in South Africa through education, housing, and other programs and services.

Those who benefited from apartheid policies should contribute toward the alleviation of poverty. A "wealth tax" and other proposals should be considered.

7. UNDERTAKE FURTHER INVESTIGATIONS

Argentina   The courts should press for investigation and verification of the depositions received by the commission.

Chile   A follow-up state body should be created to continue the search for the remains of those killed and disappeared.

El Salvador   A thorough investigation into private armed groups (death squads) should be undertaken immediately to ensure that they are disbanded and to prevent them from becoming active again.

South Africa   A comprehensive analysis should be undertaken into both the scope and the content of the remaining archival holdings of the intelligence services and all divisions of the security forces.

Guatemala   The government and judiciary, in collaboration with civil society, should initiate investigations regarding all known forced disappearances. All available legal and material resources should be utilized to clarify the whereabouts of the disappeared and to deliver the remains to the relatives.

A special commission should be established to look for children who were disappeared, illegally adopted or illegally separated from their parents. Special measures should allow for the review of adoptions that took place against the will of the natural parents.

8. MORAL COMPENSATION: ACKNOWLEDGMENT AND APOLOGY TO VICTIMS

Chile   Restore the good name of victims through a statement from the president, Parliament, or by a law.

Other symbolic reparation, which may include a monument or a public park in memory of victims

El Salvador   A national monument should be constructed bearing the names of all the victims of the conflict.

The good name of the victims and the serious crimes of which they were victims should be recognized.

El Salavador,   A national holiday in memory of the victims should be created.
continued

Chad   Erection of a monument to the memory of victims of Habré repression, and promulgation of a decree making the second Sunday of December a day of prayer and remembrance of said victims.

Conversion of former headquarters and subterranean prison into a museum to remind people of the dark reign of the past.

South Africa   The government should declare a national day of remembrance and facilitate the building of monuments and memorials to commemorate events of the past.

A public apology should be made to the people of neighboring countries for past violations suffered as a result of actions of representatives of the previous South African government. Appropriate symbolic reparations should be considered.

Guatemala   The president and ex-command of the armed opposition should acknowledge wrongs and ask pardon and forgiveness, and Congress should issue a declaration reaffirming the dignity and honor of victims.

The state should establish a day of commemmoration for the victims and construct monuments and public parks in their memory. Commemorations should take into consideration the multicultural roots of the Guatemalan nation.

9. FINANCIAL AND OTHER REPARATIONS TO VICTIMS

Argentina   Appropriate laws should be passed to provide children and/or relatives of disappeared with economic assistance, study grants, social security and employment and to authorize measures necessary to alleviate the many varied family and social problems causes by disappearances.

Chile   Reparation should be provided to the families of those victims listed in the truth commission report, equivalent to a monthly sum not lower than the average income of a family in Chile.

Specialized health care, educational benefits and housing benefits should be considered for the families, as well as cancellation of outstanding debts owed to the government by those killed or disappeared.

El Salvador   A special fund should be established to award appropriate material compensation to the victims. This fund should receive support from the State, but should also receive a substantial contribution from the international community. Not less than 1 percent of all international assistance that reaches El Salvador should be set aside for this purpose.

South Africa   A structure should be developed in the president's office whose function will be to oversee the implementation of reparation and rehabilitation policy proposals and recommendations. This body should also oversee the issuance of death certificates, expediting exhumations and burials, expunging criminal records where the political activity of individuals was criminalized, and facilitating the renaming of streets and community facilities in order to remember and honor individuals or significant events.

The State should consider some form of compensation for persons who lost their businesses or other sources of income during the period of unrest in the 1980s and 1990s, particularly those who were not insured against such loss.

Guatemala   The state should create through national legislation a National Reparations Program, to be overseen by a broadly representative board, to provide moral and material reparations, psychosocial rehabilitation, and other benefits.

CHART 6

Reparations from Truth Commissions:
A Comparision of Chilean and Argentine Benefits for Victims

The following reparations programs were based in part on the recommendations and victims lists that emerged from the truth commissions in Chile and Argentina. See chapter 11 for a full discussion of these and other reparations programs.

CHILE[5]

Cash Payments to Families of the Disappeared and Killed:

What: Monthly pension paid by check

To whom: Family members of those killed or disappeared (as determined by the National Commission on Truth and Reconciliation or its fol-low-up body, the National Corporation for Reparation and Recon-ciliation)

Amount: $481/month ($5,781/year), distributed among immediate family members.

                  If there is only one surviving family member, then $345/month ($4,140/year).

                  Additional one-time start-up payment of the total annual sum.

How distributed: 40% to spouse

                  30% to parents

                  15% to each child

                  15% to surviving parent of the person's children

For how long: Lifetime (except for the children of the victim, who receive it to age 25)[6]

Total number
of persons
receiving benefit: 4,886 (the total number of family members of 2,723 disappeared persons)

Total annual
cost to state: $13 million/year

Medical Benefits to Families of the Disappeared and Killed:

What benefits: Monthly medical allowance, calculated at 7% of the above pension.

To whom: Family members of those killed or disappeared (as determined by National Commission on Truth and Reconciliation or its follow-up body, the National Corporation for Reparation and Reconciliation).

Total cost to state: $950,000/year

Other noncash
medical benefits: Free access to special state counseling and medical program (open to relatives of those killed or disappeared and to former political prisoners).

Educational Benefits to Children of the Disappeared and Killed

What benefits: Full coverage of tuition and expenses for university training

To whom: Children of those killed or disappeared

For how long: Until age 35

Number of
beneficiaries: 837 (as of 1995)

Total cost to state: $1.2 million/year
(Average cost: $1,534/student)

Other Benefits:

Waiver of mandatory military service for children of disappeared and killed.

Those who lost a state job for political reasons may reinstate their retirement pension, with lost years credited, with the assistance of a special state office.

Those who returned from exile abroad are eligible for a waiver of reentry tax for vehicles.

Who Is Not Covered:

Survivors of torture or illegal imprisonment receive no pension, education, or health benefits, except for free access to a state-run medical and counseling program.

ARGENTINA

Monetary Reparations for Families of the Disappeared and Killed:[7]

What: One-time payment of $220,000, paid in state bonds.[8]

To whom: Distributed among family members of the disappeared that are listed in the National Commission on the Disappeared report, or those disappeared or killed that have subsequently been reported to the government's Human Rights Office.

Total number
of potential
beneficiaries: Family members of approximately 15,000 dead or disappeared.[9]

Total cost to state: Between $2 and 3 billion, estimated.[10]

How amount
was determined: $220,000 is equivalent to 100 months at the salary level of the highest-paid civil servant.

Additional
pension to
children of the
disappeared: Up to age 21, children of the disappeared also receive a monthly pension of $140/month.[11]

Monetary Reparations for Those Imprisoned for Political Reasons or Forced into Exile:[12]

To whom: Political prisoners held without trial; those who had been temporarily "disappeared" (imprisonment unrecognized by the authorities) and whose case was reported in the press, to the truth commission, or to a human rights organization at the time; those arrested and sent into exile by the authorities.

What: For each day in prison or in forced exile, paid at the daily salary rate of the highest-paid civil servant, up to a total of $220,000 (equivalent to $74/day). One-time payment in state bonds.

If died
while in prison: Family paid same daily rate up to day of death, plus equivalent of 5 years at same rate, up to a total of $220,000.

If seriously
wounded while
in prison: Paid daily rate plus equivalent of 3.5 years at same rate, up to a total of $220,000.

Number of
beneficiaries: Estimated 10,000 political prisoners held without trial and 1,000
forced into exile.

Total cost to state: Approximately $500 million.[13]

Other Reparations:

Creation of new legal category of "forcibly disappeared," which
holds the legal equivalent of death for purposes of the law (allowing
processing of wills and closing of estates), while preserving the possibility of a person's reappearance.[14]

Waiver of military service for children of the disappeared.[15]

Housing credits for children of the disappeared.

---

5. All benefits were established in the Law Creating the National Corporation for Reparation
and Reconciliation, Law No. 19,123, Chile (January 31, 1992); reprinted in Kritz, *Transitional Justice*, vol. 3, 685–95. The details of the implementation of the reparations program are reported in
the Corporation's first interim report, Corporacíon Nacional de Reparación y Reconciliación, *Informe Sobre Calificación de Victimas de Violaciones de Derecho Humanos y de la Violencia Política*
(Santiago: Corporacíon Nacional de Reparación y Reconciliación, 1996), 595-602. Figures current
as of 1995.

6. For handicapped children of the victim, reparations are paid for life.

7. Law No. 24,411, Argentina, December 7, 1994.

8. Those who cashed these bonds in immediately, as many needed to do, actually received less
than $220,000. State bonds have been valued at 50 to 70 percent of their face value in recent years.

9. Although the commission documented 8,960 disappeared, many cases were not reported to the
commission. In addition, the government's Human Rights Office has estimated that several
thousand persons were killed, with a body identified, in the course of the dictatorship. Interview
by author with staff of the Human Rights Office, Ministry of the Interior, December 1996 and
February 1999.

10. The Argentine government planned for $3 billion in state bonds to cover expected reparations
payments. Telephone interview by the author with Alejandro Kwawabatta, Human Rights Office, Ministry of the Interior, February 20, 1998.

11. Law No. 23,466, Argentina, 1987.

12. Law No. 24,043, Argentina, November 27, 1991 (also extended to political prisoners under the
state of siege that began two years before the military coup of 1976). The Argentine Commission
on the Disappeared did not investigate or document political prisoners who survived detention.
This program therefore did not rely on information from the commission, but from evidence
presented to the state by each survivor claiming reparation.

13. "Indemnizaran a cinco mil presos del régimen militar," *Clarin,* March 15, 1994.

14. Law No. 24,321, Argentina, May 11, 1994.

15. Military service is no longer mandatory in Argentina, but was when this law was enacted.

CHART 7

A Comparison of Resources and Responsibilities

Country	Total Number of Cases Presented to Commission[16]	Number of Cases or Events Investigated in Depth[17]	Length of Commission's Work	Period of Time Covered by Commission	Number of Commissioners	Number of Staff
Uganda 1974	308 disappeared	N/A[18]	1 year	3.5 years	4	N/A
Bolivia	155 disappeared	0	2–3 years	15 years	8	6
Argentina	8,960 disappeared, unspecified number of victims of torture or prolonged detention	0[19]	9 months	7 years	13	60
Uruguay	164 disappeared	0	7 months	11 years	approx. 9	N/A
Zimbabwe	N/A	N/A	several months	2 years	1	N/A
Uganda 1986	608 deponents	0	9 years	24 years	6	5–10
Nepal	100	N/A	1 year	30 years	4	N/A
Chile	3,428 disappeared, killed, tortured to death, or kidnapped[20]	2,920	9 months	16.5 years	8	60
Chad	3,800 killed, unspecified number of victims of torture or arbitrary detention	0	10 months	8 years	12–16	0[21]

South Africa (ANC 1)	32 survivors of torture and abuse in detention camps	0	7 months	11.5 years	3	N/A
Germany	N/A	0	3 years	40 years	27	approx. 20
El Salvador	22,000 disappeared, killed, tortured, or kidnapped	32	8 months	12 years	3	15–45[22]
South Africa (ANC 2)	29 disappeared; 19 "complainants" and 11 "defendants" presented their cases re: detention camp abuses	29 disappeared, 19 complainants, 11 defendants	8 months	11.5 years	3	7
Sri Lanka	27,000	0	3 years	5.5 years	3 per commission	5-20 per commission
Haiti	8,600	0	10 months	3 years	7	50-100
Burundi	N/A	N/A	10 months	2 years	5	N/A
South Africa	21,000	All cases corroborated for reparations program; thousands of amnesty applications investigated, as well as numerous other special investigations	2.5 years[23]	34 years	17	300

Country	Total Number of Cases Presented to Commission[16]	Number of Cases or Events Investigated in Depth[17]	Length of Commission's Work	Period of Time Covered by Commission	Number of Commissioners	Number of Staff
Ecuador	N/A	N/A	1 year (disbanded after 5 months)	17 years	7	N/A
Guatemala	42,275 victims, including those killed, disappeared, tortured, and raped[24]	100	1.5 years	34 years	3	Up to 200
Nigeria	still in process	still in process	1 year expected	33 years	6	N/A
Sierra Leone	still in process	still in process	1 to 1.5 years expected	9 years	7	N/A

16. These numbers provide general indications of the number of cases that were reported to each commission. For some commissions, numbers are not exact. In most countries, the actual total number of cases of human rights abuses is estimated to be far higher than the number reported to the commission.

17. The number of individual cases (such as a disappeared person or victim of torture) or events (such as a massacre) that were investigated at greater depth and reported by the commission.

18. "N/A" indicates that information is not available: the commission did not complete or did not publish a report, or information is otherwise unknown.

19. Some reports (such as those of Argentina, Chad, and ANC 1) describe at length the overall nature of human rights violations during the period at hand, including extensive quotes from testimony provided to the commission and backup documentation, but do not enter into the investigation of any one case in depth.

20. 508 of these 3,428 were determined to fall outside of the mandate of the commission.

21. The twelve (and later sixteen) "members of the commission" include secretaries and clerks.

22. Including approximately twenty temporary staff hired for one to three months for data processing and data entry.

23. The South African Truth and Reconciliation Commission worked for over two and one-half years, then was suspended for eighteen months while the Amnesty Committee completed its work; it will reconvene to submit a final report in 2000.

24. Using a variety of primary and secondary sources, the Guatemalan commission estimated a total of over 200,000 persons killed or disappeared over the thirty-four years of armed conflict.

CHART 8

What Works Best?

Large/Strong/Broad			*Small/Weak/Narrow*		*Comments*
◄─────────────────────────────────────►					

BUDGET

>$35 million	$5-35	$1-5	$500k–	<$500k	
South Africa	million	million	1 million	Chad	
	Guatemala	Chile	Uganda	ANC	
		El Salvador	(1986)	(1 and 2)	

SIZE OF STAFF

>200	101–200	51–100	11–50	1–10	
South Africa	Guatemala	Argentina	El Salvador		
		Chile	Uganda		
		Haiti	(1986)		

LENGTH OF COMMISSION

>3 years	2–3 years	1–2 years	9 months–	<9 months	Commission
Uganda	South Africa	Guatemala	1 year	El Salvador	should always
(1986)	Sri Lanka	Sierra Leone	Argentina		be given a
		Nigeria	Chile		deadline, even
			Haiti		if extendable

MANDATE: PERIOD OF TIME TO BE INVESTIGATED

>30 years	15–29 years	10–14 years	5–9 years	<5 years	Must be
South Africa	Chile	El Salvador	Argentina	Haiti	determined by
Guatemala			Sierra		circumstances
Nigeria			Leone		

Large/Strong/Broad   *Small/Weak/Narrow* | *Comments*

◄━━━━━━━━━━━━━━━━━━━━━━━━━━━━━━━━━━━━━━►

**MANDATE: POWERS OF INVESTIGATION
(SUBPOENA, SEARCH AND SEIZURE, WITNESS PROTECTION)**

South Africa	Sri Lanka	Argentina
Sierra Leone	El Salvador	Chile
	Uganda	Haiti
	(1986)	Guatemala

**MANDATE: POWERS OF REPORTING
(NAME PERPETRATORS, MAKE MANDATORY
RECOMMENDATIONS)**

Very stong:	Strong:	Some	Few	Restricted
El Salvador	South Africa	powers:	powers:	powers:
Sierra Leone		Sri Lanka	Chile	Guatemala
			Argentina	Haiti

MANDATE: BREADTH OF INVESTIGATION

Very broad:	Some abuses	Sri Lanka	Much	Narrow	Sometimes
El Salvador	excluded:		excluded:	focus:	necessary and
Chad	South Africa		Chile	Argentina	appropriate to
Guatemala					narrow mandate
Nigeria					

MANDATE: WHAT PARTIES TO BE INVESTIGATED

Complex	Two sides of		One side	Must be
conflict of	conflict:		only:	determined by
three or	El Salvador		Argentina	national
more parties:	Guatemala		Chad	circumstances
South Africa	Chile		Haiti	
			ANC	
			1 and 2	

[   ] = Ideal in most circumstances

APPENDIX 2

Interviews by the Author

This is not a complete list of persons interviewed, as some asked not to be identified. In most cases, persons are listed in the position that they held at the time of the interview, and in the location where the interview took place.

ARGENTINA
December 1996

National Commission on the Disappeared

Commissioners: **Eduardo Rabossi**, former Undersecretary of Human Rights; **Hugo Piucill**, Assemblea Permenente de Derechos Humanos; **Gregorio Klimovsky**. *Staff*: **Senator Graciela Fernández Meijide**, commission's staff director.

Human Rights Office of the Ministry of the Interior

Mercedes Assorati, Dolly Scaccheri, Gudelia Araoz, Rita Haydee Tanuz, Carlos Gonzalez Gartland, Analia Lanza, Lita Abdala.

Nongovernmental Organizations

Martin Abregú, Centro de Estudios Legales y Sociales; **Enrique Pochat**, Movimiento Ecumenico por los Derechos Humanos; **Alejandro Inchaurregui** and **Luis Fondebrider**, Equipo Argentino de Antropología Forense; **Nora Cortiñas**, Madres de la Plaza de Mayo - Linea Fundadora; **Mercedes Meroño**, Associación Madres de Plaza de Mayo; **Horacio Lynch**, Foro de Estudios sobre la Administración de Justicia; **Patricia Valdez**, Poder Ciudidano.

Media, Academics, and Other

Horacio Verbitsky, *Pagina 12;* **Luis Moreno Ocampo**, former deputy prosecutor; **Maria del Carmen Feijoó** and **Elizabeth Jelin**, sociologists; **Juan Carlos Olivera**, Editorial Universitaria de Buenos Aires; **Jorge Reinaldo Vanossi**, former member of Congress; **Juan Carlos Volnovich** and **Fernando Ulloa**, psychoanalysts; **Marcela Scilingo**.

CHILE
November–December 1996

National Commission for Truth and Reconciliation

Commissioners: **Jose Zalaquett; José Luis Cea; Laura Novoa; Monica Jimenez.** *Staff:* **Jorge Correa**, Diego Portalis University, chief of staff of commission. National Corporation for Reconciliation and Reparation **Alejandro Gonzalez**, President; **Andres Dominguez**, Chief of Staff; **Sergio Hevia**, legal counsel.

Government, Judicial, and Armed Forces

Francisco Cumplido, University of Chile, former Minister of Justice; **Carlos Cerda**, judge and professor, Diego Portalis University; **Gonzalo Garcia Pino**, Political Advisor to the Minister of Defense.

Nongovernmental Organizations and Human Rights Advocates

Sola Sierra, Group of Families of the Detained and Disappeared; **Veronica Reyna**, Fundación de Ayuda Social de las Iglesias Cristianas; **Pamela Pereira** and **Hector Salazar**, lawyers representing families of the disappeared; **Sabastian Brett**, Human Rights Watch.

Media, Academics, and Others

Felipe Portalis Cifuentes, sociologist; **Elizabeth Lira**, psychologist; **Tomás Mouliou**, Center for Social Investigation, Arcis University; **Monica Gonzalez**, Political Editor, Cosas Magazine; **Patricia Verdugo**, author and television anchor; **Nissim Sharim**, actor and director; **Augusto Varas**, Ford Foundation; **Carla Pellegrin Friedman**.

EL SALVADOR
April 1996

Nongovernmental Organizations and Academics

Benjamin Cuéllar, Instituto de Derechos Humanos de la Universidad Centroamericana; **Alicia de García**, CoMadres.

Government, Judicial, and Peace Accords Implementation Commission

Antonio Aguilar Martínez, Procuraduría para la Defensa de los Derechos Humanos; **Mirna Perla de Anaya**, Juvenile Court Judge; **General Mauricio Vargas**, Peace Accords Trilateral Commission; **Antonio Alvarez**, FMLN, Peace Accords Trilateral Commission.

International Community

Martha Doggett, UN Mission to El Salvador; **William Duncan**, Human Rights Officer, U.S. Embassy.

Other

Rufina Amaya, **Pedro Chicas**, and other current and former residents of El Mozote.

GERMANY
July 1997

Enquete Kommission

Commission members: **Rainer Eppelmann**, Chair, Member of Parliament, Christian Democratic Union Party; **Gerd Poppe**, MP, Alliance 90/Green Party; **Gerald Häfner**, MP, Alliance 90/Green Party; **Karl Wilhelm Fricke**, Historian. *Staff*: **Rolf Eising**, Director; **Marlies Jansen**, Deputy Director; **Martin Georg Goerner**; **Thomas Ammer**.

Government and Judicial

Joachim Gauck, Director, Federal Authority on the Records of the former Ministry for State Security of the German Democratic Republic (the Gauck Authority); **Johannes Legner,** Press Spokesperson, Federal Authority on the Records of the former Ministry for State Security of the German Democratic Republic; **Christoph Schaefgen,** Special Prosecutor for GDR and Unification Crimes; **Manfred Kittlaus,** Director, Office of Police Investigations into Stasi and Unification Crimes; **Dr. Falco Werkentin** and **Gebhard Klenz,** Office of the State Commissioner on Stasi Files; **Wolfgang Wiemer,** Head of Office for Wolfgang Thierse, MP, SPD; **Christa Seeliger,** Judge, Bonn.

Media, Academics, Nongovernmental Organizations, and Other

Dr. Gabriele Camphausen, Director, Berlin Hohenschönhausen Memorial; **Barbara Distel,** Director, Dachau Museum and Memorial; **Jörg Drieselmann,** Director, Normannenstrasse Stasi Museum; **Peter Alexander Hussock,** Director, Help for Victims of Political Violence in Europe; **Dr. André Brie,** PDS Party; **Dr. Ulrich Schröter,** Lutheran Church; **Ulrike Poppe; Roland Jahn,** television journalist; **Richard Schröder,** Professor of Theology, Humboldt University of Berlin; **Uwe Wesel,** Free University of Berlin; **René Schiller** and **Wolfram Theilemann,** History Department, Technical University of Berlin; **Hans Michael Kloth,** journalist; **Wuf Gruner** and **Sandra Gruner-Domic,** history students.

GUATEMALA
April 1996, May 1998

Historical Clarification Commission

Commissioners: **Christian Tomuschat,** Coordinator; **Otilia Lux de Cotí.**
Staff: **Fernando Castañón Alvarez, Marcie Mersky; Roberto Rodriguez; Felipe Sanchez; Brigitta Suhr; Joanna Crandal; Jesus Peña; Sonia Zombrano; Alessandro Preti; Jaime Esponda Fernández; Ramiro Avila; Greg Grandin; Manuel Oviedo; Melisa Stappers; Liz Oglesby; Jan Perlin.**

Nongovernmental Oganizations

Helen Mack, Myrna Mack Foundation; **Ronald Ochaeta,** Human Rights Office of the Archbishop of Guatemala; **Marcie Mersky,** Recopilación de la Memoria Histórica Project, Human Rights Office of the Archbishop of Guatemala (1996); **Hugo Cabrera** and **Orlando Blanco,** Center for the Investigation of International Human Rights; **Frank La Rue** and **Helen Duffy,** Center for Human Rights Legal Action; **Fernando Moscoso** and **Juan Alberto Charmele,** Guatemala Forensic Anthropology Team; **Mario Polanco,** Director, Mutual Support Group (GAM); **David Holiday.**

Government, Government-Affiliated, Opposition, and International Community

Julio Balconi, Minister of Defense; **Carlos Maldonado,** Human Rights Ombuds Office; **Hector Rosada,** military sociologist, and **Antonio Arenales Forno,**

former members of government's peace negotiating team; **Jim Benson**, First Secretary, U.S. Embassy; **Ana Maria Tello**, UN Mission to Guatemala; **Ricardo Ramírez de León**, URNG.

HAITI
December 1995

National Commission on Truth and Justice

Commissioners: **Freud Jean**; **Bacre Waly N'Diaye**. *Staff*: **Francoise Boucard**, Director, **Jean Claude Icart**, Executive Secretary; **Wanita Westmoreland**.

Government

Rene Magloir, Minister of Justice, former member of truth commission; **Roger Pereira**, Chief of Staff, Minister of Culture; **Camille de Blanc**, Coordinator, Legal Assistance Bureau.

Nongovernmental Organizations

Jean Claude Jean, Institut Culturel Karl Leveque; **Necker Dessables**, National Peace and Justice Commission; **Daniel Roussiere**, Justice and Peace Commission, Gonaive; **Bobby Vaval**, Ecumenical Center for Human Rights.

United Nations Mission to Haiti

Rodolfo Mattarollo, Deputy Director, Legal Unit; **Javier Zuniga**, Director, Human Rights Division; **Denis Racicot**, Legal Department; **Javier Hernandez**, Director of Investigation.

Other International Community and Misc.

Louis Gary Lissade, former president of bar association; **Mike Levy**, International Liaison Office for President Aristide; **Indiana Gonzalez**, UN Development Program; **Michelle Schimpp**, Project Officer, U.S. Agency for International Development; **Kathy Hoffman** and **Julie Wynne**, U.S. Embassy; **Dieuseule Louisejuste, Ludy Lapointe,** and **Thomas Joseph Wills**, victims of political violence.

MOZAMBIQUE
September 1996

Government, Frelimo, and Renamo

Aguiar Mazula, Minister of Defense; **Jose Ibraimo Abudo**, Minister of Justice; **Antonio Matonse**, Press Advisor to President; **Jorge Rebelo**, Frelimo Party, former Minister of Information; **Louis Cabaço**, Frelimo Party, consultant; **Raul Manuel Domingos**, Head of Renamo in Parliament.

Nongovernmental Organizations

Alice Mabota, Mozambican League of Human Rights; **Roberto Luis**, ActionAid Mozambique; **Elisa dos Santos**, War-Torn Societies Project; **Ilidio Silva**, Mozambican

Institute of Psychotrauma; **Celia Deniz**, African-American Institute; **Santos Alfredo**, Link

Academics and Media

Brazão Mazula, President, Eduardo Mondlane University; **João Paulo Borges Cuelo**, History Department, Eduardo Mondlane University; **David Hedges**, History Department, Eduardo Mondlane University; **Louis de Brito**, Social Science Department, Eduardo Mondlane University; **Carlos Cardoso**, Editor, Mediacoop; **Iain Christie**, Radio Mozambique; **Fernando Lima**, Media Institute of Southern Africa and Mediacoop; **Noe Dimande**, Demos Weekly; **Leite de Vasconcelos**, Journalist; **Ne Afonso**, Radio Mozambique.

Residents of the Village of Tres de Fevereiro

Mr. Timane, Curandeiro; **Carlos Ubisse**, Advisor to traditional leader; **Bernando Chavo**, headmaster of school; **Salvador Mahachane**.

Other

Sam Barnes, consultant; **Joao Ribeiro**, filmmaker, Ebano Company; **Jon Danilowicz**, Political Affairs Officer, U.S. Embassy.

SOUTH AFRICA
August–September 1996, October–November 1997, June 1999, January 2000

Truth and Reconciliation Commission

Commissioners: **Archbishop Desmond Tutu; Alex Boraine; Mary Burton; Chris de Jager; Richard Lyster; Wynand Malan; Hlengiwe Mkhize; Wendy Orr; Fazel Randera; Yasmin Sooka; Glenda Wildschut.** *Committee Members:* **Russell Ally; Ilan Lax; Hugh Lewin; Judge Hassen Mall; Tom Manthata; Bernhard Ngoepe; Ntsikie Sandi.** *Staff:* **Vanessa Barolski; Robin Brink; Janet Cherry; Martin Coetzee; John Daniel; Madeleine Fullard; Glenn Goosen; Thulani Grenville-Grey; Janis Grobbelaar; Patrick Kelly; Jan Kyellberg; Jan Lueks; Chris McAdam; Biki Minyuku; Lebo Molete; Themba Mzimela; Gerald O'Sullivan; Piers Pigou; Sekoati Pitso; Paul van Zyl; Wilhelm Verwoerd; Charles Villa-Vicencio; Barbara Watson; Wendy Watson.** *Designated statement takers and others:* **Rev. S. K. Mbande** and **Boniwe Mafu**, Daveyton; **Joseph Dube**, Soweto; **Lars Buur; Michelle Parlevliet.**

Government, Parliament, and Judicial

Dullah Omar, Minister of Justice; **Kader Asmal**, Minister of Water and Forestry; **Nicholas "Fink" Haysom**, Legal Counsel to President Nelson Mandela; **Johnny de Lange**, Chair, Parliamentary Committee on Justice; **Phillip Powell**, Inkatha Freedom Party, member of parliament; **Justice Richard Goldstone, Justice L.W.H. Ackerman**, and **Justice Albie Sachs**, Constitutional Court; **Howard Varney** and **Melanie Lue**, Investigative Task Unit.

Nongovernmental Organizations

Graeme Simpson, Brandon Hamber, Tlhoki Mofokeng, and **Hugo van der Merwe,** Centre for the Study of Violence and Reconciliation; **Ntombi Mosikare, Thandi Shezi, Rose Everett-Mudimu, Duma Kumalo, Mavis Kumalo, Ntombe Mosikare,** and **Rudy Mphela,** Khulumani; **Eddie Makue** and **Teboho Sejake,** South African Council of Churches; **Jody Kollapen,** Lawyers for Human Rights; **Steve Kahanovitz,** Legal Resources Center; **Janet Levy,** Institute for Democracy in South Africa; **Scott de Klerk** and **Theo de Jager,** Foundation for Equality before the Law; **Tom Winslow,** Trauma Centre for Victims of Violence and Torture; **Paddy Kearney,** Diakonia; **Rev. Danny Chetty** and staff, Practical Ministries; **Jenny Irish** and **Selvan Chetty,** Network of Independent Monitors; **Steven Zintel,** National Association of Democratic Lawyers.

Academics

Andre du Toit, University of Cape Town; **Jonathan Klaaren,** Witswatersrand University Law School; **Beth Goldblatt,** Centre for Applied Legal Studies, Witswatersrand University; **Pamela Reynolds** and **Fiona Ross,** Anthropology Department, University of Cape Town; **Mahmood Mamdani,** University of Cape Town; **Jeremy Sarkin,** Faculty of Law, University of the Western Cape; **Steven Robins,** Department of Anthropology and Sociology, University of the Western Cape.

Victims, Survivors, and Family Members

Sylvia Dlomo, Soweto; **Pauline Mbatha** and **Johannes Mbatha,** Boipatong Township, Slovo Park squatter camp; **Flora Mkhize; Albert "Mandla" Mbalekelwa Nangalembe** and **Margaret Nangalembe,** Sebokeng Township; **Chris Ribiero; Simpson Xakelka; David Alcock,** Durban; **Elizabeth Hashe** and **Monica Godolozi,** Port Elizabeth.

Media

Max DuPreez and **Jann Turner,** Truth Commission Special Report; **Claire Keeton,** The Sowetan; **Kenneth Makeitis,** SABC Radio; **Wally Mbheli,** City Press; **S'Kumbuzu Miya,** UmAfrika.

Other

Dirk Coetzee; Phyllis Naidoo, ANC Truth Commission desk; **Carole Baekey,** consultant; **Ken Wilson,** Ford Foundation.

UGANDA
October 1996

Human Rights Commissions of Inquiry

Commissioners (1986 commission): **Justice Arthur Oder,** Chair; **John Nagenda.** *Staff:* **John Ssekandi,** Legal Counsel; **Alex Okello,** Executive Secretary; **Baker Wairama,** Senior Consultant. *Staff (1974 commission):* **Joseph Mulenga,** Legal Counsel to commission (and later Attorney General/Minister of Justice).

Government, Judicial, and Opposition

Bart Katureebe, Attorney General/Minister of Justice; **Abu Mayanja**, former Attorney General/Minister of Justice; **George Kanyeihamba**, Senior Presidential Advisor for Human Rights and International Affairs, former Attorney General/Minister of Justice; **Lucian Tibaruha**, Human Rights Officer, Ministry of Justice; **Fred Egonda Ntende**, Justice of the High Court; **Alfred Nasaba**, Director, Law Development Centre; Former Director of Public Prosecutions; **Cecilia Ogwal**, Uganda People's Congress.

Nongovernmental Organizations, Church, and Academics

Rev. John Mary Waliggo, Uganda Catholic Secretariat; former Secretary General, Constitutional Commission; **Miriam Mwangi**, Foundation for Human Rights Initiative; **Twesigye Jackson Kaguri**, Human Rights Concern; **John Mugisha**, President, Uganda Law Society; **Solomy Bossa**, former President, Uganda Law Society; **Joe Oloka-Onyango** and **Fred Jjuuko**, Makarere University School of Law.

Media

Amos Kajoba, Editor, *The People;* **Charles Onyango-Obbo**, Editor, *The Monitor;* **John Kakande**, New Vision.

International Community

George Colvin, Political Affairs Officer, U.S. Embassy; **Daniel Iga**, Program Officer, DANIDA; **Albrecht Bossert**, Resident Representative, Konrad Adenauer Stiftung.

UNITED STATES

Nongovernmental Organizations

Kenneth Roth, Bronwen Manby, Wilder Tayler, Reed Brody, Jose Miguel Vivanco, and **Anne Manual**, Human Rights Watch; **Michael Posner**, Lawyers Committee for Human Rights; **Mercedes Doretti**, Argentine Forensic Anthropology Team; **George Vickers, Rachel Garst, Rachel Nield, Jeff Thale,** and **Colletta Youngers,** Washington Office on Latin America; **Tom Blanton** and **Kate Doyle**, National Security Archive; **Patrick Ball**, American Association for the Advancement of Science, Science and Human Rights Program; **Margaret Popkin**, Robert F. Kennedy Memorial Center for Human Rights; **Javier Miranda**, FEDEMAN, Uruguay.

Academics

Thomas Buergenthal, George Washington University Law School; **Robert Goldman**, American University Law School; **Steve Marks**, Columbia University; **Ben Kiernan**, Yale University.

Other

Alvaro de Soto and **Jean Arnault**, United Nations; **Juan Méndez**, Inter-American Institute for Human Rights; **Judith Lewis Herman**, Harvard Medical School;

Aryeh Neier, President, Open Society Institute; Margaret Burnham; Genoveva Hernandez; Peter Cleveland, Office of U.S. Senator Chuck Robb; Yael Danieli.

ZIMBABWE
September–October 1996

Government

Emmerson Mnangagwa, Minister of Justice; Y. Omerjee, Secretary for Justice, Legal and Parliamentary Affairs, Ministry of Justice; Bornwell Chakaodza, Director of Information, Ministry of Information.

Nongovernmental Organizations

Eileen Sawyer, National Director, Legal Resources Foundation; Tony Reeler, Amani Foundation; David Chimhini, Executive Director, Zimbabwe Human Rights Association; Elizabeth Feltoe, Legal Officer, Catholic Commission for Justice and Peace; Judith Todd, Board Member, Mafela Trust; David Coltart, Legal Resources Foundation, Bulawayo; John Stewart, Director of Southern Africa Office, American Friends Service Committee; Sharry Apple, Coordinator of Special History Research Project of the Legal Resources Foundation and the Catholic Commission for Justice and Peace, Bulawayo.

Media

Pat Made, InterPress Service; Edwina Spicer, Independent filmmaker.

LONDON AND OTHER

Alex Vines, Human Rights Watch; Ingrid Massagé, Ignacio Saiz, Nicholas Howen, Mary Rayner, Martin Hill, and Tracy Ulltveit-Moe, Amnesty International; Chidy Odinkalu, Interights; Richard Carver; JoAnne McGregor, Oxford University; Pedro Nikken.